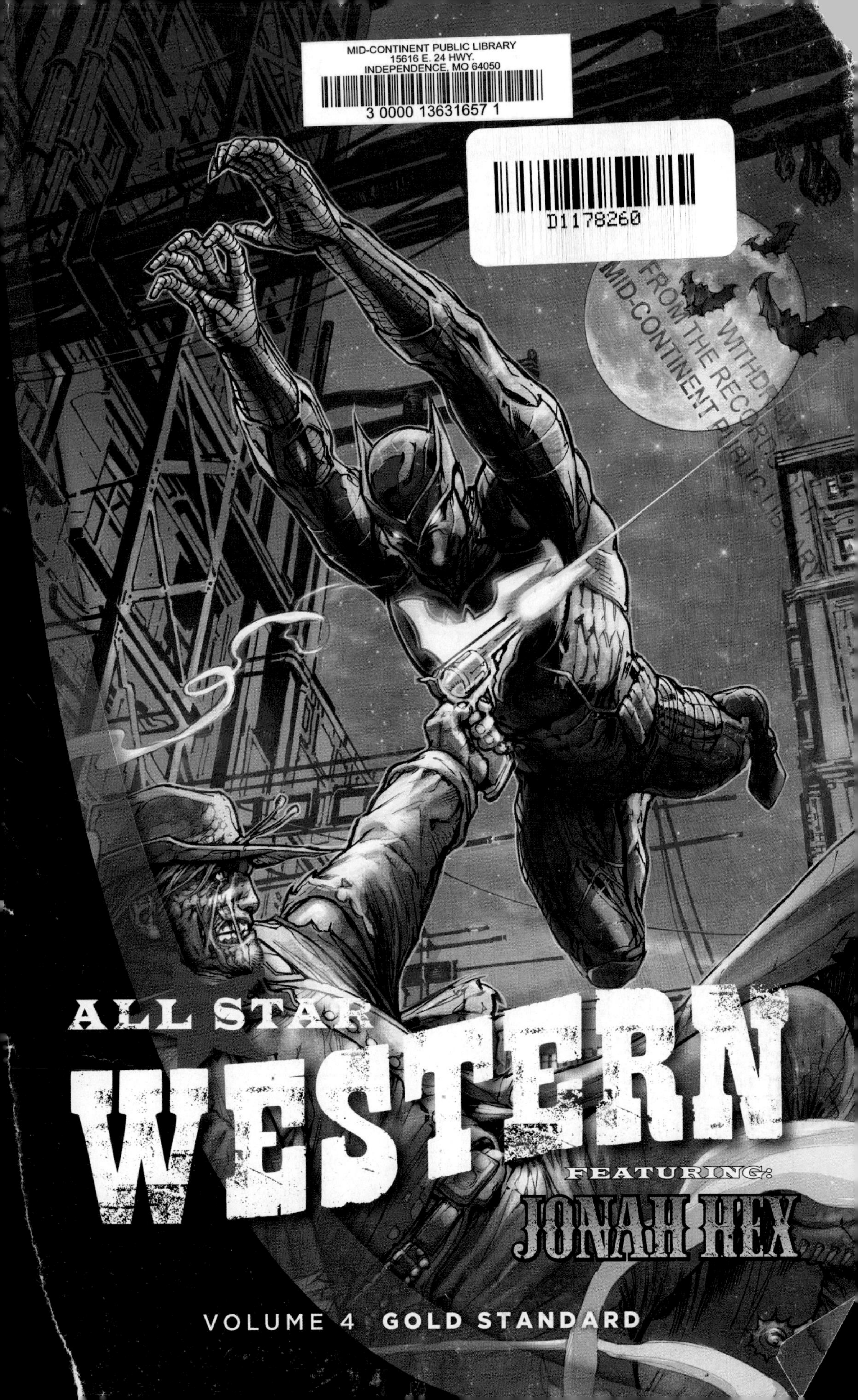
ALL STAR
WESTERN
FEATURING:
JONAH HEX
VOLUME 4 GOLD STANDARD

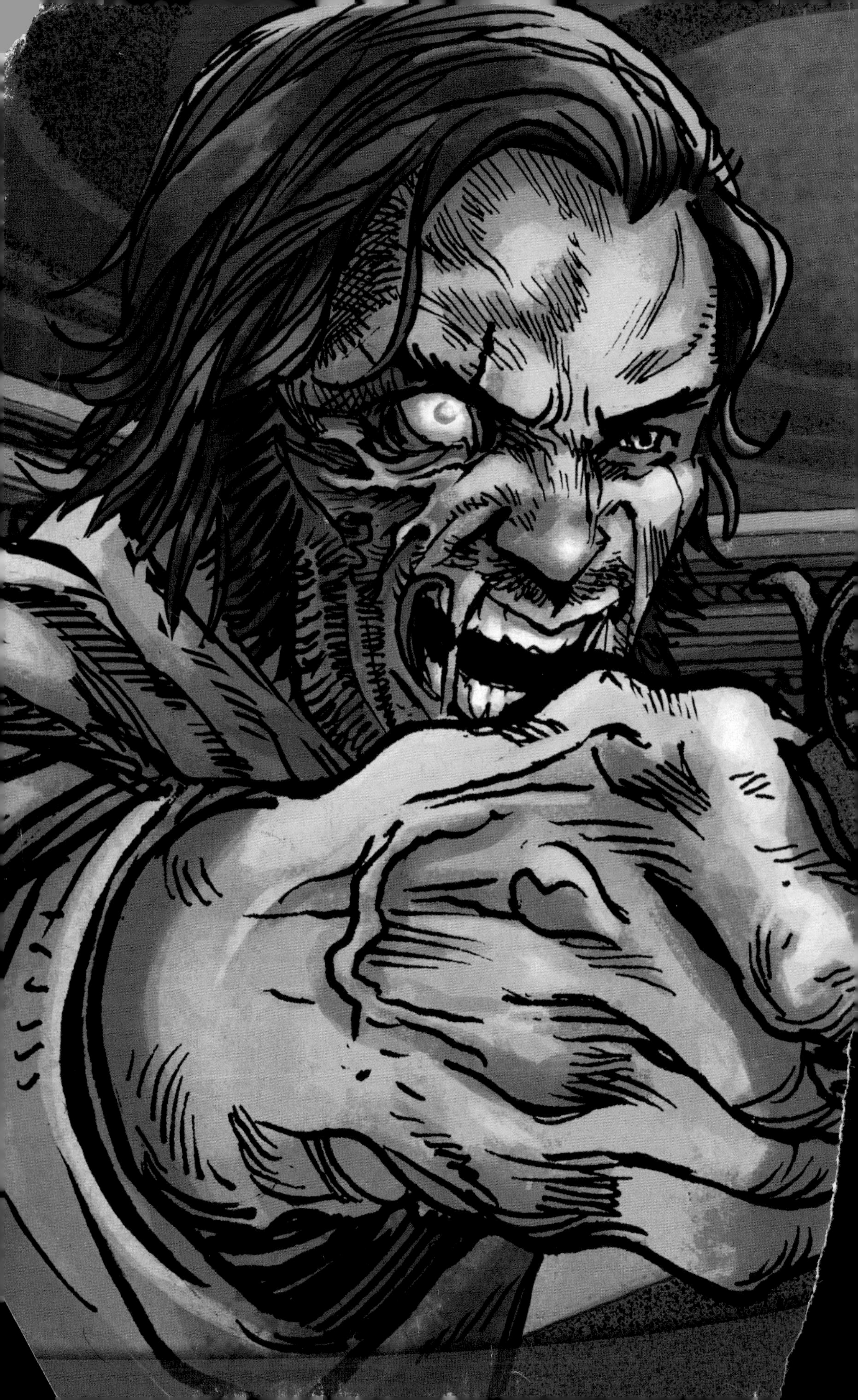

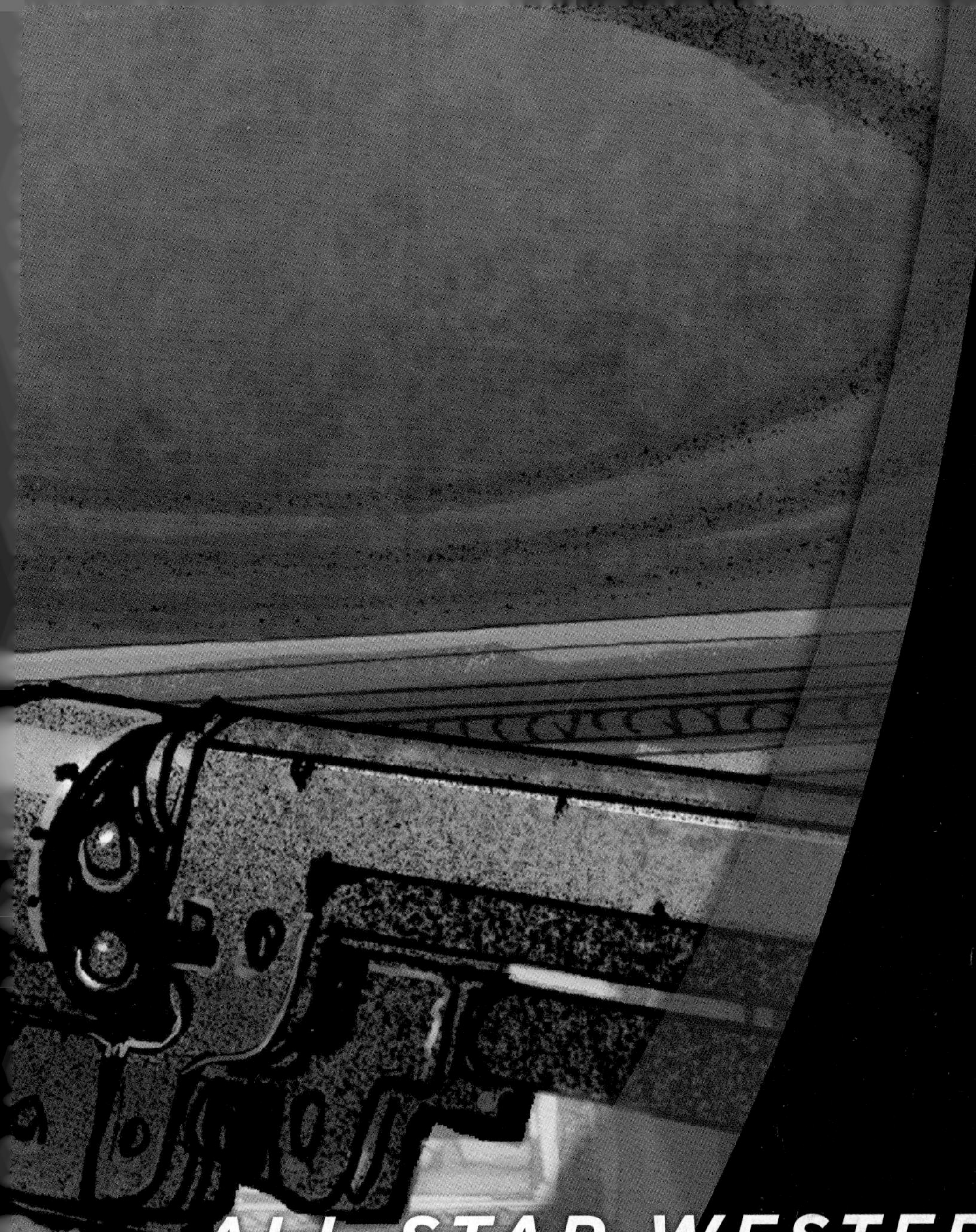

ALL STAR WESTERN
FEATURING: JONAH HEX

VOLUME 4
GOLD STANDARD

JUSTIN **GRAY** JIMMY **PALMIOTTI** writers

MORITAT STAZ **JOHNSON** artists

MIKE **ATIYEH** ANDRE **SZYMANOWICZ**
ROB **SCHWAGER** MATT **YACKEY** colorists

ROB **LEIGH** letterer

HOWARD **PORTER** collection cover artist

MIKE COTTON JOEY CAVALIERI Editors – Original Series
KATE STEWART ANTHONY MARQUES Assistant Editors – Original Series ROWENA YOW Editor
ROBBIN BROSTERMAN Design Director – Books ROBBIE BIEDERMAN Publication Design

BOB HARRAS Senior VP – Editor-in-Chief, DC Comics

ALL STAR WESTERN FEATURING: JONAH HEX VOLUME 4: GOLD STANDARD
Published by DC Comics. Copyright © 2014 DC Comics. All Rights Reserved.

Originally published in single magazine form in ALL STAR WESTERN 17-21 © 2013 DC Comics. All Rights Reserved.
All characters, their distinctive likenesses and related elements featured in this publication are trademarks of DC Comics.
The stories, characters and incidents featured in this publication are entirely fictional.
DC Comics does not read or accept unsolicited ideas, stories or artwork.

DC Comics, 1700 Broadway, New York, NY 10019
A Warner Bros. Entertainment Company.
Printed by RR Donnelley, Salem, VA, USA. 4/4/14. First Printing.
ISBN: 978-1-4012-4626-6

Library of Congress Cataloging-in-Publication Data

Palmiotti, Jimmy, author.
All Star Western. Volume 4, Gold Standard / Jimmy Palmiotti, Justin Gray ; illustrated by Moritat.
pages cm. — (The New 52!)
Collects issues #17-21"— Provided by publisher.
ISBN 978-1-4012-4626-6 (paperback)
1. Graphic novels. I. Gray, Justin, author. II. Norman, Justin, illustrator. III. Title. IV. Title: Gold Standard.
PN6728.A425P38 2014
741.5'973—dc23
2014000322

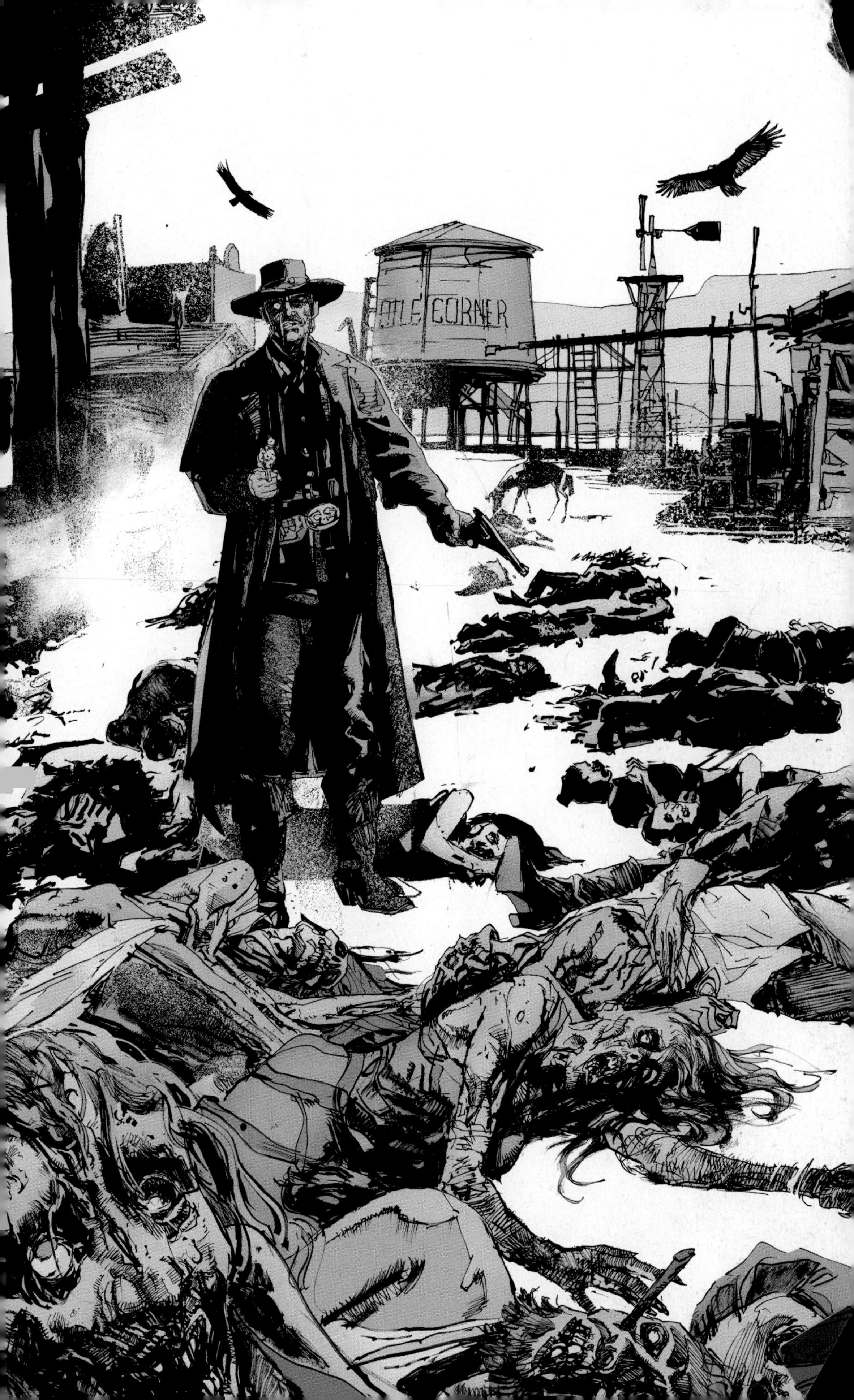
CORNER

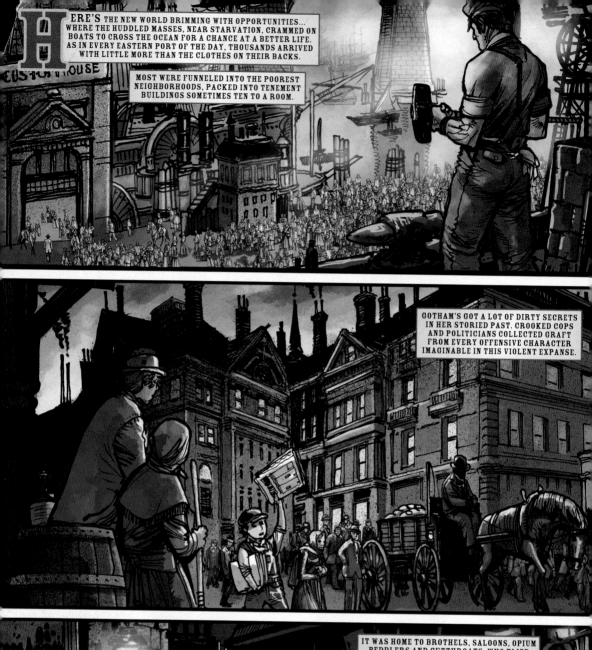

HERE'S THE NEW WORLD BRIMMING WITH OPPORTUNITIES... WHERE THE HUDDLED MASSES, NEAR STARVATION, CRAMMED ON BOATS TO CROSS THE OCEAN FOR A CHANCE AT A BETTER LIFE. AS IN EVERY EASTERN PORT OF THE DAY, THOUSANDS ARRIVED WITH LITTLE MORE THAN THE CLOTHES ON THEIR BACKS.

MOST WERE FUNNELED INTO THE POOREST NEIGHBORHOODS, PACKED INTO TENEMENT BUILDINGS SOMETIMES TEN TO A ROOM.

GOTHAM'S GOT A LOT OF DIRTY SECRETS IN HER STORIED PAST. CROOKED COPS AND POLITICIANS COLLECTED GRAFT FROM EVERY OFFENSIVE CHARACTER IMAGINABLE IN THIS VIOLENT EXPANSE.

IT WAS HOME TO BROTHELS, SALOONS, OPIUM PEDDLERS AND CUTTHROATS, WHO PLIED THEIR TRADE ALONG HARVEST, GREEN, MILLWOOD, MARTIN AND PIPER STREETS.

THE DISTRICT WAS ONCE AWASH IN VICE, A PLACE WHERE EXILED CRIMINALS FROM OTHER PARTS OF THE CITY SOUGHT REFUGE.

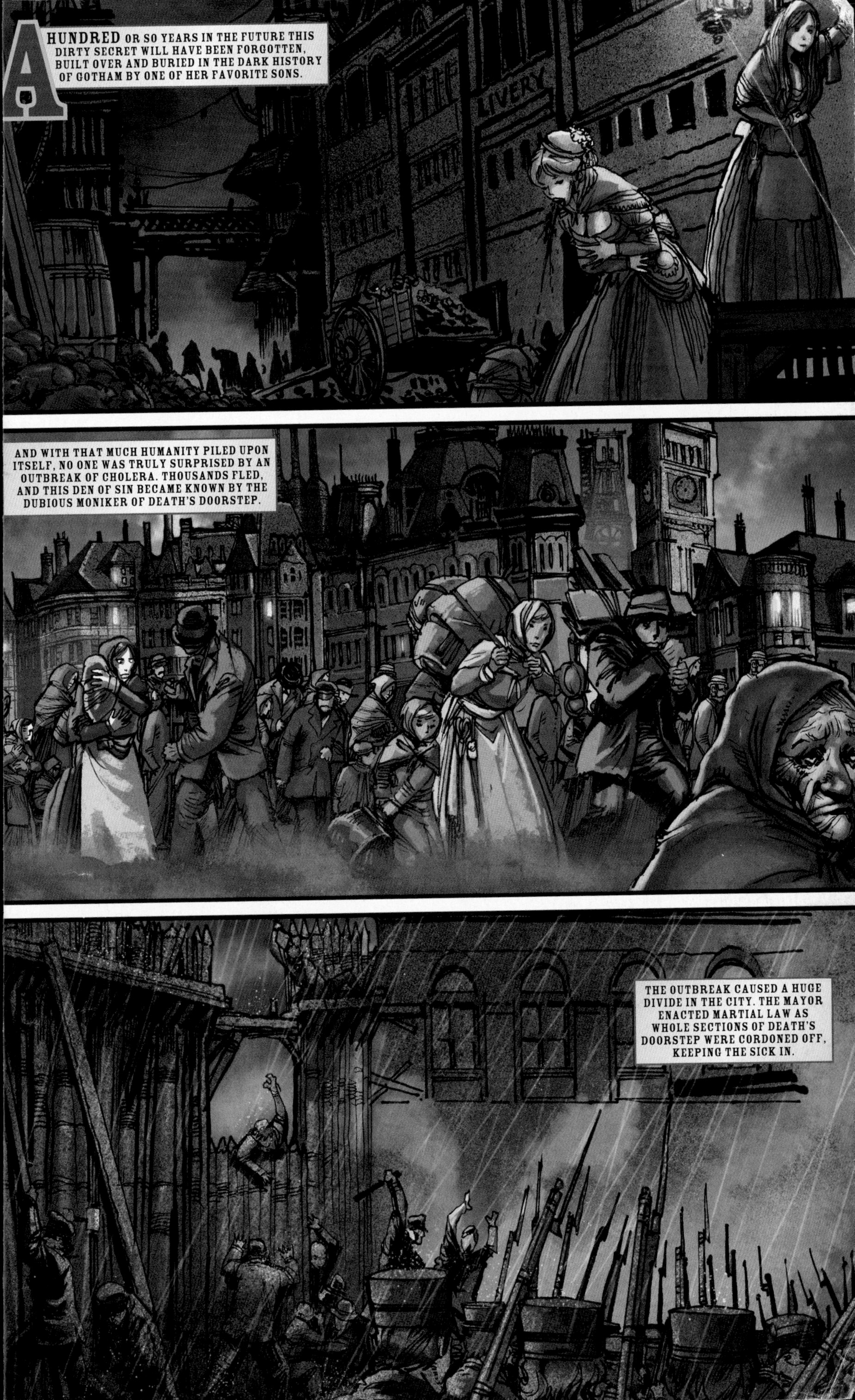
A HUNDRED OR SO YEARS IN THE FUTURE THIS DIRTY SECRET WILL HAVE BEEN FORGOTTEN, BUILT OVER AND BURIED IN THE DARK HISTORY OF GOTHAM BY ONE OF HER FAVORITE SONS.
LIVERY
AND WITH THAT MUCH HUMANITY PILED UPON ITSELF, NO ONE WAS TRULY SURPRISED BY AN OUTBREAK OF CHOLERA. THOUSANDS FLED, AND THIS DEN OF SIN BECAME KNOWN BY THE DUBIOUS MONIKER OF DEATH'S DOORSTEP.
THE OUTBREAK CAUSED A HUGE DIVIDE IN THE CITY. THE MAYOR ENACTED MARTIAL LAW AS WHOLE SECTIONS OF DEATH'S DOORSTEP WERE CORDONED OFF, KEEPING THE SICK IN.

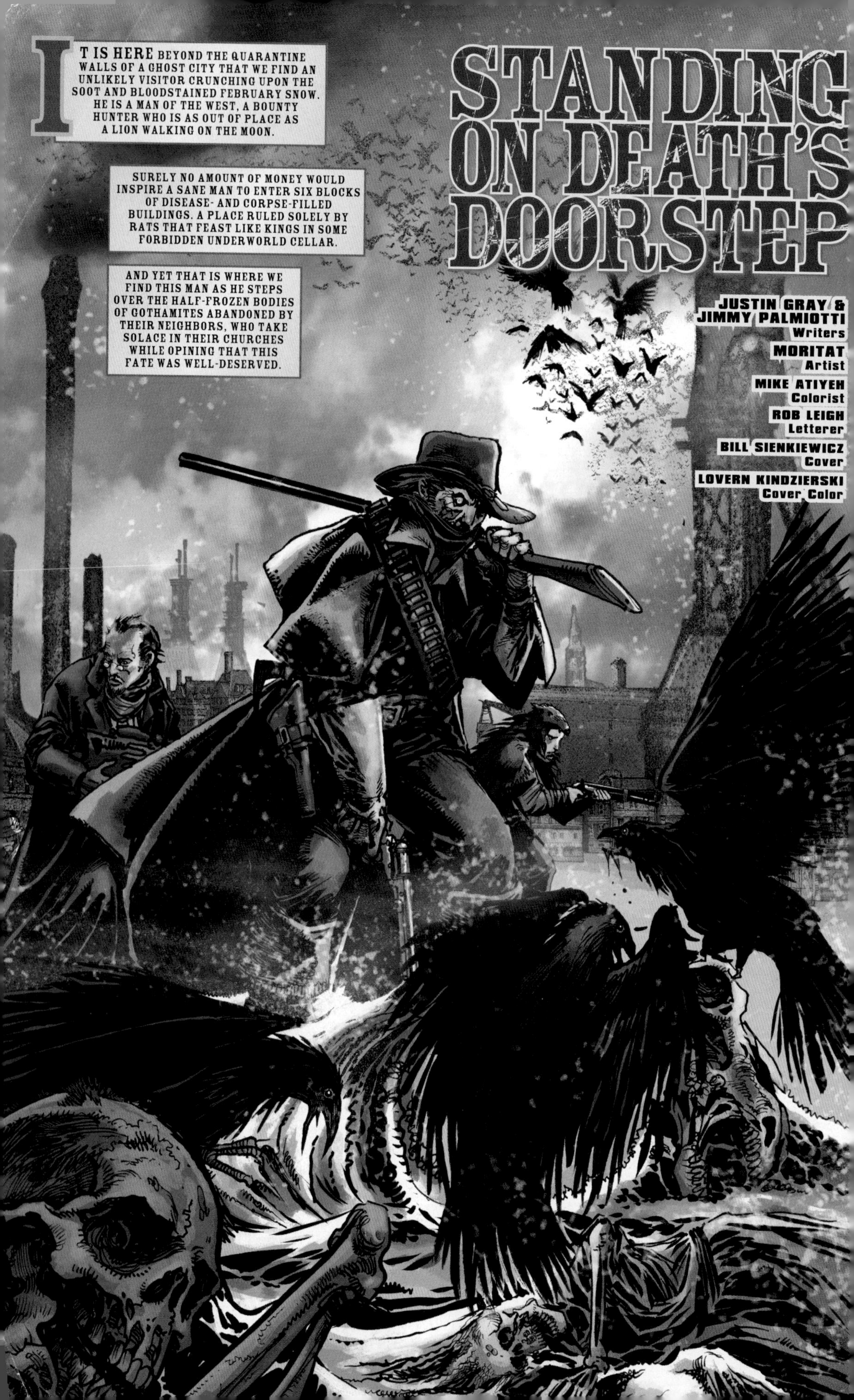

IT IS HERE BEYOND THE QUARANTINE WALLS OF A GHOST CITY THAT WE FIND AN UNLIKELY VISITOR CRUNCHING UPON THE SOOT AND BLOODSTAINED FEBRUARY SNOW. HE IS A MAN OF THE WEST, A BOUNTY HUNTER WHO IS AS OUT OF PLACE AS A LION WALKING ON THE MOON.
SURELY NO AMOUNT OF MONEY WOULD INSPIRE A SANE MAN TO ENTER SIX BLOCKS OF DISEASE- AND CORPSE-FILLED BUILDINGS. A PLACE RULED SOLELY BY RATS THAT FEAST LIKE KINGS IN SOME FORBIDDEN UNDERWORLD CELLAR.
AND YET THAT IS WHERE WE FIND THIS MAN AS HE STEPS OVER THE HALF-FROZEN BODIES OF GOTHAMITES ABANDONED BY THEIR NEIGHBORS, WHO TAKE SOLACE IN THEIR CHURCHES WHILE OPINING THAT THIS FATE WAS WELL-DESERVED.
STANDING ON DEATH'S DOORSTEP
JUSTIN GRAY & JIMMY PALMIOTTI Writers
MORITAT Artist
MIKE ATIYEH Colorist
ROB LEIGH Letterer
BILL SIENKIEWICZ Cover
LOVERN KINDZIERSKI Cover Color

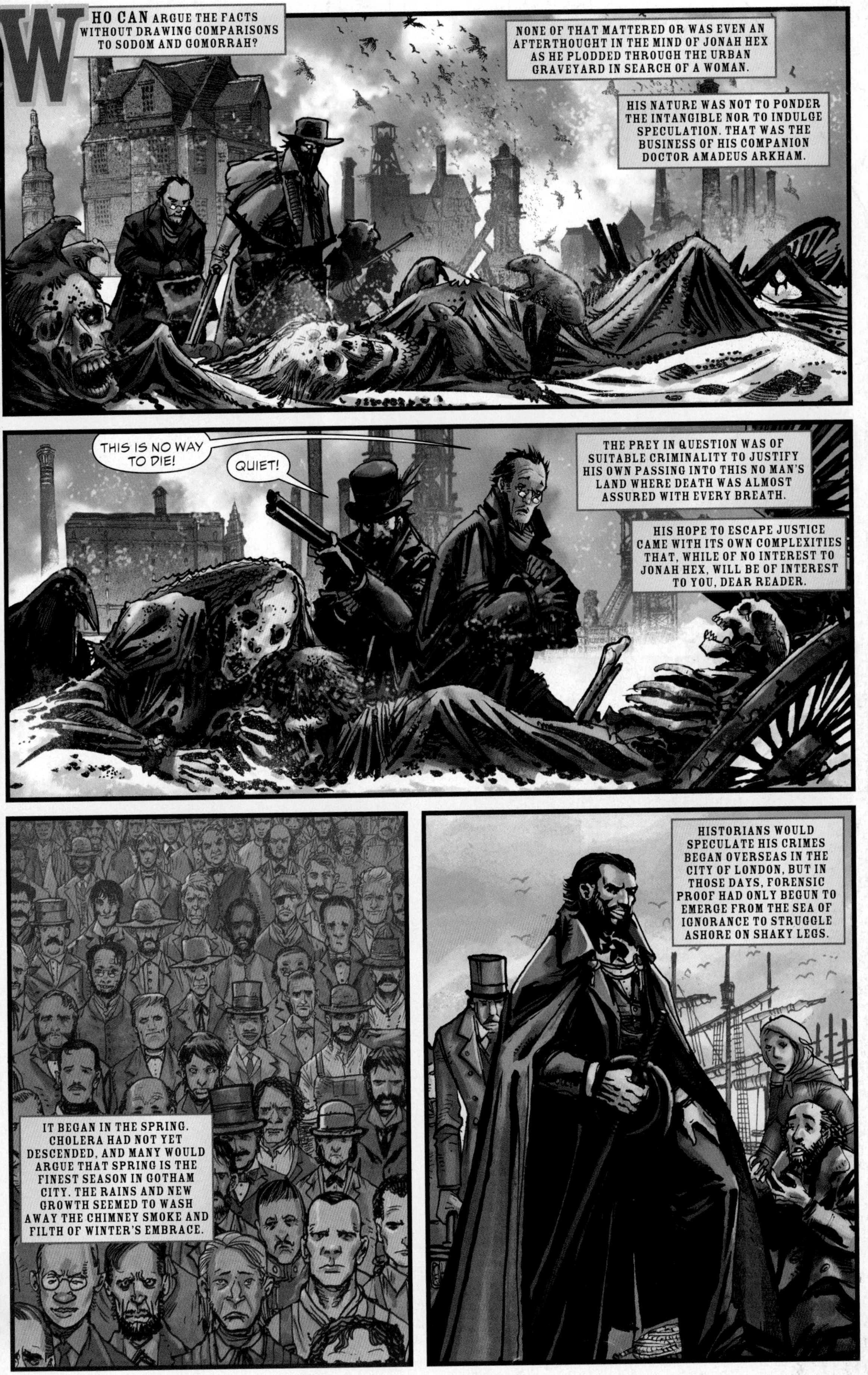
WHO CAN ARGUE THE FACTS WITHOUT DRAWING COMPARISONS TO SODOM AND GOMORRAH?
NONE OF THAT MATTERED OR WAS EVEN AN AFTERTHOUGHT IN THE MIND OF JONAH HEX AS HE PLODDED THROUGH THE URBAN GRAVEYARD IN SEARCH OF A WOMAN.
HIS NATURE WAS NOT TO PONDER THE INTANGIBLE NOR TO INDULGE SPECULATION. THAT WAS THE BUSINESS OF HIS COMPANION DOCTOR AMADEUS ARKHAM.
THIS IS NO WAY TO DIE!
QUIET!
THE PREY IN QUESTION WAS OF SUITABLE CRIMINALITY TO JUSTIFY HIS OWN PASSING INTO THIS NO MAN'S LAND WHERE DEATH WAS ALMOST ASSURED WITH EVERY BREATH.
HIS HOPE TO ESCAPE JUSTICE CAME WITH ITS OWN COMPLEXITIES THAT, WHILE OF NO INTEREST TO JONAH HEX, WILL BE OF INTEREST TO YOU, DEAR READER.
IT BEGAN IN THE SPRING. CHOLERA HAD NOT YET DESCENDED, AND MANY WOULD ARGUE THAT SPRING IS THE FINEST SEASON IN GOTHAM CITY. THE RAINS AND NEW GROWTH SEEMED TO WASH AWAY THE CHIMNEY SMOKE AND FILTH OF WINTER'S EMBRACE.
HISTORIANS WOULD SPECULATE HIS CRIMES BEGAN OVERSEAS IN THE CITY OF LONDON, BUT IN THOSE DAYS, FORENSIC PROOF HAD ONLY BEGUN TO EMERGE FROM THE SEA OF IGNORANCE TO STRUGGLE ASHORE ON SHAKY LEGS.

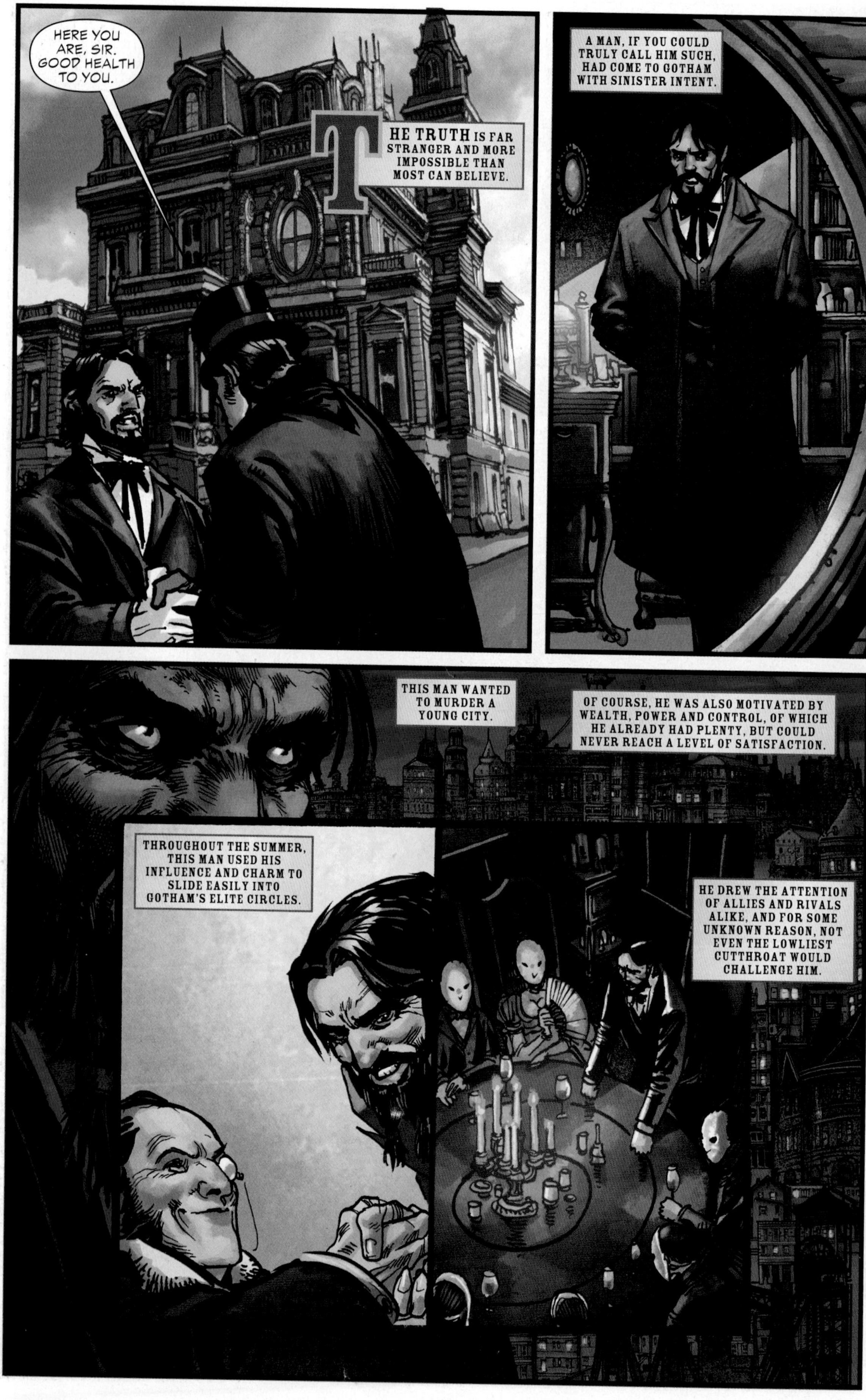

HERE YOU ARE, SIR. GOOD HEALTH TO YOU.
THE TRUTH IS FAR STRANGER AND MORE IMPOSSIBLE THAN MOST CAN BELIEVE.
A MAN, IF YOU COULD TRULY CALL HIM SUCH, HAD COME TO GOTHAM WITH SINISTER INTENT.
THIS MAN WANTED TO MURDER A YOUNG CITY.
OF COURSE, HE WAS ALSO MOTIVATED BY WEALTH, POWER AND CONTROL, OF WHICH HE ALREADY HAD PLENTY, BUT COULD NEVER REACH A LEVEL OF SATISFACTION.
THROUGHOUT THE SUMMER, THIS MAN USED HIS INFLUENCE AND CHARM TO SLIDE EASILY INTO GOTHAM'S ELITE CIRCLES.
HE DREW THE ATTENTION OF ALLIES AND RIVALS ALIKE, AND FOR SOME UNKNOWN REASON, NOT EVEN THE LOWLIEST CUTTHROAT WOULD CHALLENGE HIM.

AS HE WALKED THROUGH BOTH PALACES AND SLUMS, PEOPLE GREETED HIM WITH EQUAL RESPECT AND AN UNSPOKEN FEAR.

HE TOUCHED IN THEM SOME PRIMAL INSTINCT THAT WAS INSTILLED IN HUMANITY FROM THE EARLIEST DAYS WHEN IT SOUGHT REFUGE IN CAVES.

WAYNE CASINO

AMONG THE MANY POWERFUL MEN OF GOTHAM, ONE IN PARTICULAR WAS SUSPICIOUS OF THIS ENIGMATIC FIGURE.

PARSONS, WHO IS THAT GENTLEMAN?

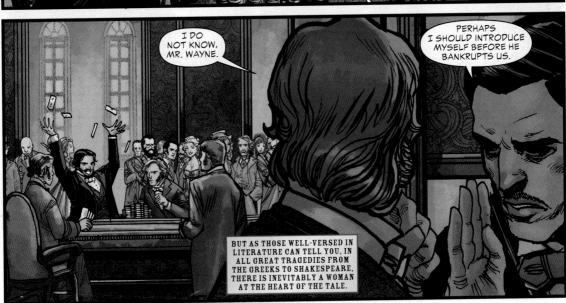

I DO NOT KNOW, MR. WAYNE.

PERHAPS I SHOULD INTRODUCE MYSELF BEFORE HE BANKRUPTS US.

BUT AS THOSE WELL-VERSED IN LITERATURE CAN TELL YOU, IN ALL GREAT TRAGEDIES FROM THE GREEKS TO SHAKESPEARE, THERE IS INEVITABLY A WOMAN AT THE HEART OF THE TALE.

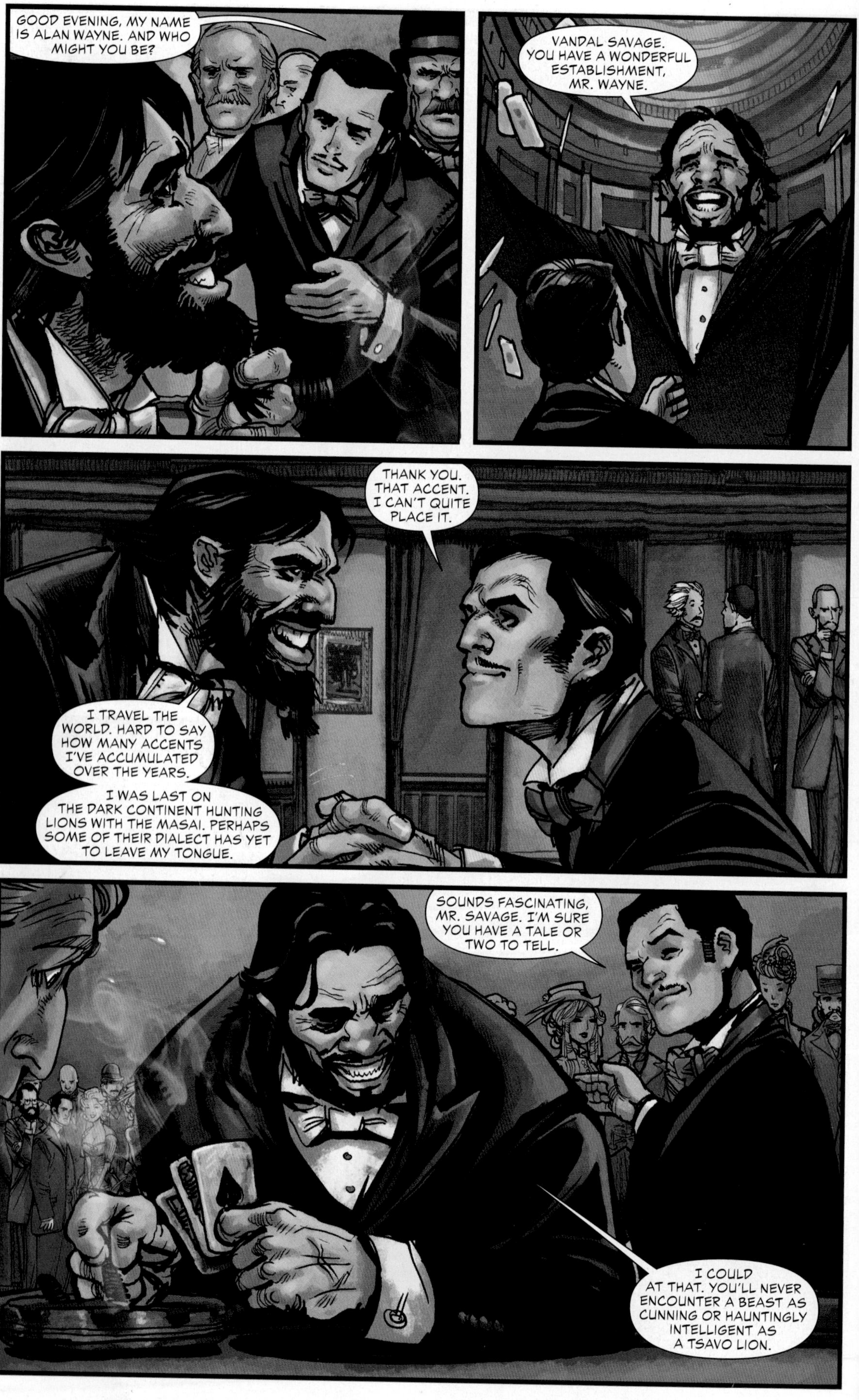
GOOD EVENING, MY NAME IS ALAN WAYNE. AND WHO MIGHT YOU BE?
VANDAL SAVAGE. YOU HAVE A WONDERFUL ESTABLISHMENT, MR. WAYNE.
THANK YOU. THAT ACCENT. I CAN'T QUITE PLACE IT.
I TRAVEL THE WORLD. HARD TO SAY HOW MANY ACCENTS I'VE ACCUMULATED OVER THE YEARS.
I WAS LAST ON THE DARK CONTINENT HUNTING LIONS WITH THE MASAI. PERHAPS SOME OF THEIR DIALECT HAS YET TO LEAVE MY TONGUE.
SOUNDS FASCINATING, MR. SAVAGE. I'M SURE YOU HAVE A TALE OR TWO TO TELL.
I COULD AT THAT. YOU'LL NEVER ENCOUNTER A BEAST AS CUNNING OR HAUNTINGLY INTELLIGENT AS A TSAVO LION.

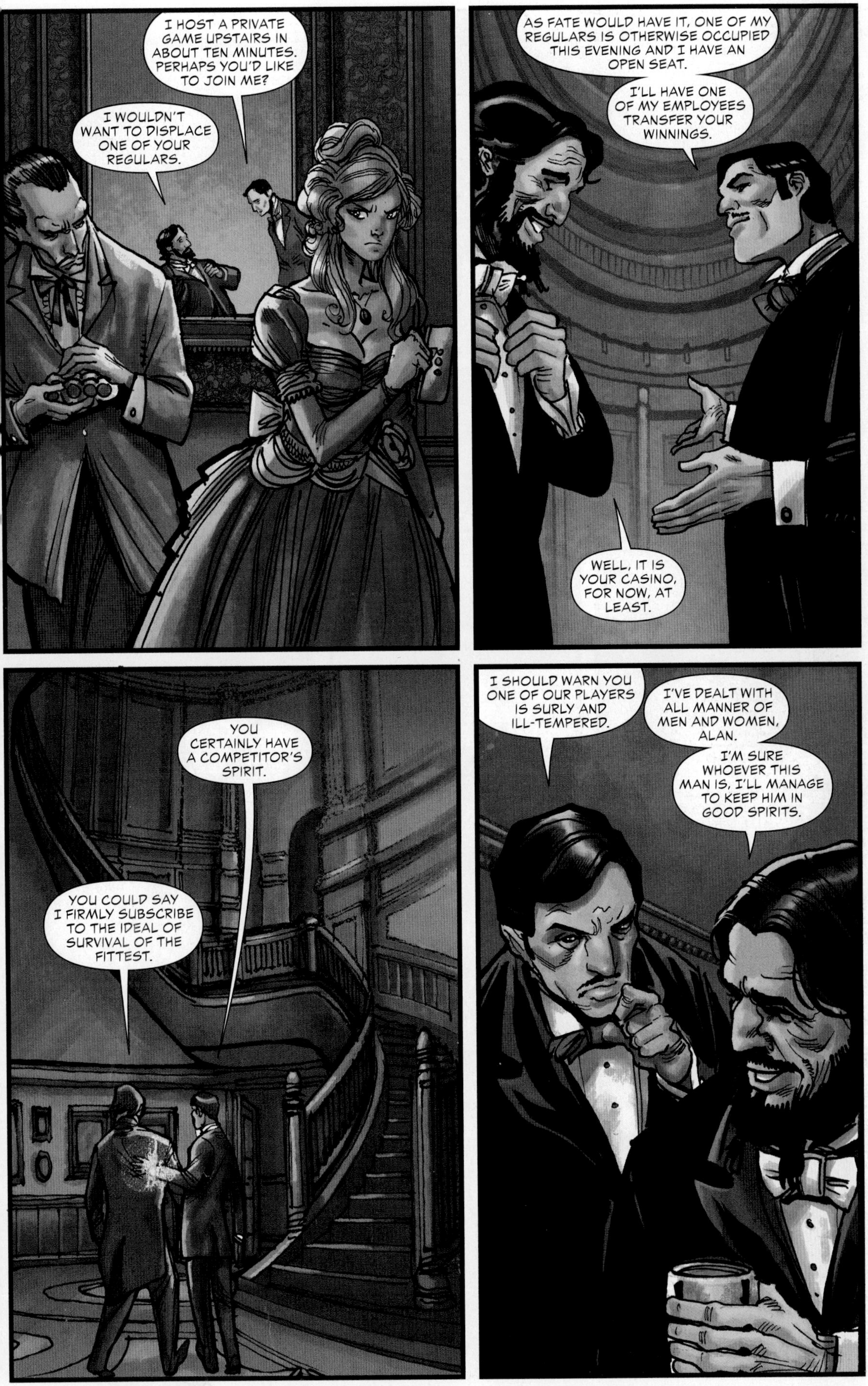
I HOST A PRIVATE GAME UPSTAIRS IN ABOUT TEN MINUTES. PERHAPS YOU'D LIKE TO JOIN ME?
I WOULDN'T WANT TO DISPLACE ONE OF YOUR REGULARS.
AS FATE WOULD HAVE IT, ONE OF MY REGULARS IS OTHERWISE OCCUPIED THIS EVENING AND I HAVE AN OPEN SEAT.
I'LL HAVE ONE OF MY EMPLOYEES TRANSFER YOUR WINNINGS.
WELL, IT IS YOUR CASINO, FOR NOW, AT LEAST.
YOU CERTAINLY HAVE A COMPETITOR'S SPIRIT.
YOU COULD SAY I FIRMLY SUBSCRIBE TO THE IDEAL OF SURVIVAL OF THE FITTEST.
I SHOULD WARN YOU ONE OF OUR PLAYERS IS SURLY AND ILL-TEMPERED.
I'VE DEALT WITH ALL MANNER OF MEN AND WOMEN, ALAN.
I'M SURE WHOEVER THIS MAN IS, I'LL MANAGE TO KEEP HIM IN GOOD SPIRITS.

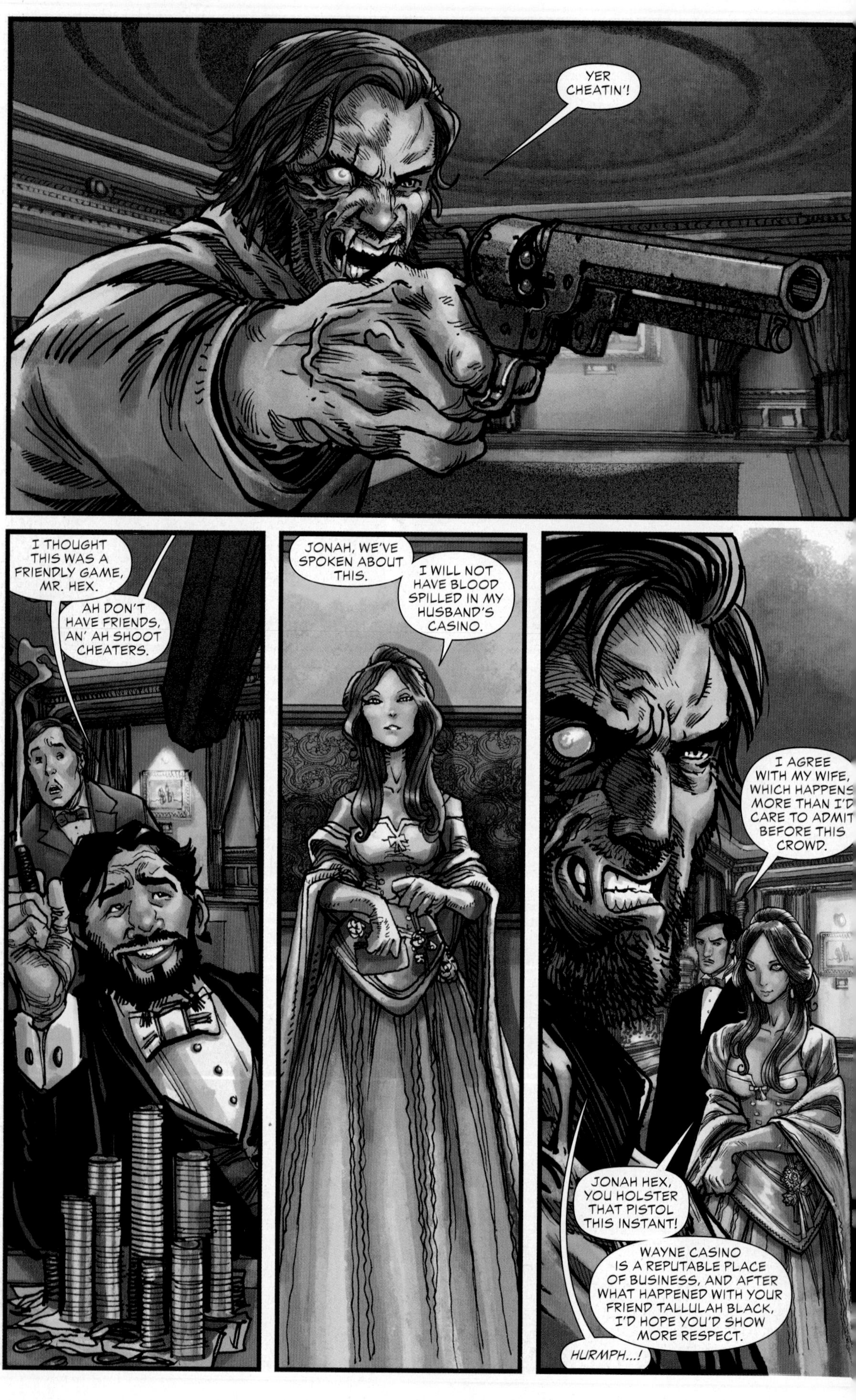

YER CHEATIN'!
I THOUGHT THIS WAS A FRIENDLY GAME, MR. HEX.
AH DON'T HAVE FRIENDS, AN' AH SHOOT CHEATERS.
JONAH, WE'VE SPOKEN ABOUT THIS.
I WILL NOT HAVE BLOOD SPILLED IN MY HUSBAND'S CASINO.
I AGREE WITH MY WIFE, WHICH HAPPENS MORE THAN I'D CARE TO ADMIT BEFORE THIS CROWD.
JONAH HEX, YOU HOLSTER THAT PISTOL THIS INSTANT!
WAYNE CASINO IS A REPUTABLE PLACE OF BUSINESS, AND AFTER WHAT HAPPENED WITH YOUR FRIEND TALLULAH BLACK, I'D HOPE YOU'D SHOW MORE RESPECT.
HURMPH...!

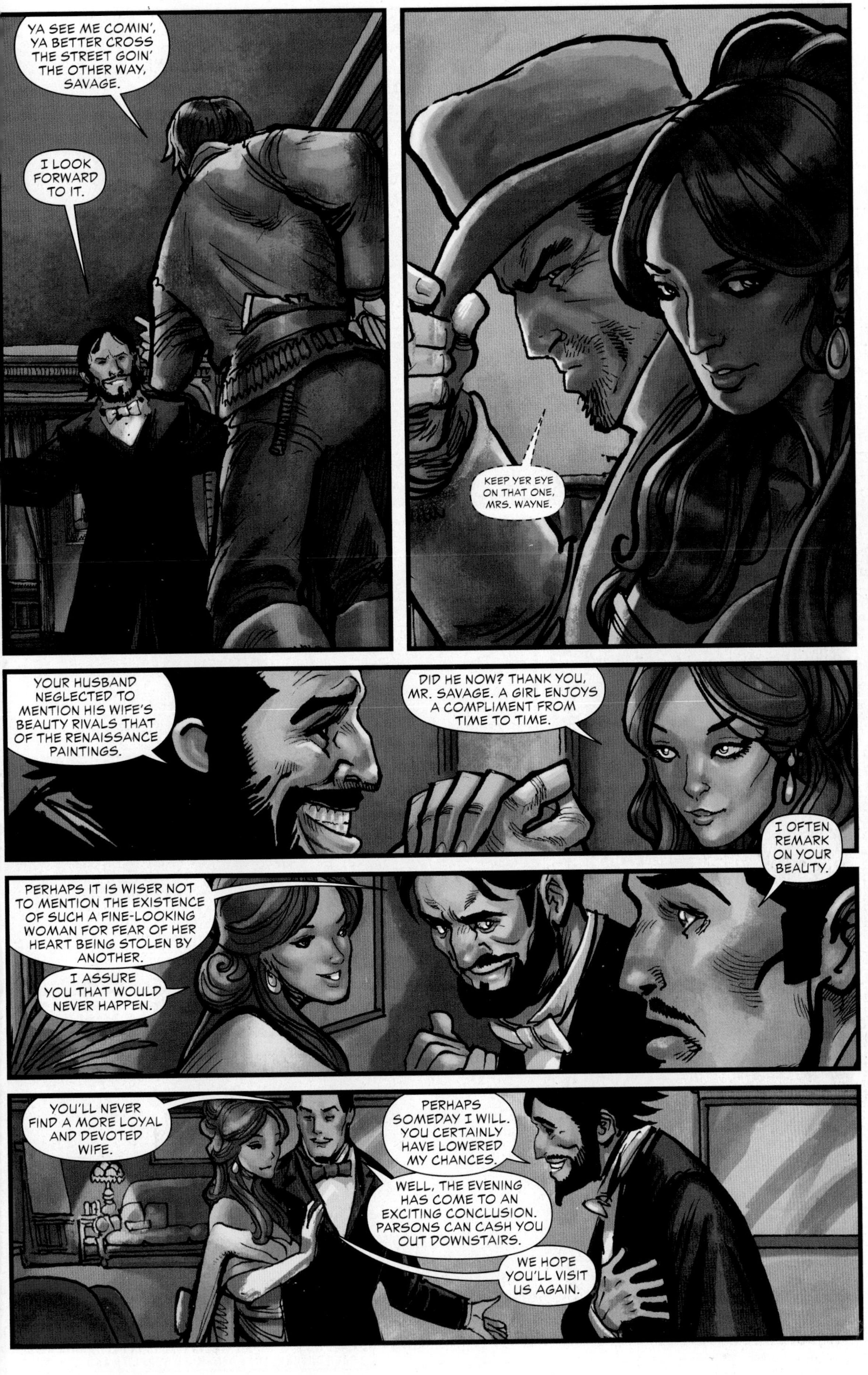
YA SEE ME COMIN', YA BETTER CROSS THE STREET GOIN' THE OTHER WAY, SAVAGE.
I LOOK FORWARD TO IT.
KEEP YER EYE ON THAT ONE, MRS. WAYNE.
YOUR HUSBAND NEGLECTED TO MENTION HIS WIFE'S BEAUTY RIVALS THAT OF THE RENAISSANCE PAINTINGS.
DID HE NOW? THANK YOU, MR. SAVAGE. A GIRL ENJOYS A COMPLIMENT FROM TIME TO TIME.
I OFTEN REMARK ON YOUR BEAUTY.
PERHAPS IT IS WISER NOT TO MENTION THE EXISTENCE OF SUCH A FINE-LOOKING WOMAN FOR FEAR OF HER HEART BEING STOLEN BY ANOTHER.
I ASSURE YOU THAT WOULD NEVER HAPPEN.
YOU'LL NEVER FIND A MORE LOYAL AND DEVOTED WIFE.
PERHAPS SOMEDAY I WILL. YOU CERTAINLY HAVE LOWERED MY CHANCES.
WELL, THE EVENING HAS COME TO AN EXCITING CONCLUSION. PARSONS CAN CASH YOU OUT DOWNSTAIRS.
WE HOPE YOU'LL VISIT US AGAIN.

PLEASE, FOR THE LOVE OF GOD, YOU CAN'T DENY US FOOD AND MEDICINE!

THOSE WHO WERE WALLED IN AND ABANDONED TO SUFFER BOTH THE WINTER AND DISEASE WERE QUITE MAD AND DESPERATE.

GET BACK! HELP ME, SOMEONE!

LIKE PACKS OF ROAMING ANIMALS THEY SOUGHT OUT FOOD.

RUMORS OF CANNIBALISM WERE RAMPANT.

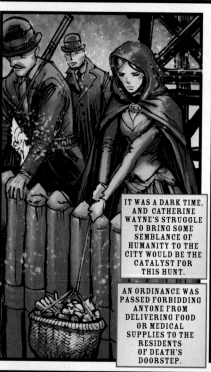

IT WAS A DARK TIME, AND CATHERINE WAYNE'S STRUGGLE TO BRING SOME SEMBLANCE OF HUMANITY TO THE CITY WOULD BE THE CATALYST FOR THIS HUNT.

AN ORDINANCE WAS PASSED FORBIDDING ANYONE FROM DELIVERING FOOD OR MEDICAL SUPPLIES TO THE RESIDENTS OF DEATH'S DOORSTEP.

NO! WHAT ARE YOU DOING?!?

DESPERATE TO HELP AND APPALLED BY THE CITY'S NEGLECT, CATHERINE MADE NIGHTLY RUNS TO THE EDGE OF DEATH'S DOORSTEP TO DELIVER ILLEGAL SUPPLIES.

NOT EVEN HER HUSBAND WAS AWARE OF HER ACTIONS.

IT WAS DURING JUST SUCH AN EVENING WHEN THE VICTIMS AND OUTCASTS TOOK CATHERINE, AND IN EXCHANGE FOR HER SAFE RETURN, THEY DEMANDED SUPPLIES AND DOCTORS.

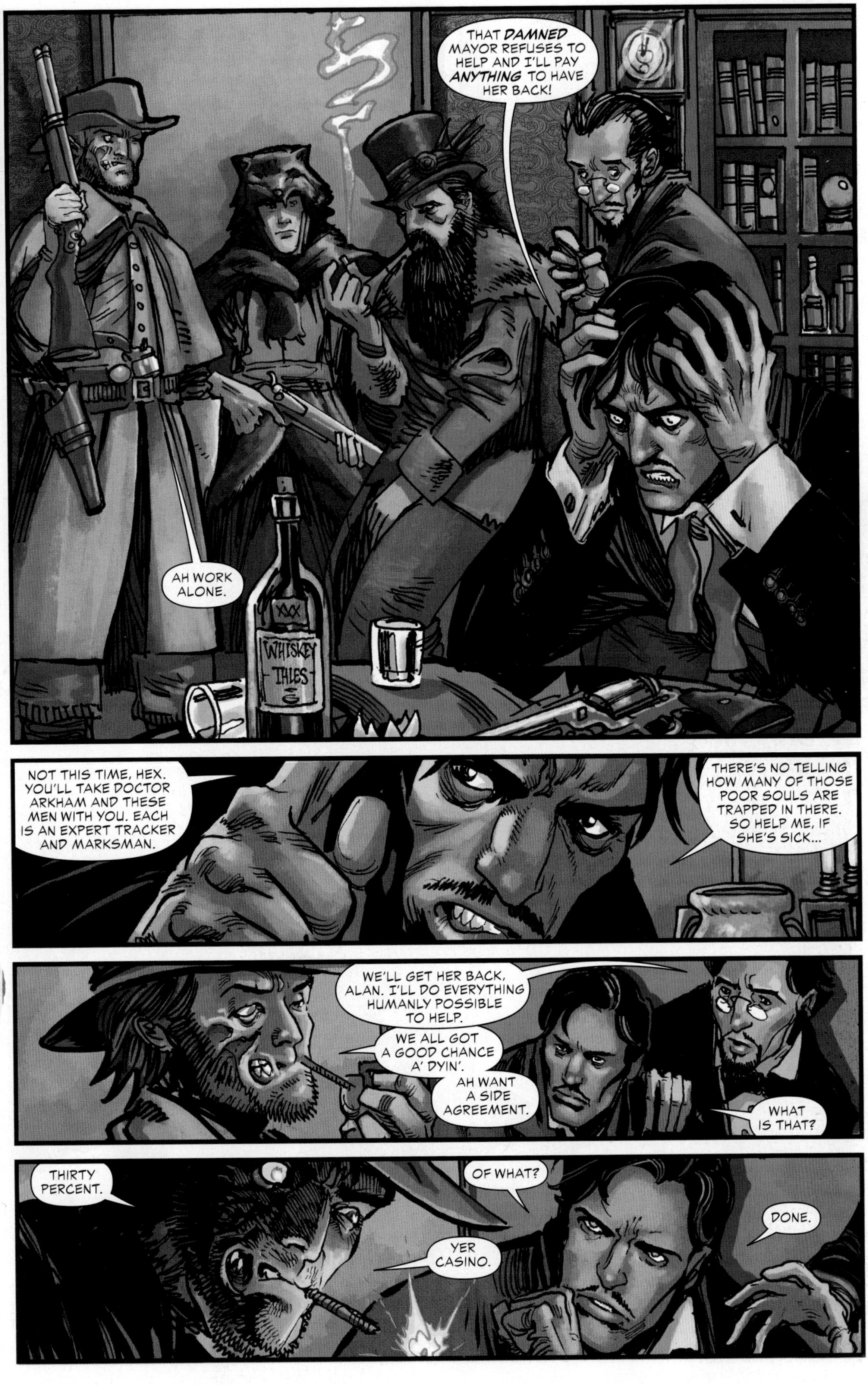
THAT DAMNED MAYOR REFUSES TO HELP AND I'LL PAY ANYTHING TO HAVE HER BACK!
AH WORK ALONE.
WHISKEY TALES
NOT THIS TIME, HEX. YOU'LL TAKE DOCTOR ARKHAM AND THESE MEN WITH YOU. EACH IS AN EXPERT TRACKER AND MARKSMAN.
THERE'S NO TELLING HOW MANY OF THOSE POOR SOULS ARE TRAPPED IN THERE. SO HELP ME, IF SHE'S SICK...
WE'LL GET HER BACK, ALAN. I'LL DO EVERYTHING HUMANLY POSSIBLE TO HELP.
WE ALL GOT A GOOD CHANCE A' DYIN'.
AH WANT A SIDE AGREEMENT.
WHAT IS THAT?
THIRTY PERCENT.
OF WHAT?
YER CASINO.
DONE.

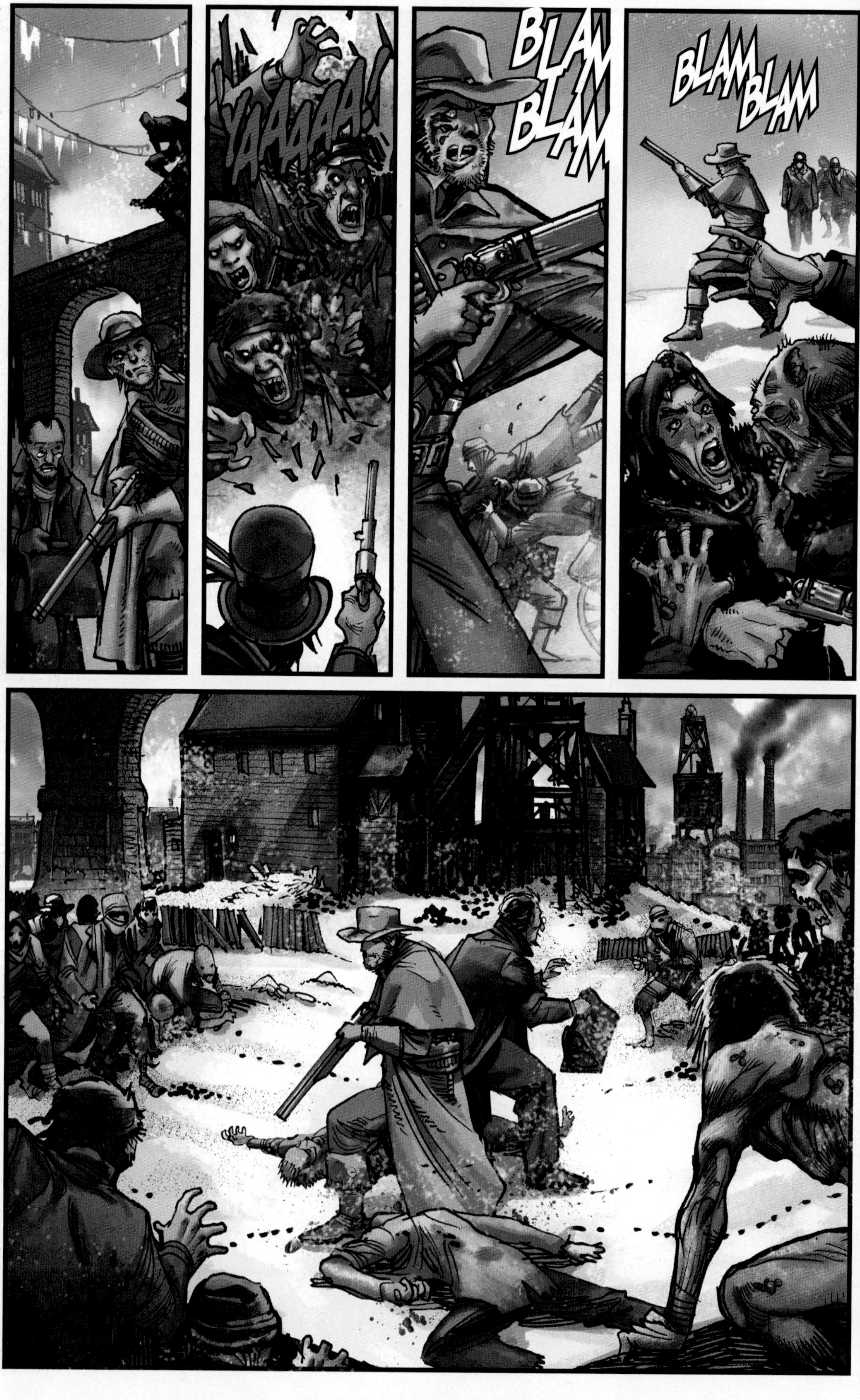
YAAAAA!
BLAM
BLAM
BLAM
BLAM
BLAM

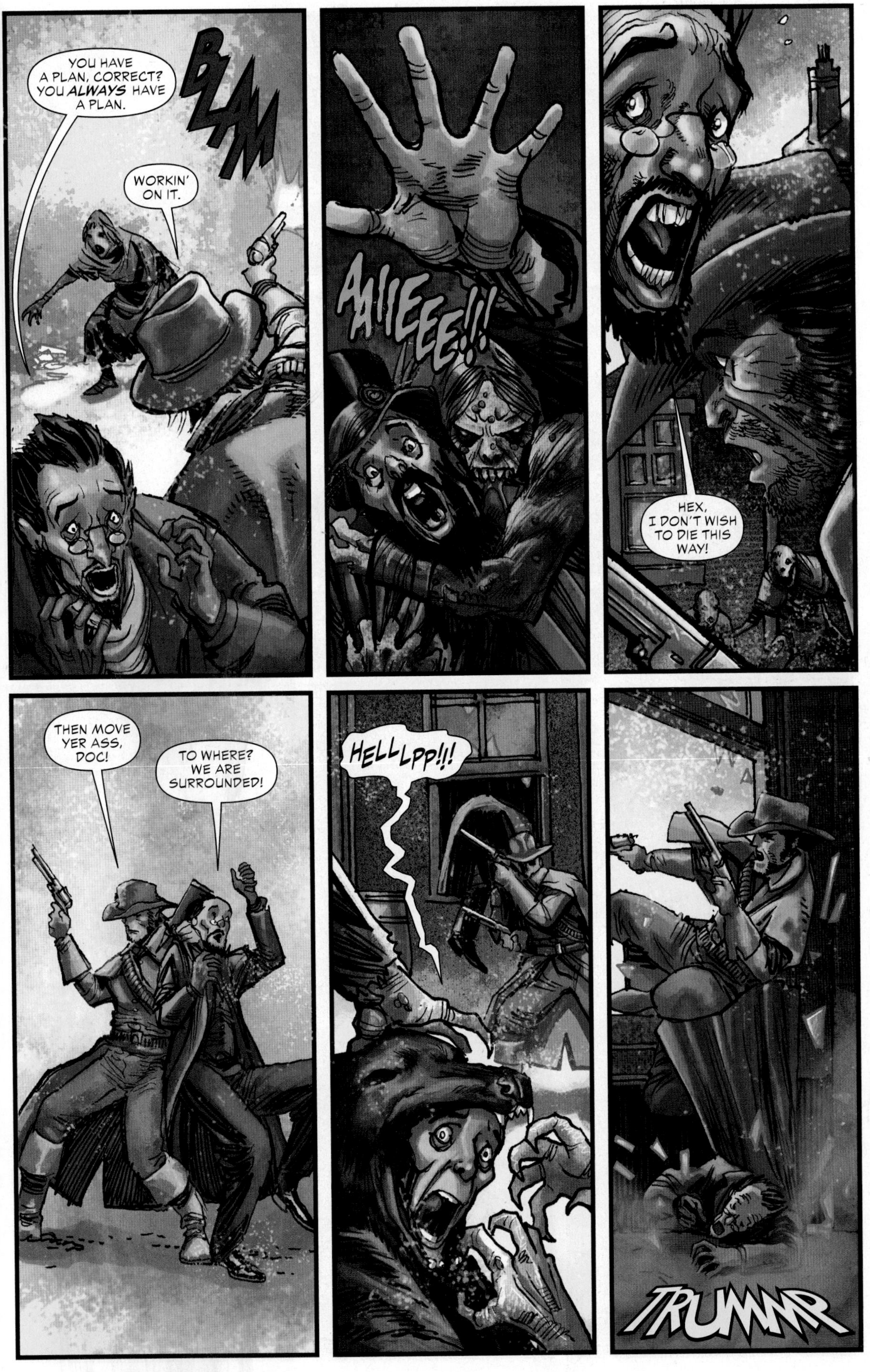
YOU HAVE A PLAN, CORRECT? YOU ALWAYS HAVE A PLAN.
BLAM
WORKIN' ON IT.
AAIIEEE!!!
HEX, I DON'T WISH TO DIE THIS WAY!
THEN MOVE YER ASS, DOC!
TO WHERE? WE ARE SURROUNDED!
HELLLPP!!!
TRUMMP

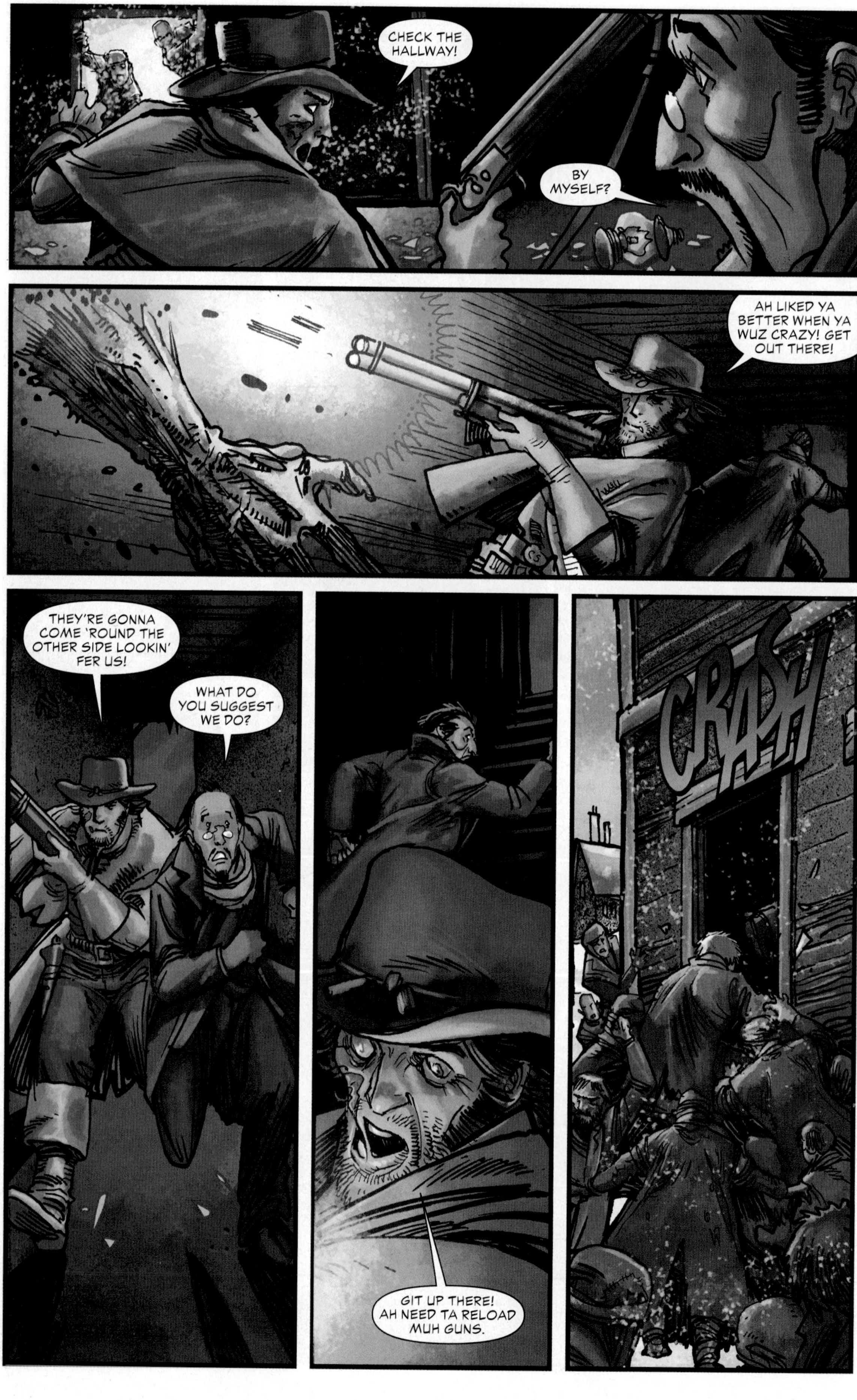
CHECK THE HALLWAY!
BY MYSELF?
AH LIKED YA BETTER WHEN YA WUZ CRAZY! GET OUT THERE!
THEY'RE GONNA COME 'ROUND THE OTHER SIDE LOOKIN' FER US!
WHAT DO YOU SUGGEST WE DO?
GIT UP THERE! AH NEED TA RELOAD MUH GUNS.
CRASH

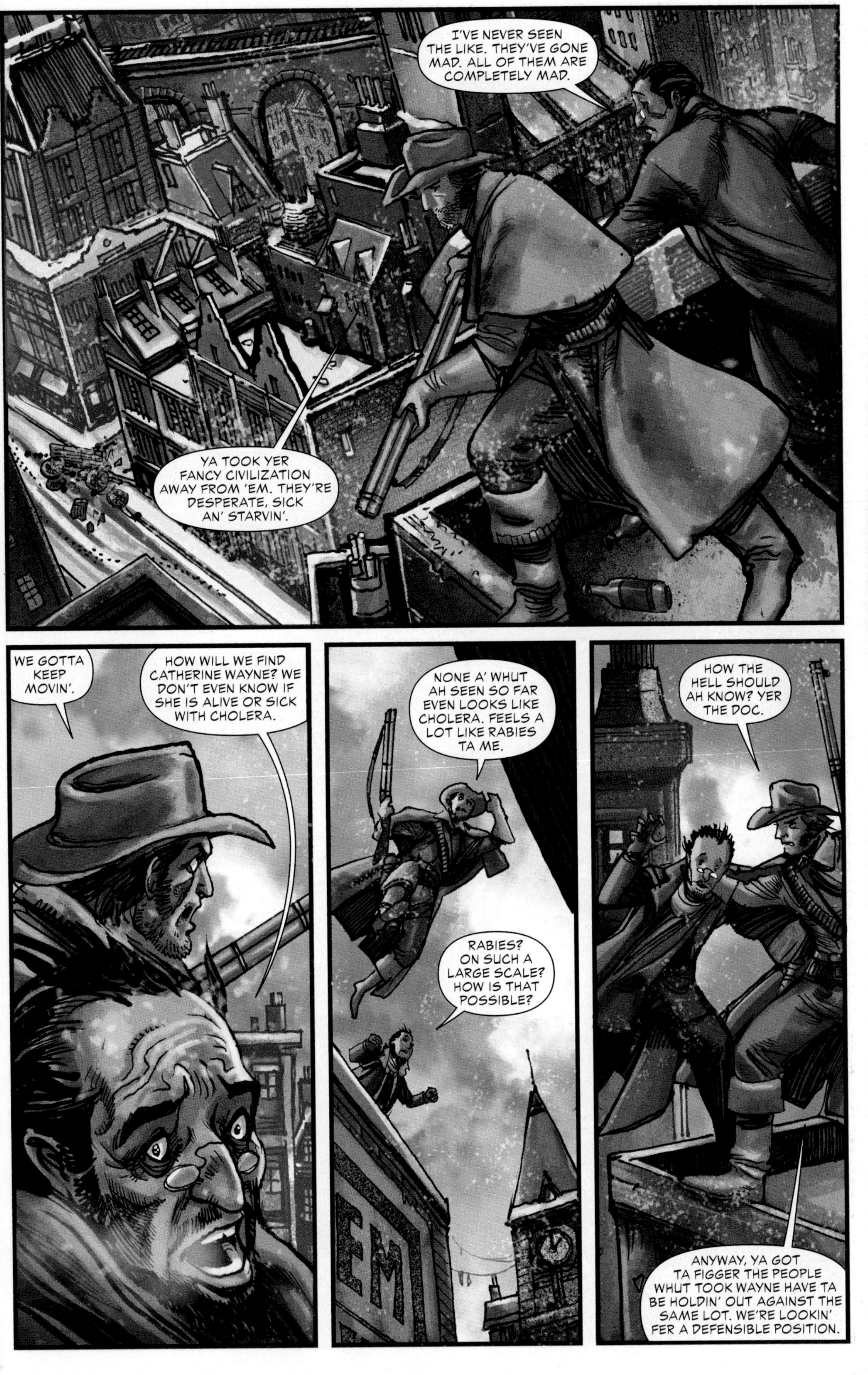
I'VE NEVER SEEN THE LIKE. THEY'VE GONE MAD. ALL OF THEM ARE COMPLETELY MAD.
YA TOOK YER FANCY CIVILIZATION AWAY FROM 'EM. THEY'RE DESPERATE, SICK AN' STARVIN'.
WE GOTTA KEEP MOVIN'.
HOW WILL WE FIND CATHERINE WAYNE? WE DON'T EVEN KNOW IF SHE IS ALIVE OR SICK WITH CHOLERA.
NONE A' WHUT AH SEEN SO FAR EVEN LOOKS LIKE CHOLERA. FEELS A LOT LIKE RABIES TA ME.
RABIES? ON SUCH A LARGE SCALE? HOW IS THAT POSSIBLE?
HOW THE HELL SHOULD AH KNOW? YER THE DOC.
ANYWAY, YA GOT TA FIGGER THE PEOPLE WHUT TOOK WAYNE HAVE TA BE HOLDIN' OUT AGAINST THE SAME LOT. WE'RE LOOKIN' FER A DEFENSIBLE POSITION.

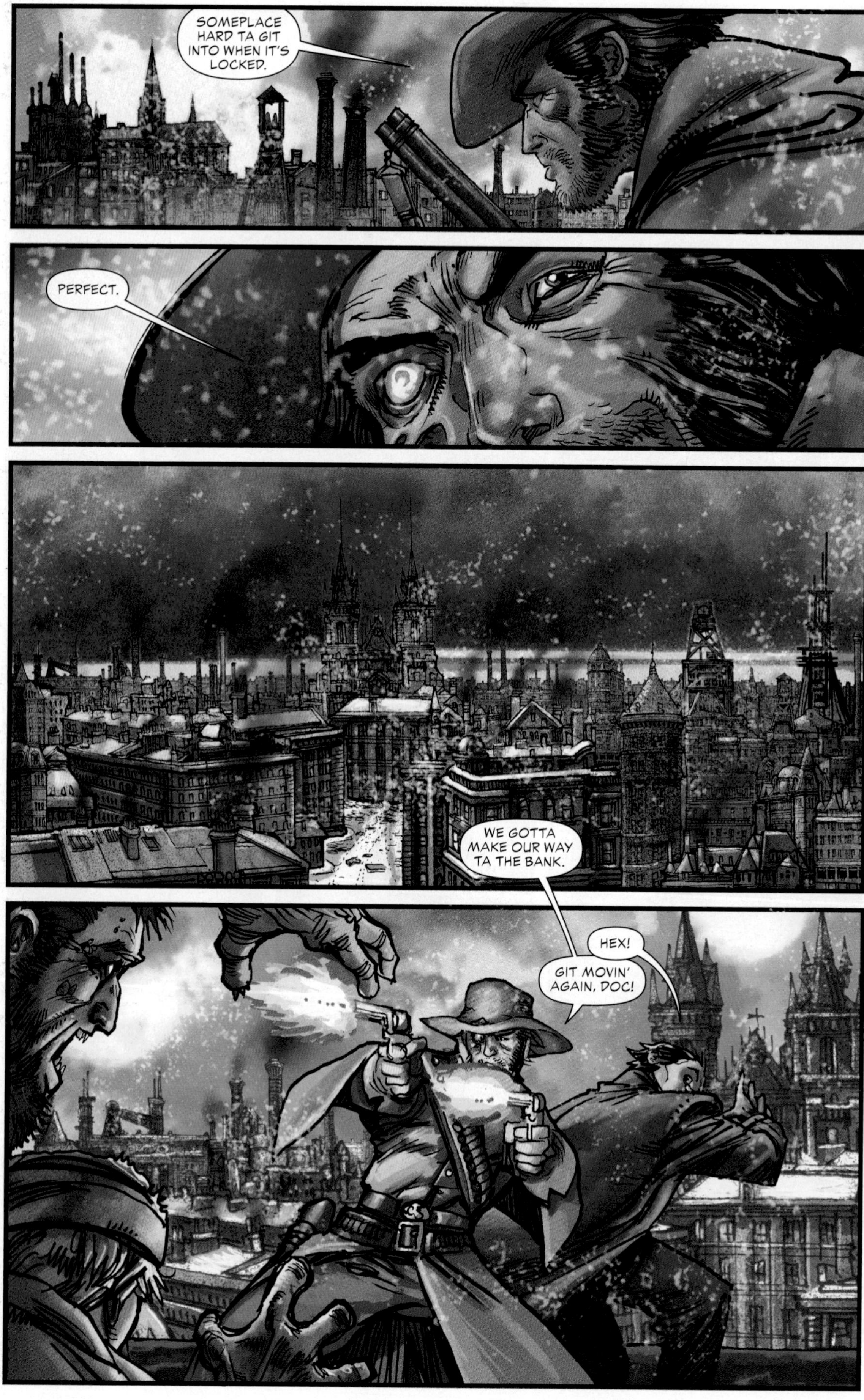
SOMEPLACE HARD TA GIT INTO WHEN IT'S LOCKED.
PERFECT.
WE GOTTA MAKE OUR WAY TA THE BANK.
HEX!
GIT MOVIN' AGAIN, DOC!

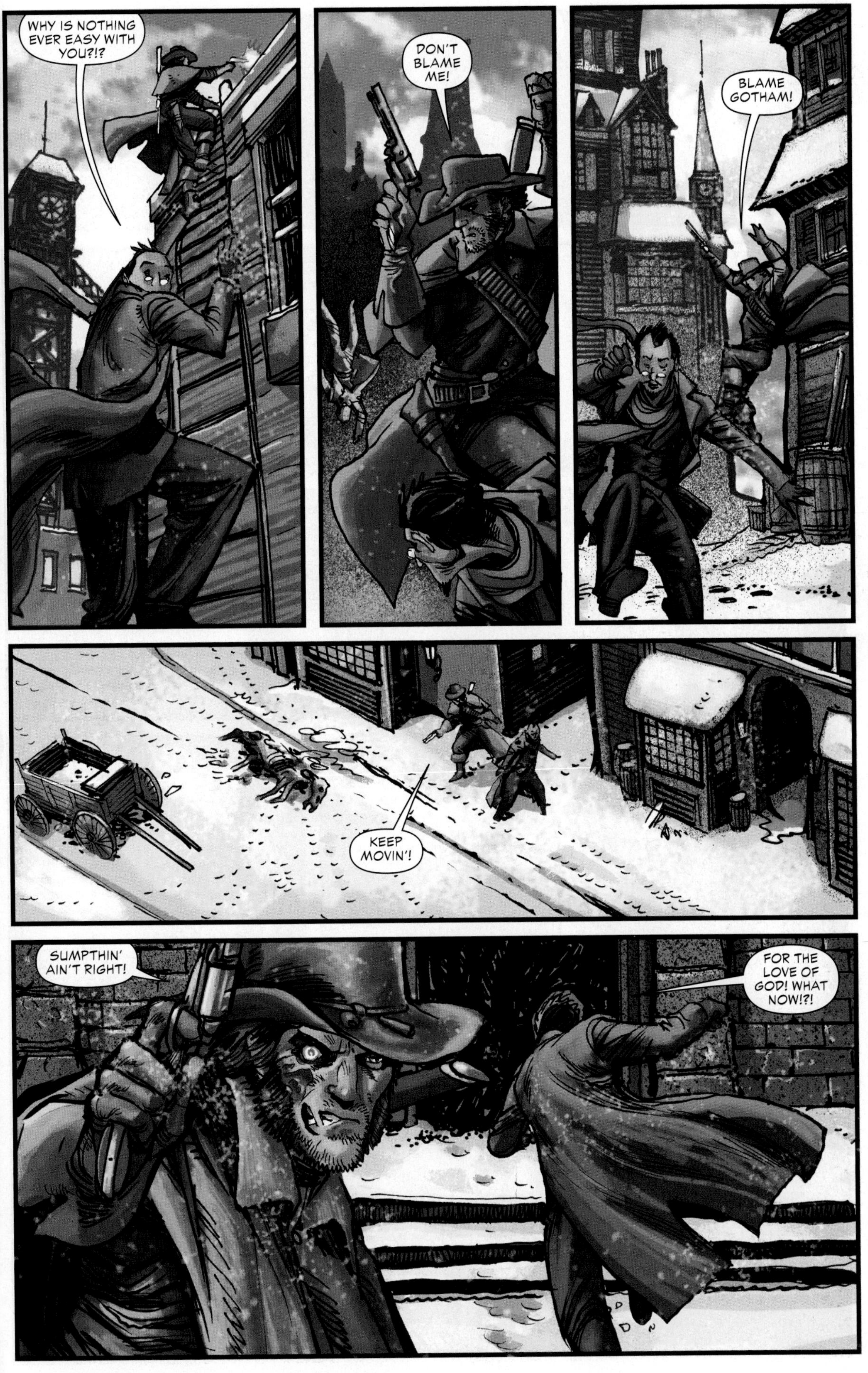
WHY IS NOTHING EVER EASY WITH YOU?!?
DON'T BLAME ME!
BLAME GOTHAM!
KEEP MOVIN'!
SUMPTHIN' AIN'T RIGHT!
FOR THE LOVE OF GOD! WHAT NOW!?!

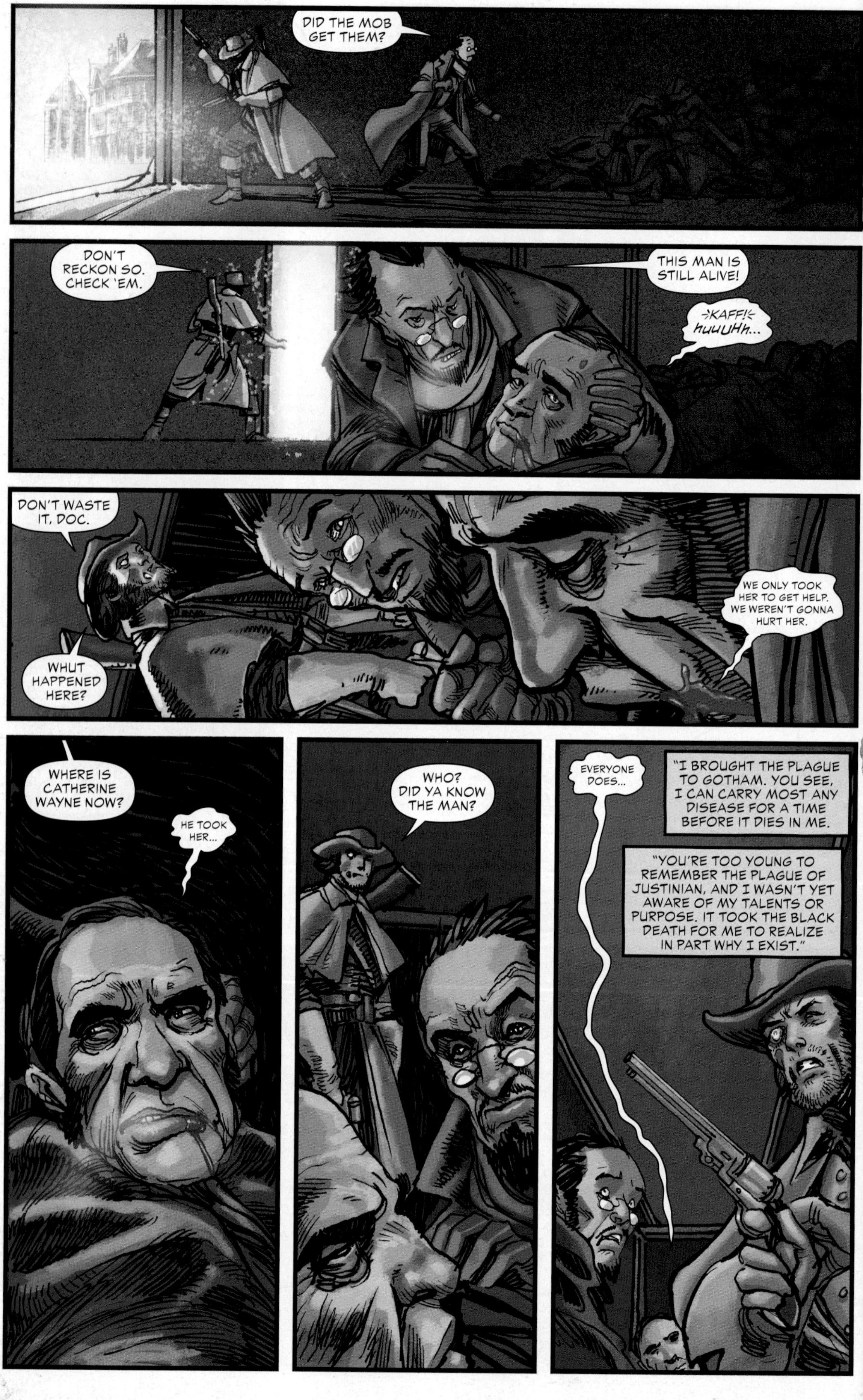
DID THE MOB GET THEM?
DON'T RECKON SO. CHECK 'EM.
THIS MAN IS STILL ALIVE!
KAFF! huuuHh...
DON'T WASTE IT, DOC.
WHUT HAPPENED HERE?
WE ONLY TOOK HER TO GET HELP. WE WEREN'T GONNA HURT HER.
WHERE IS CATHERINE WAYNE NOW?
HE TOOK HER...
WHO? DID YA KNOW THE MAN?
EVERYONE DOES...
"I BROUGHT THE PLAGUE TO GOTHAM. YOU SEE, I CAN CARRY MOST ANY DISEASE FOR A TIME BEFORE IT DIES IN ME.
"YOU'RE TOO YOUNG TO REMEMBER THE PLAGUE OF JUSTINIAN, AND I WASN'T YET AWARE OF MY TALENTS OR PURPOSE. IT TOOK THE BLACK DEATH FOR ME TO REALIZE IN PART WHY I EXIST."

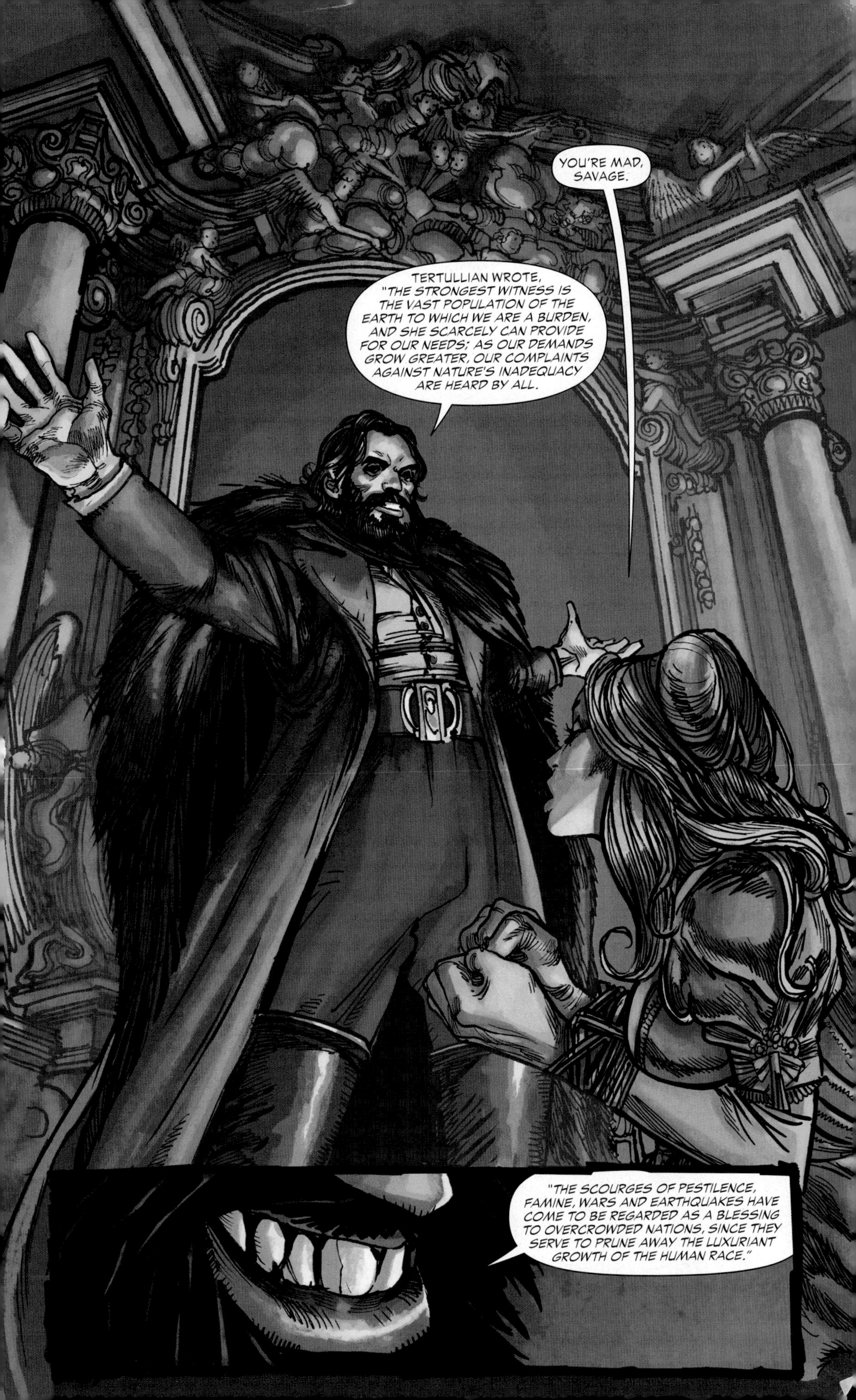
YOU'RE MAD, SAVAGE.
TERTULLIAN WROTE, "THE STRONGEST WITNESS IS THE VAST POPULATION OF THE EARTH TO WHICH WE ARE A BURDEN, AND SHE SCARCELY CAN PROVIDE FOR OUR NEEDS; AS OUR DEMANDS GROW GREATER, OUR COMPLAINTS AGAINST NATURE'S INADEQUACY ARE HEARD BY ALL.
"THE SCOURGES OF PESTILENCE, FAMINE, WARS AND EARTHQUAKES HAVE COME TO BE REGARDED AS A BLESSING TO OVERCROWDED NATIONS, SINCE THEY SERVE TO PRUNE AWAY THE LUXURIANT GROWTH OF THE HUMAN RACE."

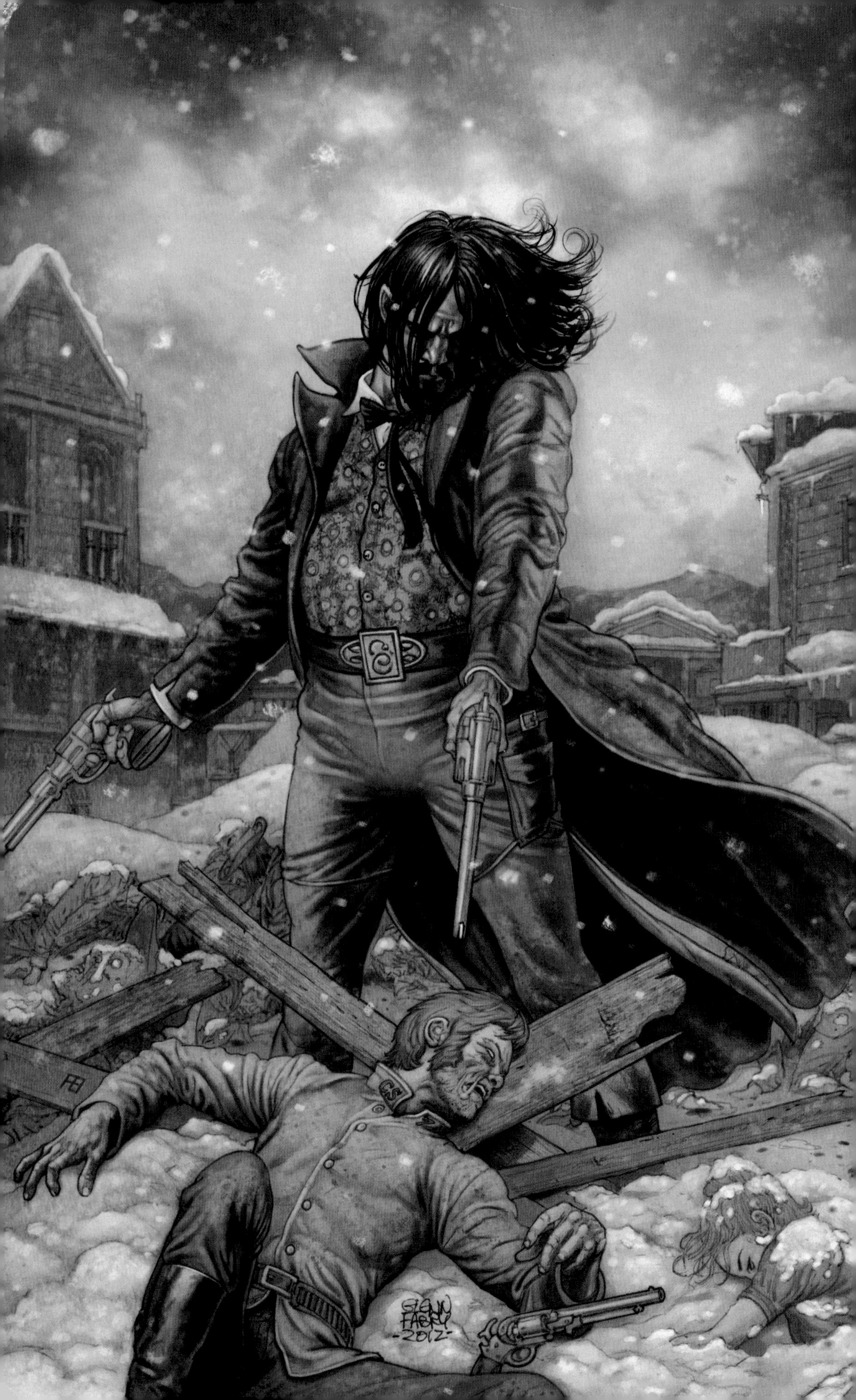
GLENN FABRY -2012-

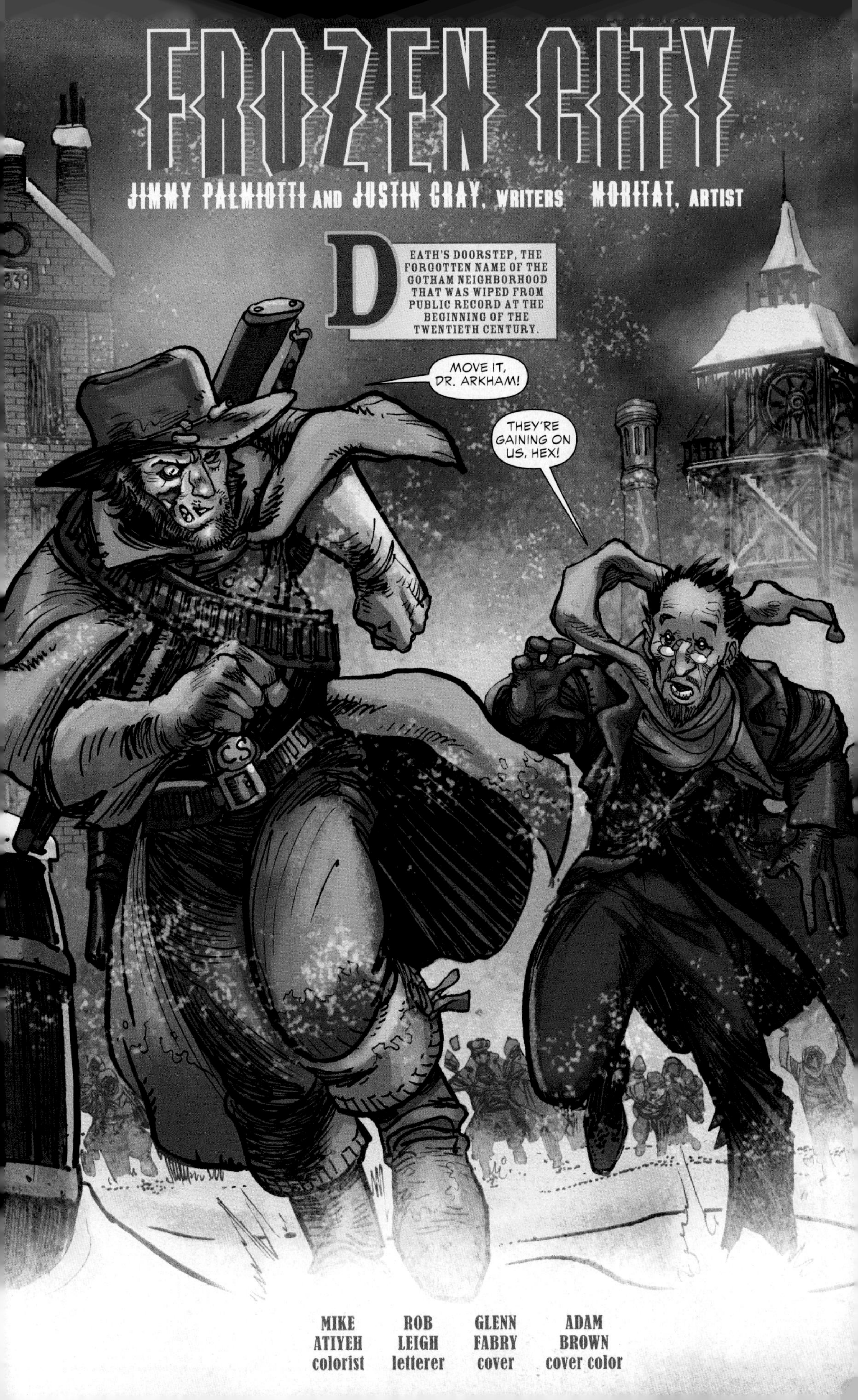
FROZEN CITY
JIMMY PALMIOTTI AND JUSTIN GRAY, WRITERS MORITAT, ARTIST
DEATH'S DOORSTEP, THE FORGOTTEN NAME OF THE GOTHAM NEIGHBORHOOD THAT WAS WIPED FROM PUBLIC RECORD AT THE BEGINNING OF THE TWENTIETH CENTURY.
MOVE IT, DR. ARKHAM!
THEY'RE GAINING ON US, HEX!
MIKE ATIYEH colorist
ROB LEIGH letterer
GLENN FABRY cover
ADAM BROWN cover color

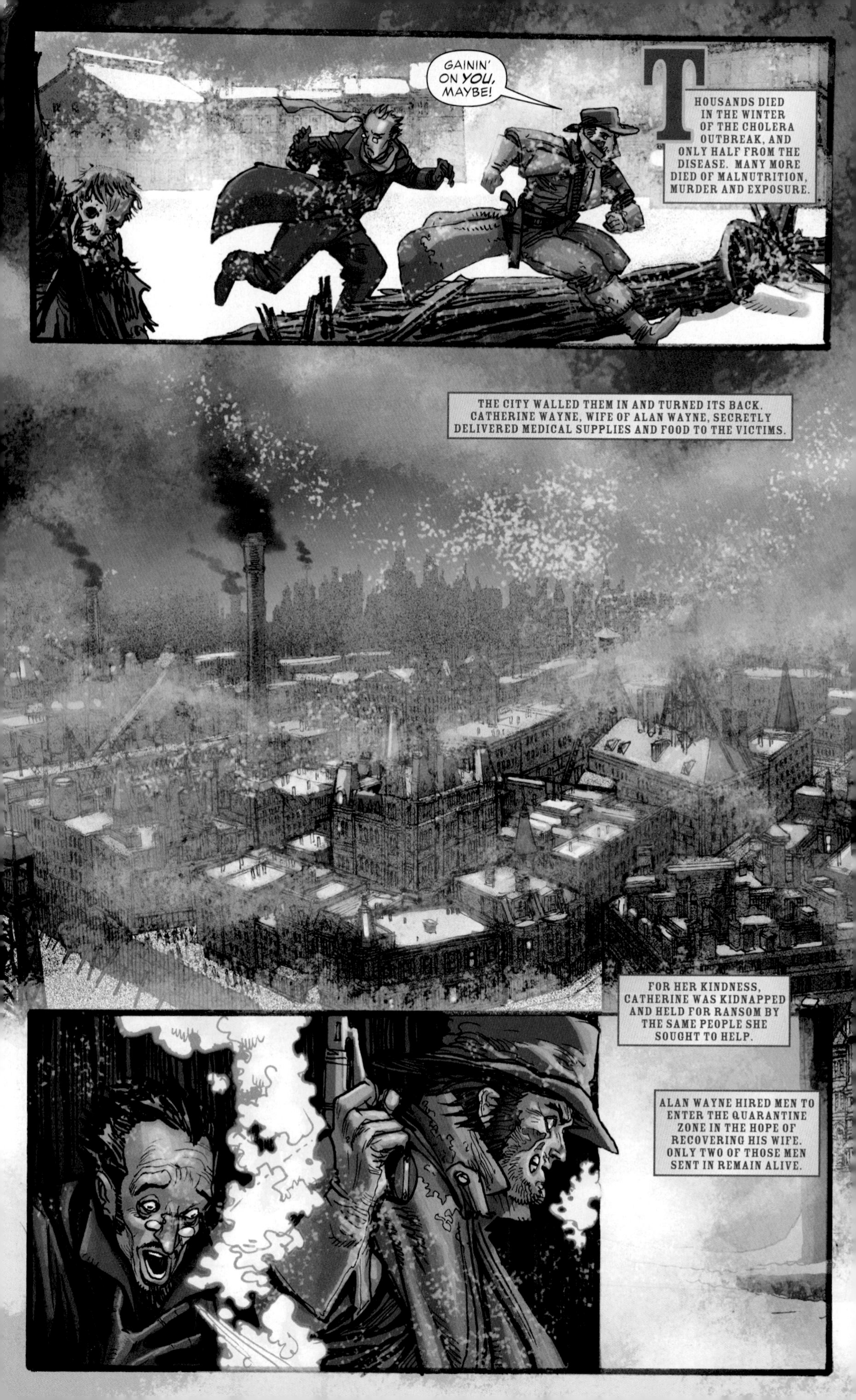
GAININ' ON YOU, MAYBE!
THOUSANDS DIED IN THE WINTER OF THE CHOLERA OUTBREAK, AND ONLY HALF FROM THE DISEASE. MANY MORE DIED OF MALNUTRITION, MURDER AND EXPOSURE.
THE CITY WALLED THEM IN AND TURNED ITS BACK. CATHERINE WAYNE, WIFE OF ALAN WAYNE, SECRETLY DELIVERED MEDICAL SUPPLIES AND FOOD TO THE VICTIMS.
FOR HER KINDNESS, CATHERINE WAS KIDNAPPED AND HELD FOR RANSOM BY THE SAME PEOPLE SHE SOUGHT TO HELP.
ALAN WAYNE HIRED MEN TO ENTER THE QUARANTINE ZONE IN THE HOPE OF RECOVERING HIS WIFE. ONLY TWO OF THOSE MEN SENT IN REMAIN ALIVE.

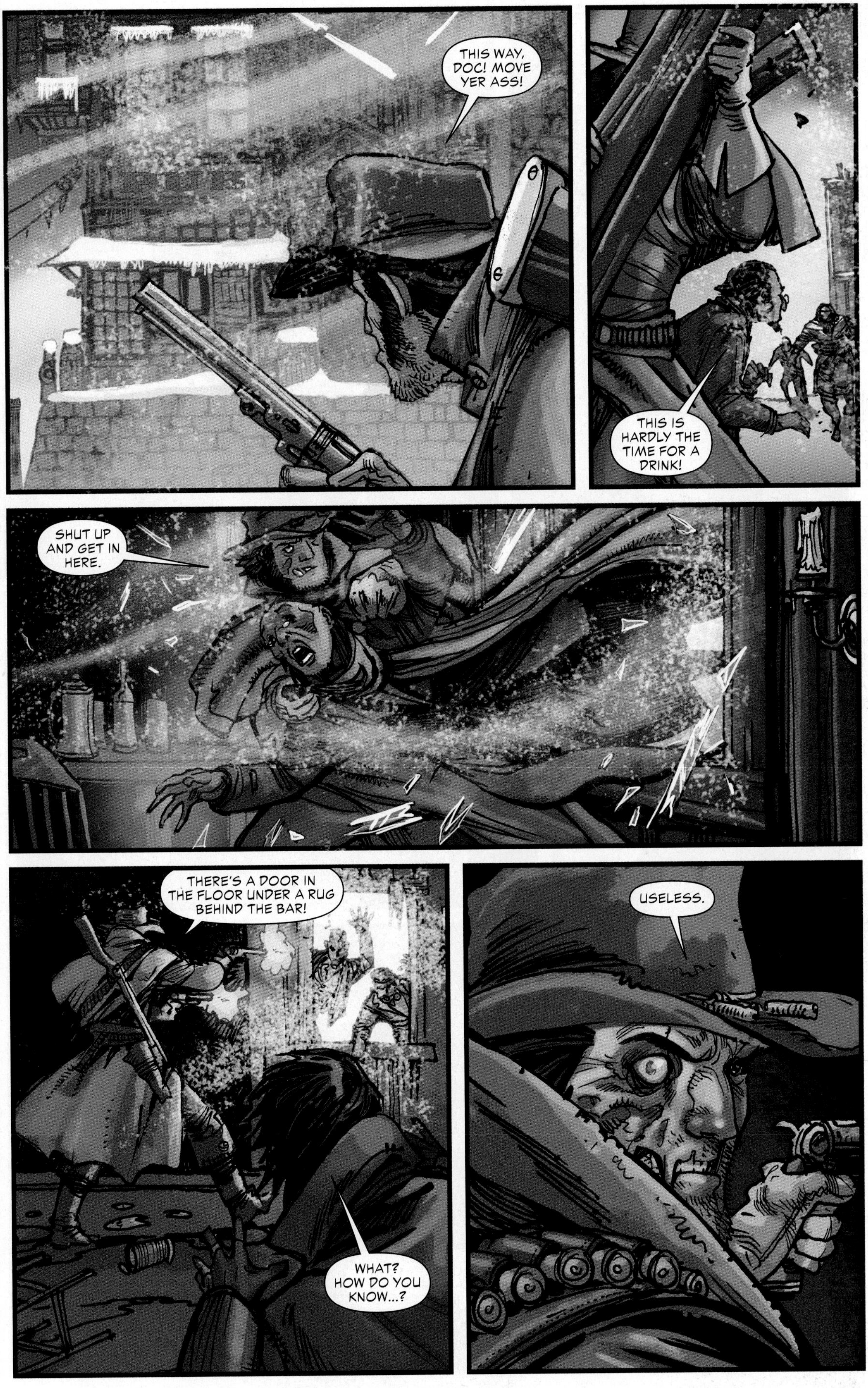
THIS WAY, DOC! MOVE YER ASS!
THIS IS HARDLY THE TIME FOR A DRINK!
SHUT UP AND GET IN HERE.
THERE'S A DOOR IN THE FLOOR UNDER A RUG BEHIND THE BAR!
WHAT? HOW DO YOU KNOW...?
USELESS.

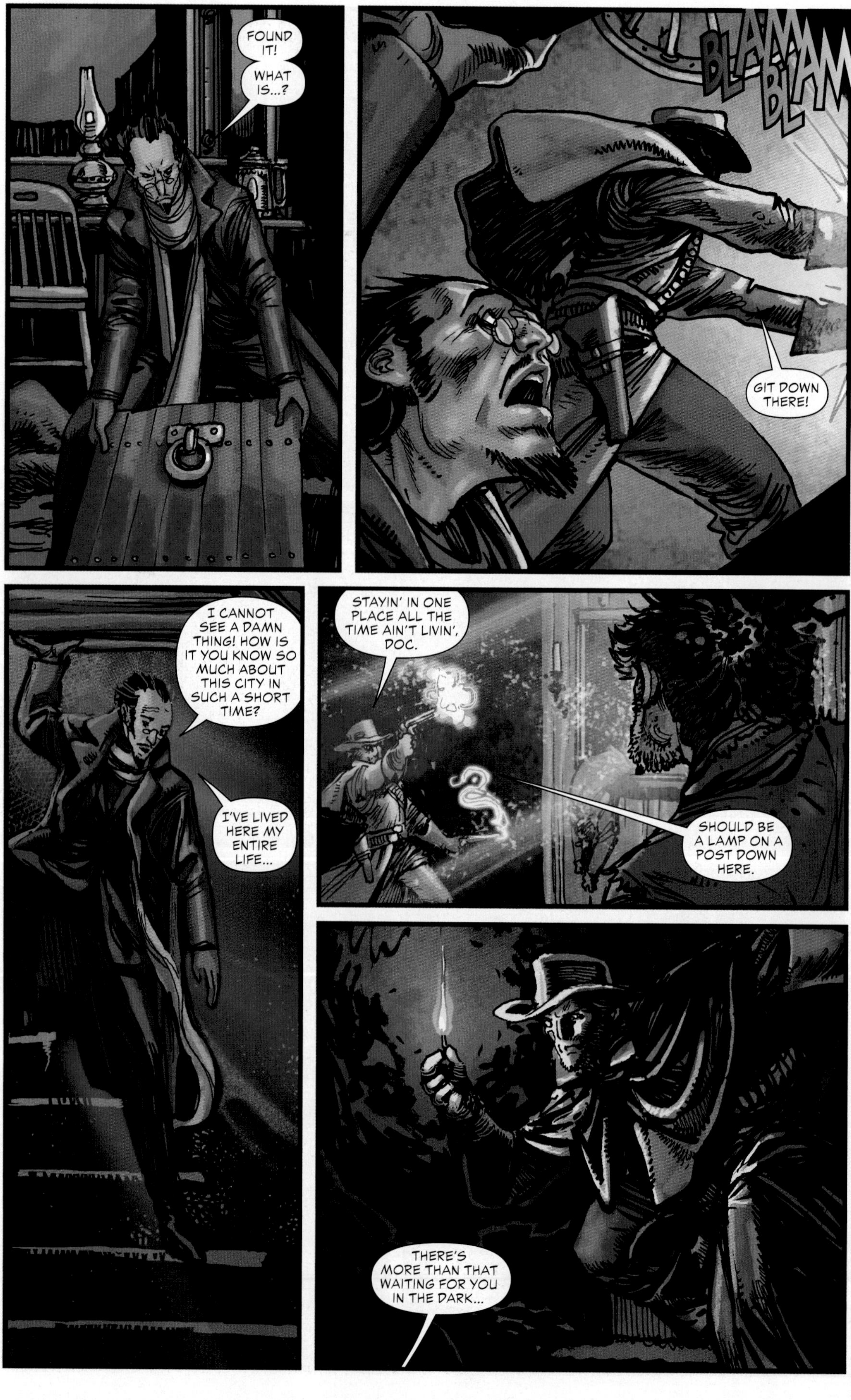
FOUND IT!
WHAT IS...?
BLAM BLAM
GIT DOWN THERE!
I CANNOT SEE A DAMN THING! HOW IS IT YOU KNOW SO MUCH ABOUT THIS CITY IN SUCH A SHORT TIME?
I'VE LIVED HERE MY ENTIRE LIFE...
STAYIN' IN ONE PLACE ALL THE TIME AIN'T LIVIN', DOC.
SHOULD BE A LAMP ON A POST DOWN HERE.
THERE'S MORE THAN THAT WAITING FOR YOU IN THE DARK...

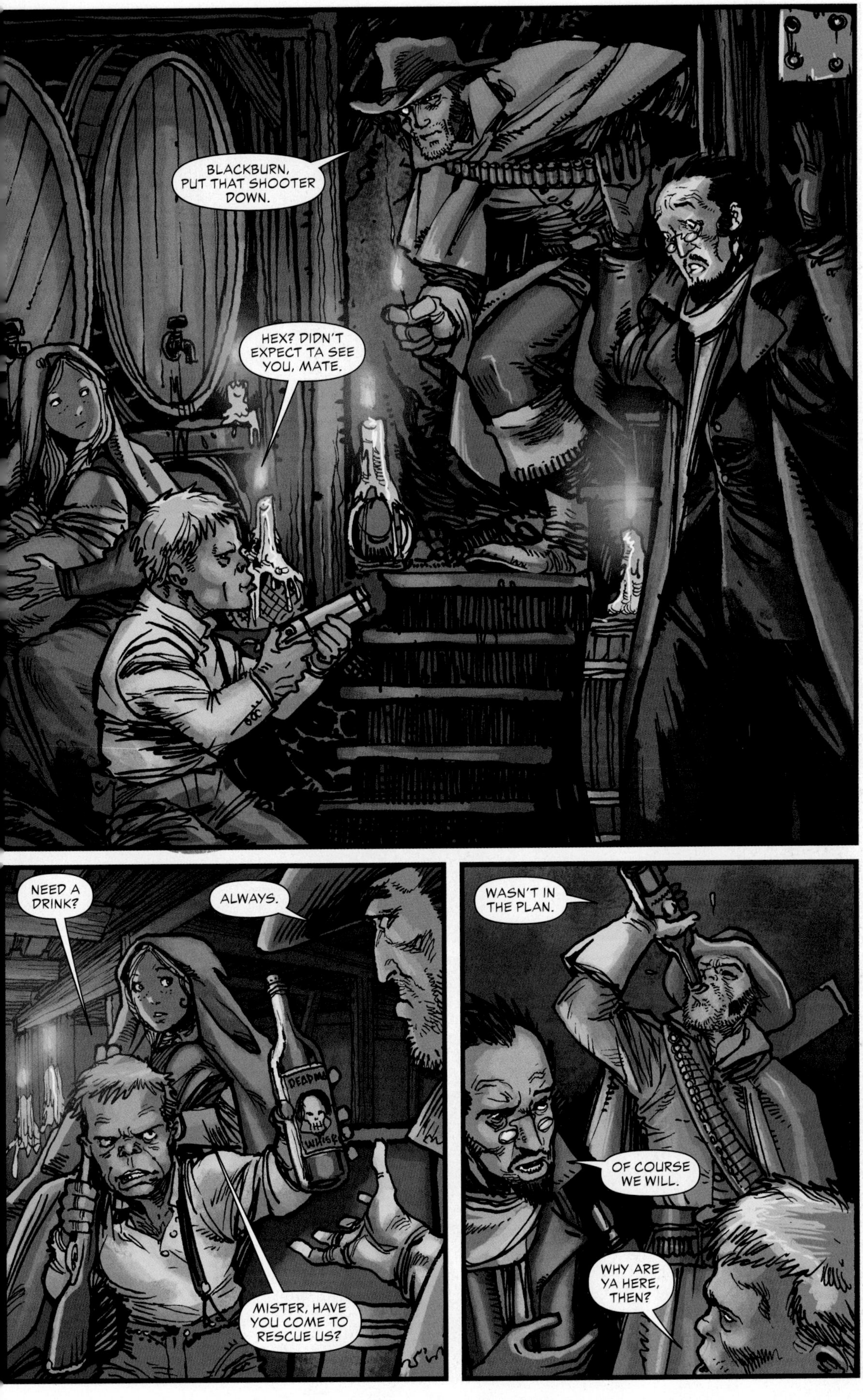
BLACKBURN, PUT THAT SHOOTER DOWN.
HEX? DIDN'T EXPECT TA SEE YOU, MATE.
NEED A DRINK?
ALWAYS.
MISTER, HAVE YOU COME TO RESCUE US?
WASN'T IN THE PLAN.
OF COURSE WE WILL.
WHY ARE YA HERE, THEN?

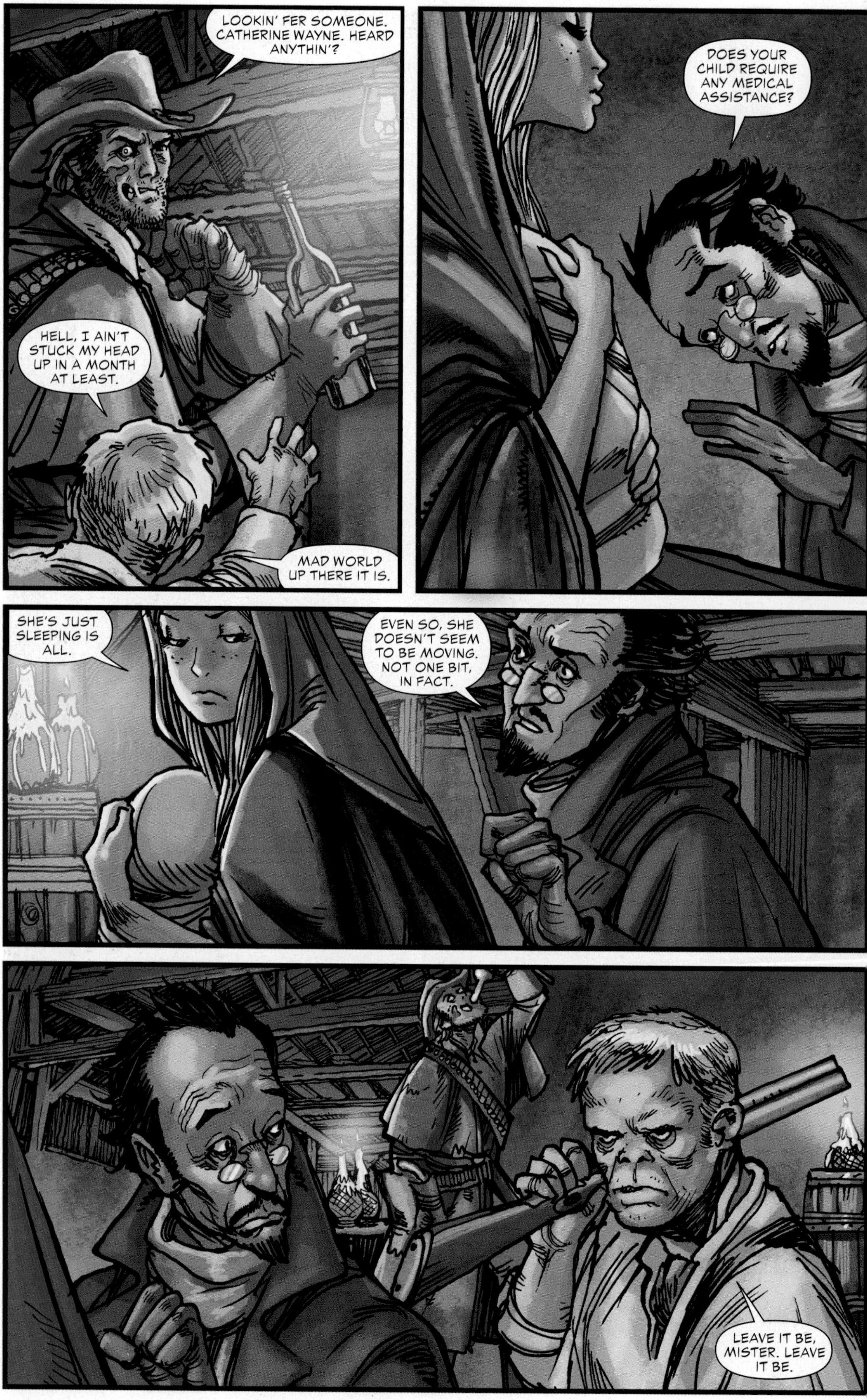
LOOKIN' FER SOMEONE. CATHERINE WAYNE. HEARD ANYTHIN'?
HELL, I AIN'T STUCK MY HEAD UP IN A MONTH AT LEAST.
MAD WORLD UP THERE IT IS.
DOES YOUR CHILD REQUIRE ANY MEDICAL ASSISTANCE?
SHE'S JUST SLEEPING IS ALL.
EVEN SO, SHE DOESN'T SEEM TO BE MOVING. NOT ONE BIT, IN FACT.
LEAVE IT BE, MISTER. LEAVE IT BE.

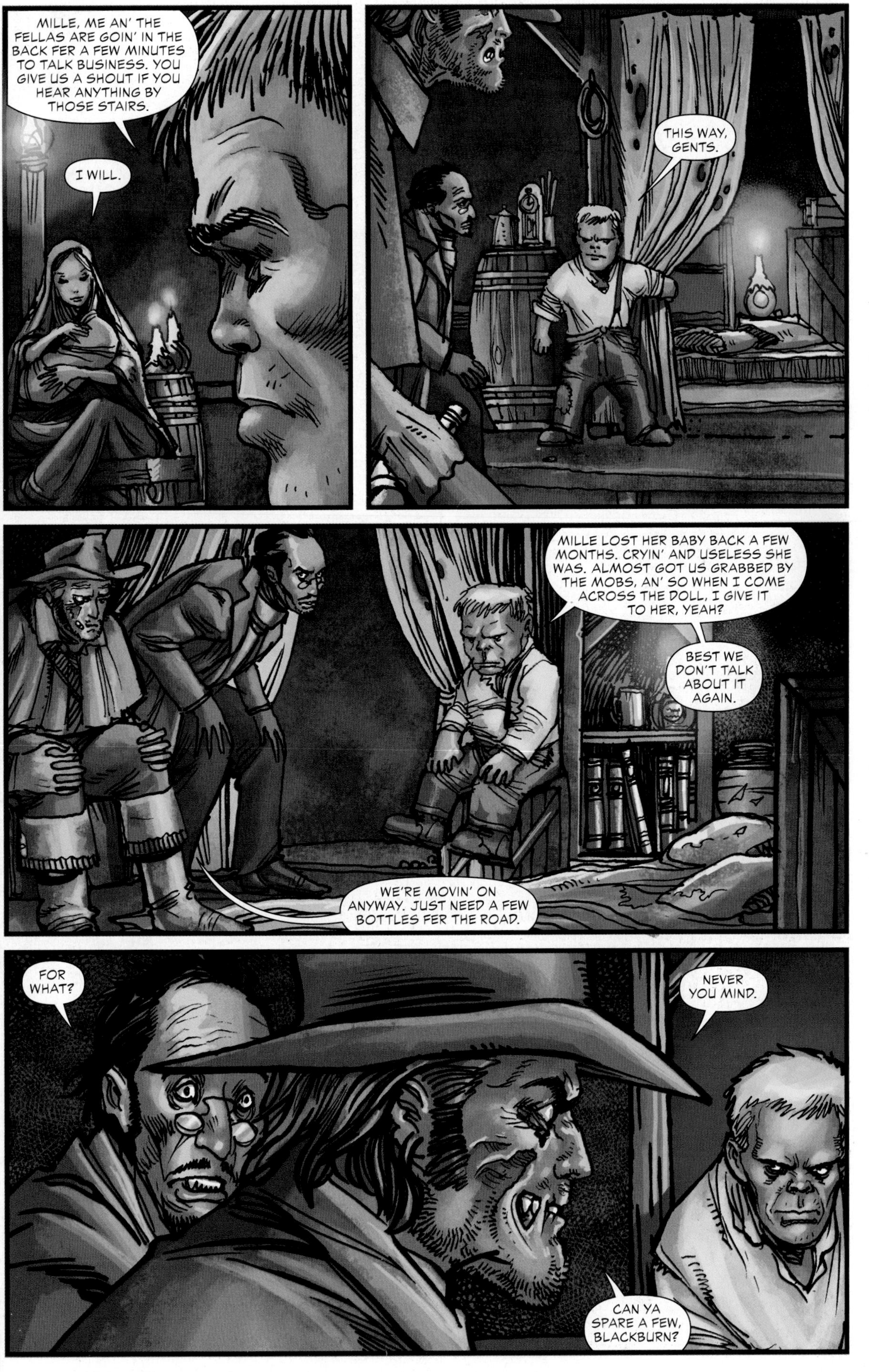
MILLE, ME AN' THE FELLAS ARE GOIN' IN THE BACK FER A FEW MINUTES TO TALK BUSINESS. YOU GIVE US A SHOUT IF YOU HEAR ANYTHING BY THOSE STAIRS.
I WILL.
THIS WAY, GENTS.
MILLE LOST HER BABY BACK A FEW MONTHS. CRYIN' AND USELESS SHE WAS. ALMOST GOT US GRABBED BY THE MOBS, AN' SO WHEN I COME ACROSS THE DOLL, I GIVE IT TO HER, YEAH?
BEST WE DON'T TALK ABOUT IT AGAIN.
WE'RE MOVIN' ON ANYWAY. JUST NEED A FEW BOTTLES FER THE ROAD.
FOR WHAT?
NEVER YOU MIND.
CAN YA SPARE A FEW, BLACKBURN?

I'LL GIVE YOU ALL YOU CAN CARRY IF YOU TAKE US WITH YOU.

CAN'T DO IT. THEM LITTLE LEGS WILL SLOW ME DOWN TOO MUCH.

WE CAN'T LEAVE THEM HERE, HEX! BE REASONABLE.

WHO'S WE? YA WANNA SAVE 'EM, GO ON AHEAD. AH GOT TA FIND WAYNE.

YOU ARE A HEARTLESS BASTARD SOMETIMES.

AH'M FOCUSED ON THE TASK AT HAND. YA OUGHTA DO THE SAME.

OF COURSE YOU CAN COME WITH US, MR. BLACKBURN. WE'LL DO OUR BEST TO GET YOU OUT OF THE CITY.

I APPRECIATE THAT, BUT I AIN'T AS HELPLESS AS HEX SUGGESTS.

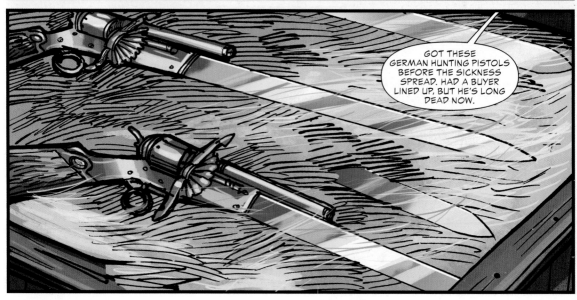

GOT THESE GERMAN HUNTING PISTOLS BEFORE THE SICKNESS SPREAD. HAD A BUYER LINED UP, BUT HE'S LONG DEAD NOW.

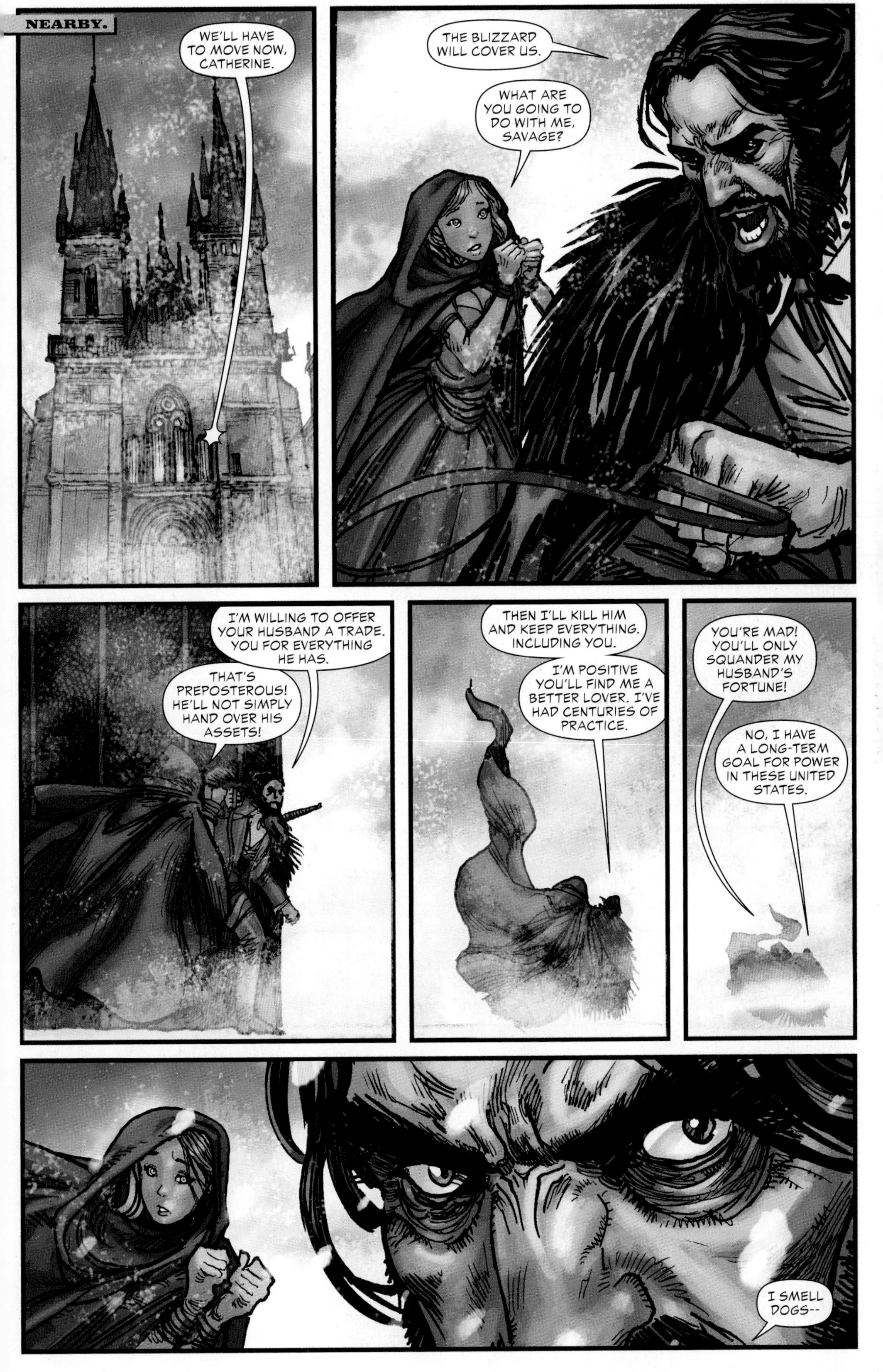
NEARBY.
WE'LL HAVE TO MOVE NOW, CATHERINE.
THE BLIZZARD WILL COVER US.
WHAT ARE YOU GOING TO DO WITH ME, SAVAGE?
I'M WILLING TO OFFER YOUR HUSBAND A TRADE. YOU FOR EVERYTHING HE HAS.
THAT'S PREPOSTEROUS! HE'LL NOT SIMPLY HAND OVER HIS ASSETS!
THEN I'LL KILL HIM AND KEEP EVERYTHING. INCLUDING YOU.
I'M POSITIVE YOU'LL FIND ME A BETTER LOVER. I'VE HAD CENTURIES OF PRACTICE.
YOU'RE MAD! YOU'LL ONLY SQUANDER MY HUSBAND'S FORTUNE!
NO, I HAVE A LONG-TERM GOAL FOR POWER IN THESE UNITED STATES.
I SMELL DOGS--

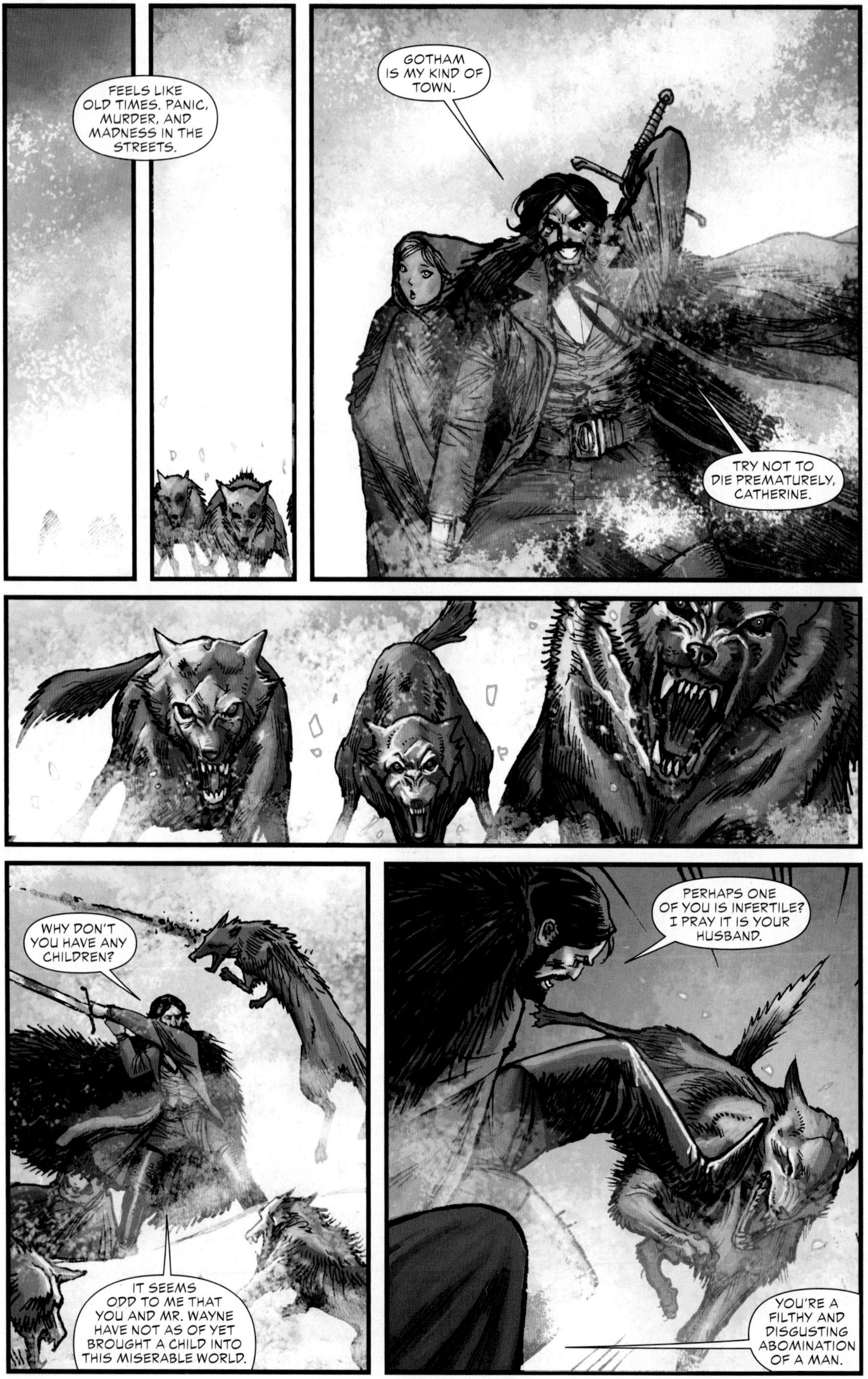
FEELS LIKE OLD TIMES. PANIC, MURDER, AND MADNESS IN THE STREETS.
GOTHAM IS MY KIND OF TOWN.
TRY NOT TO DIE PREMATURELY, CATHERINE.
WHY DON'T YOU HAVE ANY CHILDREN?
IT SEEMS ODD TO ME THAT YOU AND MR. WAYNE HAVE NOT AS OF YET BROUGHT A CHILD INTO THIS MISERABLE WORLD.
PERHAPS ONE OF YOU IS INFERTILE? I PRAY IT IS YOUR HUSBAND.
YOU'RE A FILTHY AND DISGUSTING ABOMINATION OF A MAN.

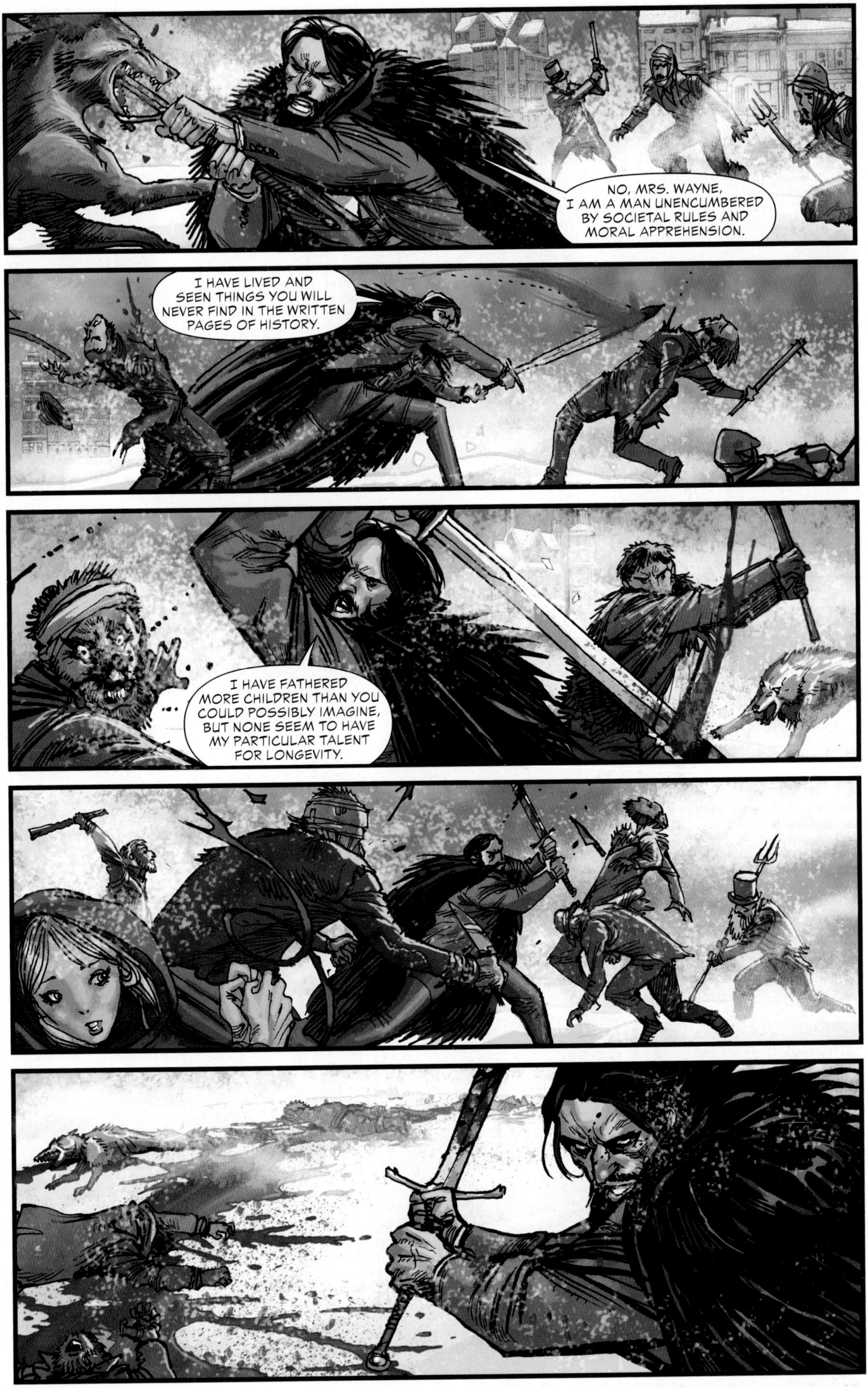
NO, MRS. WAYNE, I AM A MAN UNENCUMBERED BY SOCIETAL RULES AND MORAL APPREHENSION.
I HAVE LIVED AND SEEN THINGS YOU WILL NEVER FIND IN THE WRITTEN PAGES OF HISTORY.
I HAVE FATHERED MORE CHILDREN THAN YOU COULD POSSIBLY IMAGINE, BUT NONE SEEM TO HAVE MY PARTICULAR TALENT FOR LONGEVITY.

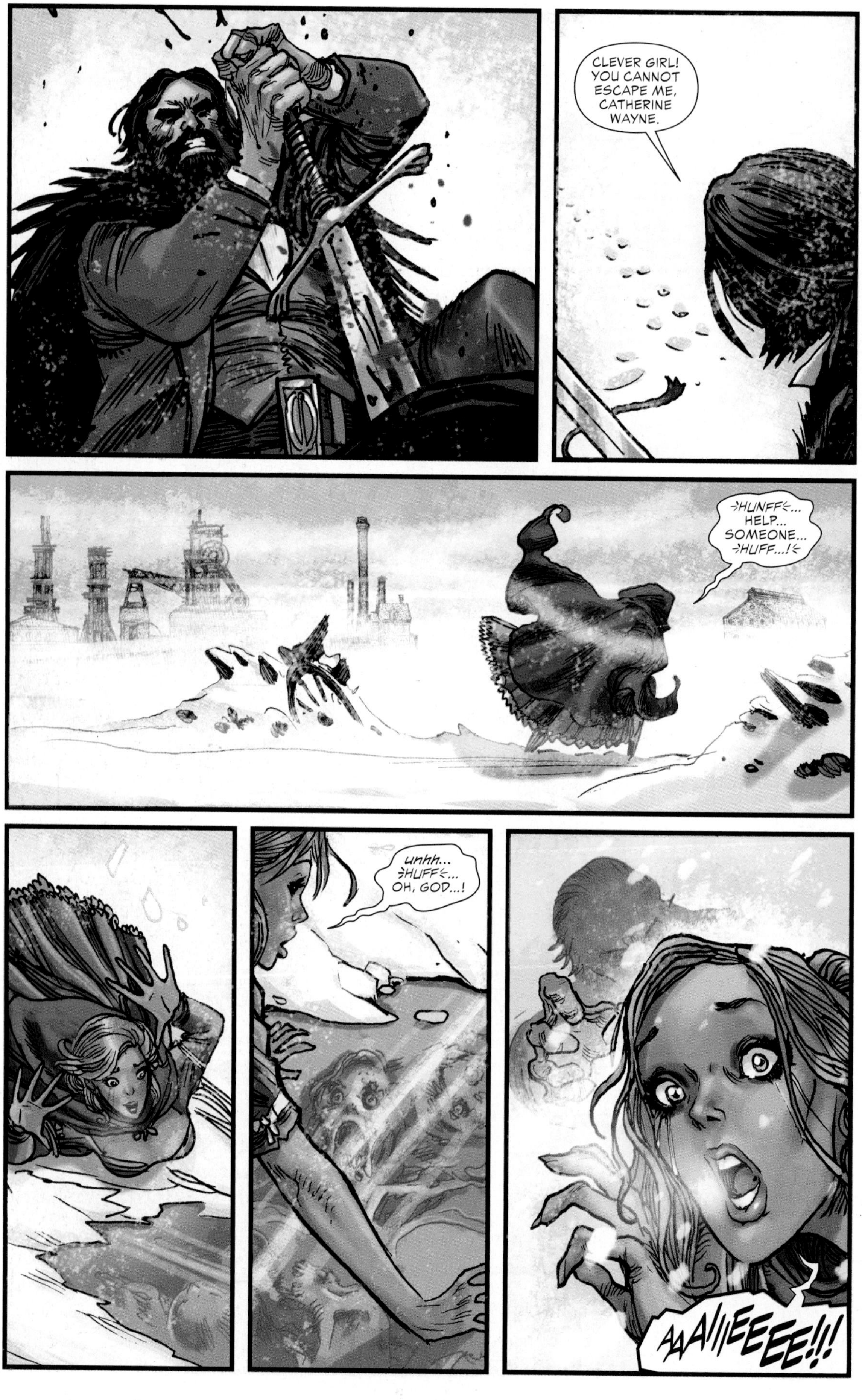
CLEVER GIRL! YOU CANNOT ESCAPE ME, CATHERINE WAYNE.
HUNFF... HELP... SOMEONE... HUFF...!
unhh... HUFF... OH, GOD...!
AAAIIIEEEEE!!!

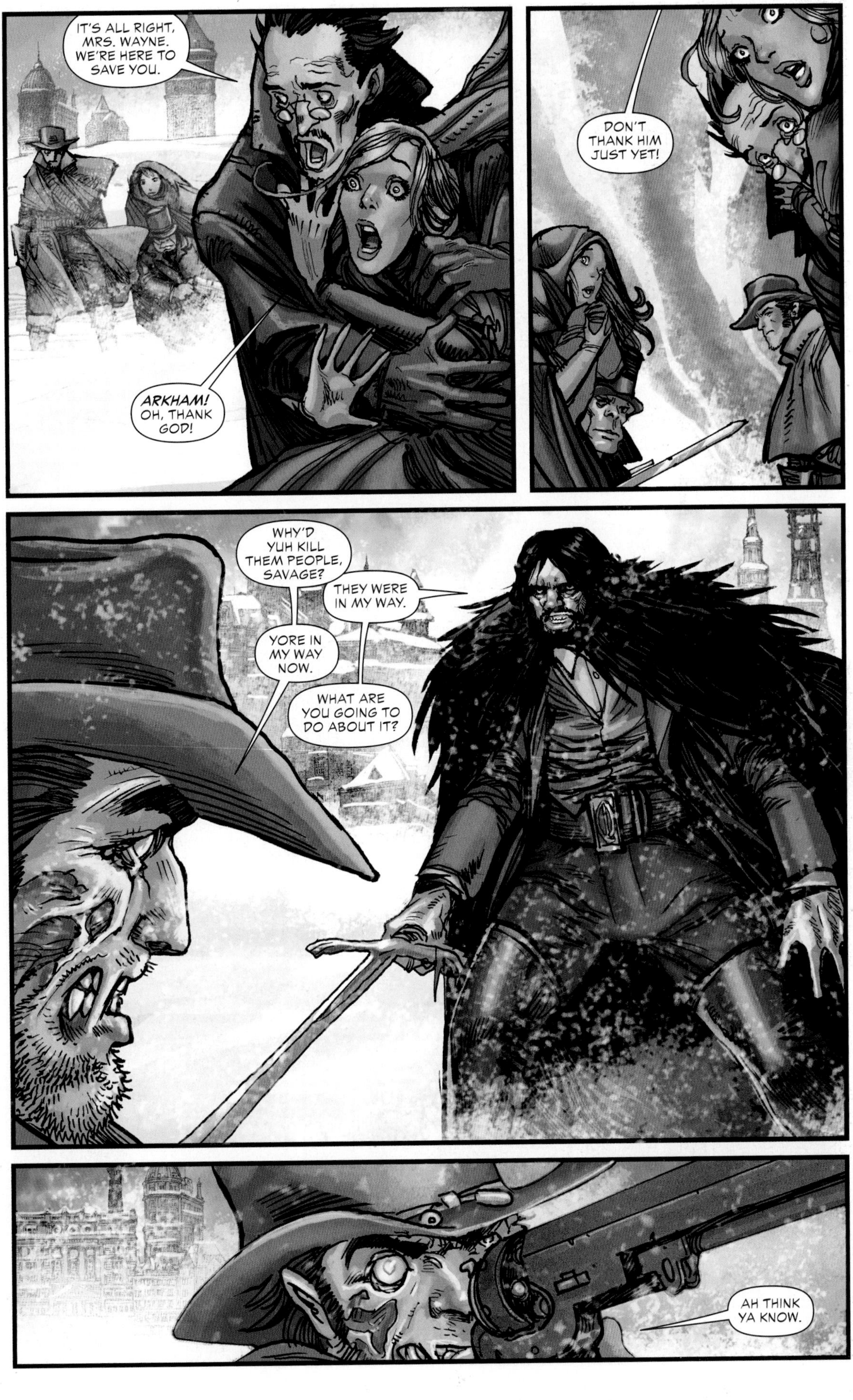
IT'S ALL RIGHT, MRS. WAYNE. WE'RE HERE TO SAVE YOU.
ARKHAM! OH, THANK GOD!
DON'T THANK HIM JUST YET!
WHY'D YUH KILL THEM PEOPLE, SAVAGE?
THEY WERE IN MY WAY.
YORE IN MY WAY NOW.
WHAT ARE YOU GOING TO DO ABOUT IT?
AH THINK YA KNOW.

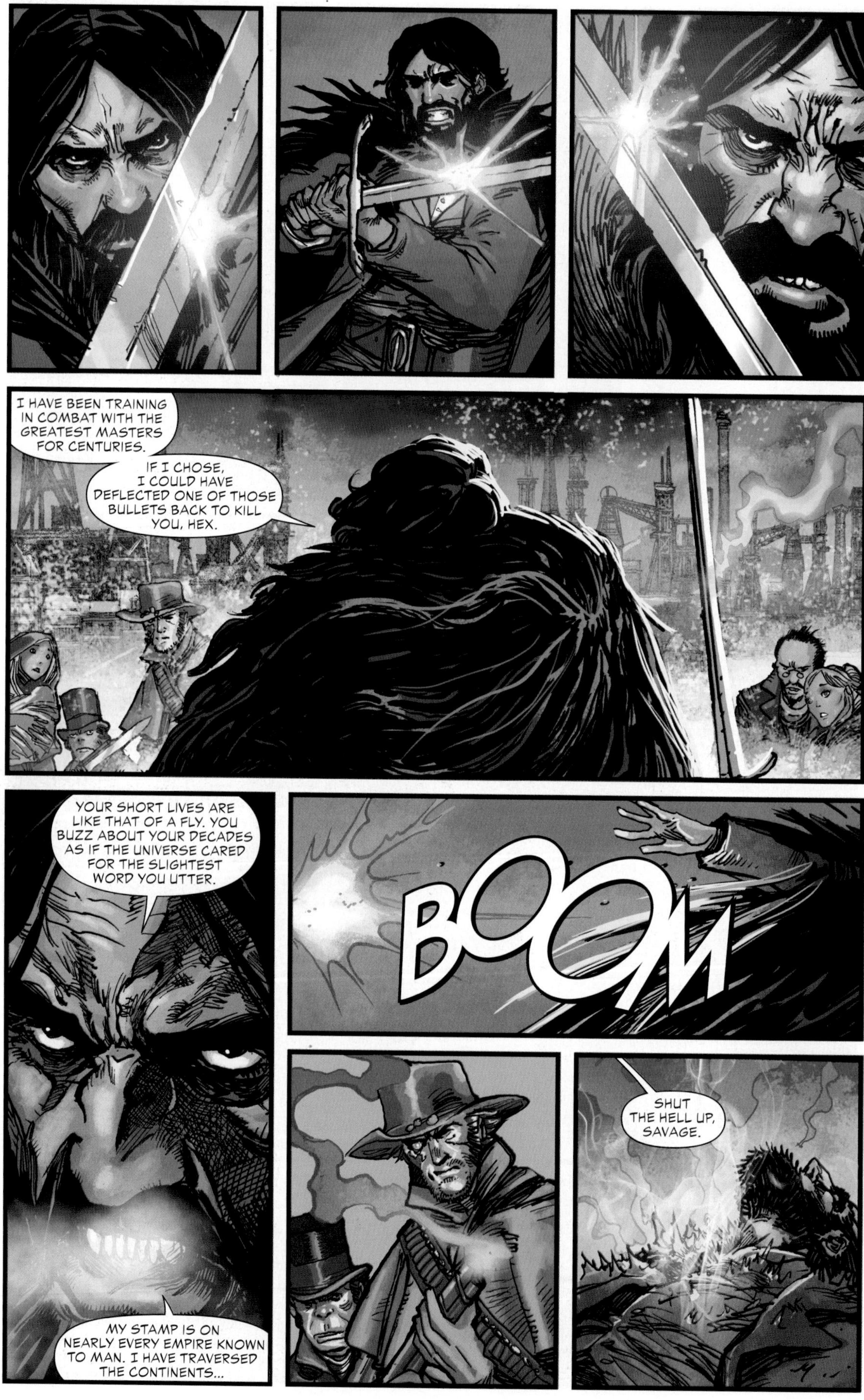
I HAVE BEEN TRAINING IN COMBAT WITH THE GREATEST MASTERS FOR CENTURIES.
IF I CHOSE, I COULD HAVE DEFLECTED ONE OF THOSE BULLETS BACK TO KILL YOU, HEX.
YOUR SHORT LIVES ARE LIKE THAT OF A FLY. YOU BUZZ ABOUT YOUR DECADES AS IF THE UNIVERSE CARED FOR THE SLIGHTEST WORD YOU UTTER.
MY STAMP IS ON NEARLY EVERY EMPIRE KNOWN TO MAN. I HAVE TRAVERSED THE CONTINENTS...
BOOM
SHUT THE HELL UP, SAVAGE.

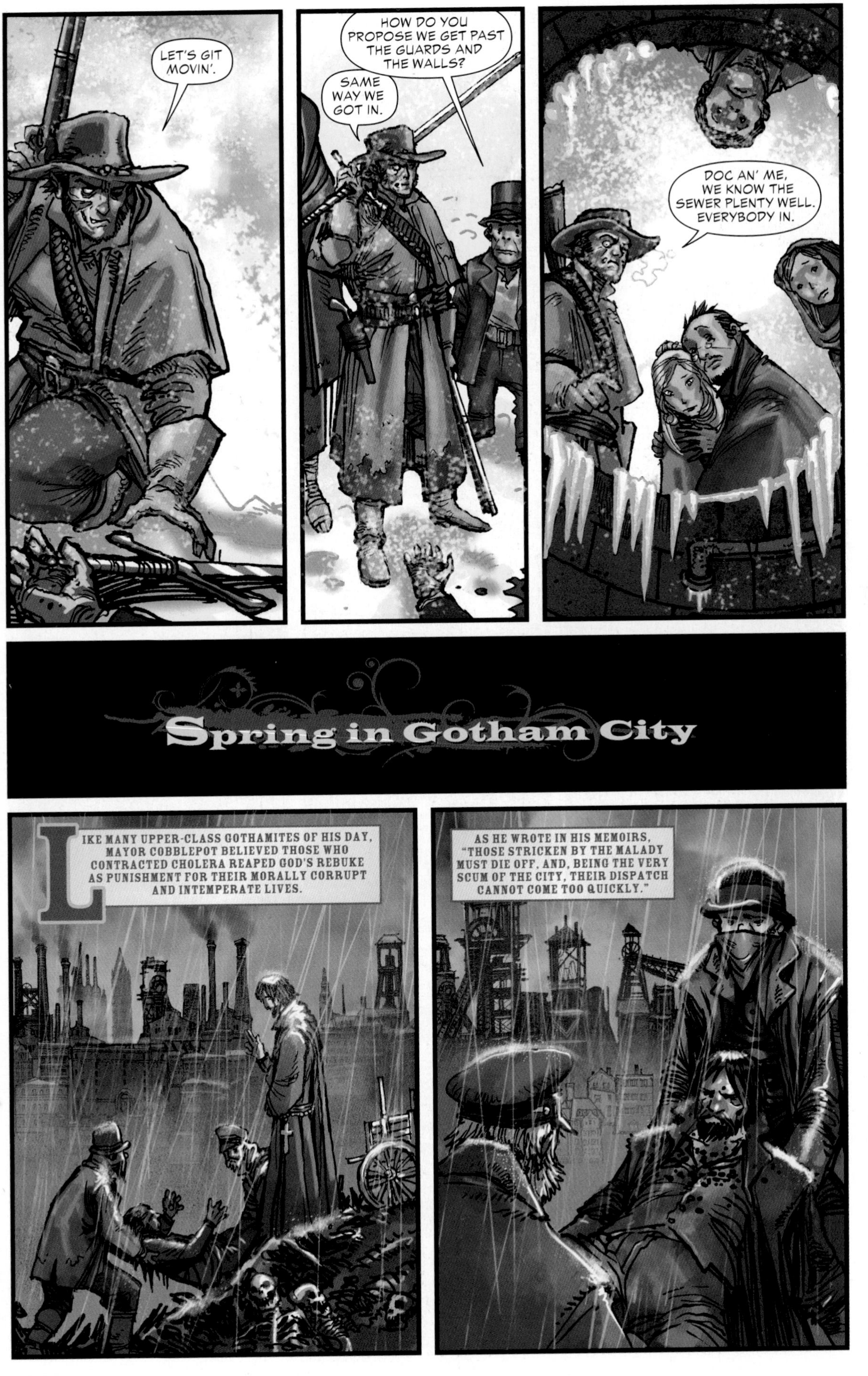
LET'S GIT MOVIN'.
HOW DO YOU PROPOSE WE GET PAST THE GUARDS AND THE WALLS?
SAME WAY WE GOT IN.
DOC AN' ME, WE KNOW THE SEWER PLENTY WELL. EVERYBODY IN.
Spring in Gotham City
LIKE MANY UPPER-CLASS GOTHAMITES OF HIS DAY, MAYOR COBBLEPOT BELIEVED THOSE WHO CONTRACTED CHOLERA REAPED GOD'S REBUKE AS PUNISHMENT FOR THEIR MORALLY CORRUPT AND INTEMPERATE LIVES.
AS HE WROTE IN HIS MEMOIRS, "THOSE STRICKEN BY THE MALADY MUST DIE OFF, AND, BEING THE VERY SCUM OF THE CITY, THEIR DISPATCH CANNOT COME TOO QUICKLY."

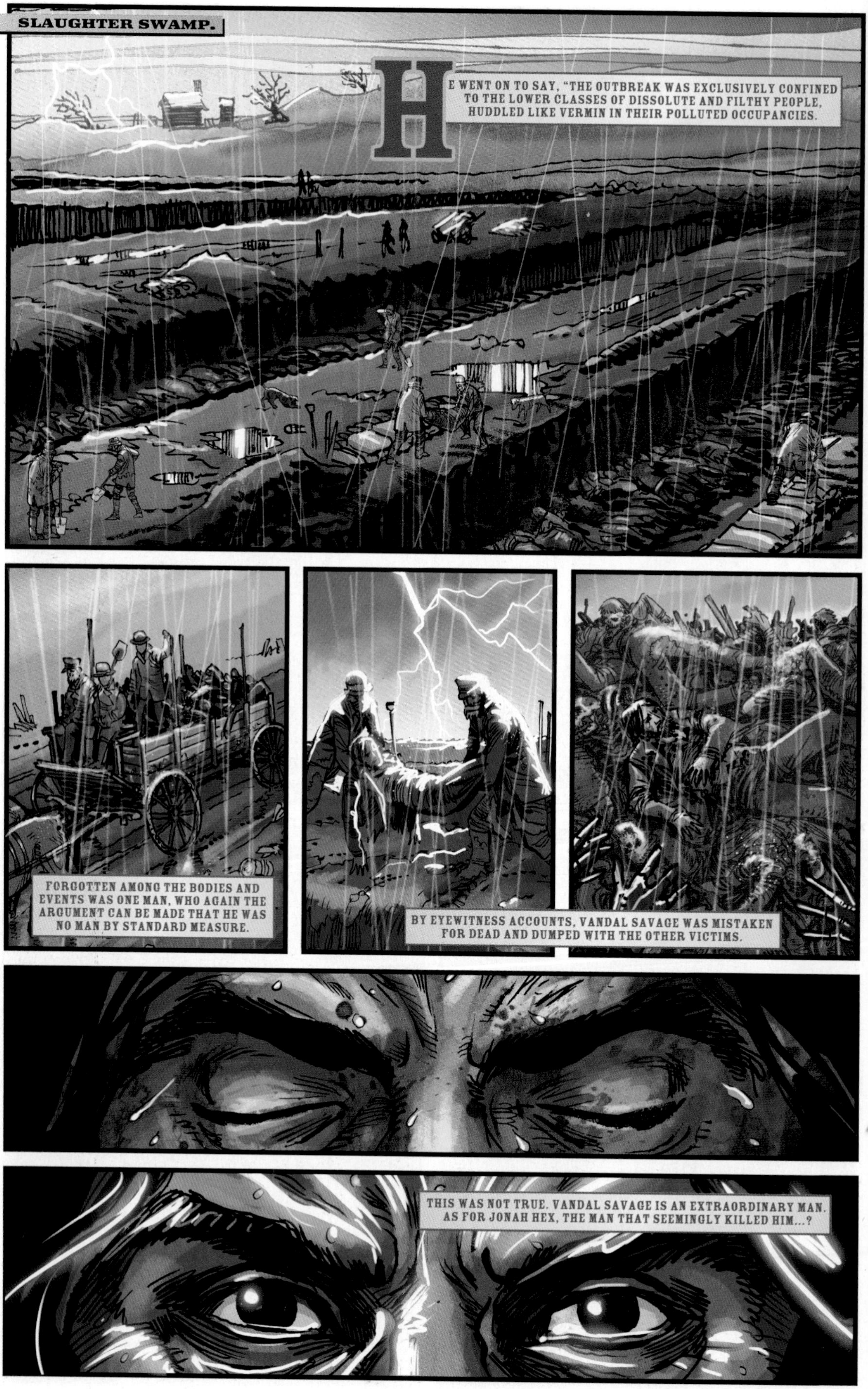
SLAUGHTER SWAMP.
HE WENT ON TO SAY, "THE OUTBREAK WAS EXCLUSIVELY CONFINED TO THE LOWER CLASSES OF DISSOLUTE AND FILTHY PEOPLE, HUDDLED LIKE VERMIN IN THEIR POLLUTED OCCUPANCIES.
FORGOTTEN AMONG THE BODIES AND EVENTS WAS ONE MAN, WHO AGAIN THE ARGUMENT CAN BE MADE THAT HE WAS NO MAN BY STANDARD MEASURE.
BY EYEWITNESS ACCOUNTS, VANDAL SAVAGE WAS MISTAKEN FOR DEAD AND DUMPED WITH THE OTHER VICTIMS.
THIS WAS NOT TRUE. VANDAL SAVAGE IS AN EXTRAORDINARY MAN. AS FOR JONAH HEX, THE MAN THAT SEEMINGLY KILLED HIM...?

Getting the Hex out of Gotham

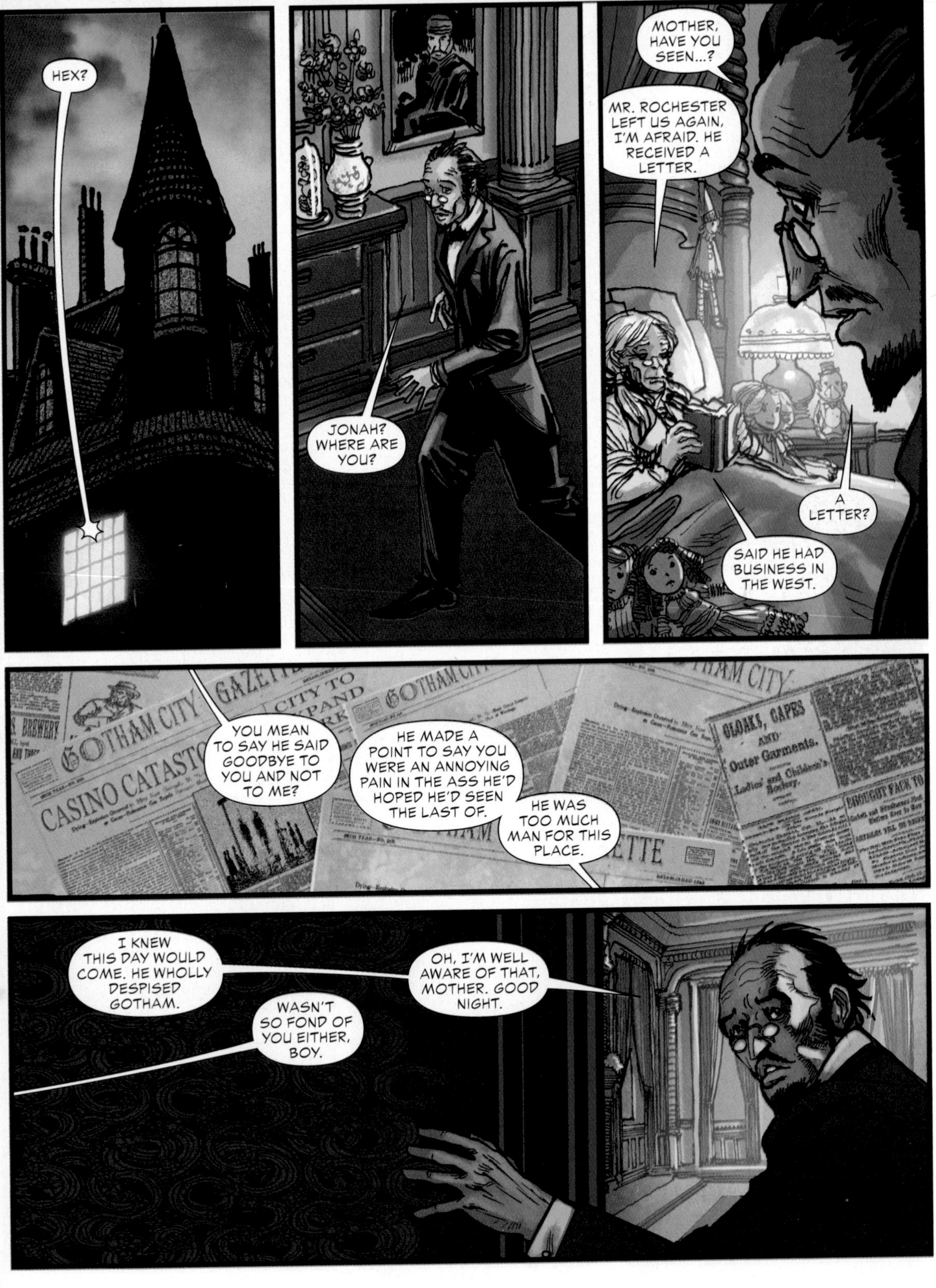

HEX?
JONAH? WHERE ARE YOU?
MOTHER, HAVE YOU SEEN...?
MR. ROCHESTER LEFT US AGAIN, I'M AFRAID. HE RECEIVED A LETTER.
A LETTER?
SAID HE HAD BUSINESS IN THE WEST.
YOU MEAN TO SAY HE SAID GOODBYE TO YOU AND NOT TO ME?
HE MADE A POINT TO SAY YOU WERE AN ANNOYING PAIN IN THE ASS HE'D HOPED HE'D SEEN THE LAST OF.
HE WAS TOO MUCH MAN FOR THIS PLACE.
I KNEW THIS DAY WOULD COME. HE WHOLLY DESPISED GOTHAM.
OH, I'M WELL AWARE OF THAT, MOTHER. GOOD NIGHT.
WASN'T SO FOND OF YOU EITHER, BOY.

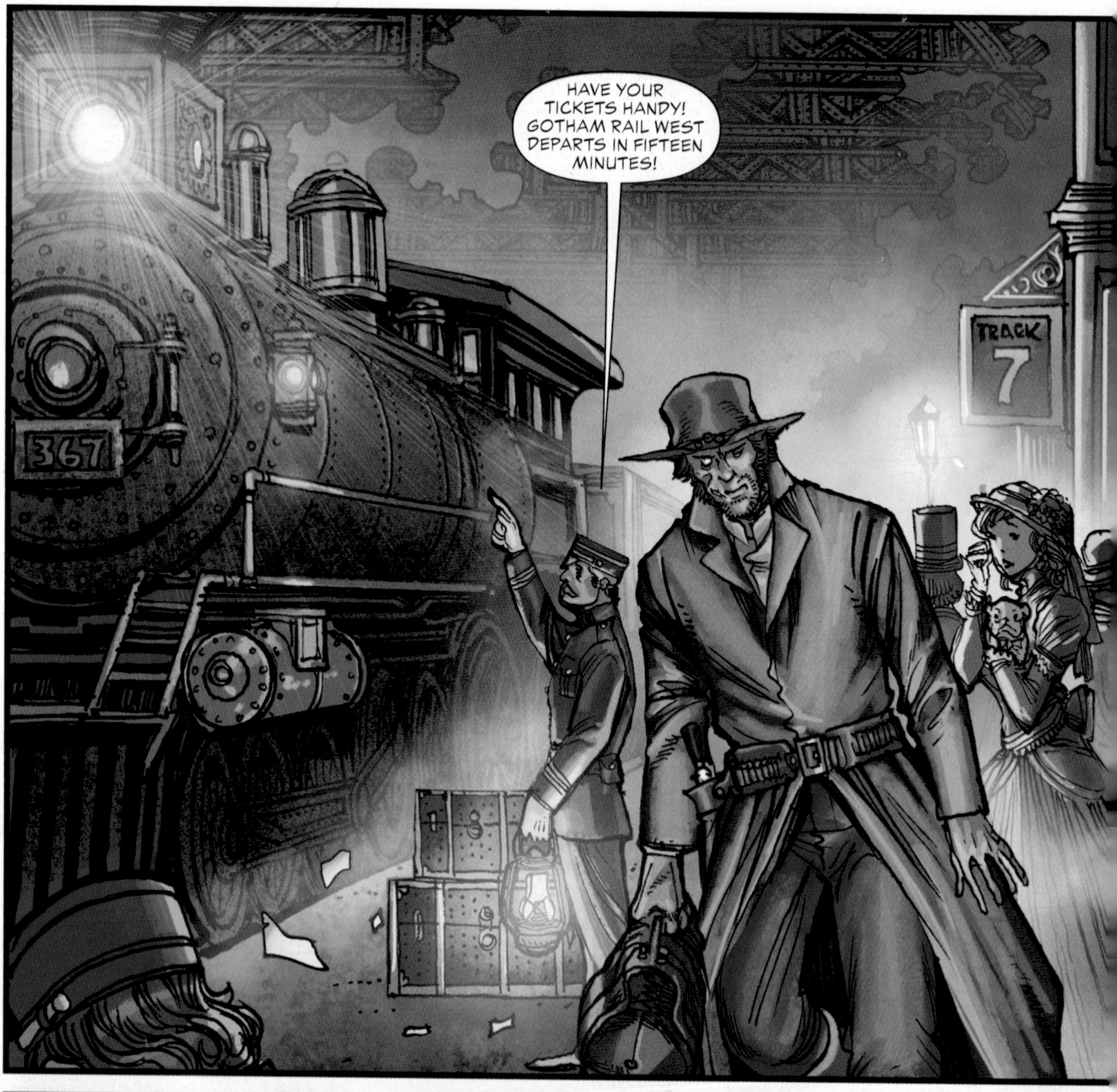
HAVE YOUR TICKETS HANDY! GOTHAM RAIL WEST DEPARTS IN FIFTEEN MINUTES!
TRACK 7
367

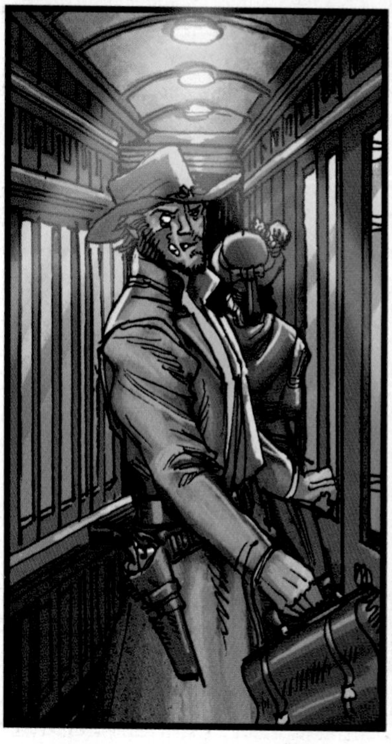

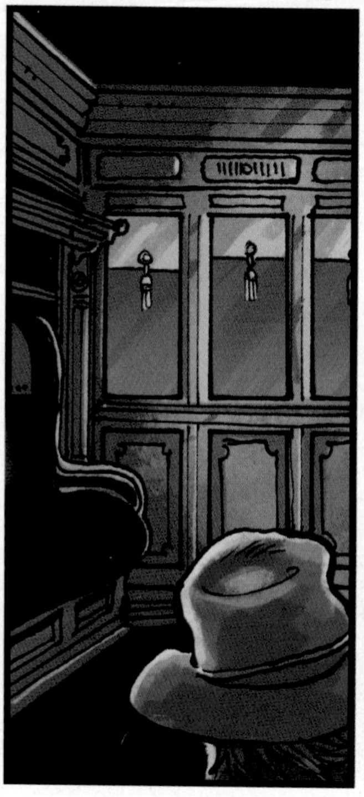

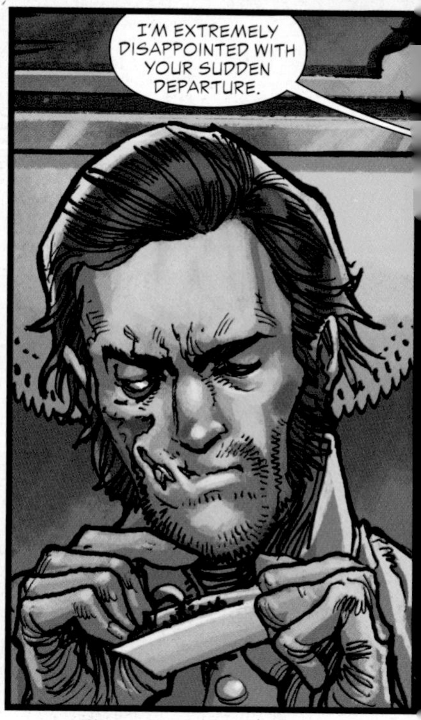
I'M EXTREMELY DISAPPOINTED WITH YOUR SUDDEN DEPARTURE.

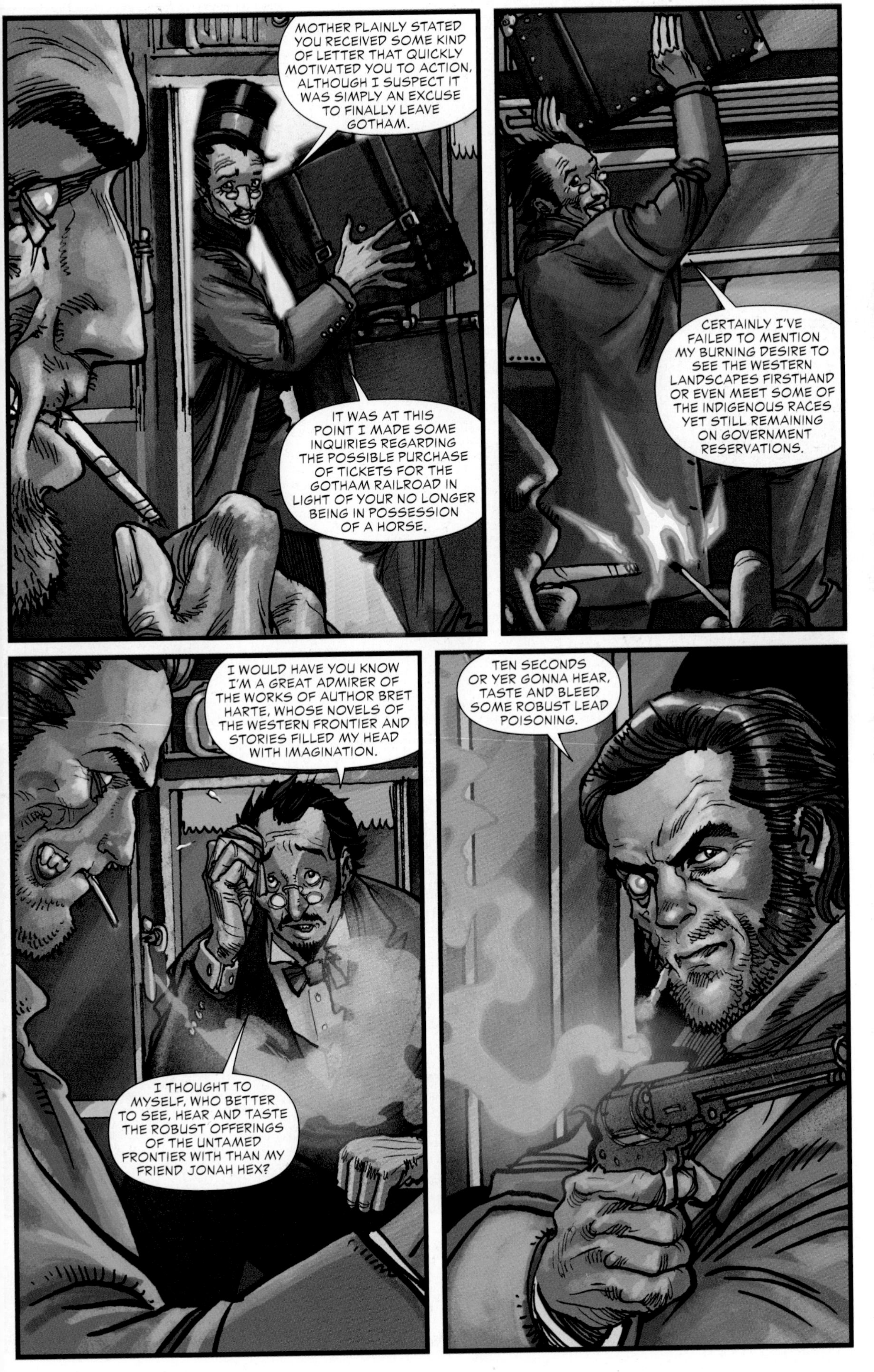
MOTHER PLAINLY STATED YOU RECEIVED SOME KIND OF LETTER THAT QUICKLY MOTIVATED YOU TO ACTION, ALTHOUGH I SUSPECT IT WAS SIMPLY AN EXCUSE TO FINALLY LEAVE GOTHAM.
IT WAS AT THIS POINT I MADE SOME INQUIRIES REGARDING THE POSSIBLE PURCHASE OF TICKETS FOR THE GOTHAM RAILROAD IN LIGHT OF YOUR NO LONGER BEING IN POSSESSION OF A HORSE.
CERTAINLY I'VE FAILED TO MENTION MY BURNING DESIRE TO SEE THE WESTERN LANDSCAPES FIRSTHAND OR EVEN MEET SOME OF THE INDIGENOUS RACES YET STILL REMAINING ON GOVERNMENT RESERVATIONS.
I WOULD HAVE YOU KNOW I'M A GREAT ADMIRER OF THE WORKS OF AUTHOR BRET HARTE, WHOSE NOVELS OF THE WESTERN FRONTIER AND STORIES FILLED MY HEAD WITH IMAGINATION.
I THOUGHT TO MYSELF, WHO BETTER TO SEE, HEAR AND TASTE THE ROBUST OFFERINGS OF THE UNTAMED FRONTIER WITH THAN MY FRIEND JONAH HEX?
TEN SECONDS OR YER GONNA HEAR, TASTE AND BLEED SOME ROBUST LEAD POISONING.

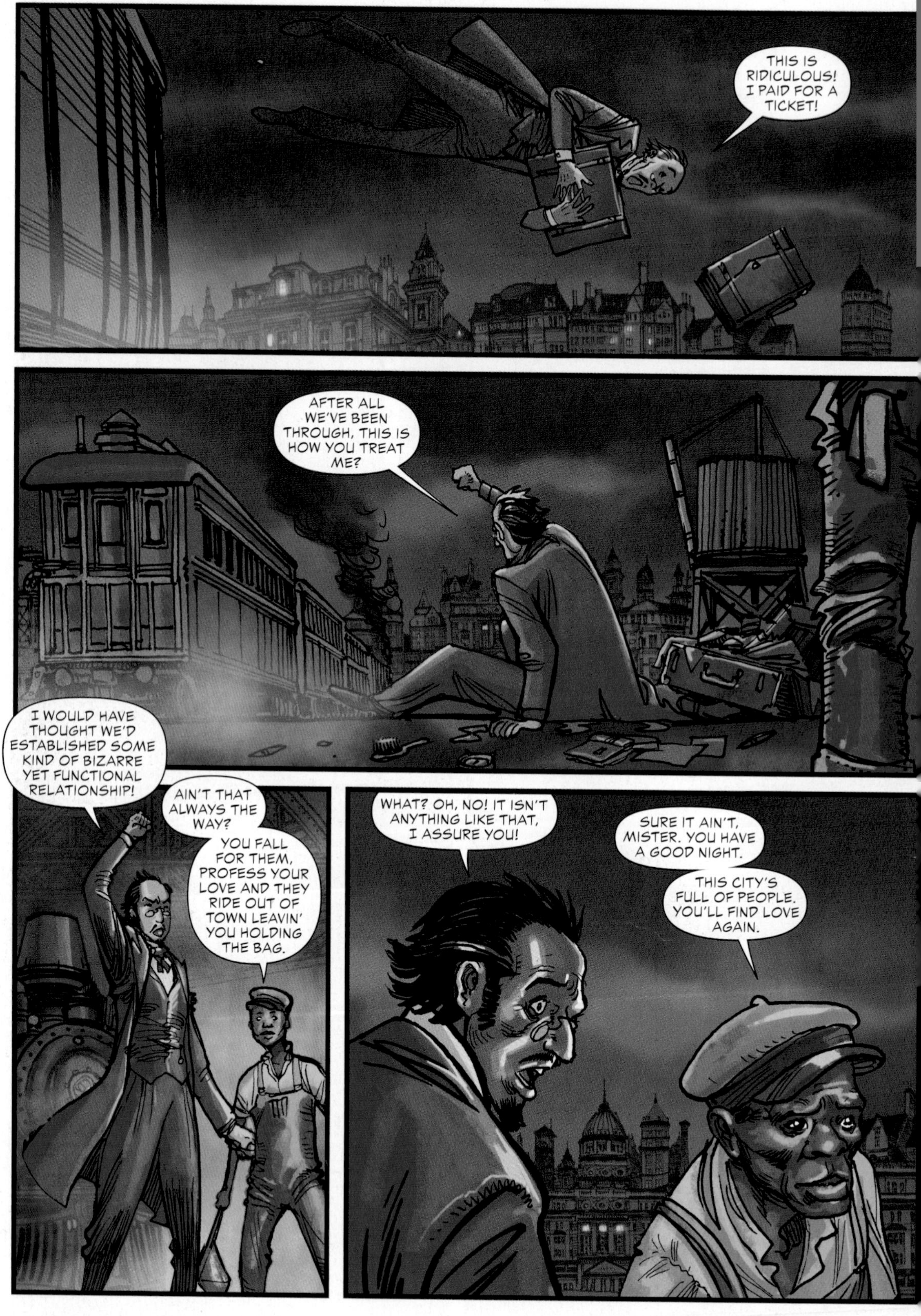
THIS IS RIDICULOUS! I PAID FOR A TICKET!
AFTER ALL WE'VE BEEN THROUGH, THIS IS HOW YOU TREAT ME?
I WOULD HAVE THOUGHT WE'D ESTABLISHED SOME KIND OF BIZARRE YET FUNCTIONAL RELATIONSHIP!
AIN'T THAT ALWAYS THE WAY?
YOU FALL FOR THEM, PROFESS YOUR LOVE AND THEY RIDE OUT OF TOWN LEAVIN' YOU HOLDING THE BAG.
WHAT? OH, NO! IT ISN'T ANYTHING LIKE THAT, I ASSURE YOU!
SURE IT AIN'T, MISTER. YOU HAVE A GOOD NIGHT.
THIS CITY'S FULL OF PEOPLE. YOU'LL FIND LOVE AGAIN.

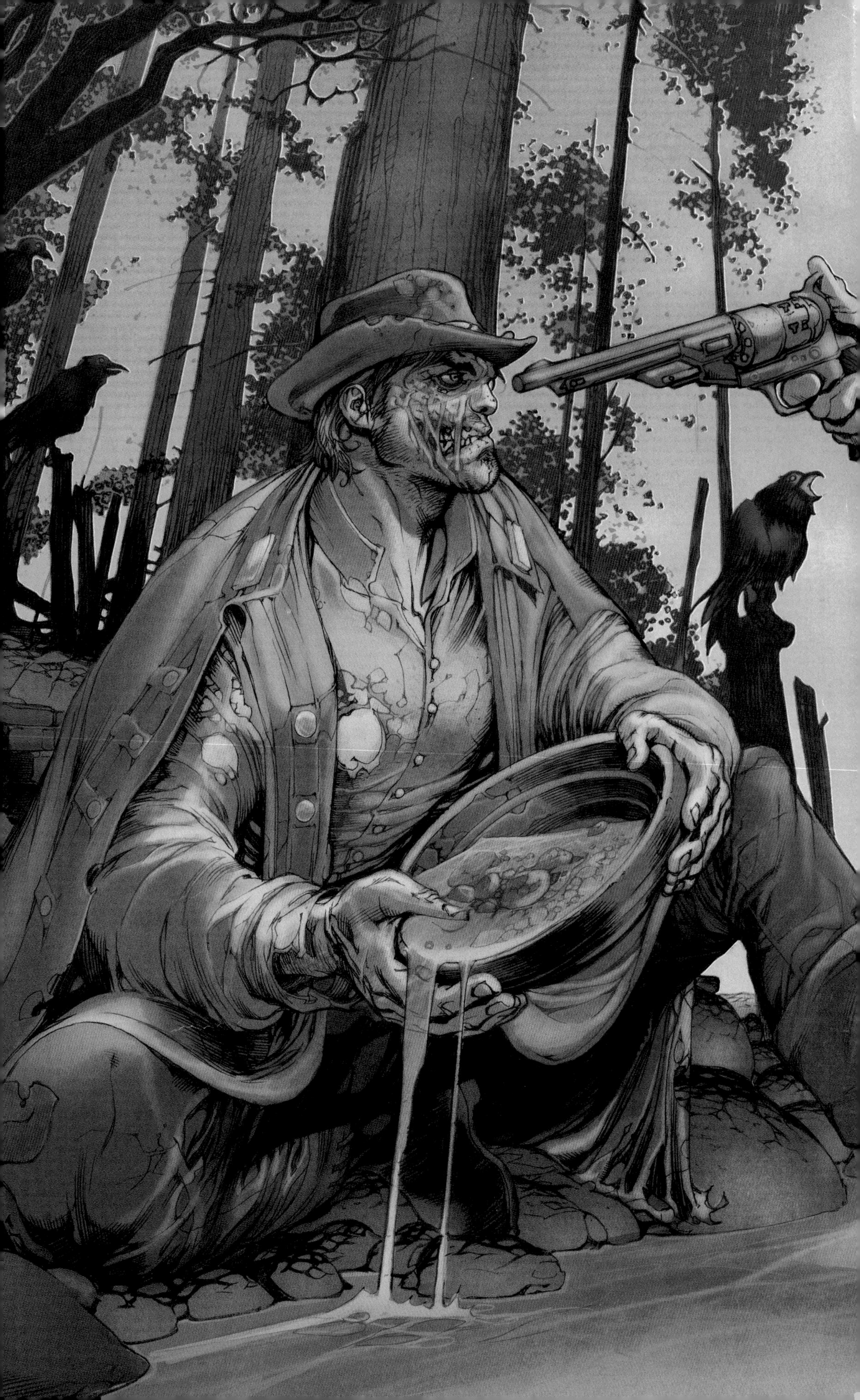

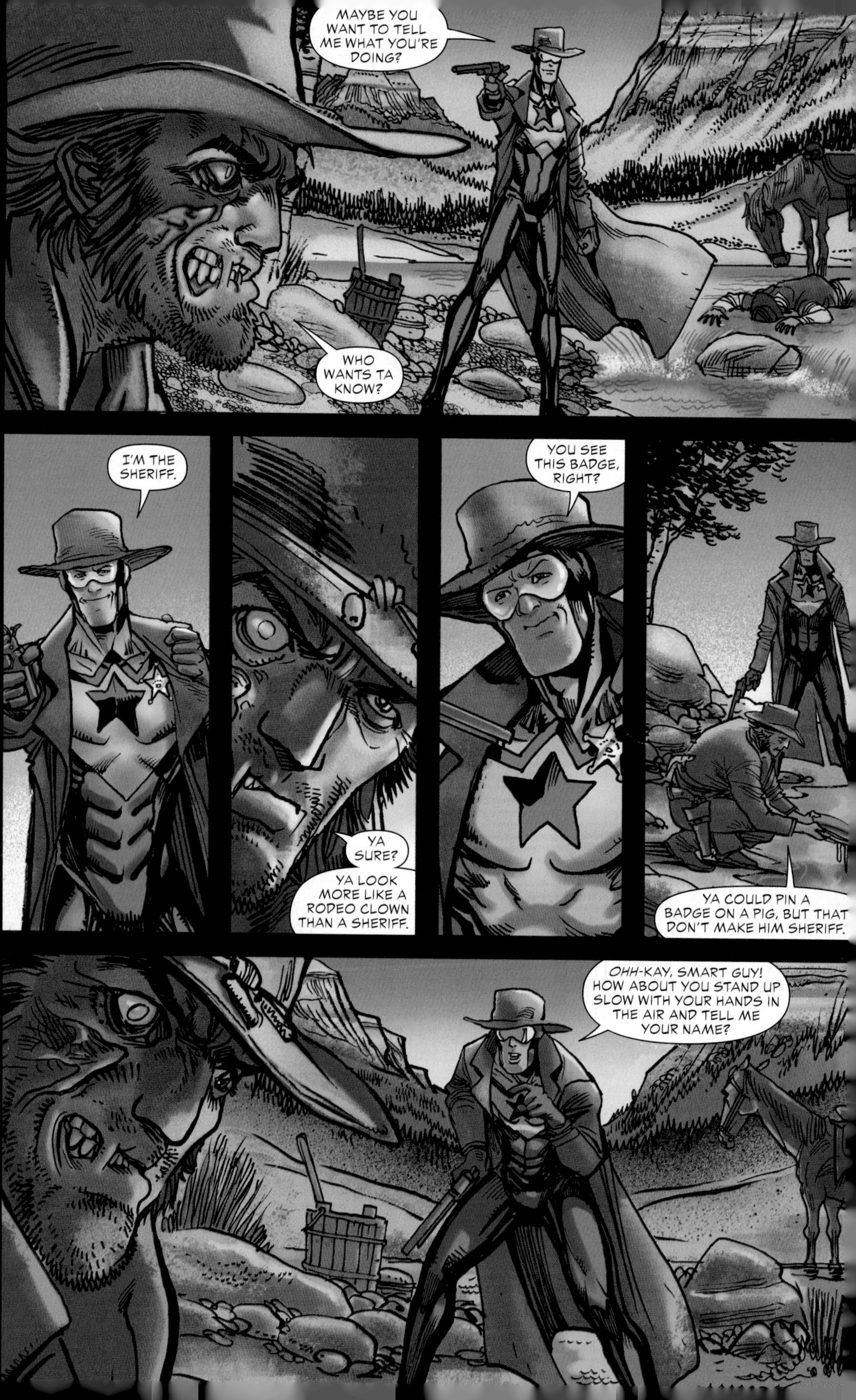
MAYBE YOU WANT TO TELL ME WHAT YOU'RE DOING?
WHO WANTS TA KNOW?
I'M THE SHERIFF.
YA SURE?
YA LOOK MORE LIKE A RODEO CLOWN THAN A SHERIFF.
YOU SEE THIS BADGE, RIGHT?
YA COULD PIN A BADGE ON A PIG, BUT THAT DON'T MAKE HIM SHERIFF.
OHH-KAY, SMART GUY! HOW ABOUT YOU STAND UP SLOW WITH YOUR HANDS IN THE AIR AND TELL ME YOUR NAME?

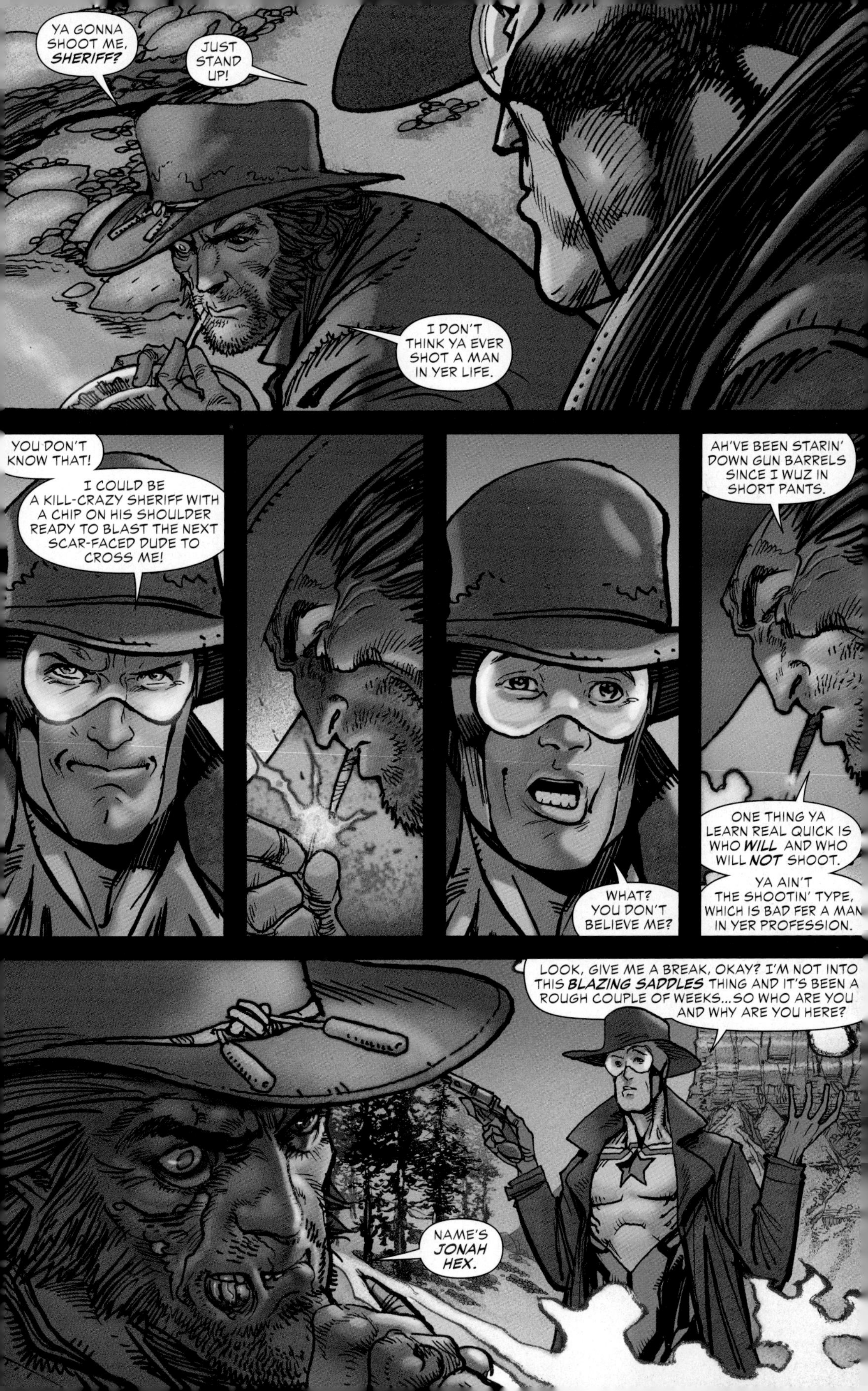

YA GONNA SHOOT ME, SHERIFF?
JUST STAND UP!
I DON'T THINK YA EVER SHOT A MAN IN YER LIFE.
YOU DON'T KNOW THAT!
I COULD BE A KILL-CRAZY SHERIFF WITH A CHIP ON HIS SHOULDER READY TO BLAST THE NEXT SCAR-FACED DUDE TO CROSS ME!
WHAT? YOU DON'T BELIEVE ME?
AH'VE BEEN STARIN' DOWN GUN BARRELS SINCE I WUZ IN SHORT PANTS.
ONE THING YA LEARN REAL QUICK IS WHO WILL AND WHO WILL NOT SHOOT.
YA AIN'T THE SHOOTIN' TYPE, WHICH IS BAD FER A MAN IN YER PROFESSION.
LOOK, GIVE ME A BREAK, OKAY? I'M NOT INTO THIS BLAZING SADDLES THING AND IT'S BEEN A ROUGH COUPLE OF WEEKS...SO WHO ARE YOU AND WHY ARE YOU HERE?
NAME'S JONAH HEX.

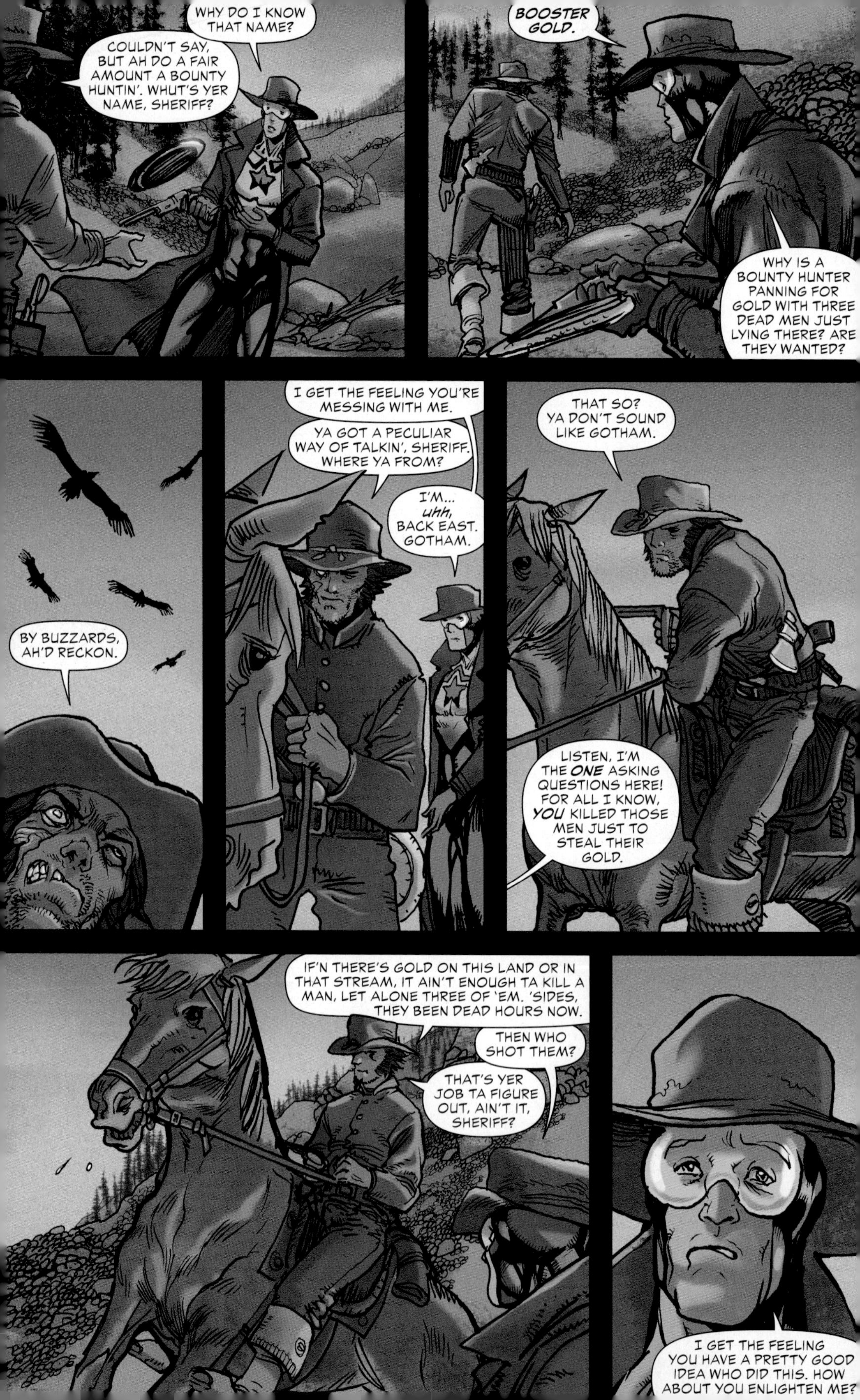
WHY DO I KNOW THAT NAME?
COULDN'T SAY, BUT AH DO A FAIR AMOUNT A BOUNTY HUNTIN'. WHUT'S YER NAME, SHERIFF?
BOOSTER GOLD.
WHY IS A BOUNTY HUNTER PANNING FOR GOLD WITH THREE DEAD MEN JUST LYING THERE? ARE THEY WANTED?
BY BUZZARDS, AH'D RECKON.
I GET THE FEELING YOU'RE MESSING WITH ME.
YA GOT A PECULIAR WAY OF TALKIN', SHERIFF. WHERE YA FROM?
I'M... uhh, BACK EAST. GOTHAM.
THAT SO? YA DON'T SOUND LIKE GOTHAM.
LISTEN, I'M THE ONE ASKING QUESTIONS HERE! FOR ALL I KNOW, YOU KILLED THOSE MEN JUST TO STEAL THEIR GOLD.
IF'N THERE'S GOLD ON THIS LAND OR IN THAT STREAM, IT AIN'T ENOUGH TA KILL A MAN, LET ALONE THREE OF 'EM. 'SIDES, THEY BEEN DEAD HOURS NOW.
THEN WHO SHOT THEM?
THAT'S YER JOB TA FIGURE OUT, AIN'T IT, SHERIFF?
I GET THE FEELING YOU HAVE A PRETTY GOOD IDEA WHO DID THIS. HOW ABOUT YOU ENLIGHTEN ME?

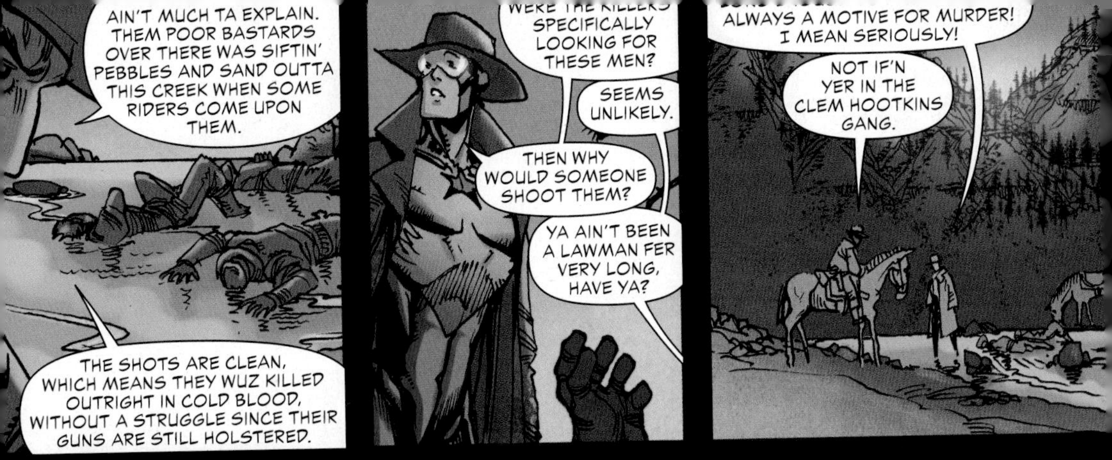
AIN'T MUCH TA EXPLAIN. THEM POOR BASTARDS OVER THERE WAS SIFTIN' PEBBLES AND SAND OUTTA THIS CREEK WHEN SOME RIDERS COME UPON THEM.
THE SHOTS ARE CLEAN, WHICH MEANS THEY WUZ KILLED OUTRIGHT IN COLD BLOOD, WITHOUT A STRUGGLE SINCE THEIR GUNS ARE STILL HOLSTERED.
WERE THE KILLERS SPECIFICALLY LOOKING FOR THESE MEN?
SEEMS UNLIKELY.
THEN WHY WOULD SOMEONE SHOOT THEM?
YA AIN'T BEEN A LAWMAN FER VERY LONG, HAVE YA?
ALWAYS A MOTIVE FOR MURDER! I MEAN SERIOUSLY!
NOT IF'N YER IN THE CLEM HOOTKINS GANG.

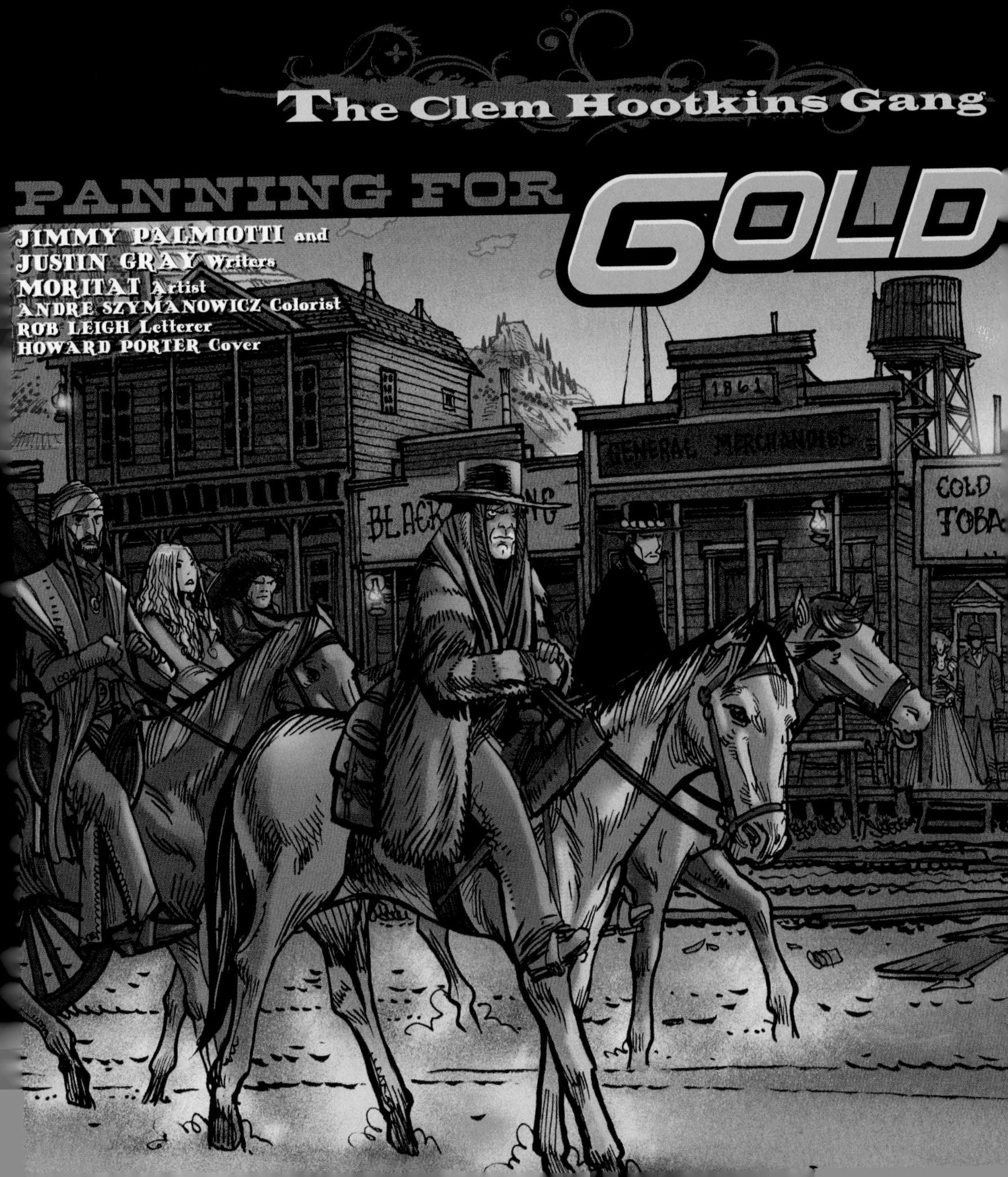
The Clem Hootkins Gang
PANNING FOR GOLD
JIMMY PALMIOTTI and JUSTIN GRAY Writers
MORITAT Artist
ANDRE SZYMANOWICZ Colorist
ROB LEIGH Letterer
HOWARD PORTER Cover
1861
GENERAL MERCHANDISE

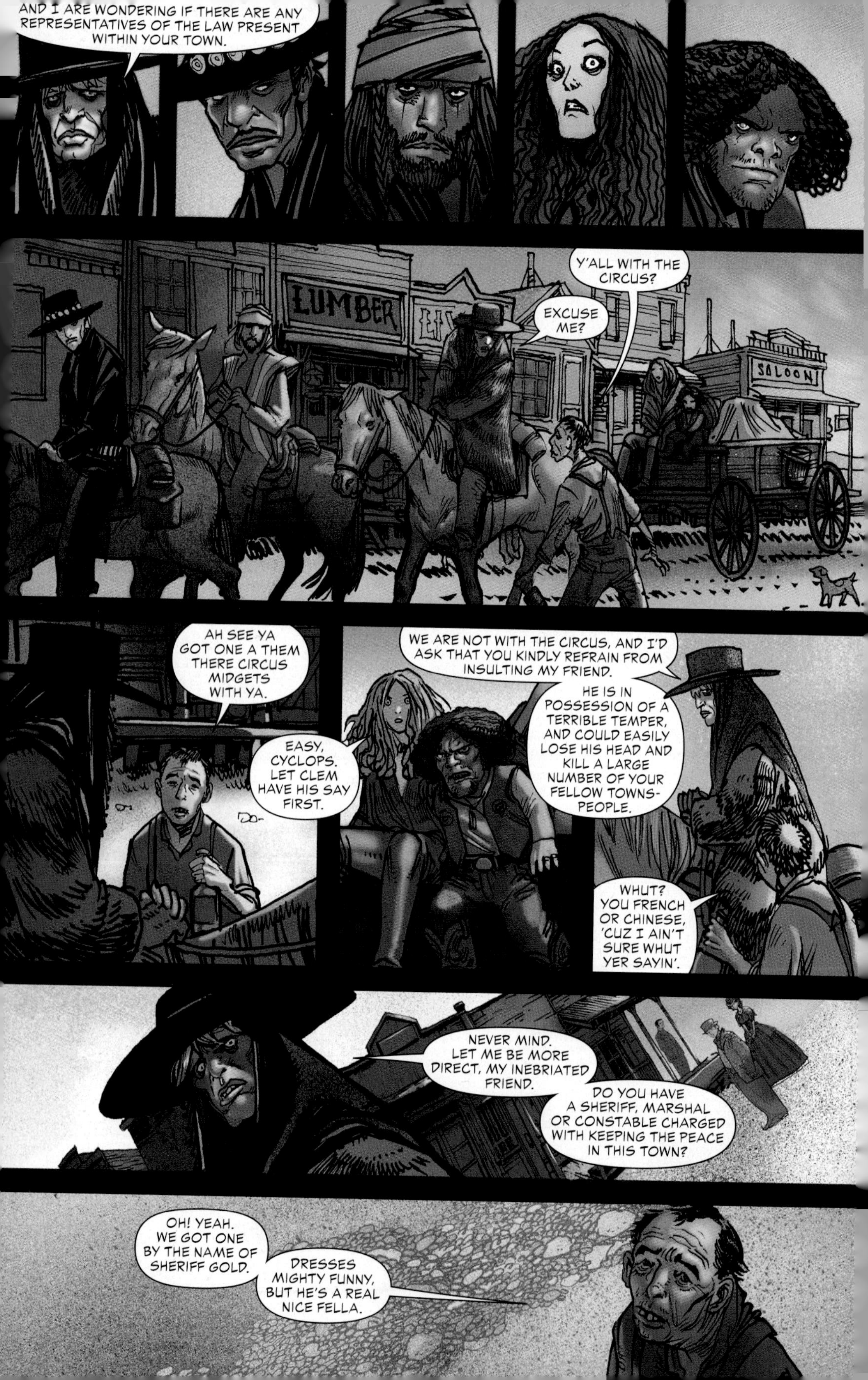
AND I ARE WONDERING IF THERE ARE ANY REPRESENTATIVES OF THE LAW PRESENT WITHIN YOUR TOWN.
LUMBER
SALOON
Y'ALL WITH THE CIRCUS?
EXCUSE ME?
AH SEE YA GOT ONE A THEM THERE CIRCUS MIDGETS WITH YA.
EASY, CYCLOPS. LET CLEM HAVE HIS SAY FIRST.
WE ARE NOT WITH THE CIRCUS, AND I'D ASK THAT YOU KINDLY REFRAIN FROM INSULTING MY FRIEND.
HE IS IN POSSESSION OF A TERRIBLE TEMPER, AND COULD EASILY LOSE HIS HEAD AND KILL A LARGE NUMBER OF YOUR FELLOW TOWNS-PEOPLE.
WHUT? YOU FRENCH OR CHINESE, 'CUZ I AIN'T SURE WHUT YER SAYIN'.
NEVER MIND. LET ME BE MORE DIRECT, MY INEBRIATED FRIEND.
DO YOU HAVE A SHERIFF, MARSHAL OR CONSTABLE CHARGED WITH KEEPING THE PEACE IN THIS TOWN?
OH! YEAH. WE GOT ONE BY THE NAME OF SHERIFF GOLD.
DRESSES MIGHTY FUNNY, BUT HE'S A REAL NICE FELLA.

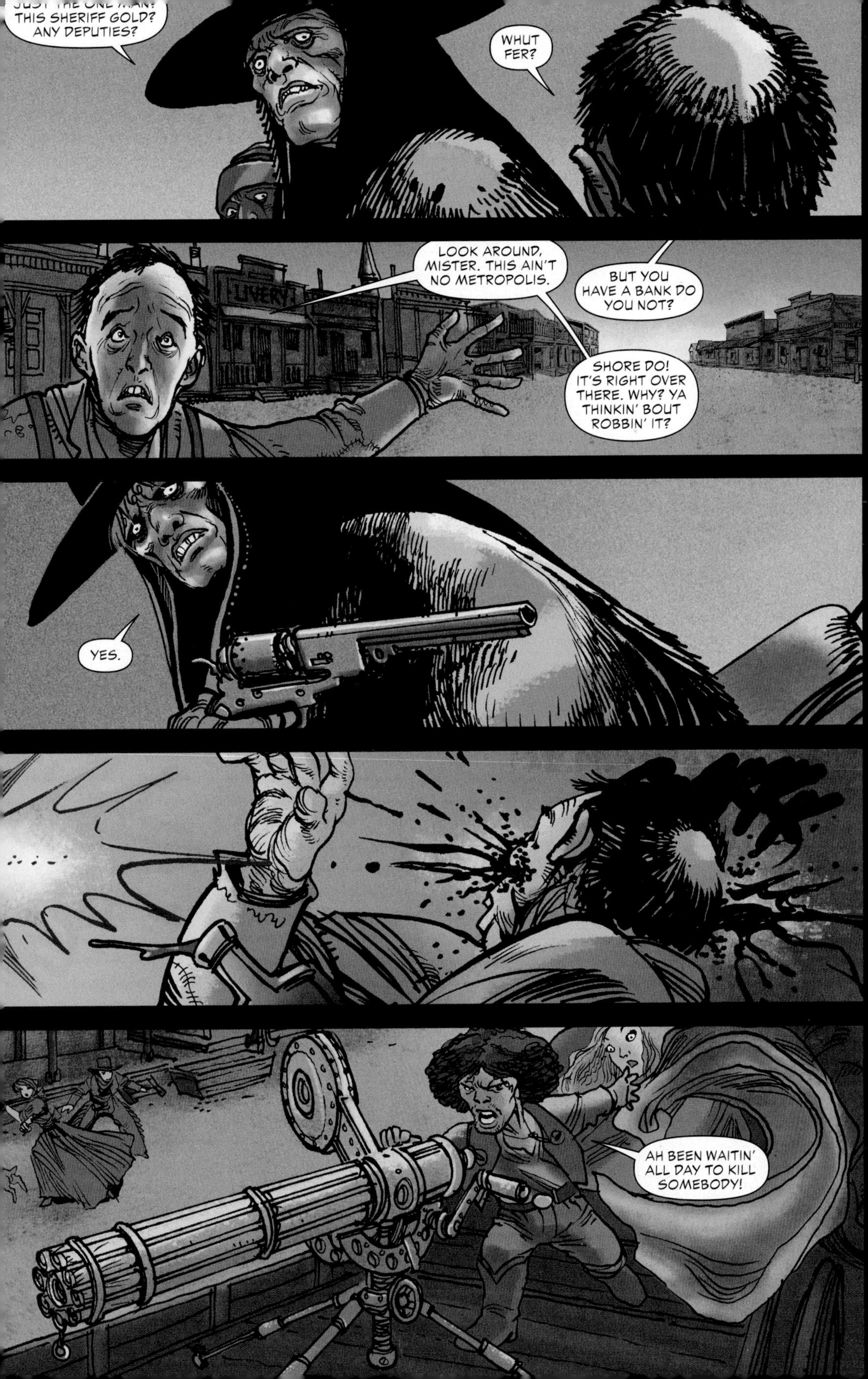
JUST THE ONE MAN? THIS SHERIFF GOLD? ANY DEPUTIES?
WHUT FER?
LIVERY
LOOK AROUND, MISTER. THIS AIN'T NO METROPOLIS.
BUT YOU HAVE A BANK DO YOU NOT?
SHORE DO! IT'S RIGHT OVER THERE. WHY? YA THINKIN' BOUT ROBBIN' IT?
YES.
AH BEEN WAITIN' ALL DAY TO KILL SOMEBODY!

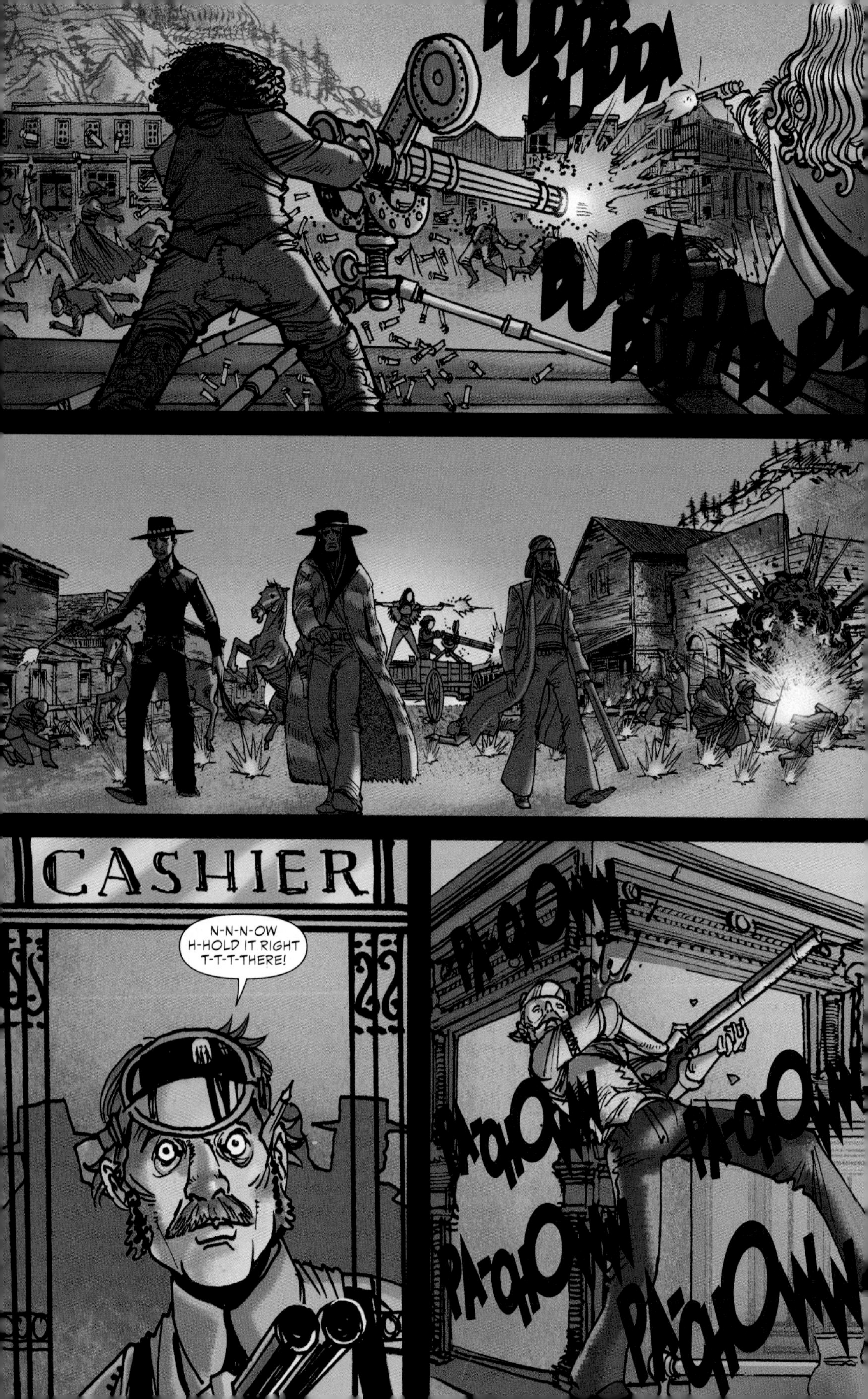
CASHIER
N-N-N-OW H-HOLD IT RIGHT T-T-T-THERE!

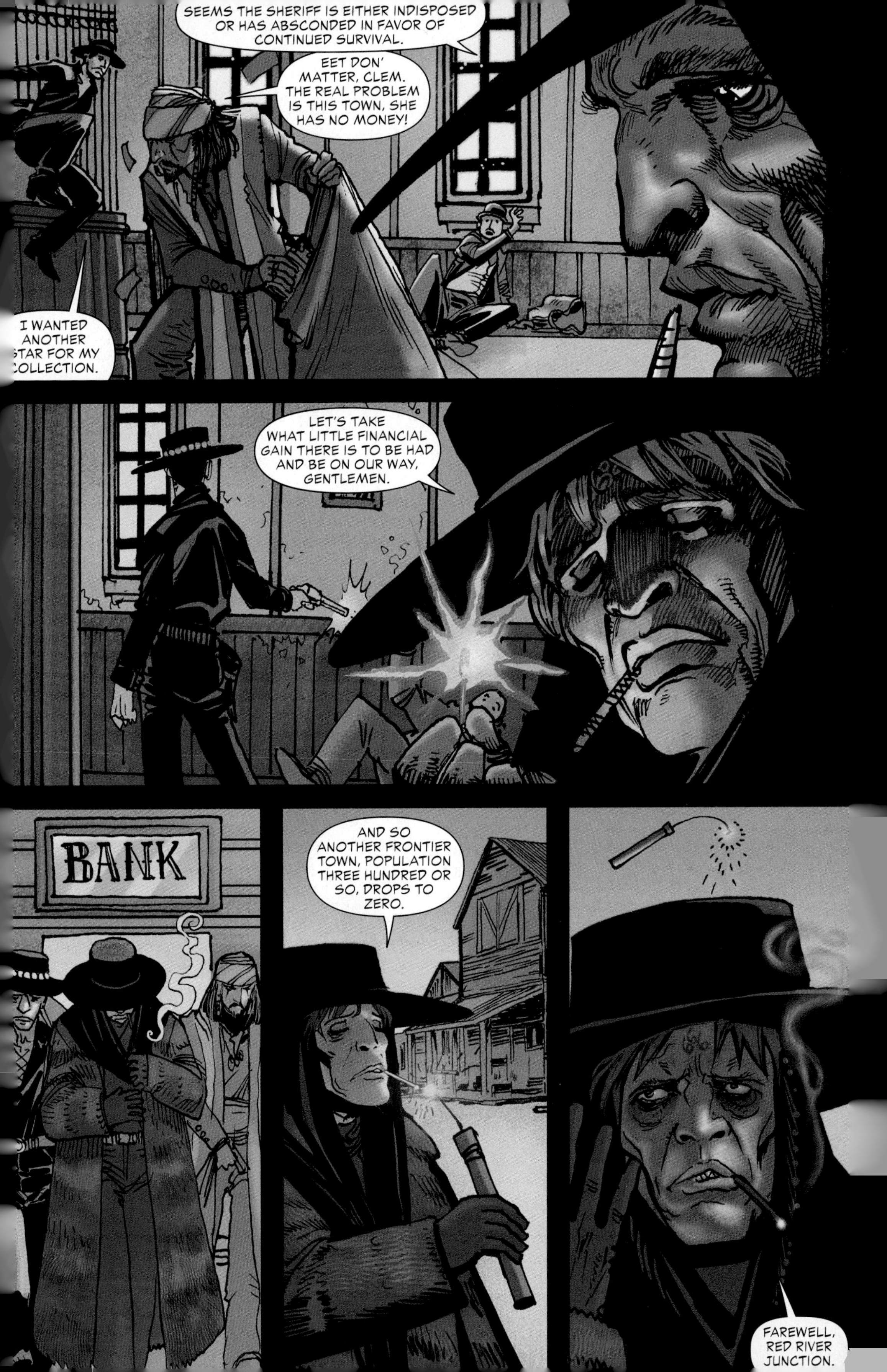
SEEMS THE SHERIFF IS EITHER INDISPOSED OR HAS ABSCONDED IN FAVOR OF CONTINUED SURVIVAL.
EET DON' MATTER, CLEM. THE REAL PROBLEM IS THIS TOWN, SHE HAS NO MONEY!
I WANTED ANOTHER STAR FOR MY COLLECTION.
LET'S TAKE WHAT LITTLE FINANCIAL GAIN THERE IS TO BE HAD AND BE ON OUR WAY, GENTLEMEN.
BANK
AND SO ANOTHER FRONTIER TOWN, POPULATION THREE HUNDRED OR SO, DROPS TO ZERO.
FAREWELL, RED RIVER JUNCTION.

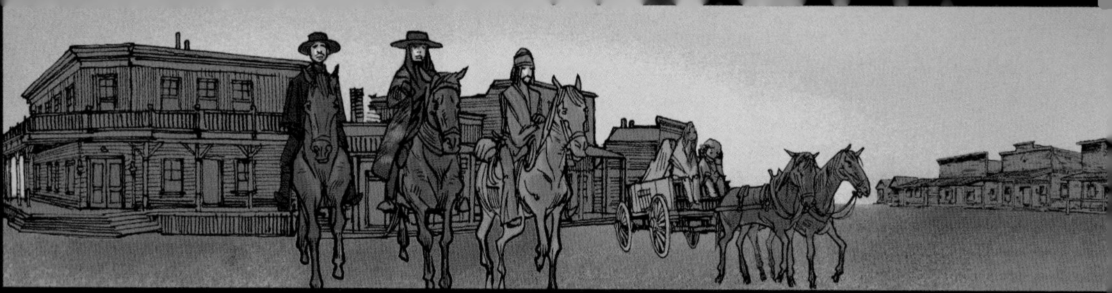

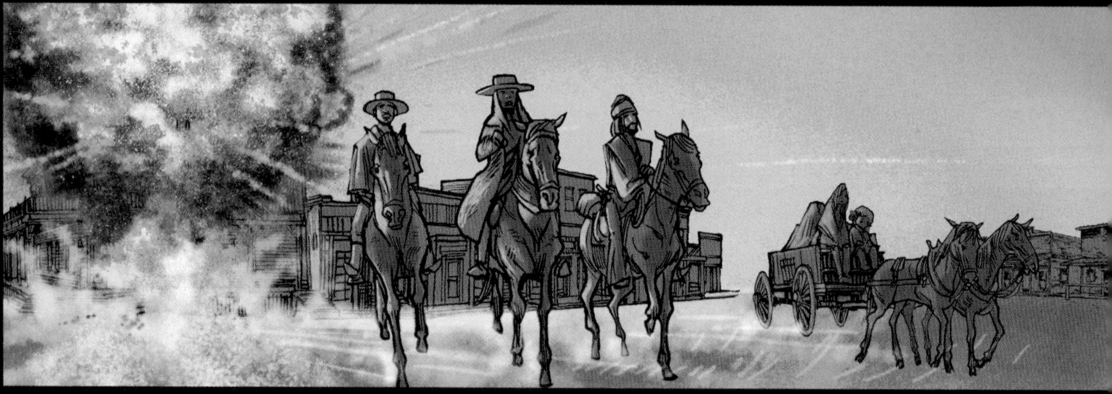

Introductions and explanations

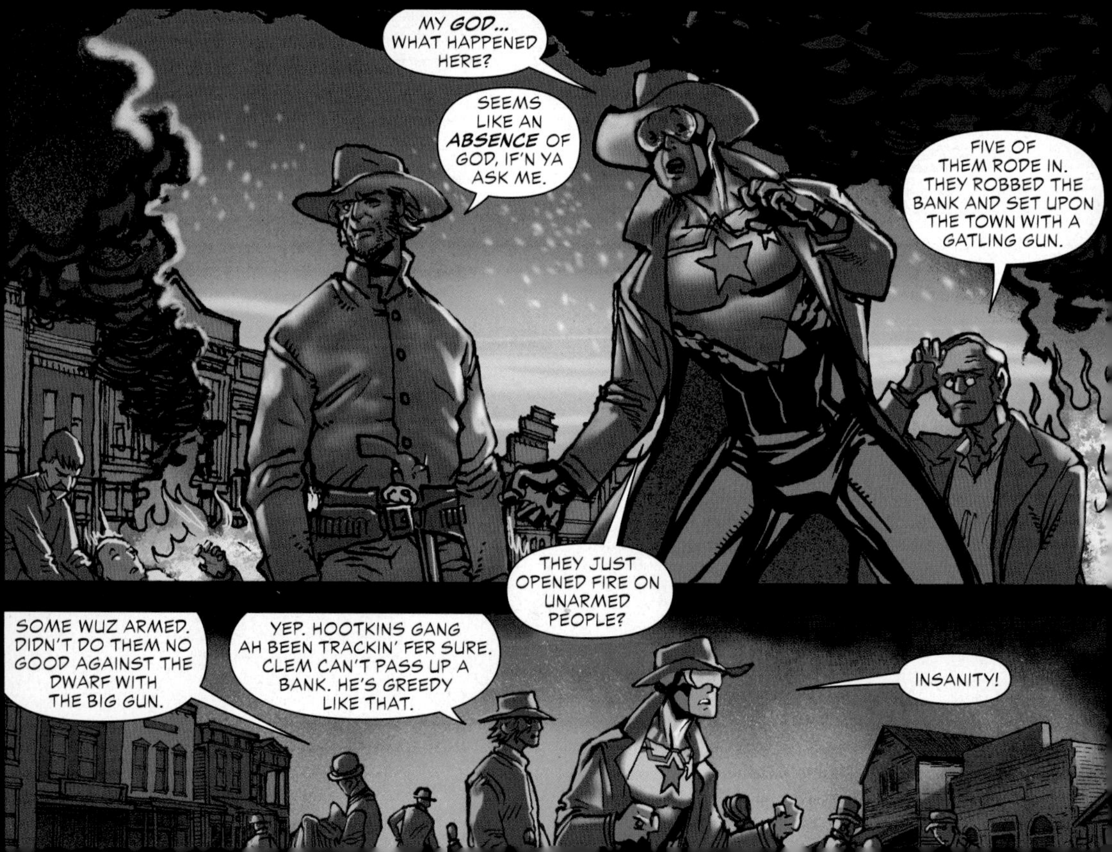
MY GOD... WHAT HAPPENED HERE?
SEEMS LIKE AN ABSENCE OF GOD, IF'N YA ASK ME.
FIVE OF THEM RODE IN. THEY ROBBED THE BANK AND SET UPON THE TOWN WITH A GATLING GUN.
THEY JUST OPENED FIRE ON UNARMED PEOPLE?
SOME WUZ ARMED. DIDN'T DO THEM NO GOOD AGAINST THE DWARF WITH THE BIG GUN.
YEP. HOOTKINS GANG AH BEEN TRACKIN' FER SURE. CLEM CAN'T PASS UP A BANK. HE'S GREEDY LIKE THAT.
INSANITY!

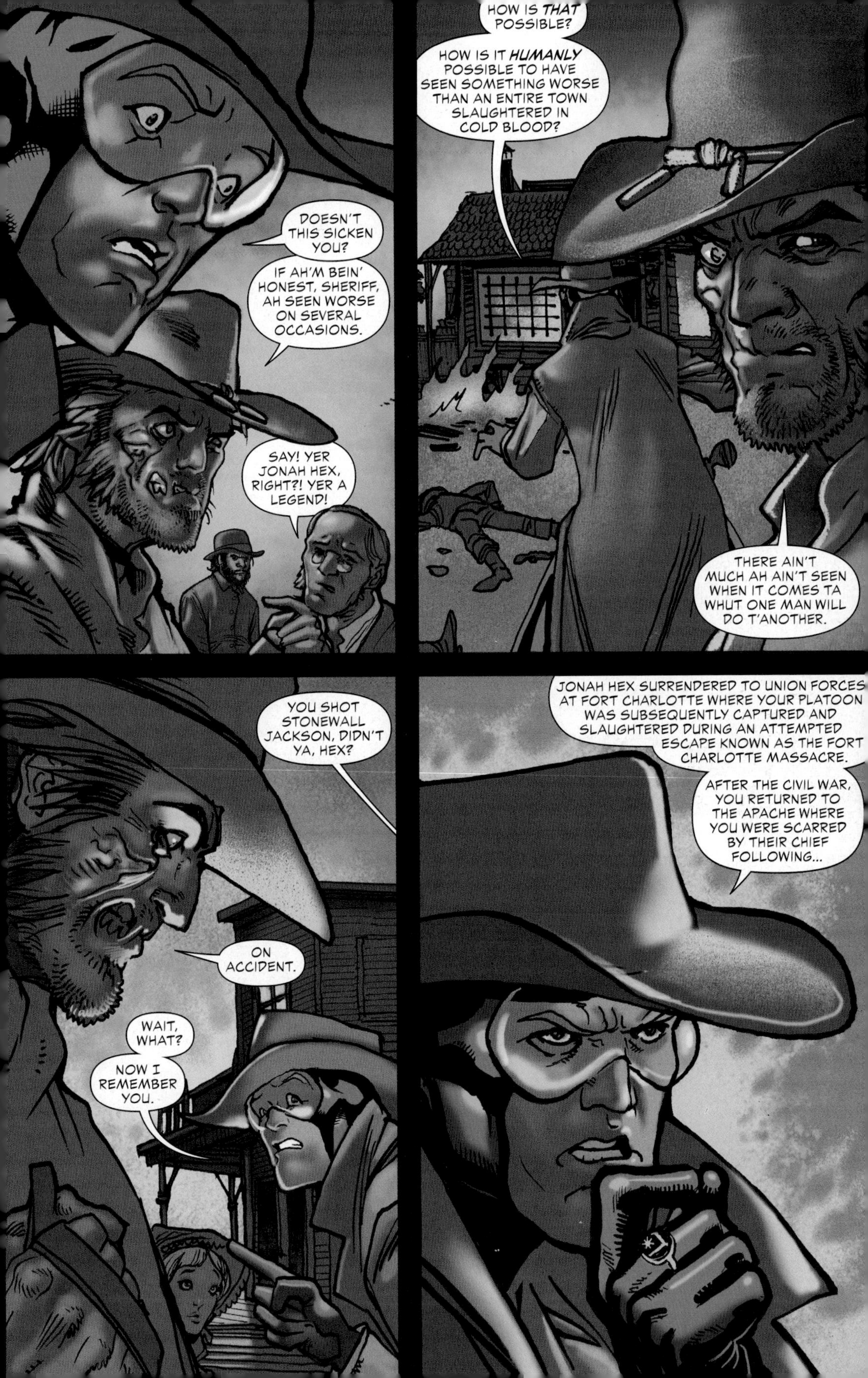
DOESN'T THIS SICKEN YOU?
IF AH'M BEIN' HONEST, SHERIFF, AH SEEN WORSE ON SEVERAL OCCASIONS.
SAY! YER JONAH HEX, RIGHT?! YER A LEGEND!
HOW IS *THAT* POSSIBLE?
HOW IS IT *HUMANLY* POSSIBLE TO HAVE SEEN SOMETHING WORSE THAN AN ENTIRE TOWN SLAUGHTERED IN COLD BLOOD?
THERE AIN'T MUCH AH AIN'T SEEN WHEN IT COMES TA WHUT ONE MAN WILL DO T'ANOTHER.
YOU SHOT STONEWALL JACKSON, DIDN'T YA, HEX?
ON ACCIDENT.
WAIT, WHAT?
NOW I REMEMBER YOU.
JONAH HEX SURRENDERED TO UNION FORCES AT FORT CHARLOTTE WHERE YOUR PLATOON WAS SUBSEQUENTLY CAPTURED AND SLAUGHTERED DURING AN ATTEMPTED ESCAPE KNOWN AS THE FORT CHARLOTTE MASSACRE.
AFTER THE CIVIL WAR, YOU RETURNED TO THE APACHE WHERE YOU WERE SCARRED BY THEIR CHIEF FOLLOWING...

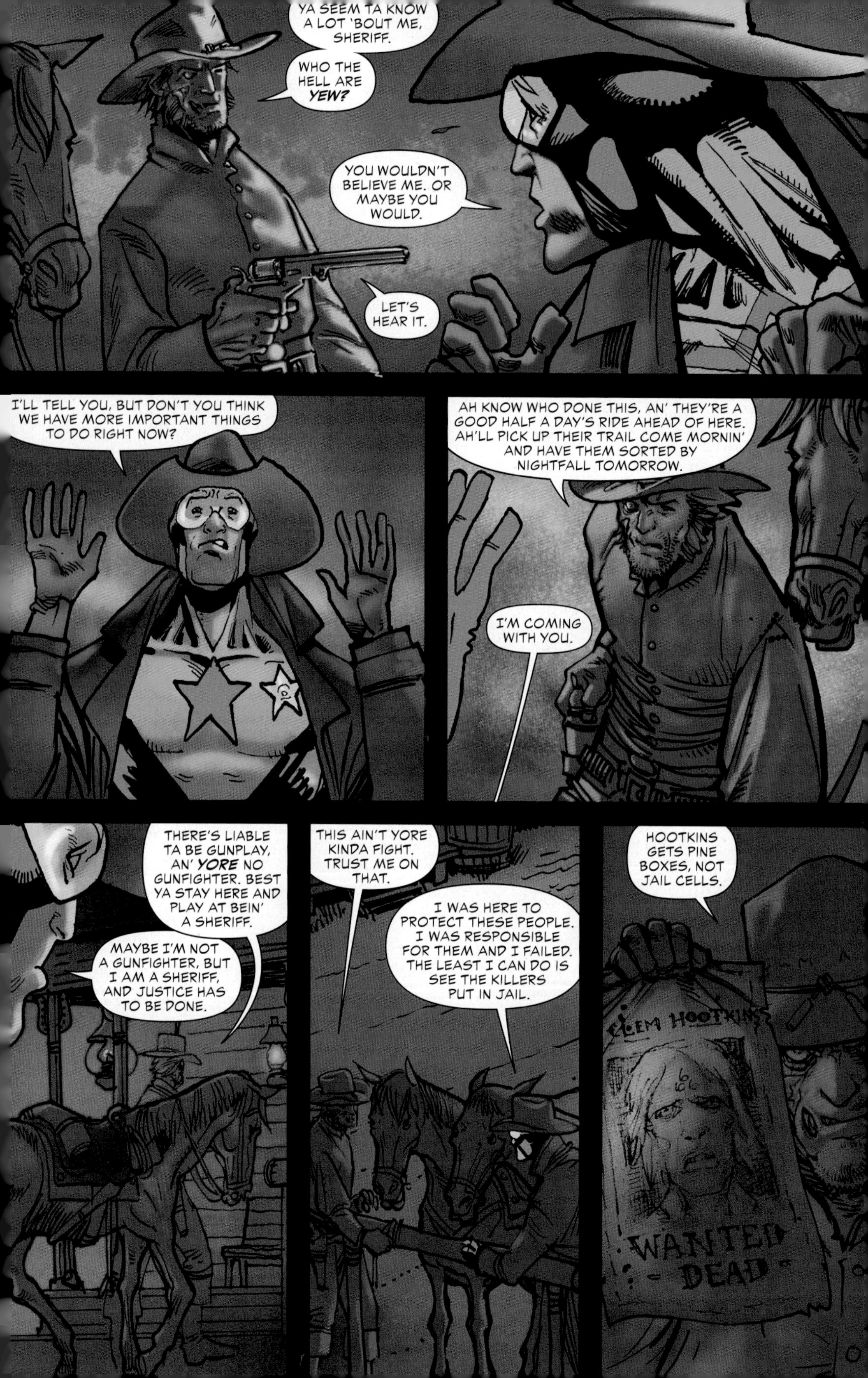
YA SEEM TA KNOW A LOT 'BOUT ME, SHERIFF.
WHO THE HELL ARE *YEW?*
YOU WOULDN'T BELIEVE ME. OR MAYBE YOU WOULD.
LET'S HEAR IT.
I'LL TELL YOU, BUT DON'T YOU THINK WE HAVE MORE IMPORTANT THINGS TO DO RIGHT NOW?
AH KNOW WHO DONE THIS, AN' THEY'RE A GOOD HALF A DAY'S RIDE AHEAD OF HERE. AH'LL PICK UP THEIR TRAIL COME MORNIN' AND HAVE THEM SORTED BY NIGHTFALL TOMORROW.
I'M COMING WITH YOU.
THERE'S LIABLE TA BE GUNPLAY, AN' *YORE* NO GUNFIGHTER. BEST YA STAY HERE AND PLAY AT BEIN' A SHERIFF.
MAYBE I'M NOT A GUNFIGHTER, BUT I AM A SHERIFF, AND JUSTICE HAS TO BE DONE.
THIS AIN'T YORE KINDA FIGHT. TRUST ME ON THAT.
I WAS HERE TO PROTECT THESE PEOPLE. I WAS RESPONSIBLE FOR THEM AND I FAILED. THE LEAST I CAN DO IS SEE THE KILLERS PUT IN JAIL.
HOOTKINS GETS PINE BOXES, NOT JAIL CELLS.
CLEM HOOTKINS
WANTED DEAD

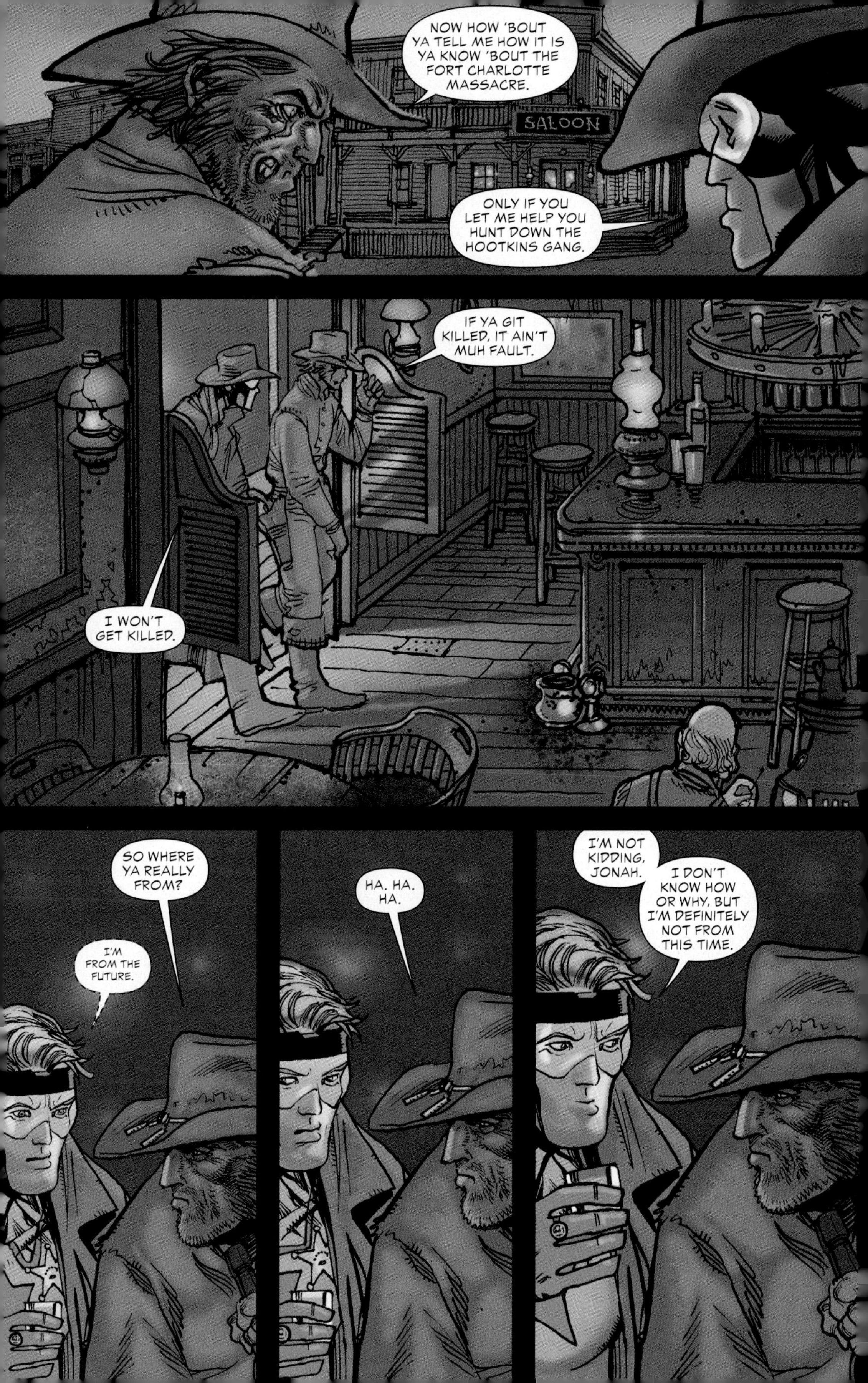
NOW HOW 'BOUT YA TELL ME HOW IT IS YA KNOW 'BOUT THE FORT CHARLOTTE MASSACRE.
SALOON
ONLY IF YOU LET ME HELP YOU HUNT DOWN THE HOOTKINS GANG.
IF YA GIT KILLED, IT AIN'T MUH FAULT.
I WON'T GET KILLED.
SO WHERE YA REALLY FROM?
I'M FROM THE FUTURE.
HA. HA. HA.
I'M NOT KIDDING, JONAH.
I DON'T KNOW HOW OR WHY, BUT I'M DEFINITELY NOT FROM THIS TIME.

How I became sheriff of Red River Junction

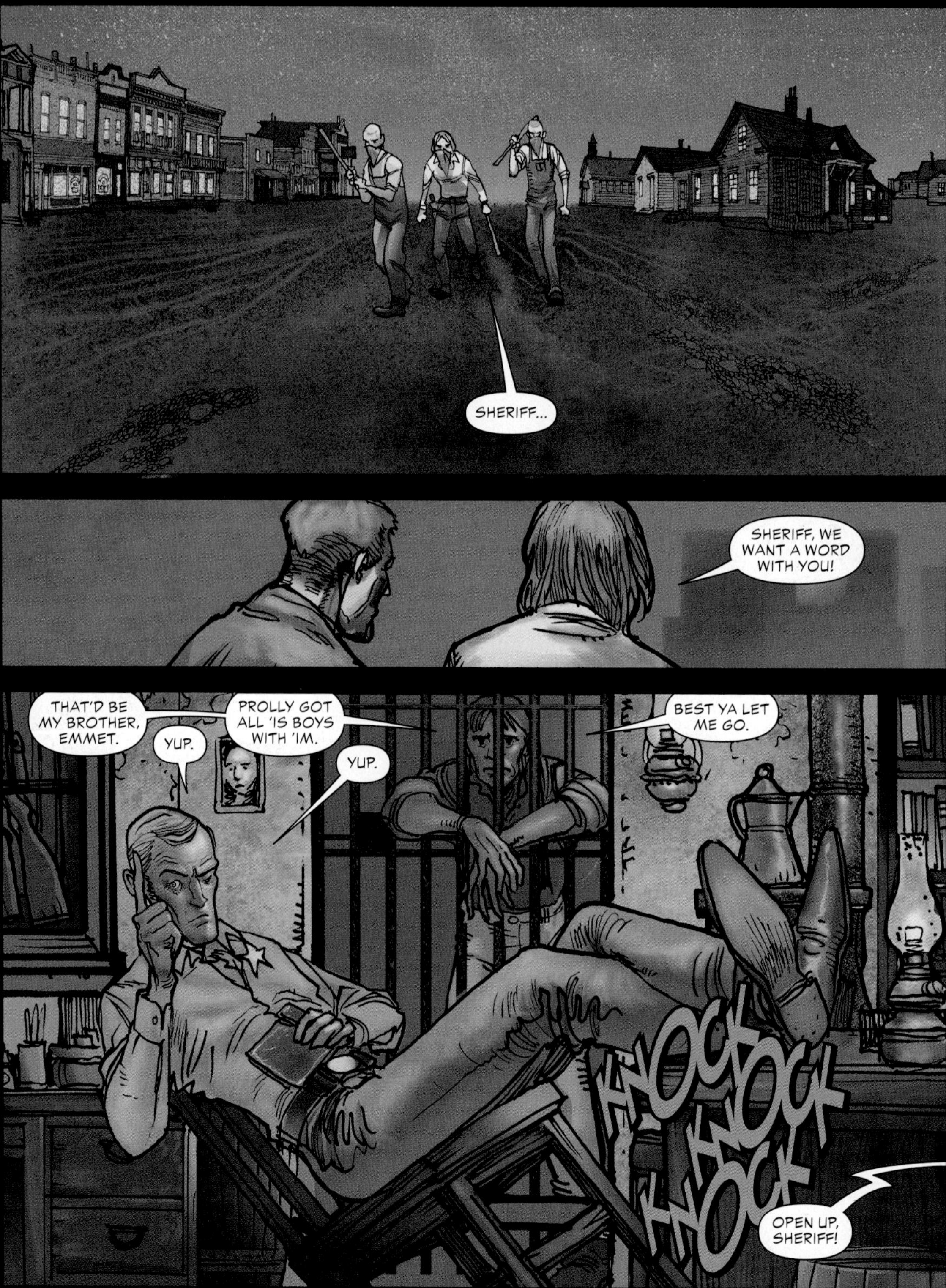
SHERIFF...
SHERIFF, WE WANT A WORD WITH YOU!
THAT'D BE MY BROTHER, EMMET.
YUP.
PROLLY GOT ALL 'IS BOYS WITH 'IM.
YUP.
BEST YA LET ME GO.
KNOCK KNOCK KNOCK
OPEN UP, SHERIFF!

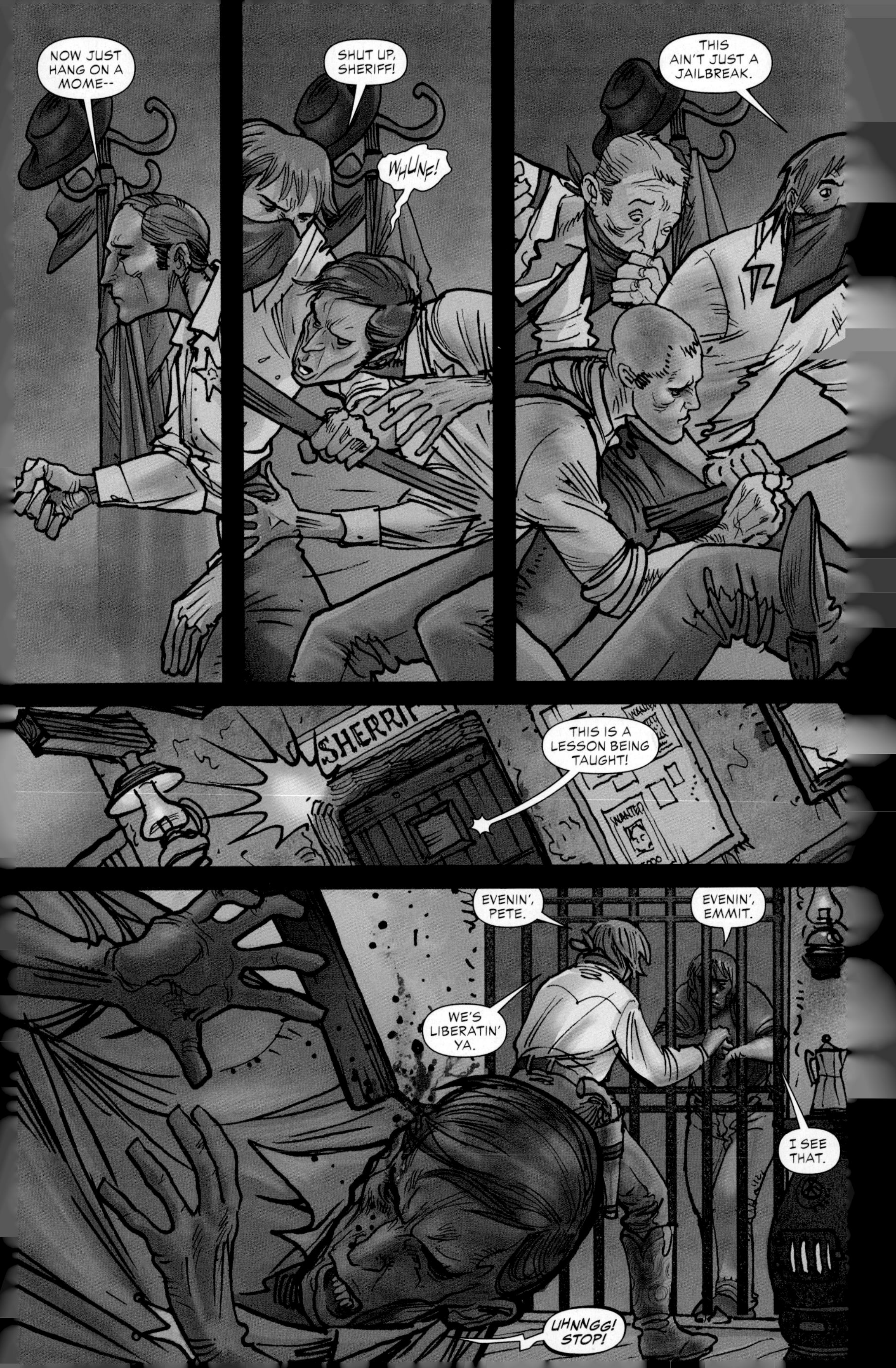
NOW JUST HANG ON A MOME--
SHUT UP, SHERIFF!
WHUNF!
THIS AIN'T JUST A JAILBREAK.
SHERRI
THIS IS A LESSON BEING TAUGHT!
EVENIN', PETE.
EVENIN', EMMIT.
WE'S LIBERATIN' YA.
I SEE THAT.
UHNNGG! STOP!

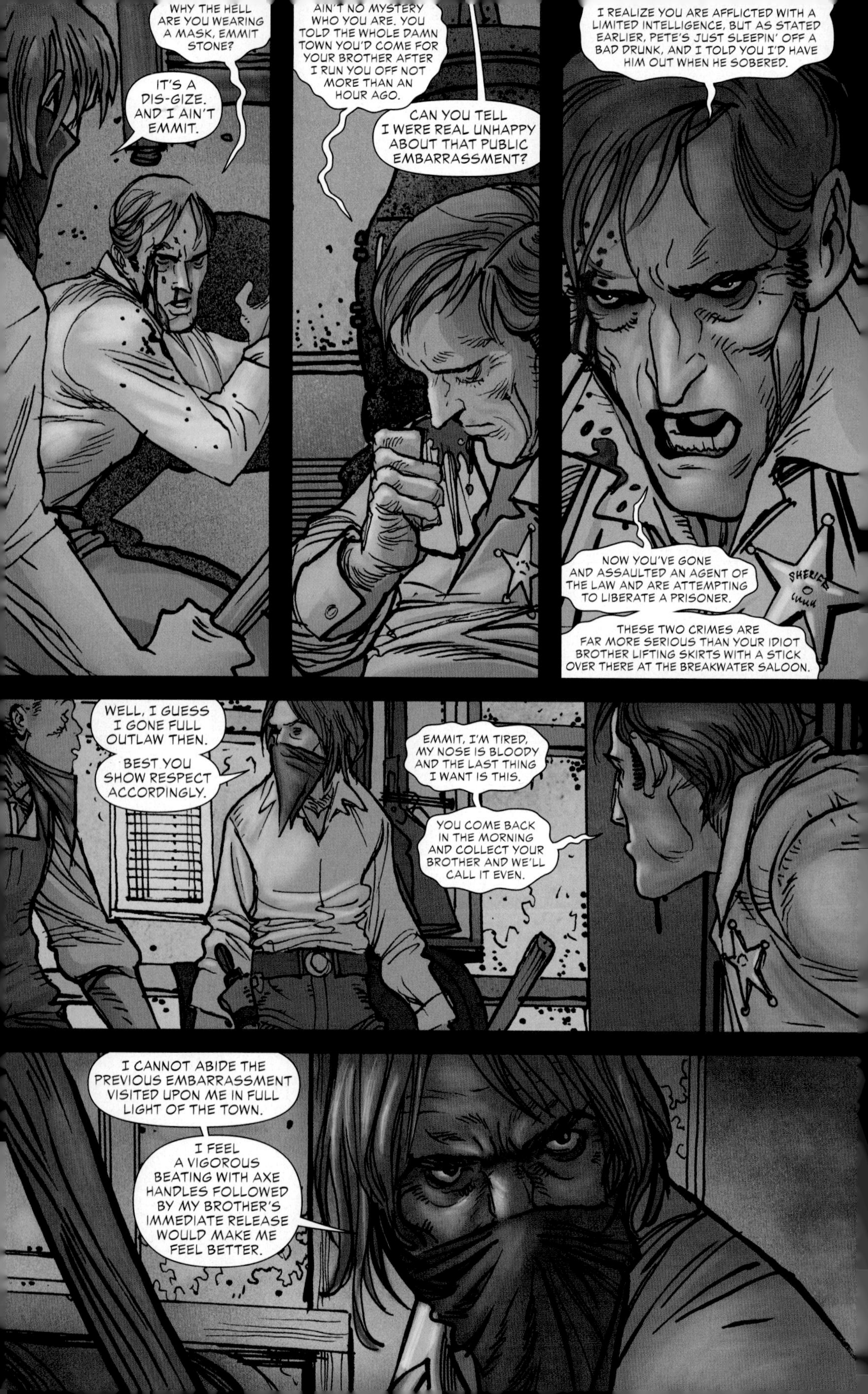
WHY THE HELL ARE YOU WEARING A MASK, EMMIT STONE?
IT'S A DIS-GIZE. AND I AIN'T EMMIT.
AIN'T NO MYSTERY WHO YOU ARE. YOU TOLD THE WHOLE DAMN TOWN YOU'D COME FOR YOUR BROTHER AFTER I RUN YOU OFF NOT MORE THAN AN HOUR AGO.
CAN YOU TELL I WERE REAL UNHAPPY ABOUT THAT PUBLIC EMBARRASSMENT?
I REALIZE YOU ARE AFFLICTED WITH A LIMITED INTELLIGENCE, BUT AS STATED EARLIER, PETE'S JUST SLEEPIN' OFF A BAD DRUNK, AND I TOLD YOU I'D HAVE HIM OUT WHEN HE SOBERED.
NOW YOU'VE GONE AND ASSAULTED AN AGENT OF THE LAW AND ARE ATTEMPTING TO LIBERATE A PRISONER.
THESE TWO CRIMES ARE FAR MORE SERIOUS THAN YOUR IDIOT BROTHER LIFTING SKIRTS WITH A STICK OVER THERE AT THE BREAKWATER SALOON.
SHERIFF
WELL, I GUESS I GONE FULL OUTLAW THEN.
BEST YOU SHOW RESPECT ACCORDINGLY.
EMMIT, I'M TIRED, MY NOSE IS BLOODY AND THE LAST THING I WANT IS THIS.
YOU COME BACK IN THE MORNING AND COLLECT YOUR BROTHER AND WE'LL CALL IT EVEN.
I CANNOT ABIDE THE PREVIOUS EMBARRASSMENT VISITED UPON ME IN FULL LIGHT OF THE TOWN.
I FEEL A VIGOROUS BEATING WITH AXE HANDLES FOLLOWED BY MY BROTHER'S IMMEDIATE RELEASE WOULD MAKE ME FEEL BETTER.

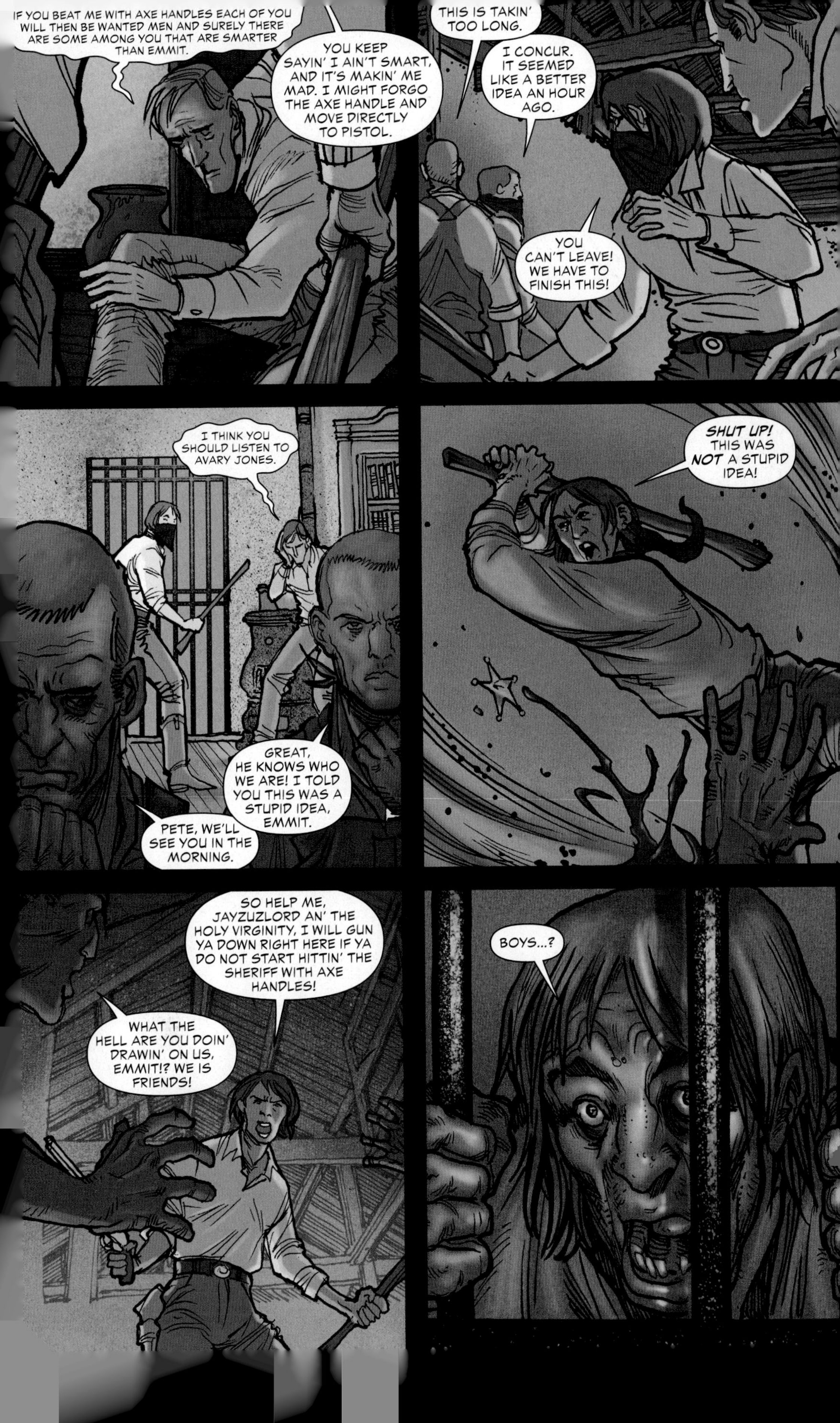
IF YOU BEAT ME WITH AXE HANDLES EACH OF YOU WILL THEN BE WANTED MEN AND SURELY THERE ARE SOME AMONG YOU THAT ARE SMARTER THAN EMMIT.
YOU KEEP SAYIN' I AIN'T SMART, AND IT'S MAKIN' ME MAD. I MIGHT FORGO THE AXE HANDLE AND MOVE DIRECTLY TO PISTOL.
THIS IS TAKIN' TOO LONG.
I CONCUR. IT SEEMED LIKE A BETTER IDEA AN HOUR AGO.
YOU CAN'T LEAVE! WE HAVE TO FINISH THIS!
I THINK YOU SHOULD LISTEN TO AVARY JONES.
GREAT, HE KNOWS WHO WE ARE! I TOLD YOU THIS WAS A STUPID IDEA, EMMIT.
PETE, WE'LL SEE YOU IN THE MORNING.
SHUT UP! THIS WAS NOT A STUPID IDEA!
SO HELP ME, JAYZUZLORD AN' THE HOLY VIRGINITY, I WILL GUN YA DOWN RIGHT HERE IF YA DO NOT START HITTIN' THE SHERIFF WITH AXE HANDLES!
WHAT THE HELL ARE YOU DOIN' DRAWIN' ON US, EMMIT!? WE IS FRIENDS!
BOYS...?

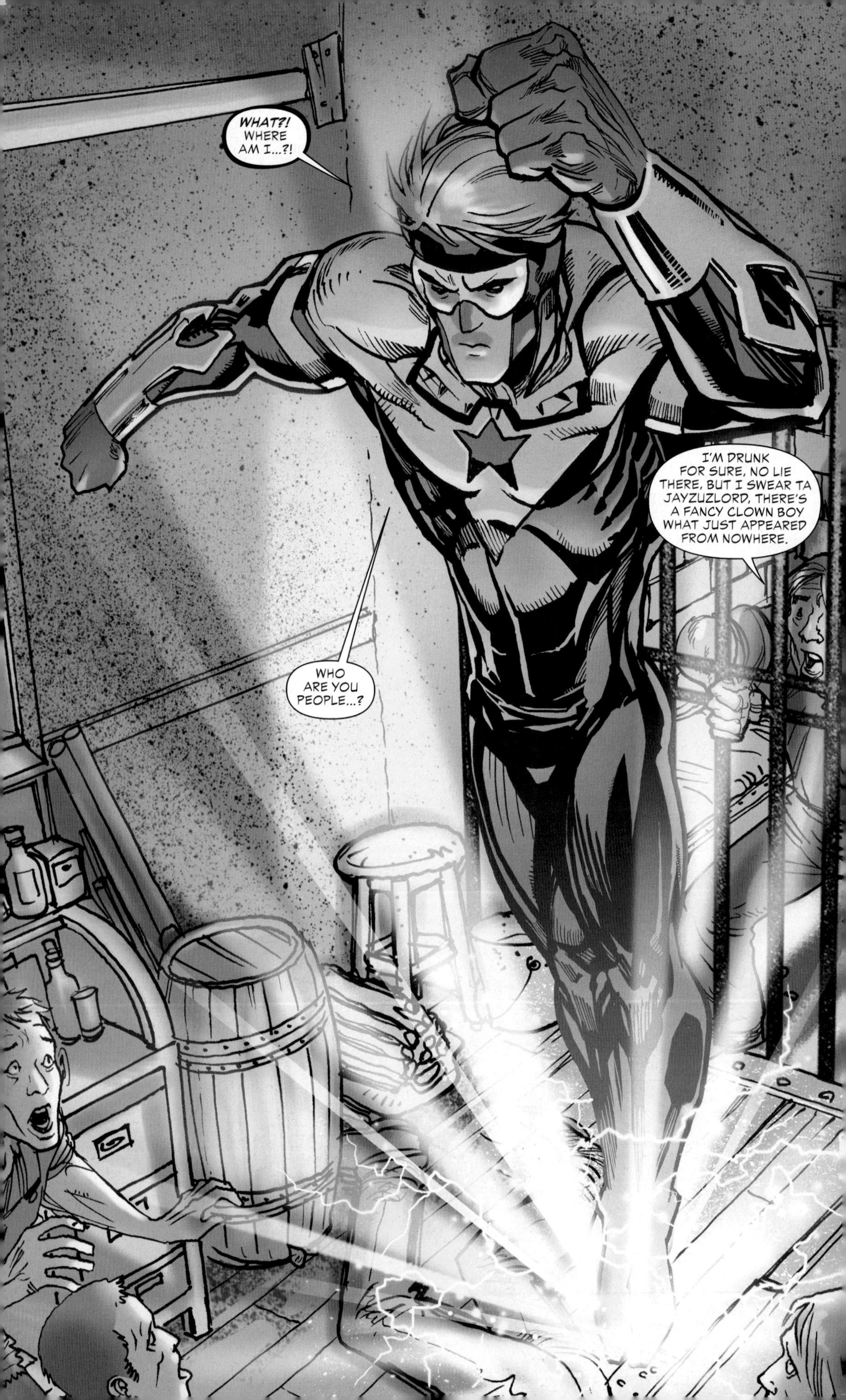
WHAT?! WHERE AM I...?!
I'M DRUNK FOR SURE, NO LIE THERE, BUT I SWEAR TA JAYZUZLORD, THERE'S A FANCY CLOWN BOY WHAT JUST APPEARED FROM NOWHERE.
WHO ARE YOU PEOPLE...?

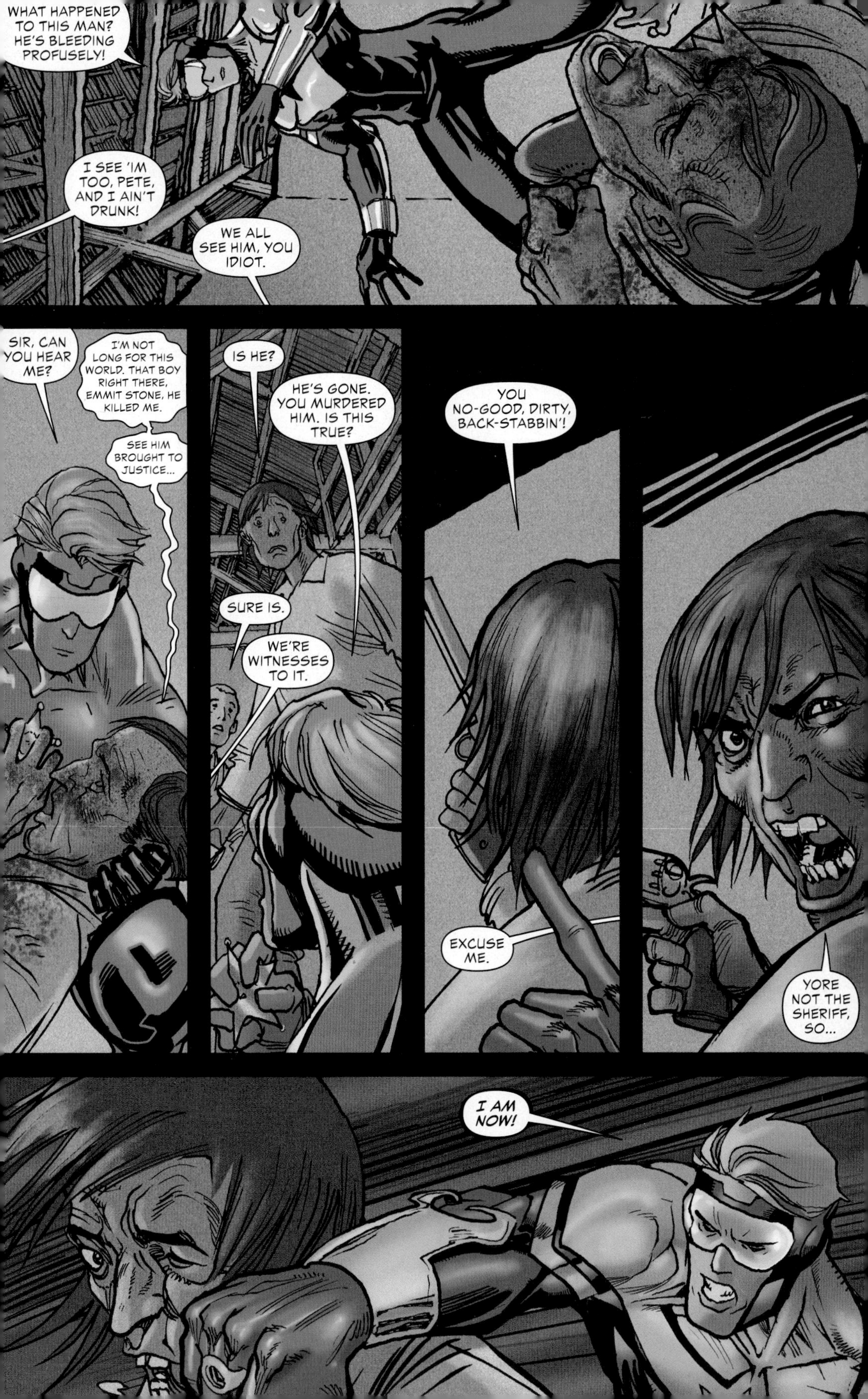
WHAT HAPPENED TO THIS MAN? HE'S BLEEDING PROFUSELY!
I SEE 'IM TOO, PETE, AND I AIN'T DRUNK!
WE ALL SEE HIM, YOU IDIOT.
SIR, CAN YOU HEAR ME?
I'M NOT LONG FOR THIS WORLD. THAT BOY RIGHT THERE, EMMIT STONE, HE KILLED ME.
SEE HIM BROUGHT TO JUSTICE...
IS HE?
HE'S GONE. YOU MURDERED HIM. IS THIS TRUE?
SURE IS.
WE'RE WITNESSES TO IT.
YOU NO-GOOD, DIRTY, BACK-STABBIN'!
EXCUSE ME.
YORE NOT THE SHERIFF, SO...
I AM NOW!

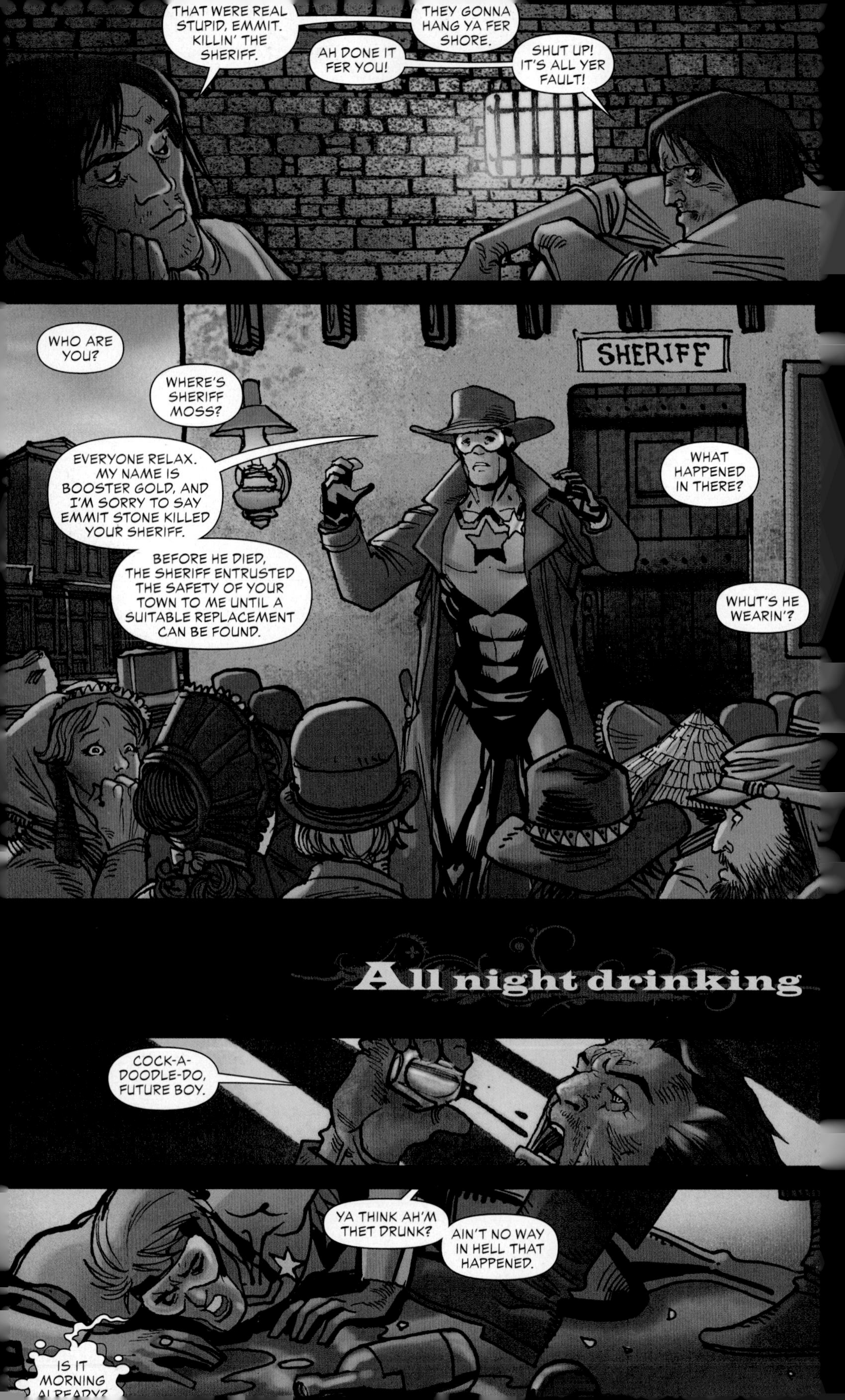
THAT WERE REAL STUPID, EMMIT. KILLIN' THE SHERIFF.
THEY GONNA HANG YA FER SHORE.
AH DONE IT FER YOU!
SHUT UP! IT'S ALL YER FAULT!
WHO ARE YOU?
WHERE'S SHERIFF MOSS?
SHERIFF
EVERYONE RELAX. MY NAME IS BOOSTER GOLD, AND I'M SORRY TO SAY EMMIT STONE KILLED YOUR SHERIFF.
BEFORE HE DIED, THE SHERIFF ENTRUSTED THE SAFETY OF YOUR TOWN TO ME UNTIL A SUITABLE REPLACEMENT CAN BE FOUND.
WHAT HAPPENED IN THERE?
WHUT'S HE WEARIN'?
All night drinking
COCK-A-DOODLE-DO, FUTURE BOY.
YA THINK AH'M THET DRUNK?
AIN'T NO WAY IN HELL THAT HAPPENED.
IS IT MORNING

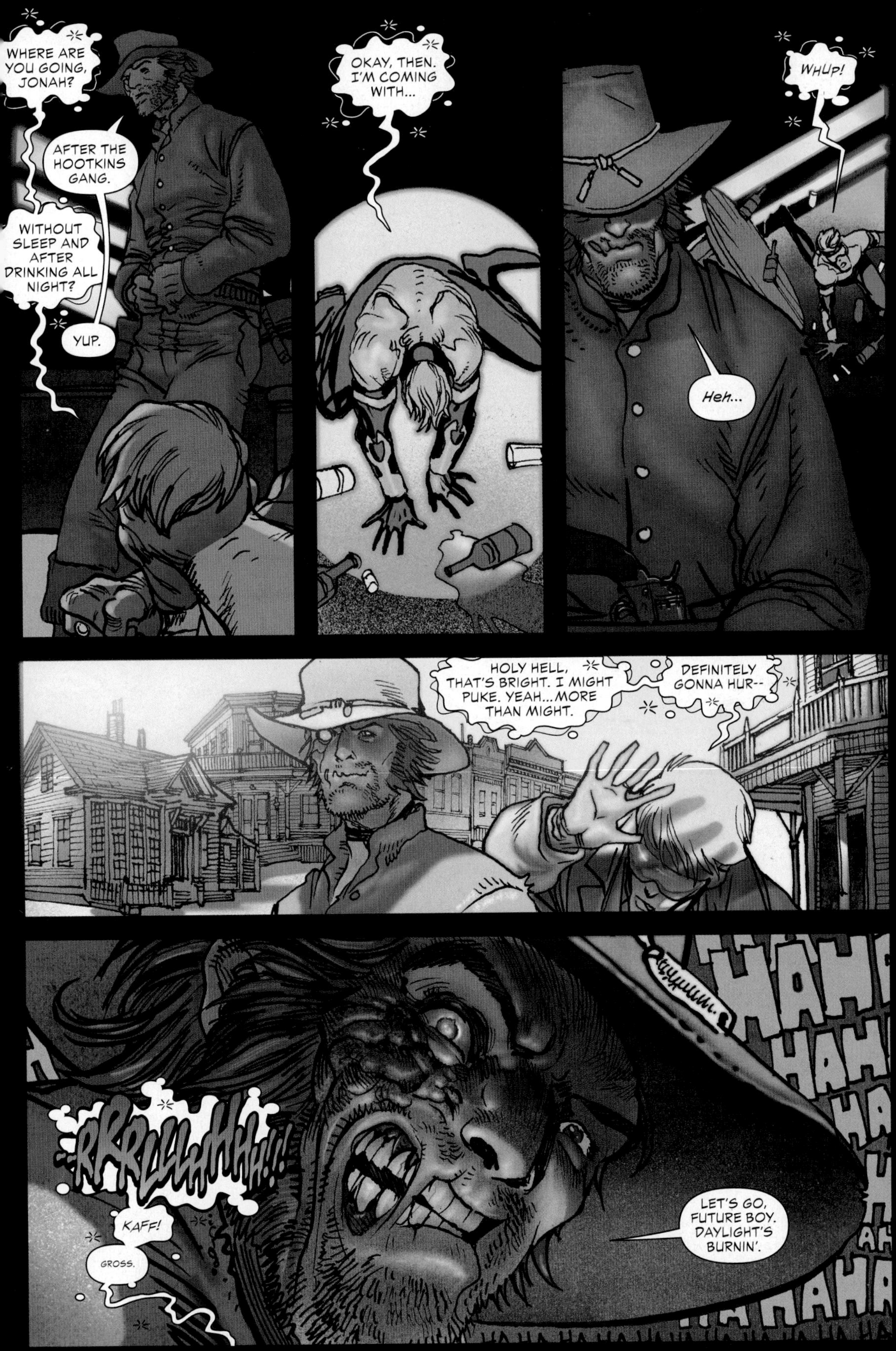

WHERE ARE YOU GOING, JONAH?
AFTER THE HOOTKINS GANG.
WITHOUT SLEEP AND AFTER DRINKING ALL NIGHT?
YUP.
OKAY, THEN. I'M COMING WITH...
WHUP!
Heh...
HOLY HELL, THAT'S BRIGHT. I MIGHT PUKE. YEAH...MORE THAN MIGHT.
DEFINITELY GONNA HUR--
RRRLLLHHHH!!!
KAFF!
GROSS.
LET'S GO, FUTURE BOY. DAYLIGHT'S BURNIN'.

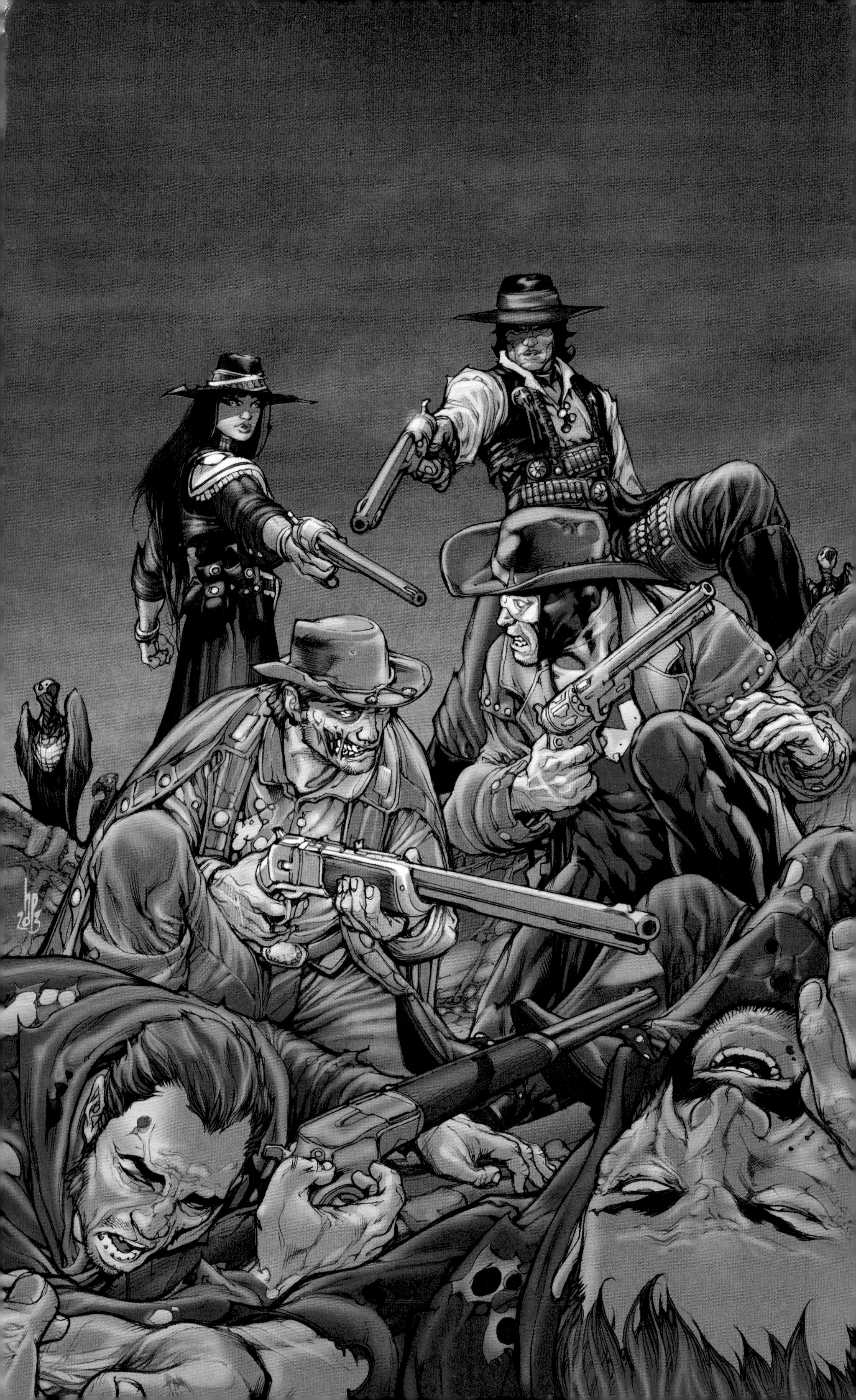

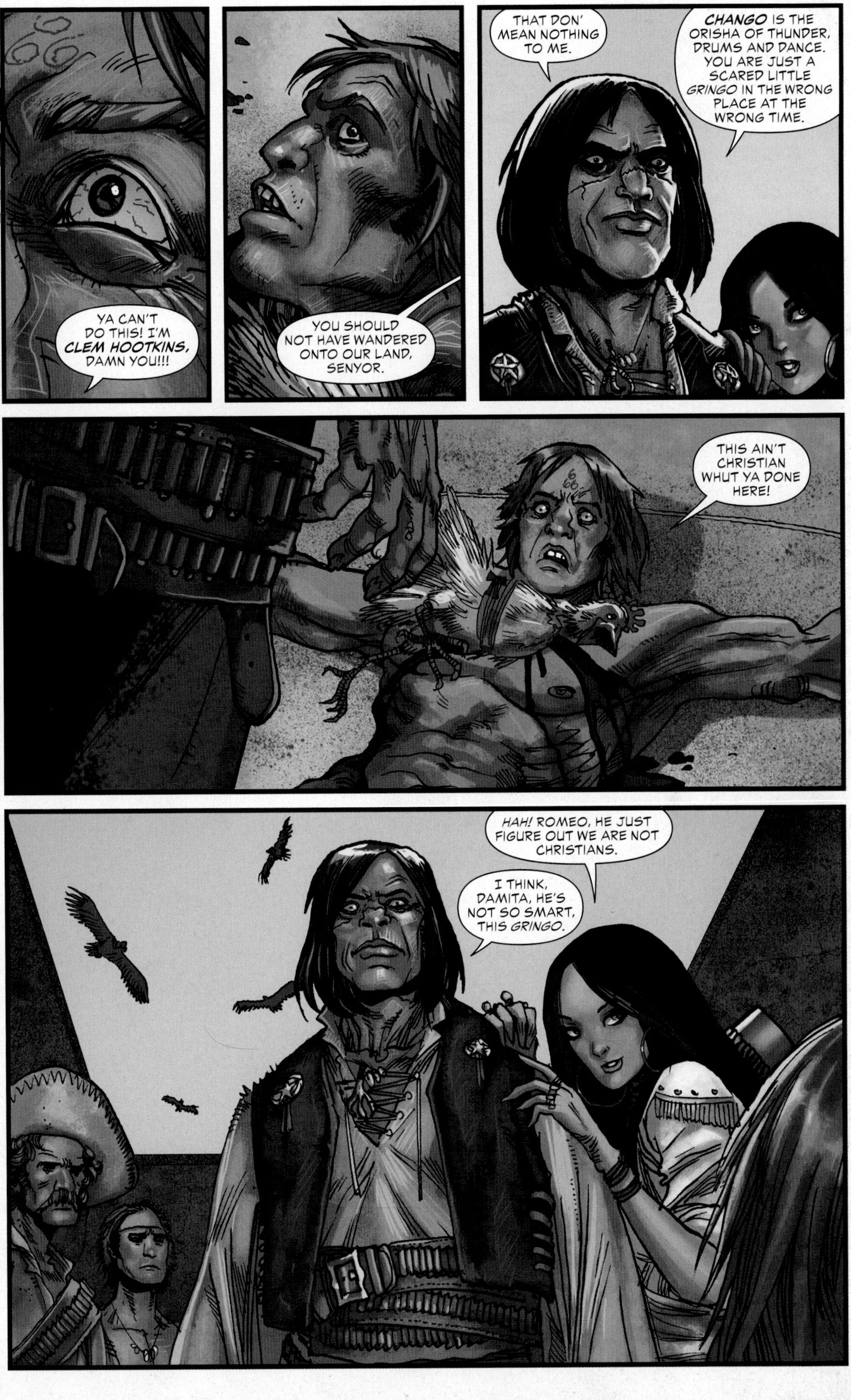
YA CAN'T DO THIS! I'M **CLEM HOOTKINS,** DAMN YOU!!!
YOU SHOULD NOT HAVE WANDERED ONTO OUR LAND, SENYOR.
THAT DON' MEAN NOTHING TO ME.
CHANGO IS THE ORISHA OF THUNDER, DRUMS AND DANCE. YOU ARE JUST A SCARED LITTLE *GRINGO* IN THE WRONG PLACE AT THE WRONG TIME.
THIS AIN'T CHRISTIAN WHUT YA DONE HERE!
HAH! ROMEO, HE JUST FIGURE OUT WE ARE NOT CHRISTIANS.
I THINK, DAMITA, HE'S NOT SO SMART, THIS *GRINGO*.

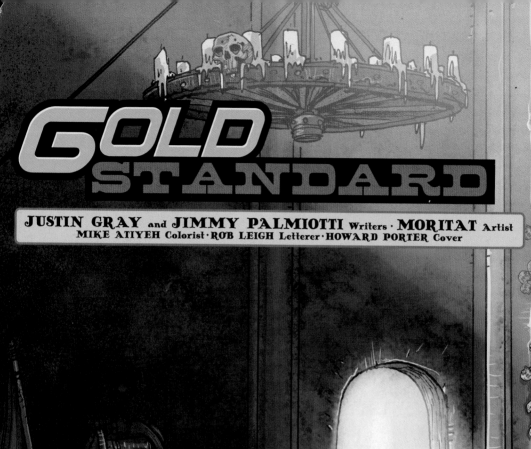

GOLD STANDARD

JUSTIN GRAY and **JIMMY PALMIOTTI** Writers · **MORITAT** Artist
MIKE ATIYEH Colorist · **ROB LEIGH** Letterer · **HOWARD PORTER** Cover

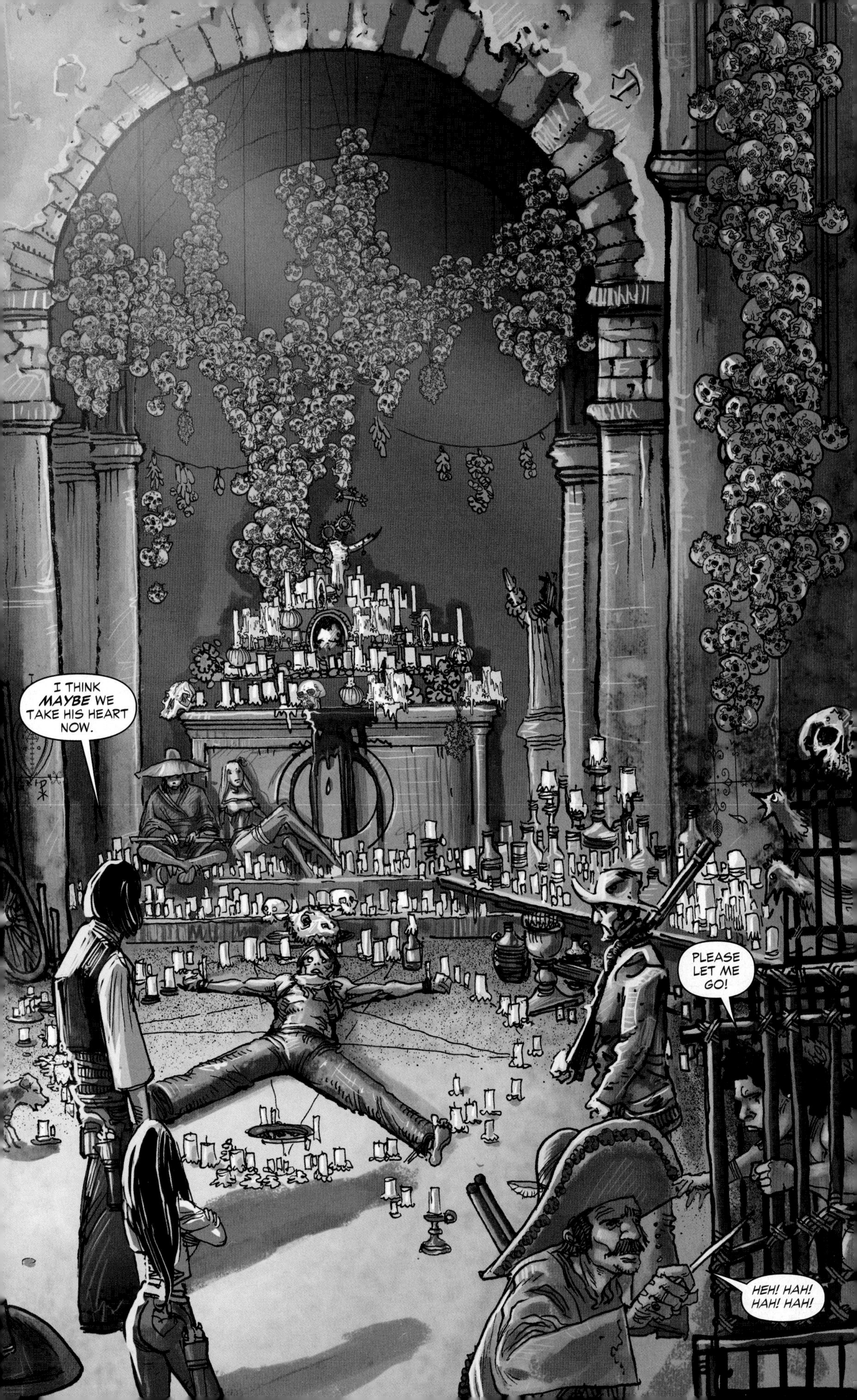
I THINK MAYBE WE TAKE HIS HEART NOW.
PLEASE LET ME GO!
HEH! HAH! HAH! HAH!

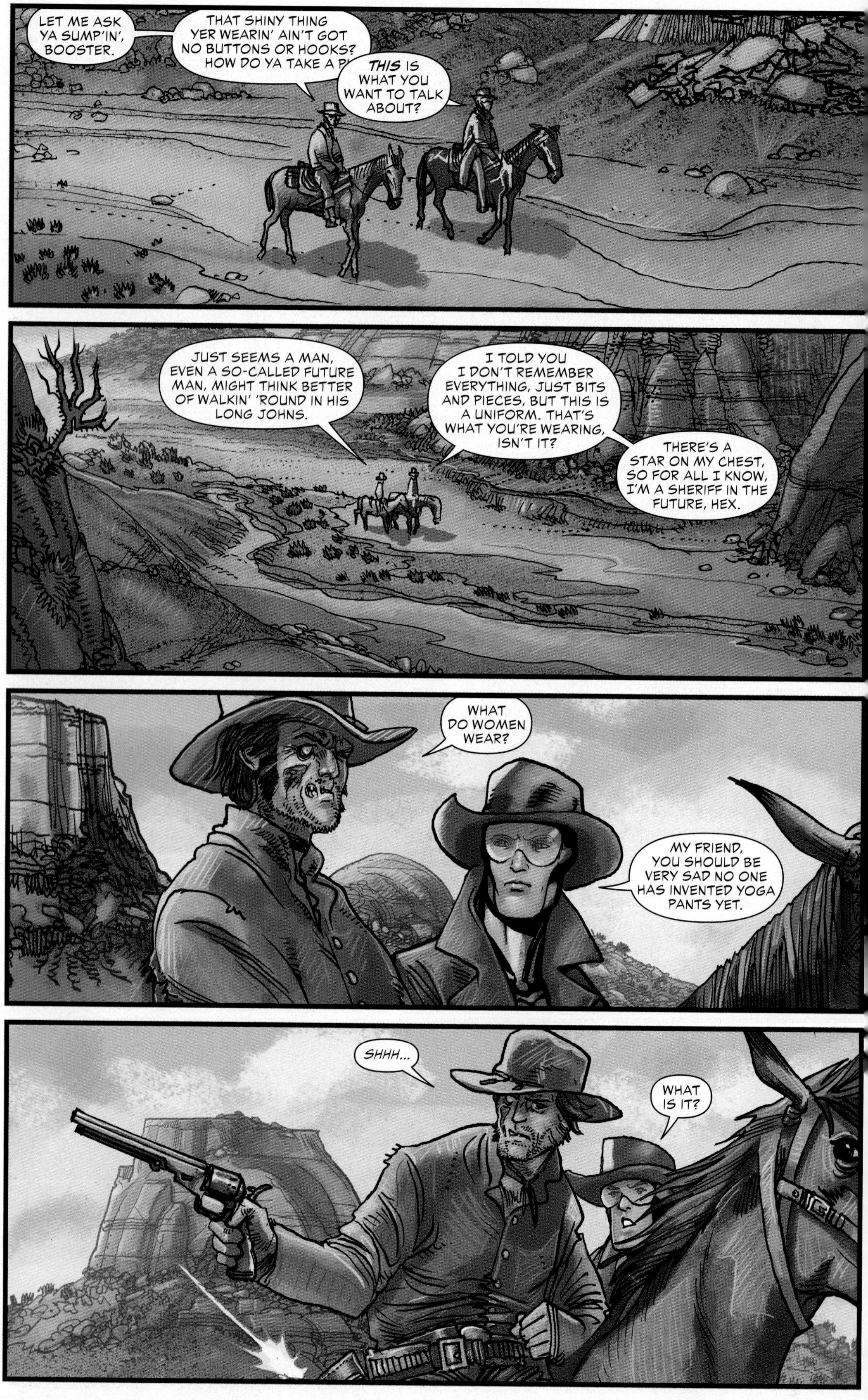
LET ME ASK YA SUMP'IN', BOOSTER.
THAT SHINY THING YER WEARIN' AIN'T GOT NO BUTTONS OR HOOKS? HOW DO YA TAKE A P
THIS IS WHAT YOU WANT TO TALK ABOUT?
JUST SEEMS A MAN, EVEN A SO-CALLED FUTURE MAN, MIGHT THINK BETTER OF WALKIN' 'ROUND IN HIS LONG JOHNS.
I TOLD YOU I DON'T REMEMBER EVERYTHING, JUST BITS AND PIECES, BUT THIS IS A UNIFORM. THAT'S WHAT YOU'RE WEARING, ISN'T IT?
THERE'S A STAR ON MY CHEST, SO FOR ALL I KNOW, I'M A SHERIFF IN THE FUTURE, HEX.
WHAT DO WOMEN WEAR?
MY FRIEND, YOU SHOULD BE VERY SAD NO ONE HAS INVENTED YOGA PANTS YET.
SHHH...
WHAT IS IT?

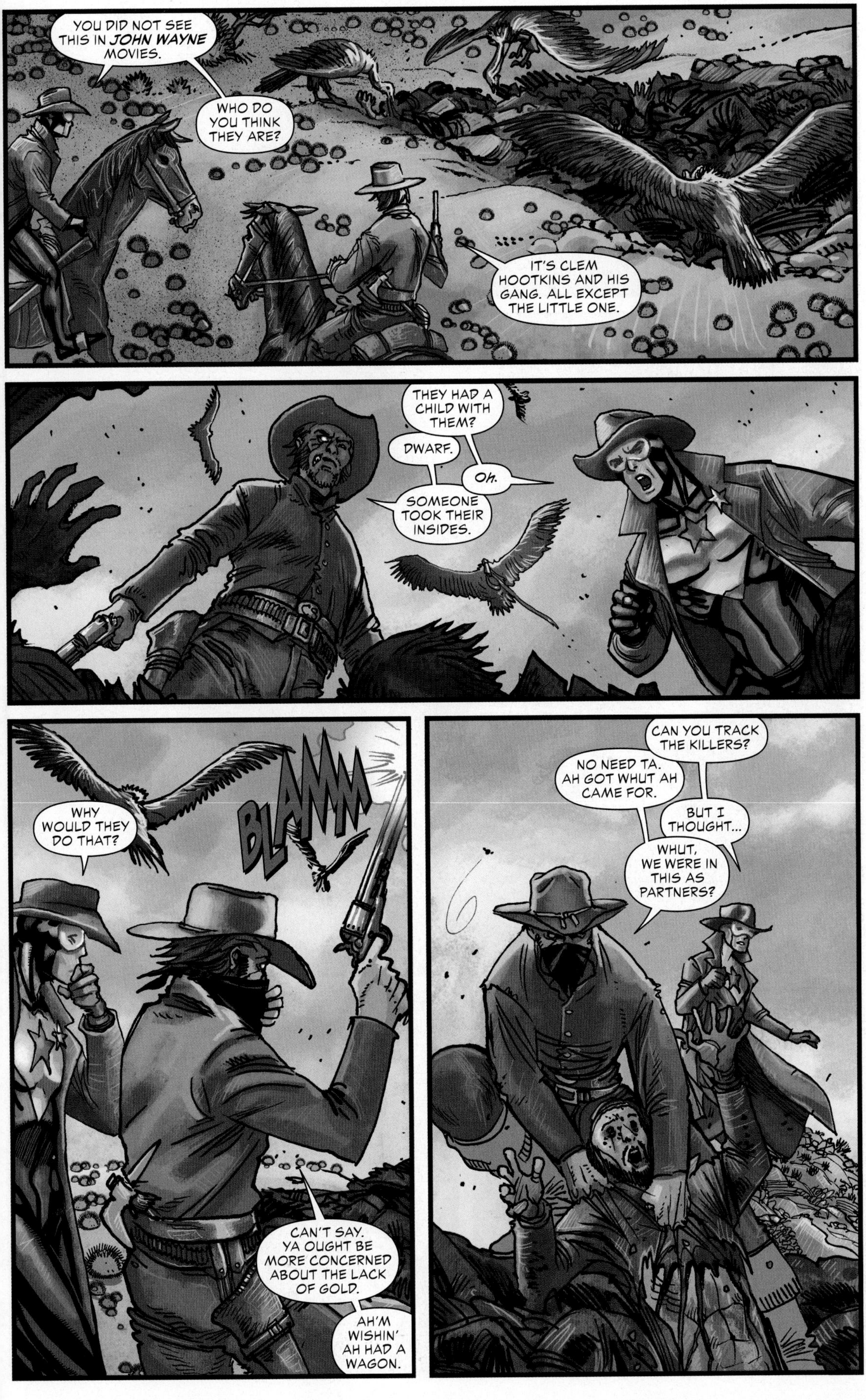
YOU DID NOT SEE THIS IN JOHN WAYNE MOVIES.
WHO DO YOU THINK THEY ARE?
IT'S CLEM HOOTKINS AND HIS GANG. ALL EXCEPT THE LITTLE ONE.
THEY HAD A CHILD WITH THEM?
DWARF.
Oh.
SOMEONE TOOK THEIR INSIDES.
WHY WOULD THEY DO THAT?
BLAMM
CAN'T SAY. YA OUGHT BE MORE CONCERNED ABOUT THE LACK OF GOLD.
AH'M WISHIN' AH HAD A WAGON.
CAN YOU TRACK THE KILLERS?
NO NEED TA. AH GOT WHUT AH CAME FOR.
BUT I THOUGHT...
WHUT, WE WERE IN THIS AS PARTNERS?

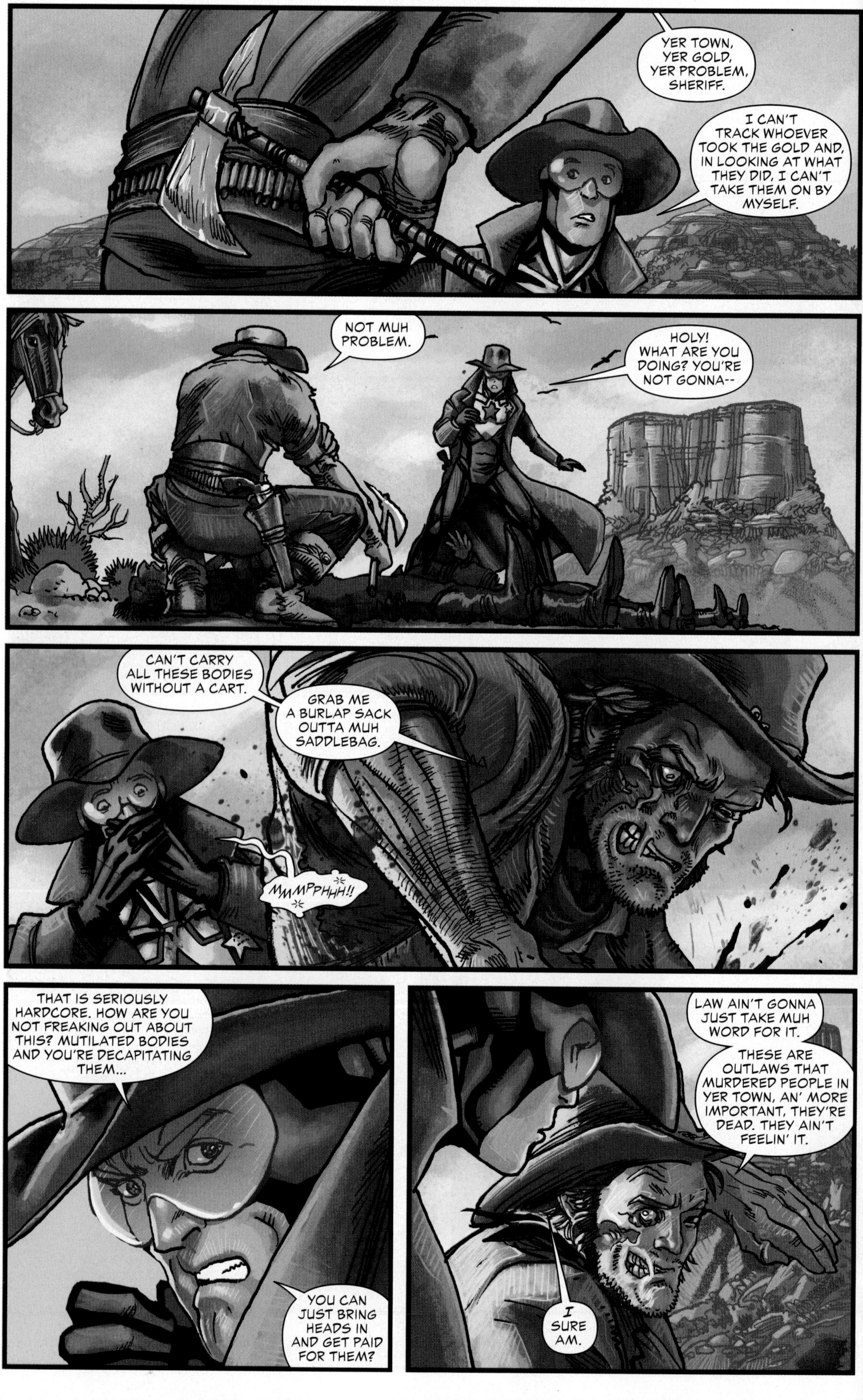
YER TOWN, YER GOLD, YER PROBLEM, SHERIFF.
I CAN'T TRACK WHOEVER TOOK THE GOLD AND, IN LOOKING AT WHAT THEY DID, I CAN'T TAKE THEM ON BY MYSELF.
NOT MUH PROBLEM.
HOLY! WHAT ARE YOU DOING? YOU'RE NOT GONNA--
CAN'T CARRY ALL THESE BODIES WITHOUT A CART.
GRAB ME A BURLAP SACK OUTTA MUH SADDLEBAG.
MMMPHHH!!
THAT IS SERIOUSLY HARDCORE. HOW ARE YOU NOT FREAKING OUT ABOUT THIS? MUTILATED BODIES AND YOU'RE DECAPITATING THEM...
YOU CAN JUST BRING HEADS IN AND GET PAID FOR THEM?
LAW AIN'T GONNA JUST TAKE MUH WORD FOR IT.
THESE ARE OUTLAWS THAT MURDERED PEOPLE IN YER TOWN, AN' MORE IMPORTANT, THEY'RE DEAD. THEY AIN'T FEELIN' IT.
I SURE AM.

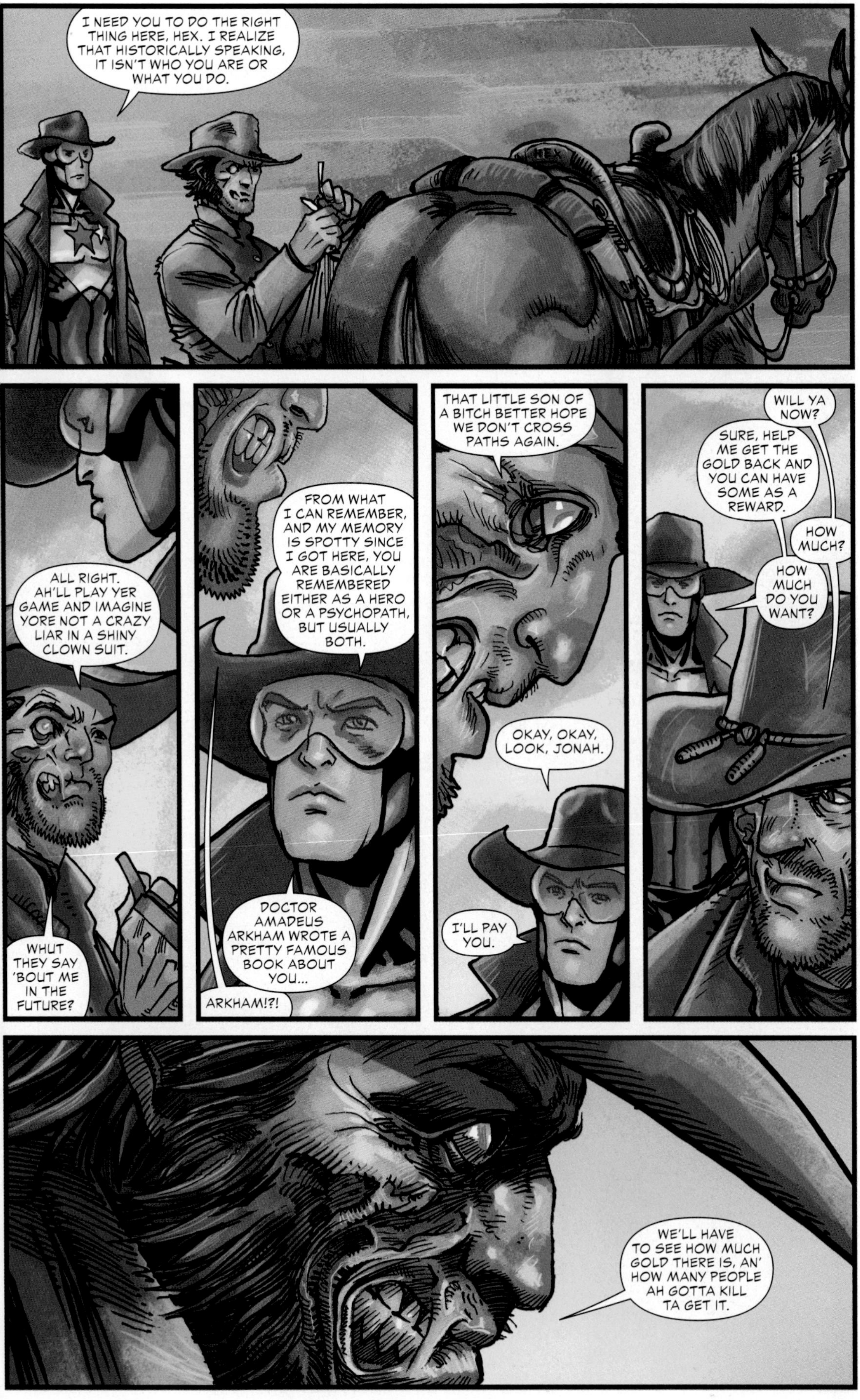
I NEED YOU TO DO THE RIGHT THING HERE, HEX. I REALIZE THAT HISTORICALLY SPEAKING, IT ISN'T WHO YOU ARE OR WHAT YOU DO.
ALL RIGHT. AH'LL PLAY YER GAME AND IMAGINE YORE NOT A CRAZY LIAR IN A SHINY CLOWN SUIT.
WHUT THEY SAY 'BOUT ME IN THE FUTURE?
FROM WHAT I CAN REMEMBER, AND MY MEMORY IS SPOTTY SINCE I GOT HERE, YOU ARE BASICALLY REMEMBERED EITHER AS A HERO OR A PSYCHOPATH, BUT USUALLY BOTH.
DOCTOR AMADEUS ARKHAM WROTE A PRETTY FAMOUS BOOK ABOUT YOU...
ARKHAM!?!
THAT LITTLE SON OF A BITCH BETTER HOPE WE DON'T CROSS PATHS AGAIN.
OKAY, OKAY, LOOK, JONAH.
I'LL PAY YOU.
WILL YA NOW?
SURE, HELP ME GET THE GOLD BACK AND YOU CAN HAVE SOME AS A REWARD.
HOW MUCH?
HOW MUCH DO YOU WANT?
WE'LL HAVE TO SEE HOW MUCH GOLD THERE IS, AN' HOW MANY PEOPLE AH GOTTA KILL TA GET IT.

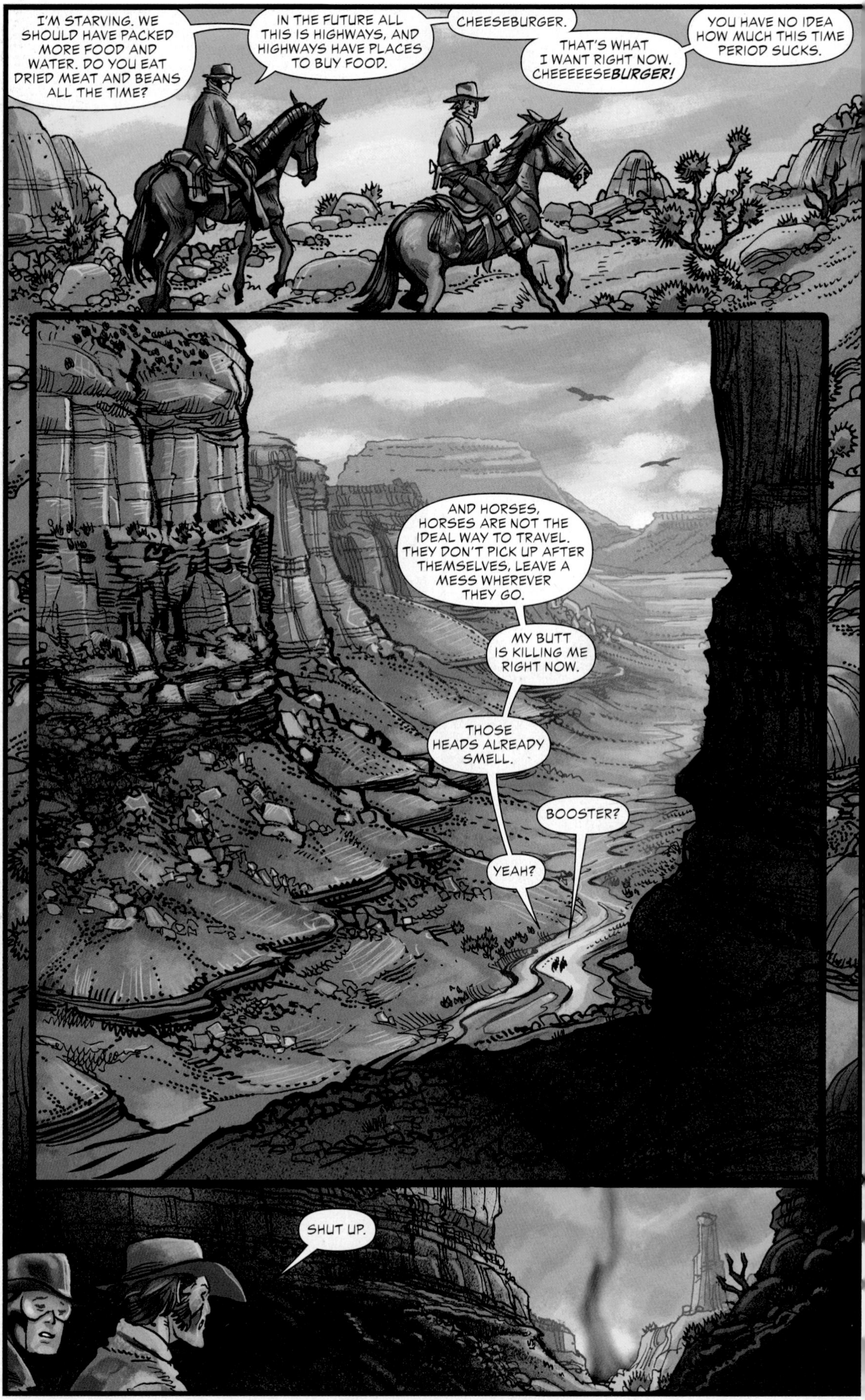
I'M STARVING. WE SHOULD HAVE PACKED MORE FOOD AND WATER. DO YOU EAT DRIED MEAT AND BEANS ALL THE TIME?
IN THE FUTURE ALL THIS IS HIGHWAYS, AND HIGHWAYS HAVE PLACES TO BUY FOOD.
CHEESEBURGER.
THAT'S WHAT I WANT RIGHT NOW. CHEEEEESE**BURGER!**
YOU HAVE NO IDEA HOW MUCH THIS TIME PERIOD SUCKS.
AND HORSES, HORSES ARE NOT THE IDEAL WAY TO TRAVEL. THEY DON'T PICK UP AFTER THEMSELVES, LEAVE A MESS WHEREVER THEY GO.
MY BUTT IS KILLING ME RIGHT NOW.
THOSE HEADS ALREADY SMELL.
BOOSTER?
YEAH?
SHUT UP.

Crazy for you

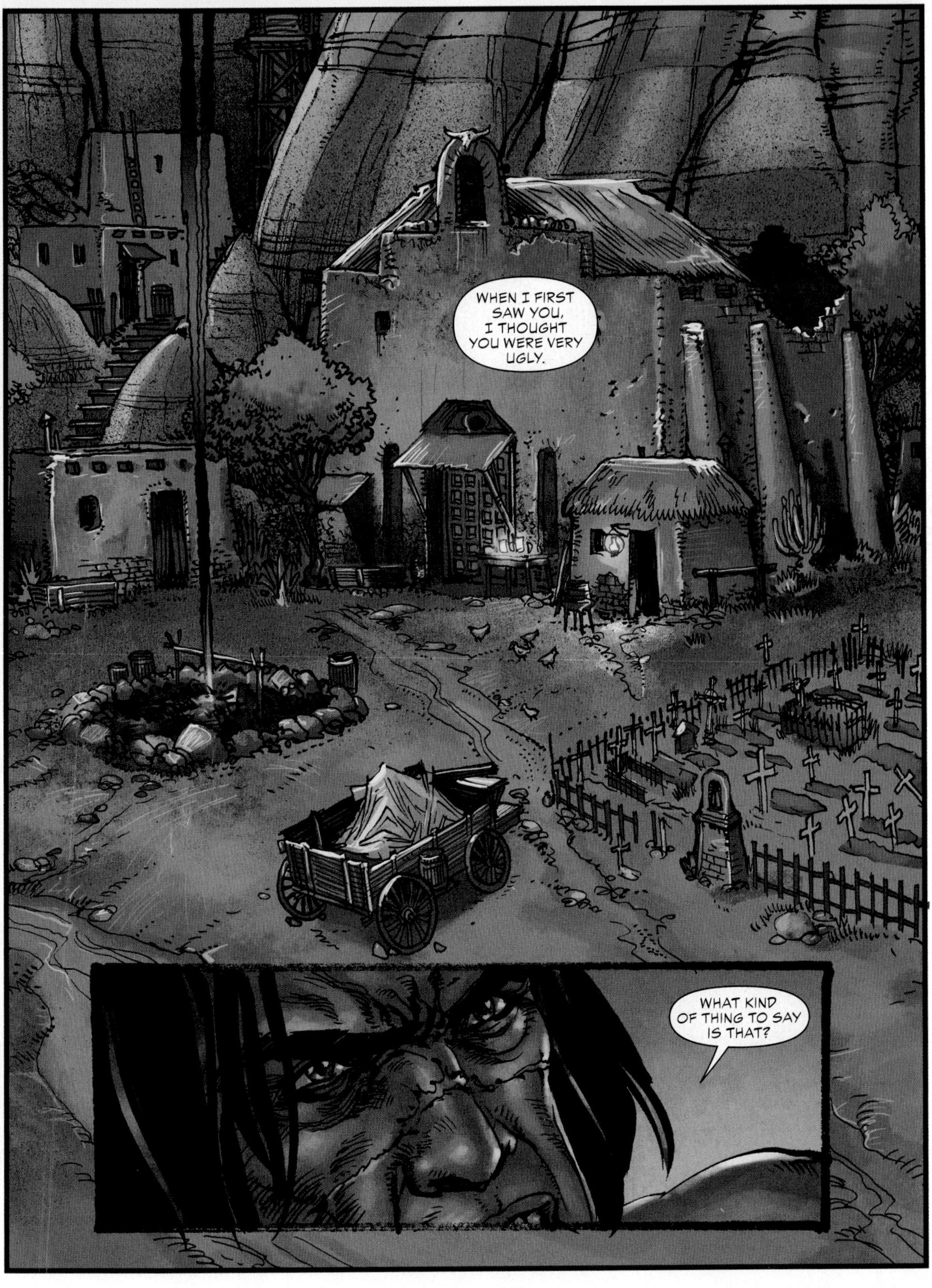
WHEN I FIRST SAW YOU, I THOUGHT YOU WERE VERY UGLY.
WHAT KIND OF THING TO SAY IS THAT?

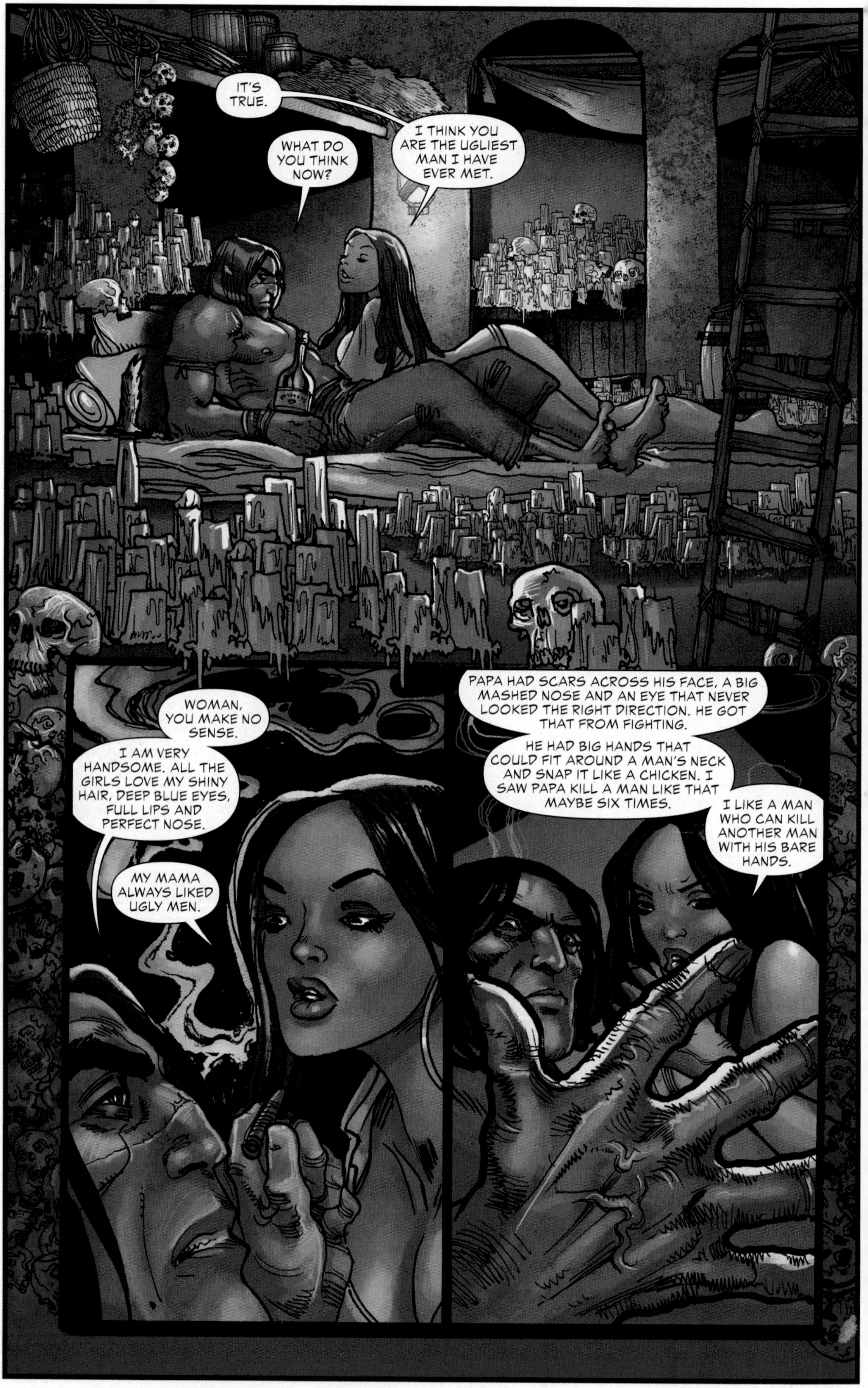
IT'S TRUE.
WHAT DO YOU THINK NOW?
I THINK YOU ARE THE UGLIEST MAN I HAVE EVER MET.
WOMAN, YOU MAKE NO SENSE.
I AM VERY HANDSOME. ALL THE GIRLS LOVE MY SHINY HAIR, DEEP BLUE EYES, FULL LIPS AND PERFECT NOSE.
MY MAMA ALWAYS LIKED UGLY MEN.
PAPA HAD SCARS ACROSS HIS FACE, A BIG MASHED NOSE AND AN EYE THAT NEVER LOOKED THE RIGHT DIRECTION. HE GOT THAT FROM FIGHTING.
HE HAD BIG HANDS THAT COULD FIT AROUND A MAN'S NECK AND SNAP IT LIKE A CHICKEN. I SAW PAPA KILL A MAN LIKE THAT MAYBE SIX TIMES.
I LIKE A MAN WHO CAN KILL ANOTHER MAN WITH HIS BARE HANDS.

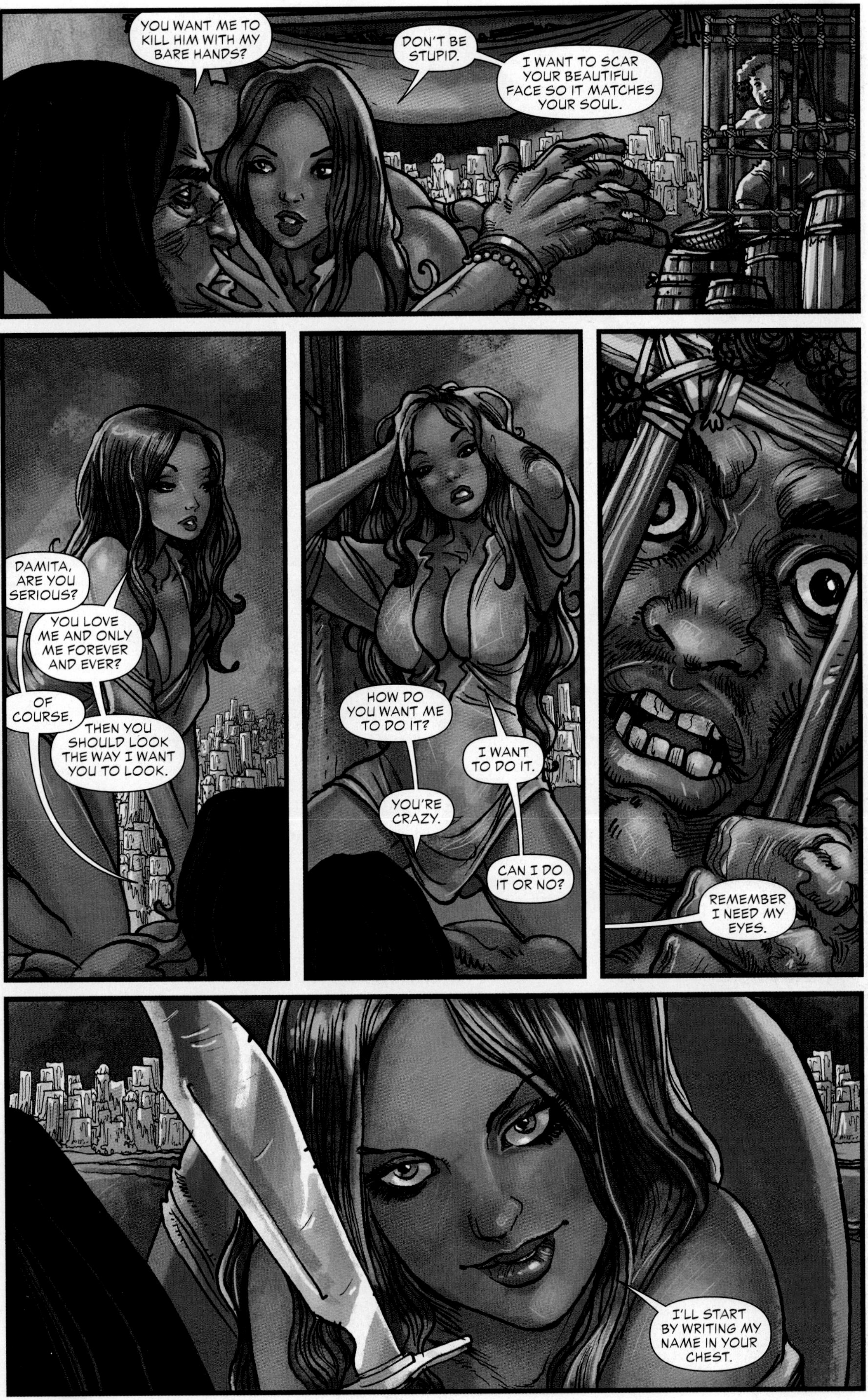
YOU WANT ME TO KILL HIM WITH MY BARE HANDS?
DON'T BE STUPID.
I WANT TO SCAR YOUR BEAUTIFUL FACE SO IT MATCHES YOUR SOUL.
DAMITA, ARE YOU SERIOUS?
YOU LOVE ME AND ONLY ME FOREVER AND EVER?
OF COURSE.
THEN YOU SHOULD LOOK THE WAY I WANT YOU TO LOOK.
HOW DO YOU WANT ME TO DO IT?
I WANT TO DO IT.
YOU'RE CRAZY.
CAN I DO IT OR NO?
REMEMBER I NEED MY EYES.
I'LL START BY WRITING MY NAME IN YOUR CHEST.

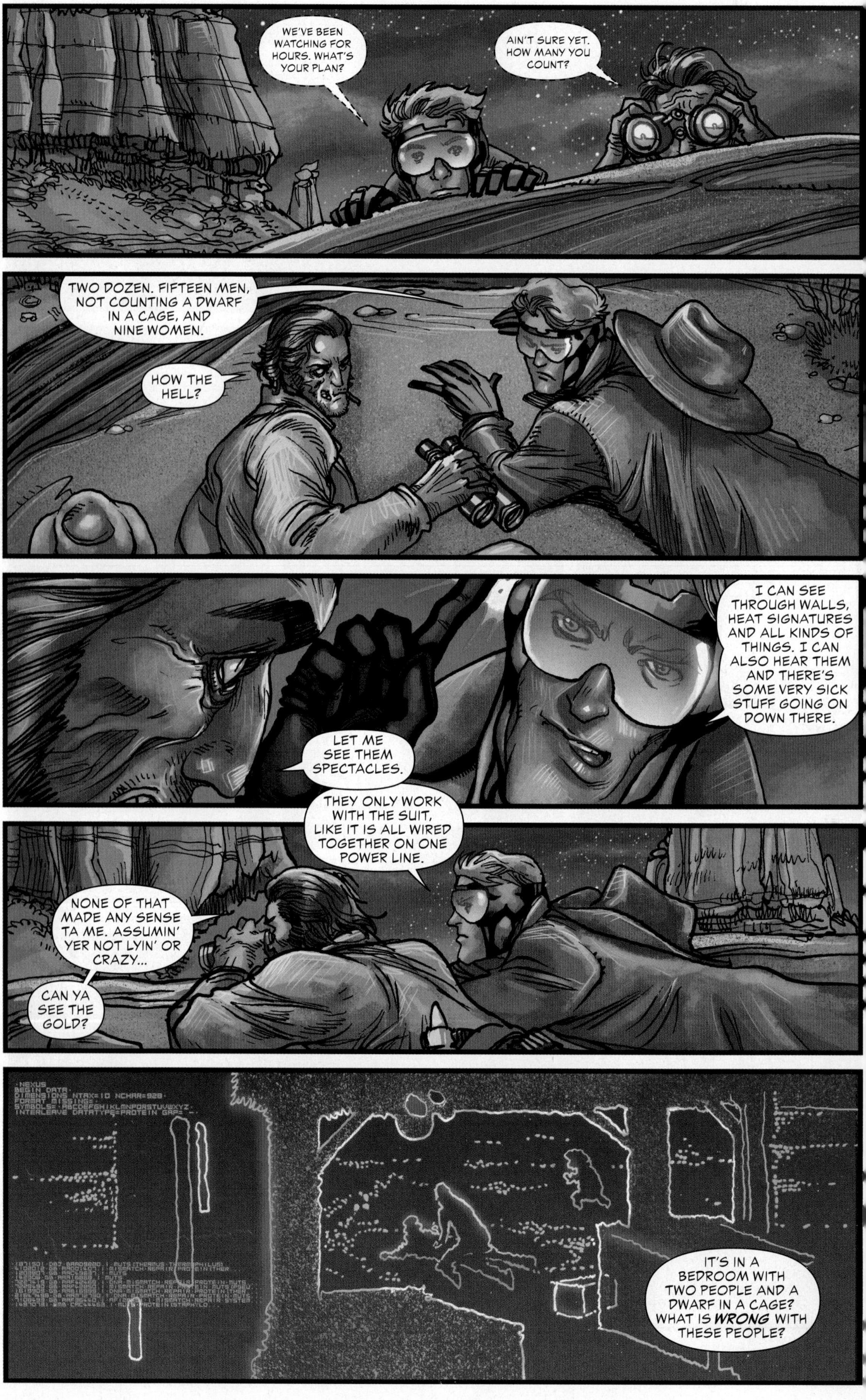
WE'VE BEEN WATCHING FOR HOURS. WHAT'S YOUR PLAN?
AIN'T SURE YET. HOW MANY YOU COUNT?
TWO DOZEN. FIFTEEN MEN, NOT COUNTING A DWARF IN A CAGE, AND NINE WOMEN.
HOW THE HELL?
I CAN SEE THROUGH WALLS, HEAT SIGNATURES AND ALL KINDS OF THINGS. I CAN ALSO HEAR THEM AND THERE'S SOME VERY SICK STUFF GOING ON DOWN THERE.
LET ME SEE THEM SPECTACLES.
THEY ONLY WORK WITH THE SUIT, LIKE IT IS ALL WIRED TOGETHER ON ONE POWER LINE.
NONE OF THAT MADE ANY SENSE TA ME. ASSUMIN' YER NOT LYIN' OR CRAZY...
CAN YA SEE THE GOLD?
IT'S IN A BEDROOM WITH TWO PEOPLE AND A DWARF IN A CAGE? WHAT IS *WRONG* WITH THESE PEOPLE?

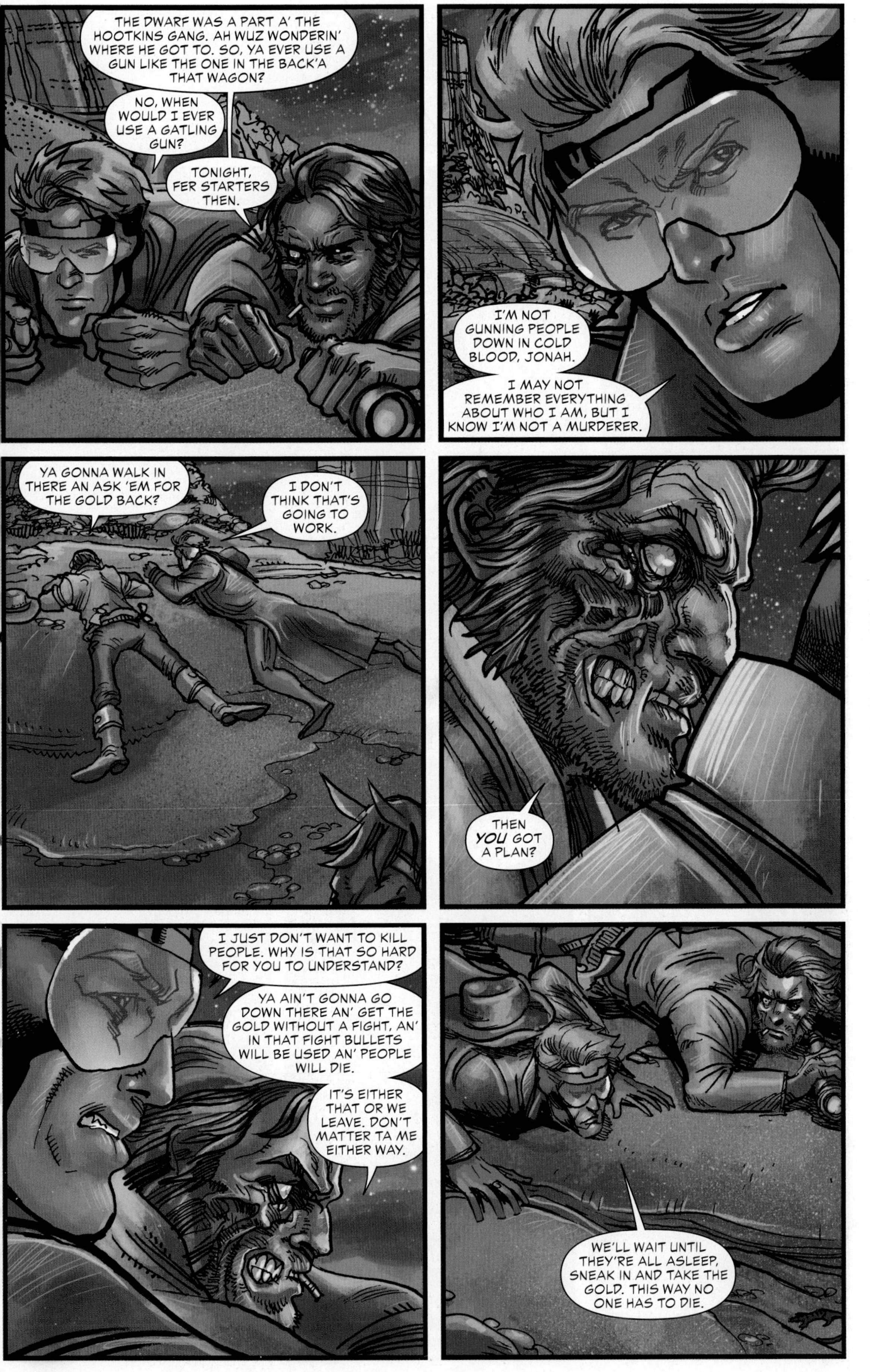
THE DWARF WAS A PART A' THE HOOTKINS GANG. AH WUZ WONDERIN' WHERE HE GOT TO. SO, YA EVER USE A GUN LIKE THE ONE IN THE BACK'A THAT WAGON?
NO, WHEN WOULD I EVER USE A GATLING GUN?
TONIGHT, FER STARTERS THEN.
I'M NOT GUNNING PEOPLE DOWN IN COLD BLOOD, JONAH.
I MAY NOT REMEMBER EVERYTHING ABOUT WHO I AM, BUT I KNOW I'M NOT A MURDERER.
YA GONNA WALK IN THERE AN ASK 'EM FOR THE GOLD BACK?
I DON'T THINK THAT'S GOING TO WORK.
THEN *YOU* GOT A PLAN?
I JUST DON'T WANT TO KILL PEOPLE. WHY IS THAT SO HARD FOR YOU TO UNDERSTAND?
YA AIN'T GONNA GO DOWN THERE AN' GET THE GOLD WITHOUT A FIGHT, AN' IN THAT FIGHT BULLETS WILL BE USED AN' PEOPLE WILL DIE.
IT'S EITHER THAT OR WE LEAVE. DON'T MATTER TA ME EITHER WAY.
WE'LL WAIT UNTIL THEY'RE ALL ASLEEP, SNEAK IN AND TAKE THE GOLD. THIS WAY NO ONE HAS TO DIE.

You're not gonna believe what happened

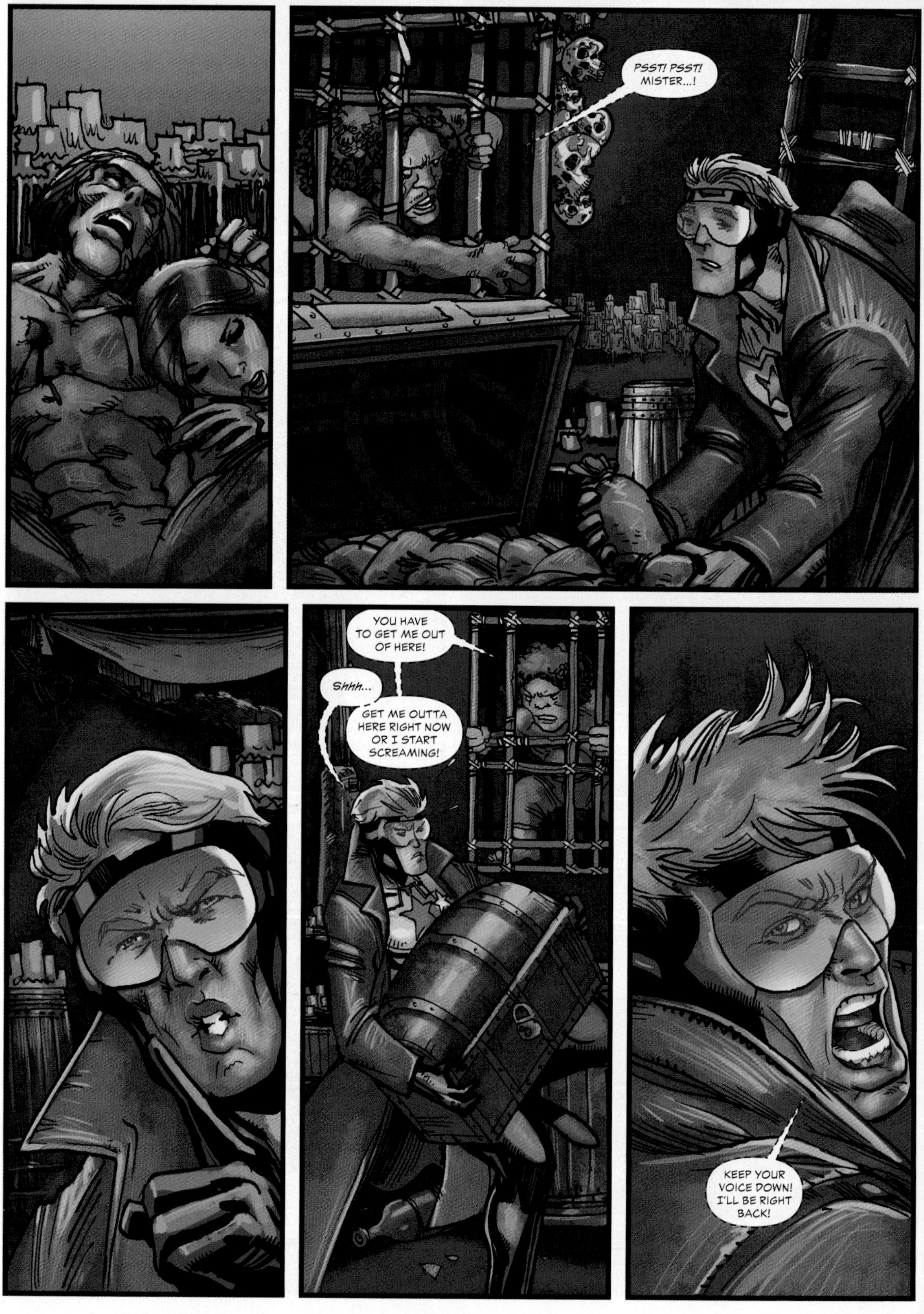
PSST! PSST! MISTER...!
YOU HAVE TO GET ME OUT OF HERE!
Shhh...
GET ME OUTTA HERE RIGHT NOW OR I START SCREAMING!
KEEP YOUR VOICE DOWN! I'LL BE RIGHT BACK!

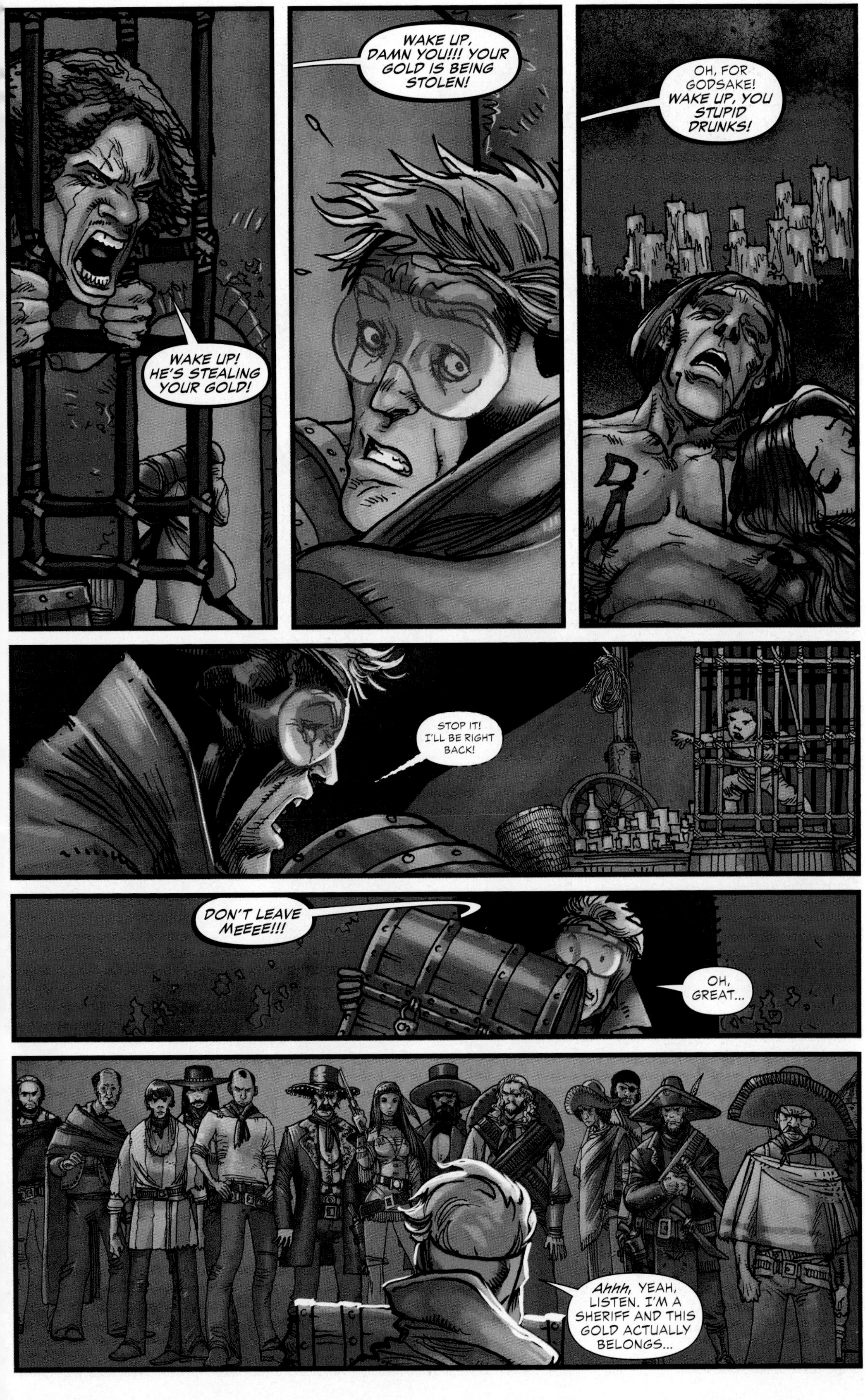
WAKE UP! HE'S STEALING YOUR GOLD!
WAKE UP, DAMN YOU!!! YOUR GOLD IS BEING STOLEN!
OH, FOR GODSAKE! WAKE UP, YOU STUPID DRUNKS!
STOP IT! I'LL BE RIGHT BACK!
DON'T LEAVE MEEEE!!!
OH, GREAT...
Ahhh, YEAH, LISTEN. I'M A SHERIFF AND THIS GOLD ACTUALLY BELONGS...

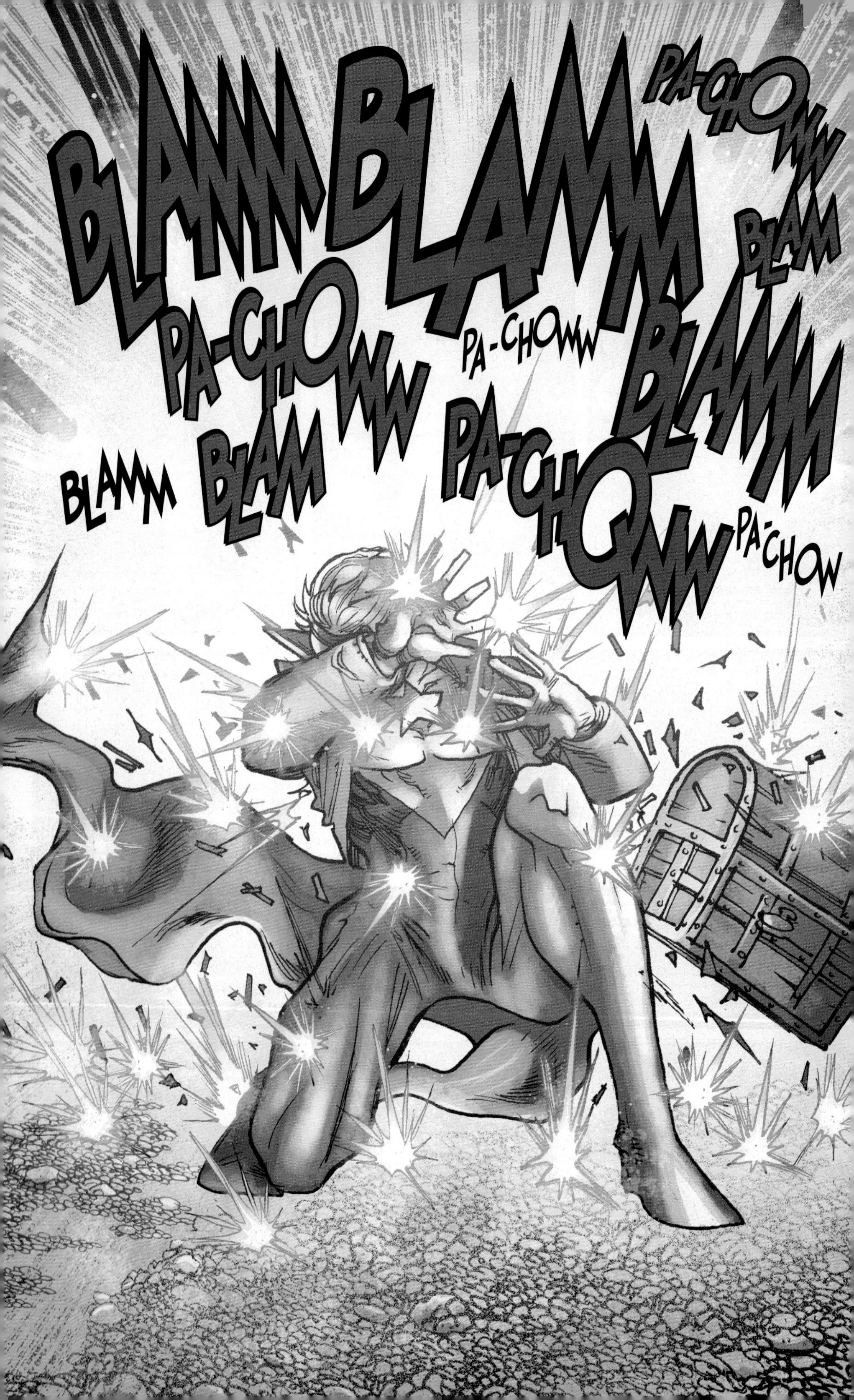
BLAMM BLAMM
PA-CHOWW
BLAM
PA-CHOWW
PA-CHOWW
BLAMM
BLAMM
BLAM
PA-CHOWW
PA-CHOW

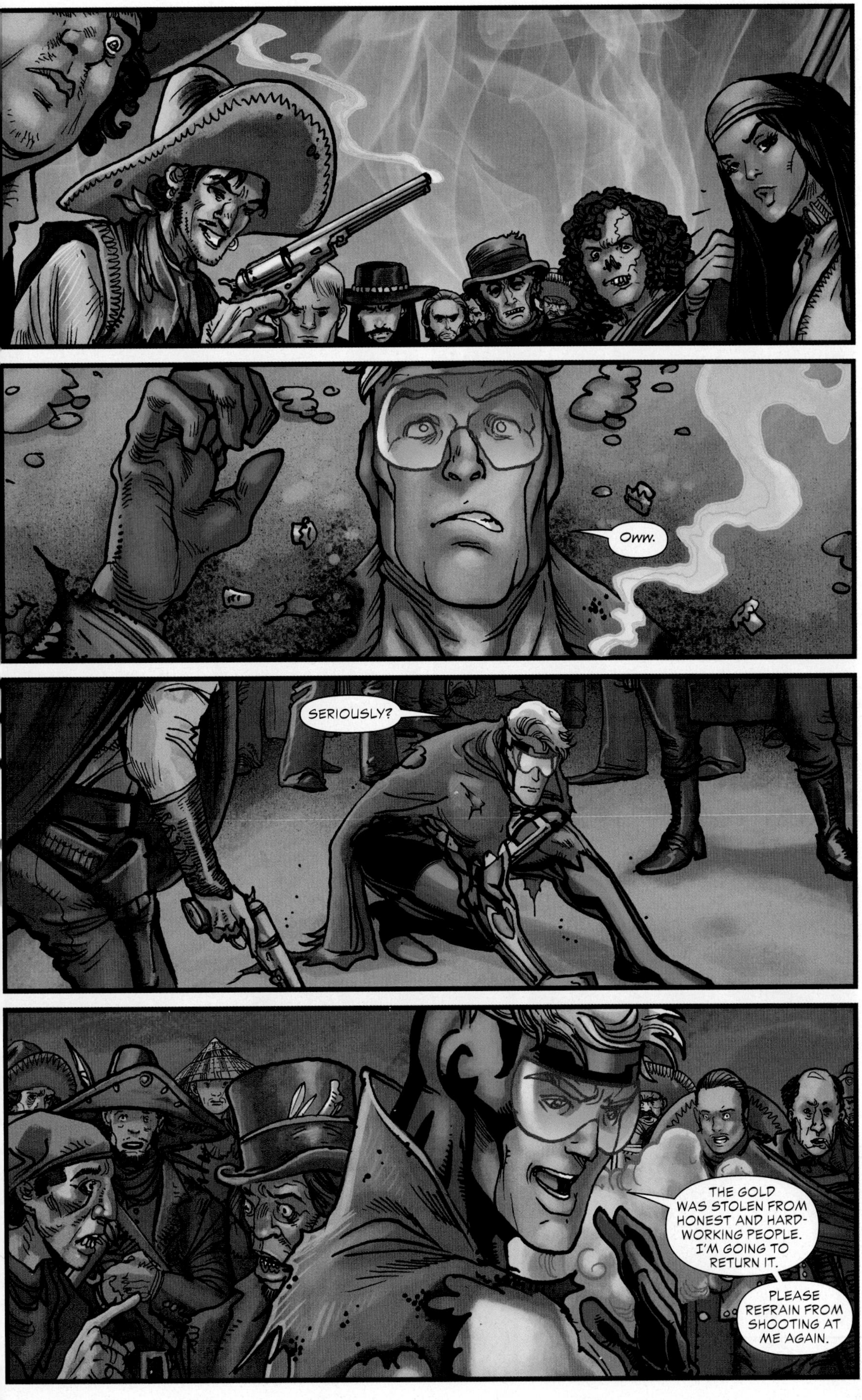
OWW.
SERIOUSLY?
THE GOLD WAS STOLEN FROM HONEST AND HARD-WORKING PEOPLE. I'M GOING TO RETURN IT.
PLEASE REFRAIN FROM SHOOTING AT ME AGAIN.

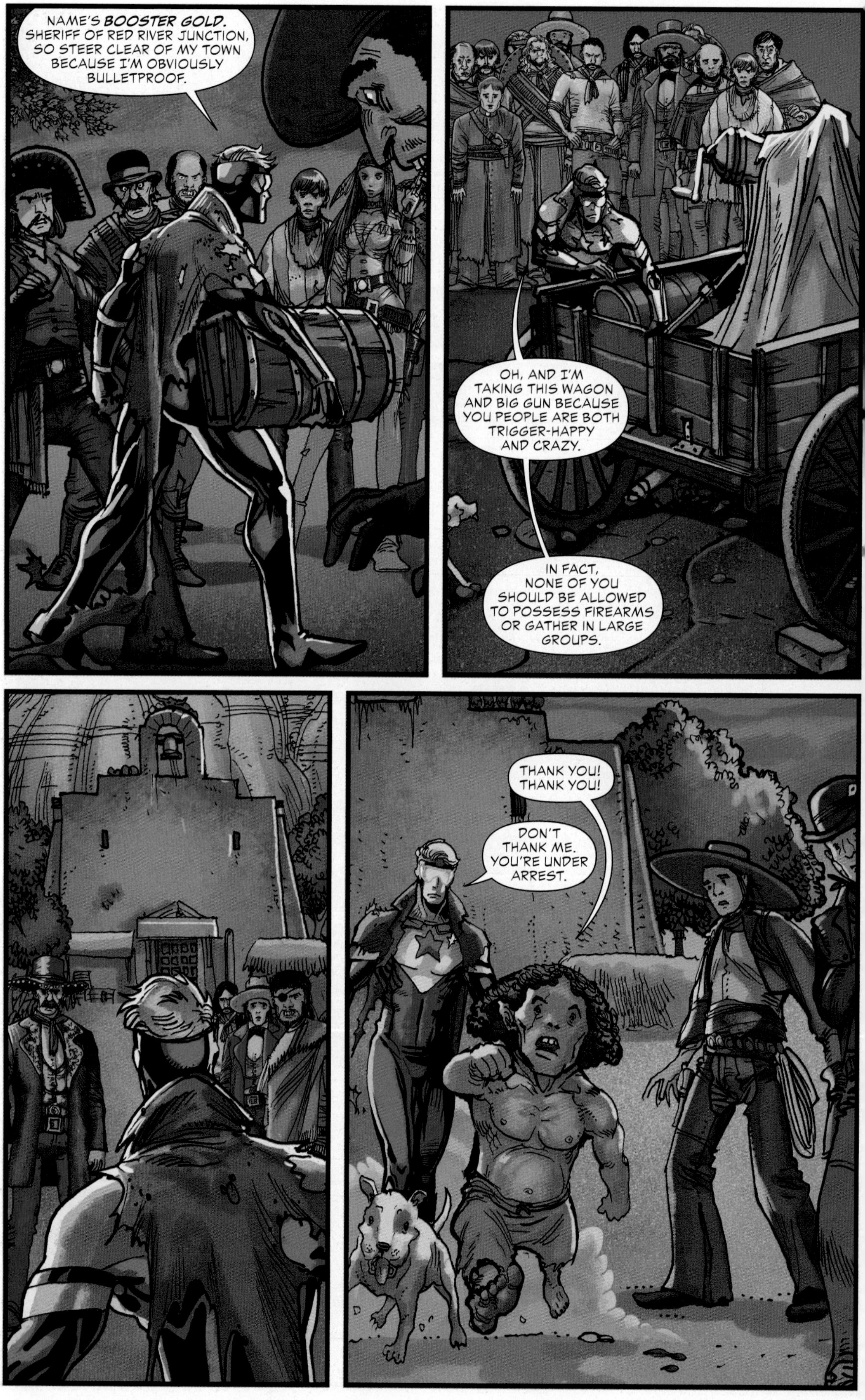
NAME'S **BOOSTER GOLD.** SHERIFF OF RED RIVER JUNCTION, SO STEER CLEAR OF MY TOWN BECAUSE I'M OBVIOUSLY BULLETPROOF.
OH, AND I'M TAKING THIS WAGON AND BIG GUN BECAUSE YOU PEOPLE ARE BOTH TRIGGER-HAPPY AND CRAZY.
IN FACT, NONE OF YOU SHOULD BE ALLOWED TO POSSESS FIREARMS OR GATHER IN LARGE GROUPS.
THANK YOU! THANK YOU!
DON'T THANK ME. YOU'RE UNDER ARREST.

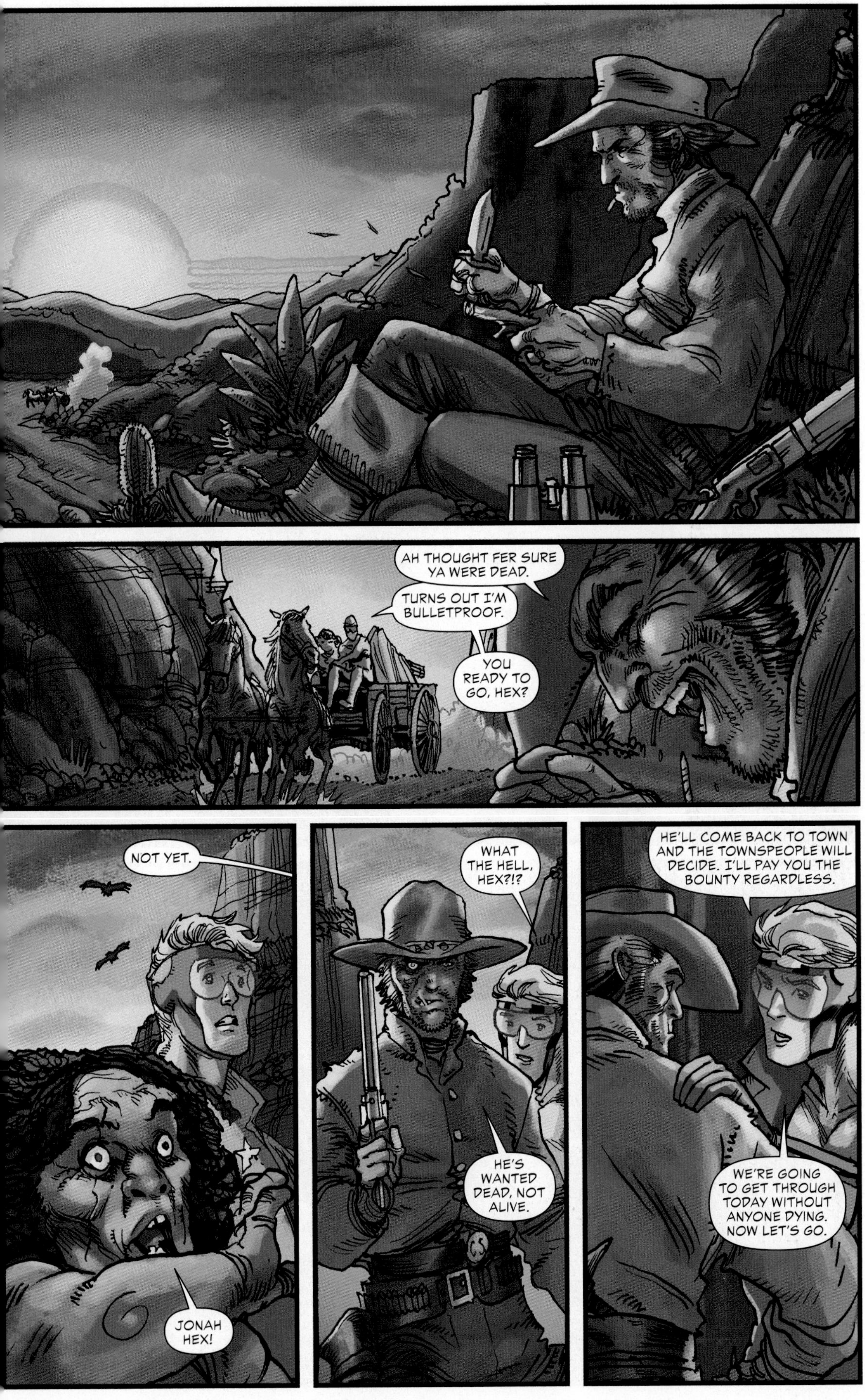
AH THOUGHT FER SURE YA WERE DEAD.
TURNS OUT I'M BULLETPROOF.
YOU READY TO GO, HEX?
NOT YET.
JONAH HEX!
WHAT THE HELL, HEX?!?
HE'S WANTED DEAD, NOT ALIVE.
HE'LL COME BACK TO TOWN AND THE TOWNSPEOPLE WILL DECIDE. I'LL PAY YOU THE BOUNTY REGARDLESS.
WE'RE GOING TO GET THROUGH TODAY WITHOUT ANYONE DYING. NOW LET'S GO.

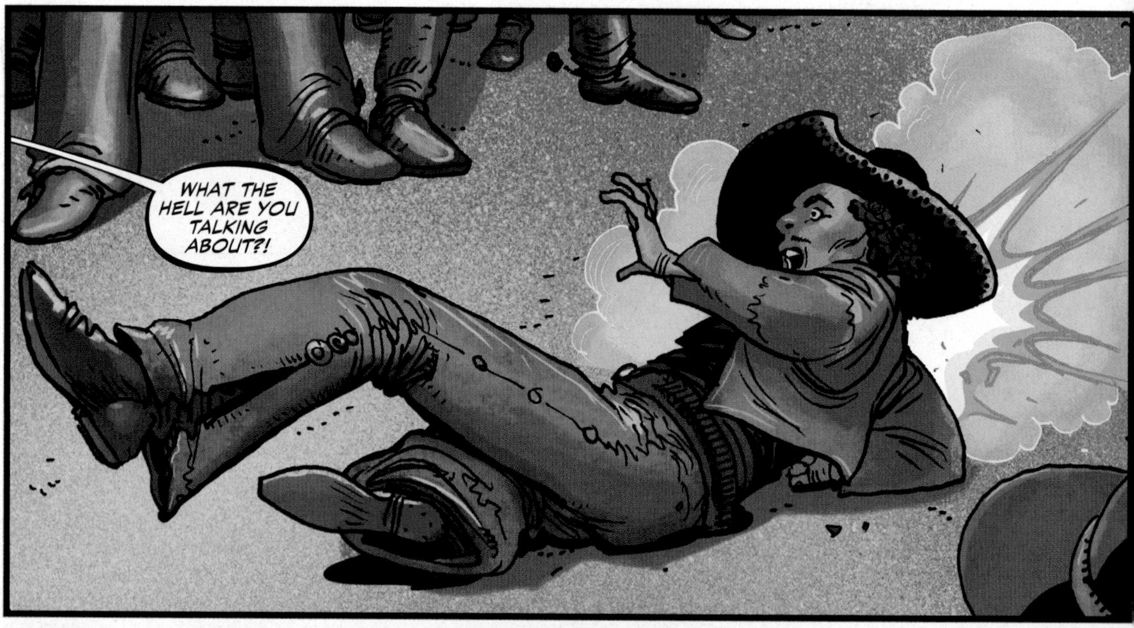
WHAT THE HELL ARE YOU TALKING ABOUT?!

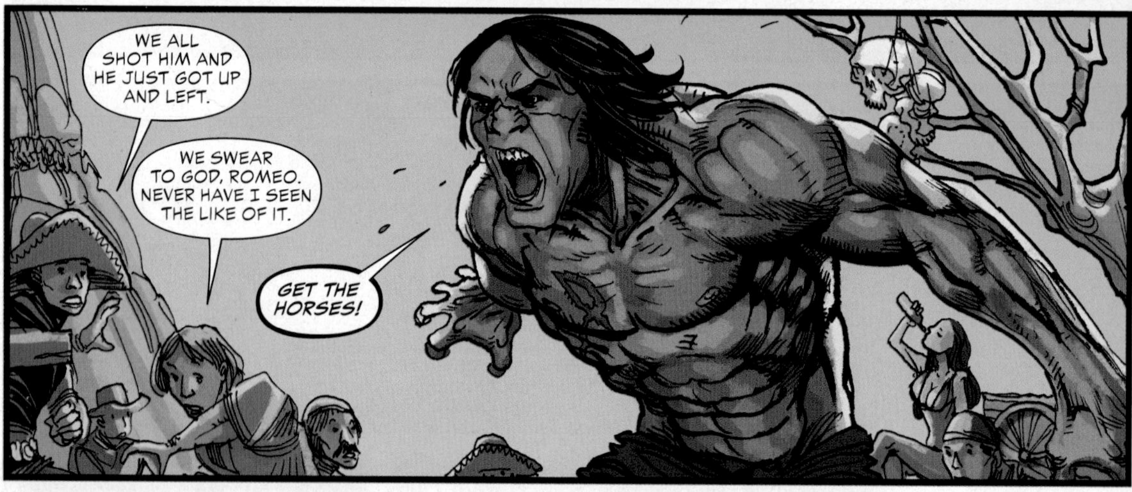
WE ALL SHOT HIM AND HE JUST GOT UP AND LEFT.
WE SWEAR TO GOD, ROMEO. NEVER HAVE I SEEN THE LIKE OF IT.
GET THE HORSES!

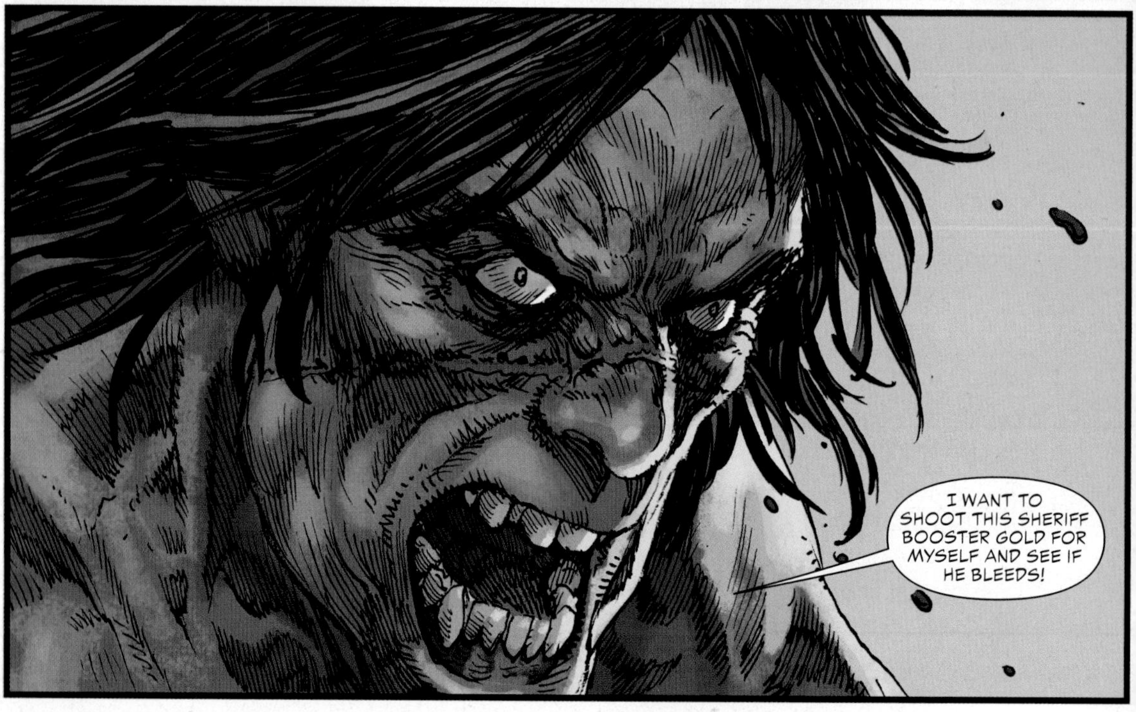
I WANT TO SHOOT THIS SHERIFF BOOSTER GOLD FOR MYSELF AND SEE IF HE BLEEDS!

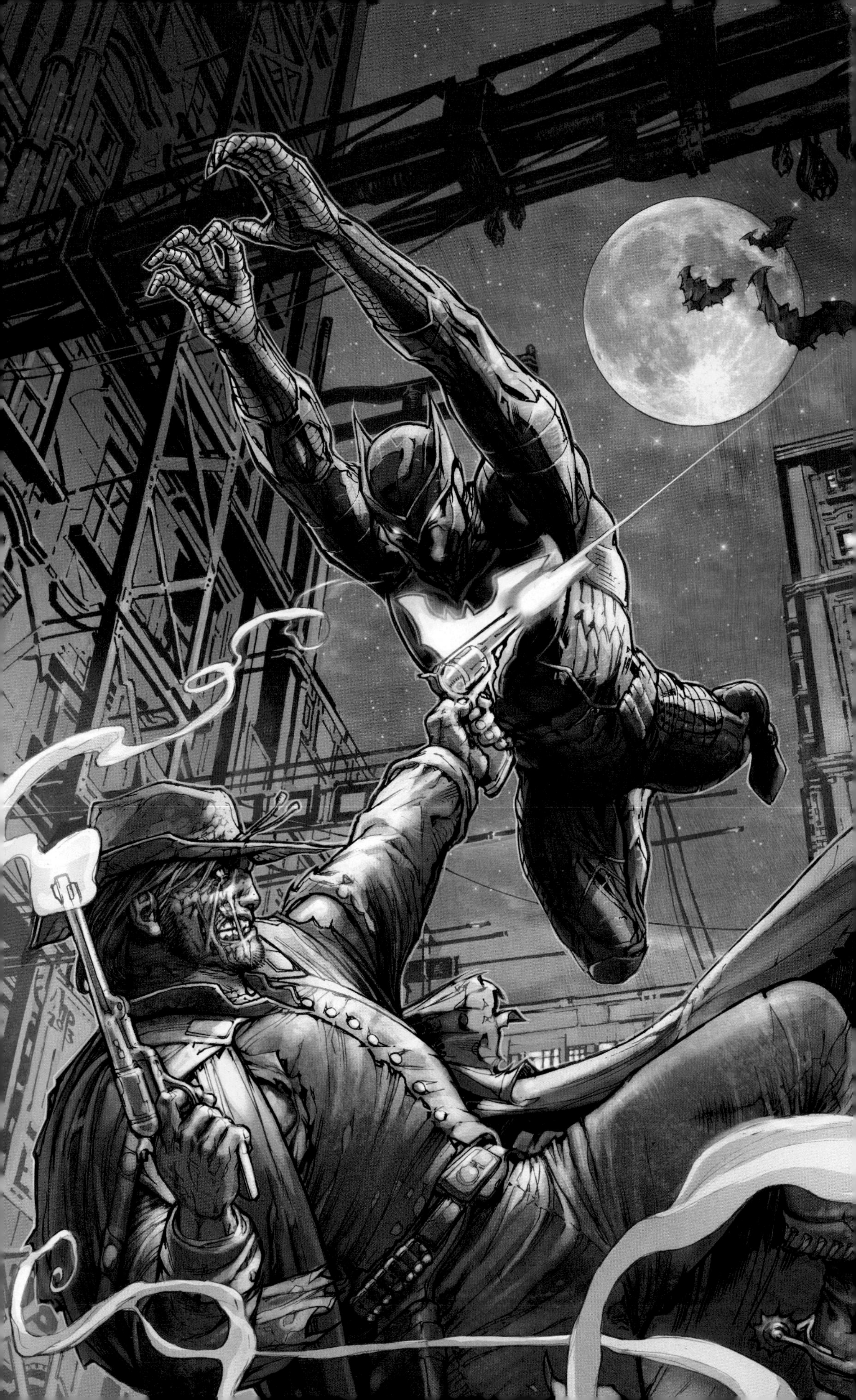

WHERE DO WE GO FROM HERE?

JUSTIN GRAY and
JIMMY PALMIOTTI writers
MORITAT artist

MIKE ATIYEH colorist **ROB LEIGH** letterer
HOWARD PORTER cover

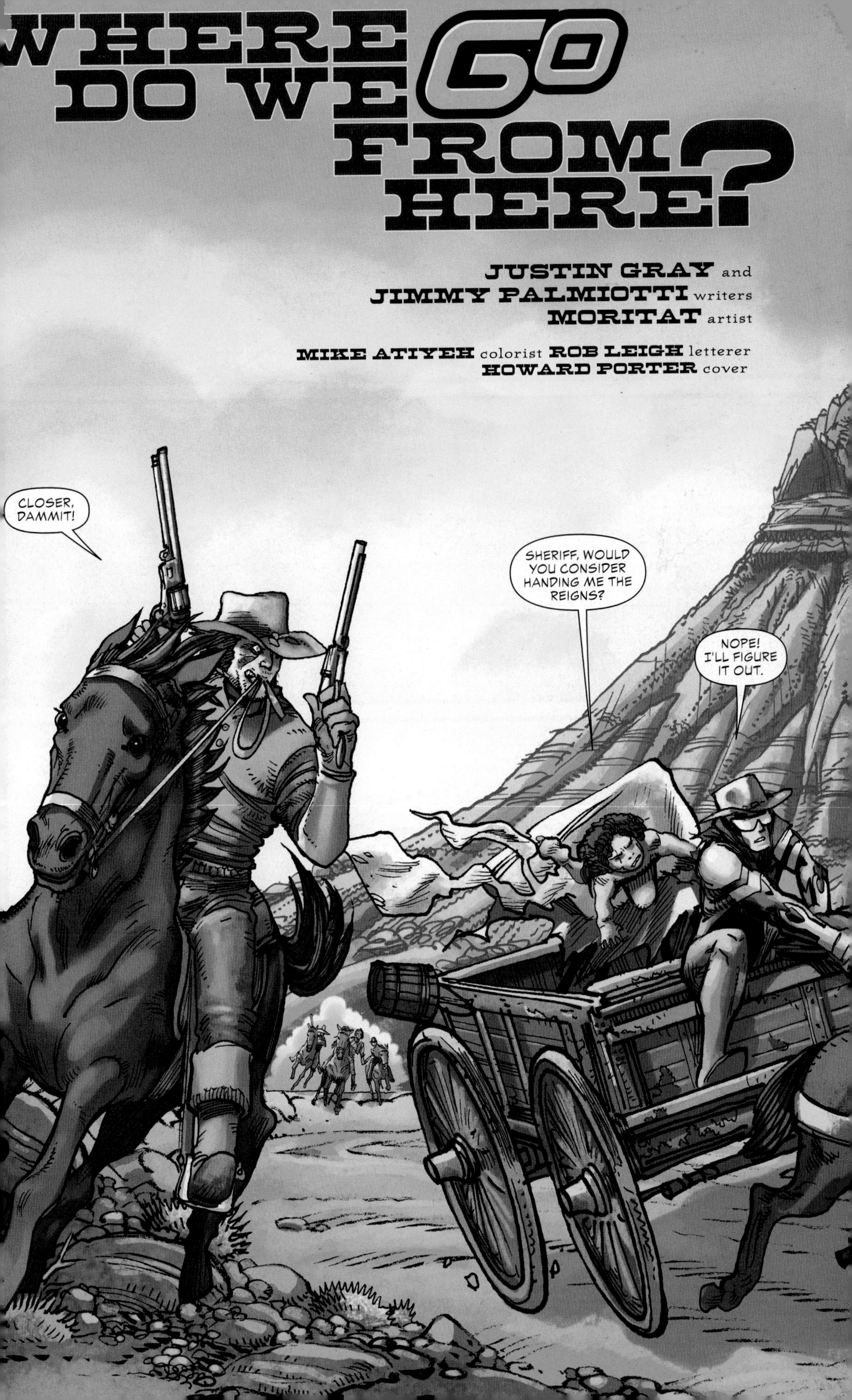
CLOSER, DAMMIT!
SHERIFF, WOULD YOU CONSIDER HANDING ME THE REIGNS?
NOPE! I'LL FIGURE IT OUT.

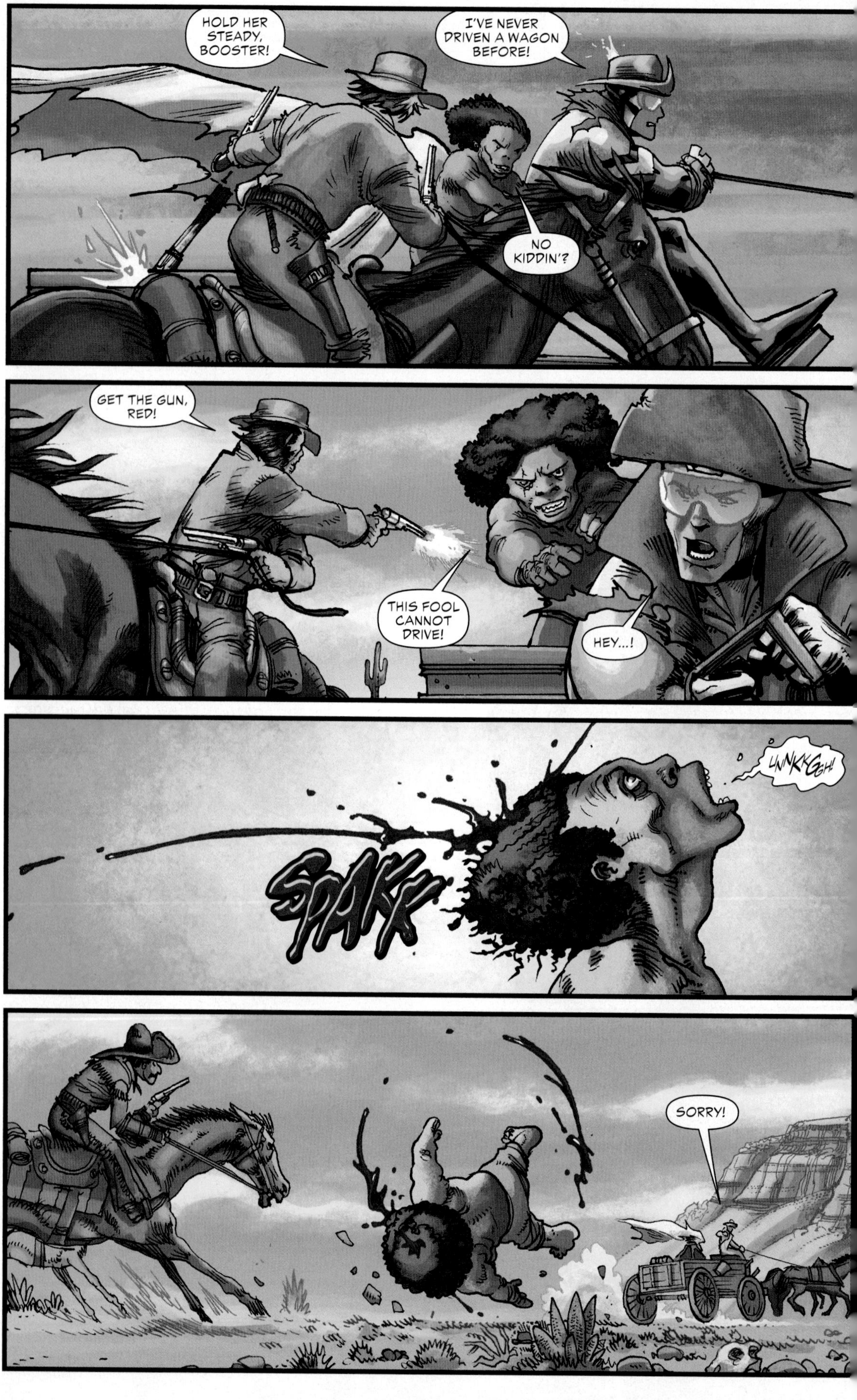
HOLD HER STEADY, BOOSTER!
I'VE NEVER DRIVEN A WAGON BEFORE!
NO KIDDIN'?
GET THE GUN, RED!
THIS FOOL CANNOT DRIVE!
HEY...!
UNNKKGGH!
SPAKK
SORRY!

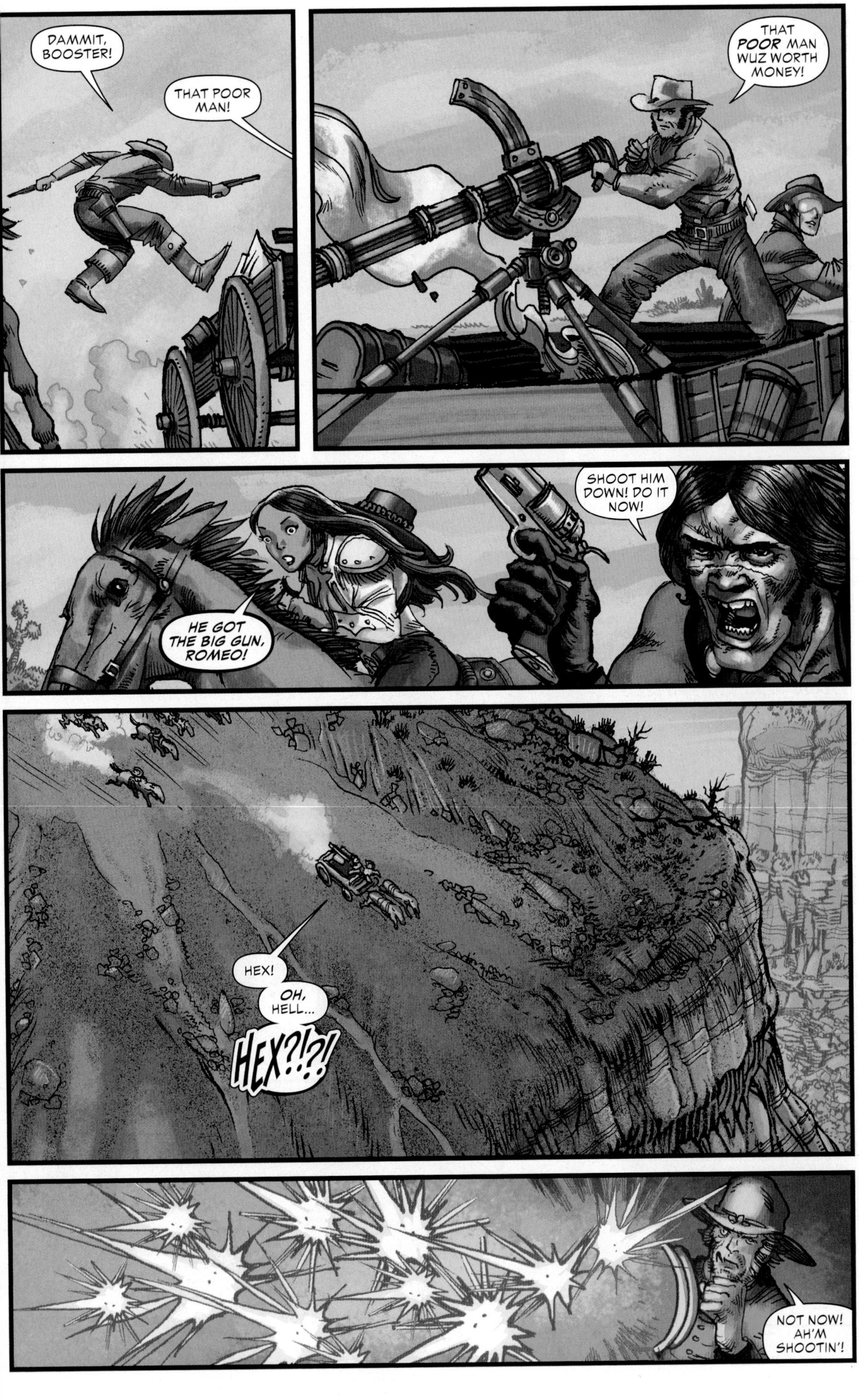
DAMMIT, BOOSTER!
THAT POOR MAN!
THAT POOR MAN WUZ WORTH MONEY!
SHOOT HIM DOWN! DO IT NOW!
HE GOT THE BIG GUN, ROMEO!
HEX!
OH, HELL...
HEX?!?!
NOT NOW! AH'M SHOOTIN'!

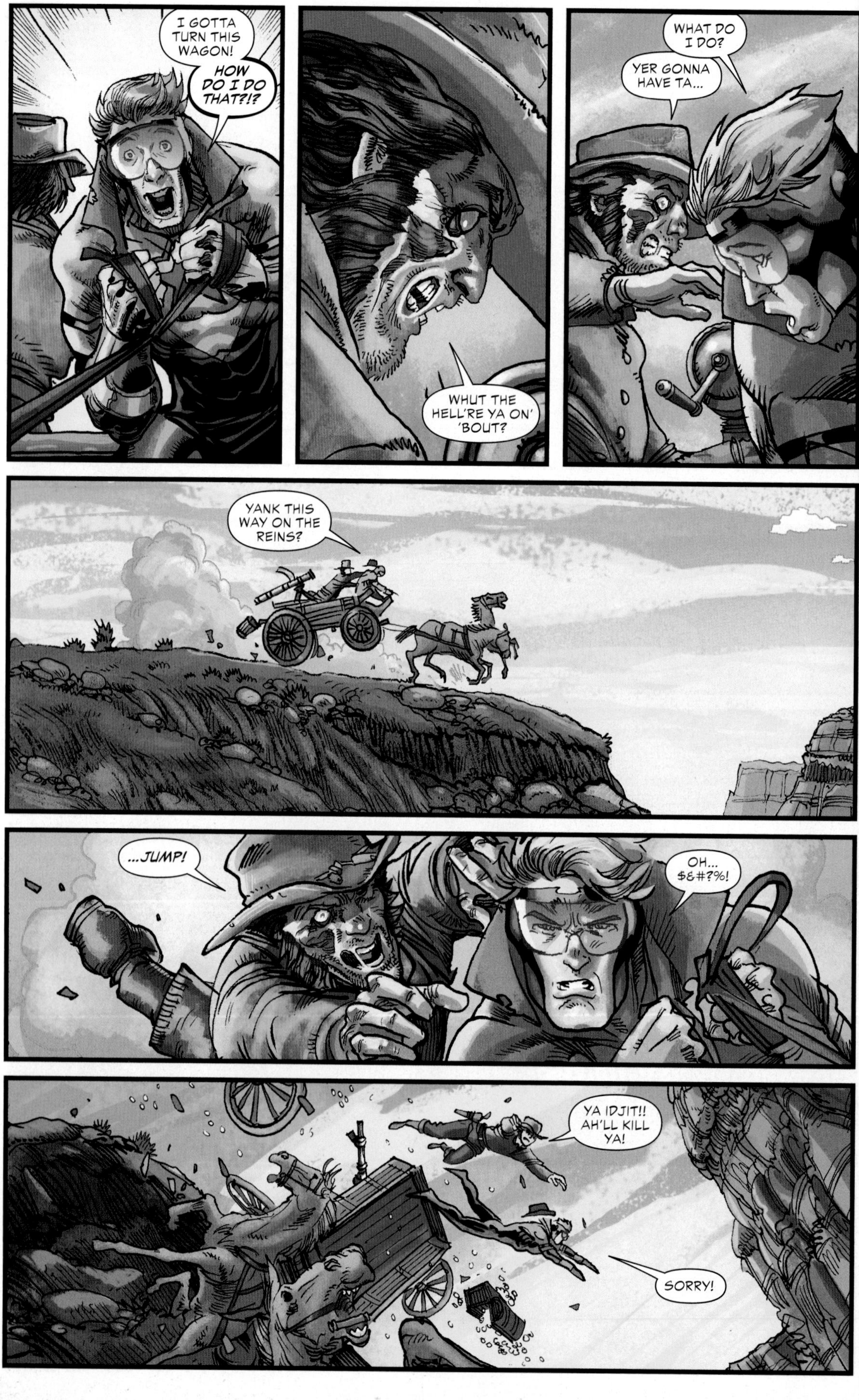
I GOTTA TURN THIS WAGON!
HOW DO I DO THAT?!?
WHUT THE HELL'RE YA ON' 'BOUT?
WHAT DO I DO?
YER GONNA HAVE TA...
YANK THIS WAY ON THE REINS?
...JUMP!
OH... $&#?%!
YA IDJIT!! AH'LL KILL YA!
SORRY!

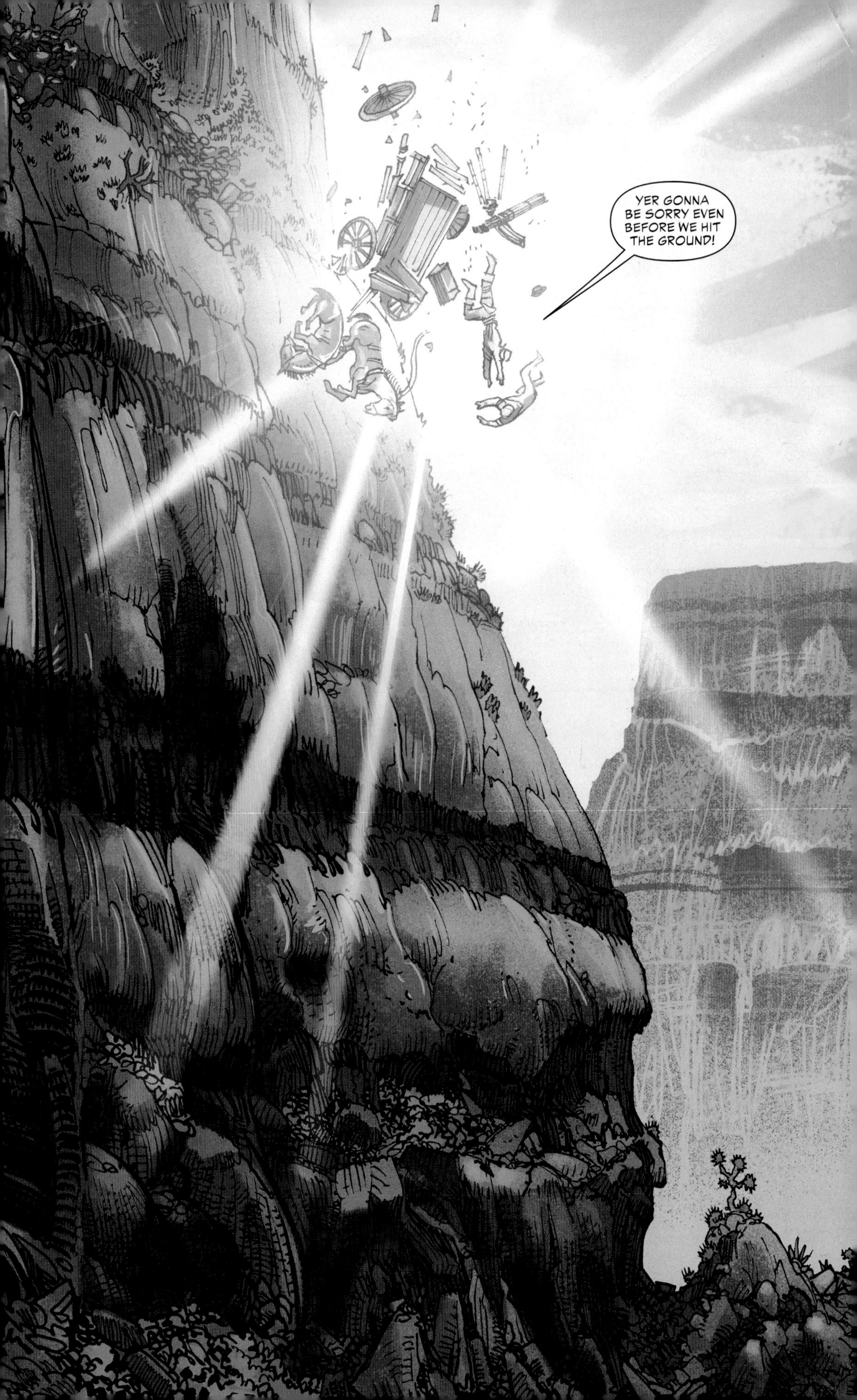
YER GONNA BE SORRY EVEN BEFORE WE HIT THE GROUND!

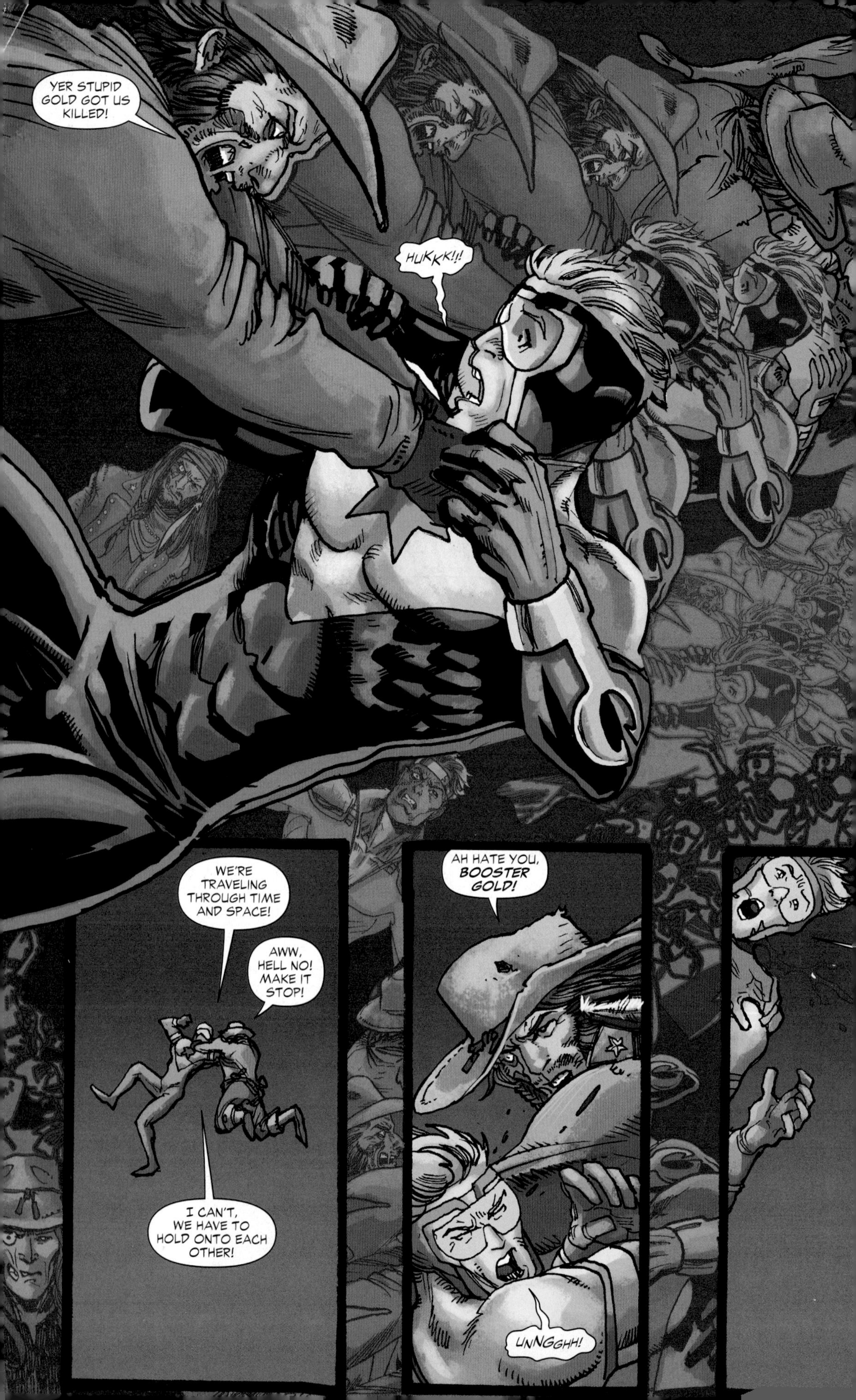
YER STUPID GOLD GOT US KILLED!
HUKKK!!!
WE'RE TRAVELING THROUGH TIME AND SPACE!
AWW, HELL NO! MAKE IT STOP!
I CAN'T, WE HAVE TO HOLD ONTO EACH OTHER!
AH HATE YOU, BOOSTER GOLD!
UNNGGHH!

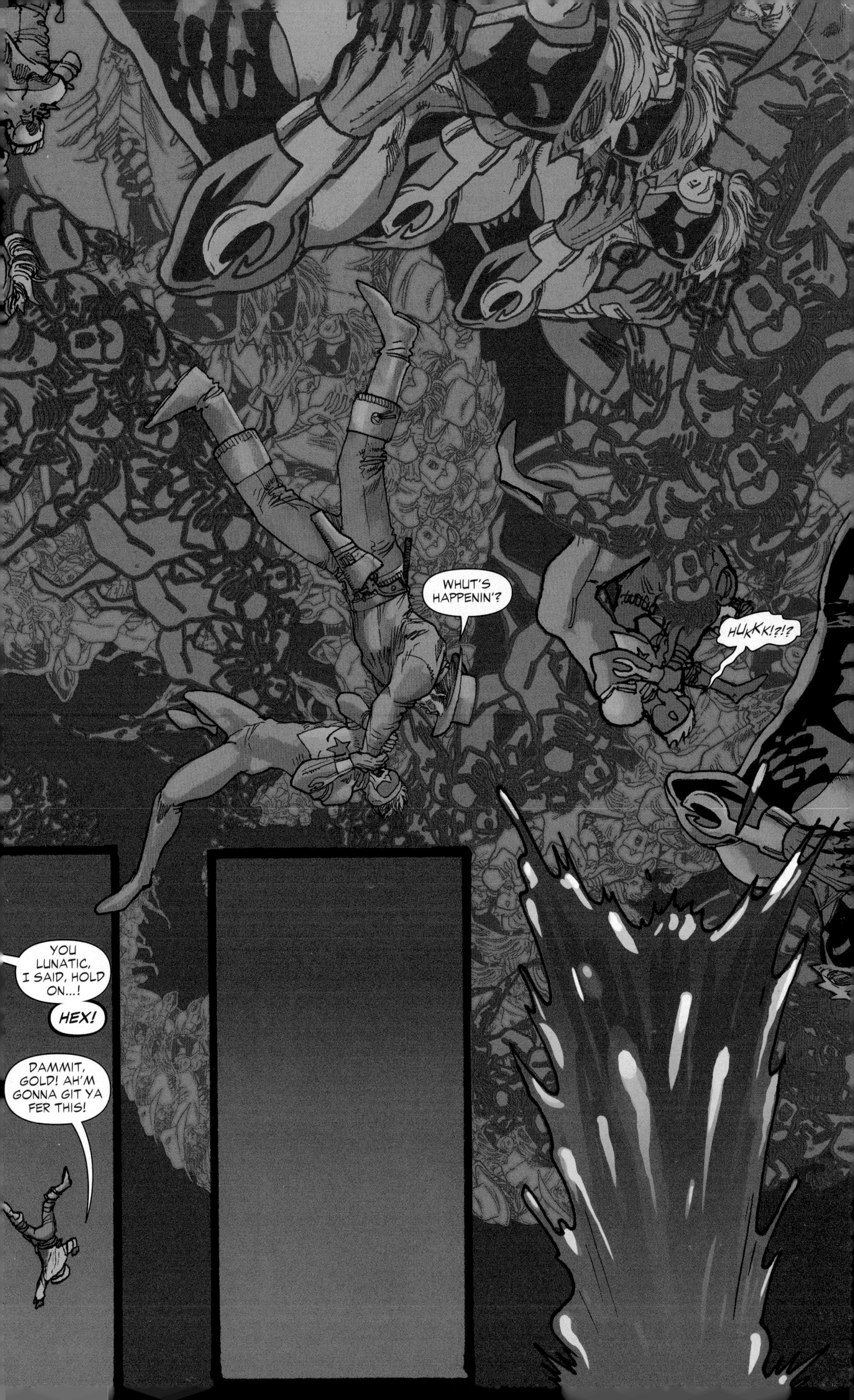
WHUT'S HAPPENIN'?
HUKKK!?!?
YOU LUNATIC, I SAID, HOLD ON...!
HEX!
DAMMIT, GOLD! AH'M GONNA GIT YA FER THIS!

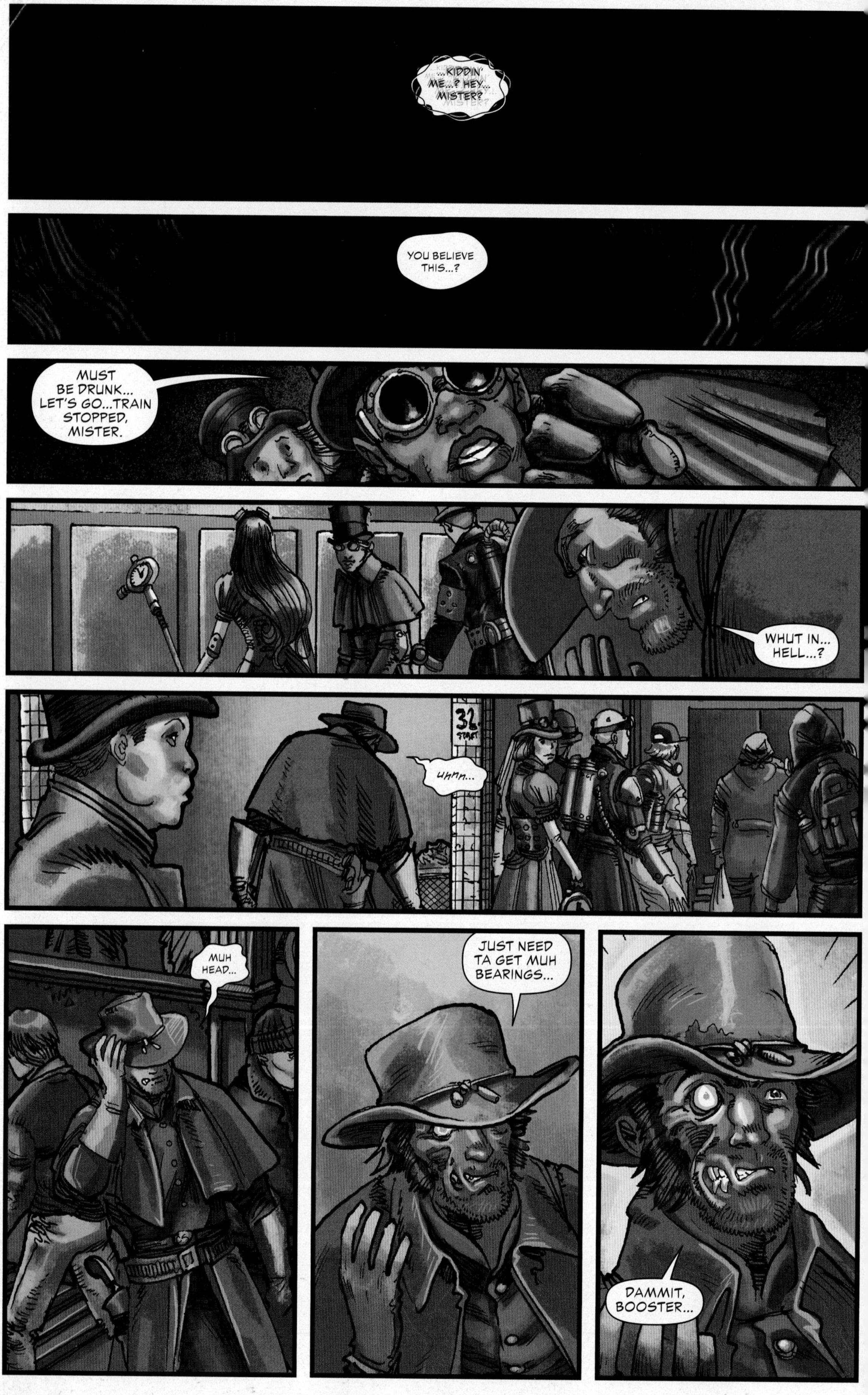
...KIDDIN' ME...? HEY... MISTER?
YOU BELIEVE THIS...?
MUST BE DRUNK... LET'S GO...TRAIN STOPPED, MISTER.
WHUT IN... HELL...?
32 STREET
uhnn...
MUH HEAD...
JUST NEED TA GET MUH BEARINGS...
DAMMIT, BOOSTER...

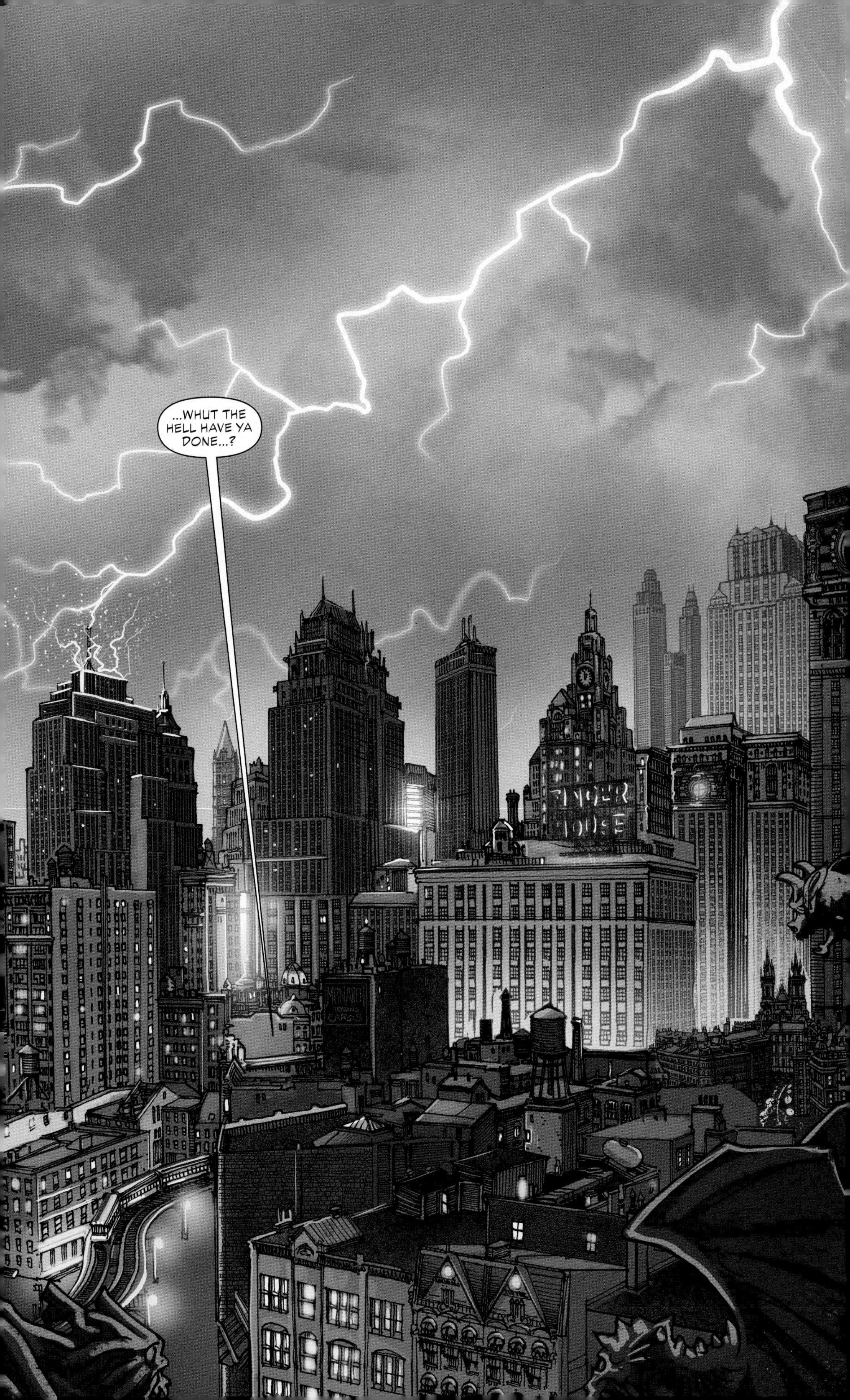
...WHUT THE HELL HAVE YA DONE...?

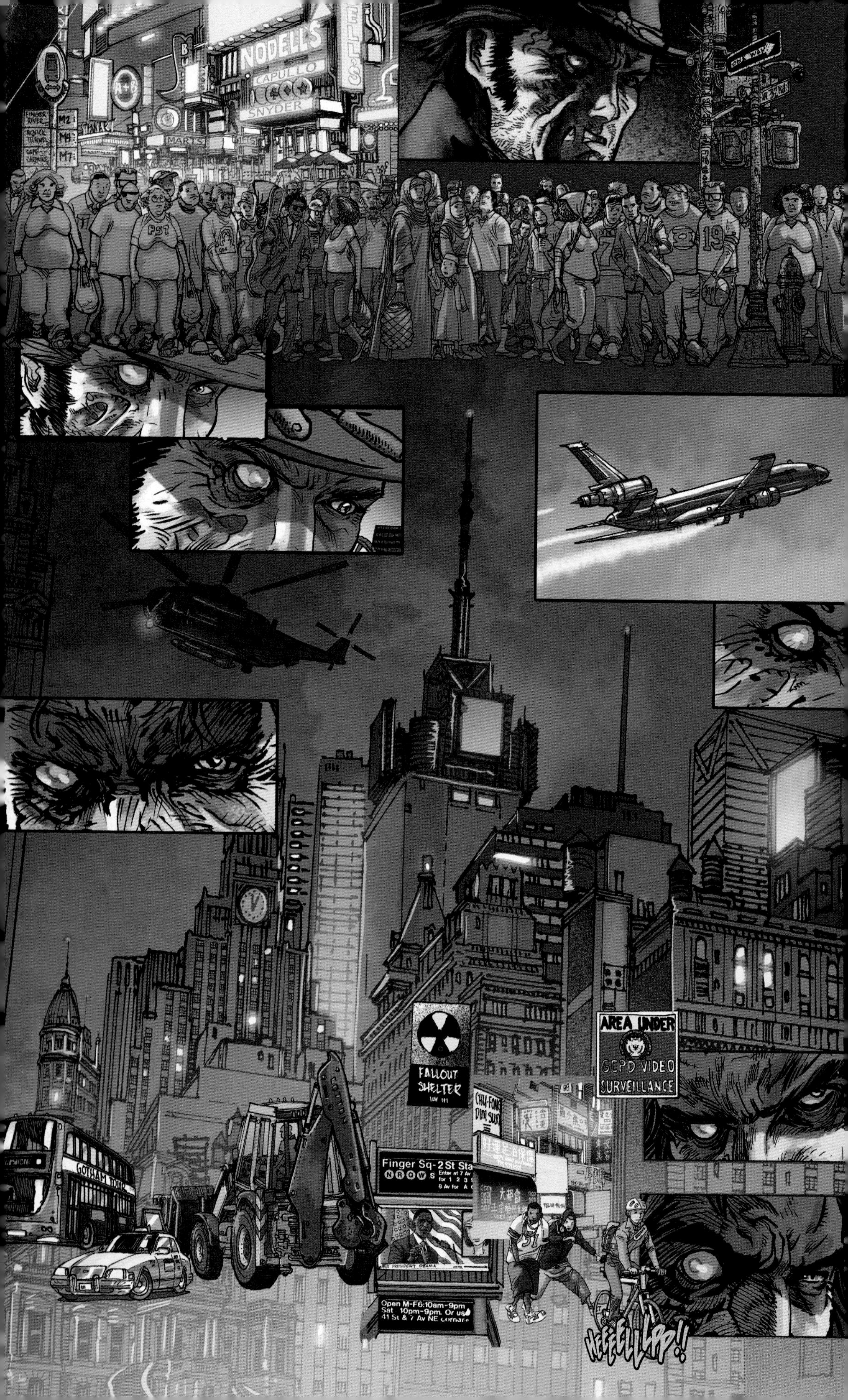
NODELL'S
CAPULLO
SNYDER
MARTS
ONE WAY
FALLOUT SHELTER
AREA UNDER GCPD VIDEO SURVEILLANCE
CHU-FONG DIM SUM
GOTHAM TOUR
Finger Sq-2St Sta
N R Q W S
PRESIDENT OBAMA
Open M-F6:10am-9pm
Sat 10pm-9pm. Or us
41 St & 7 Av NE corner
HEEELLLP!!

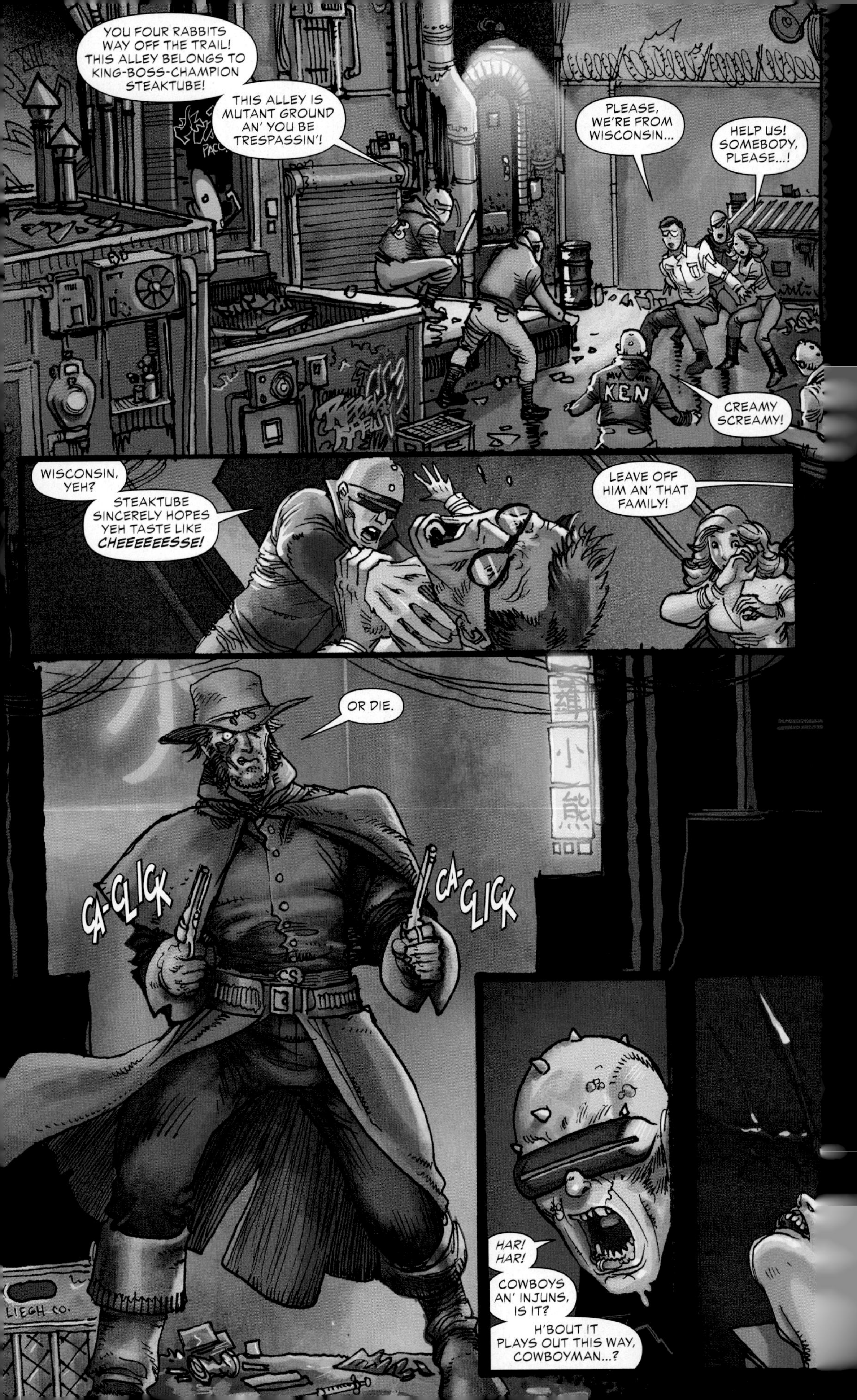
YOU FOUR RABBITS WAY OFF THE TRAIL! THIS ALLEY BELONGS TO KING-BOSS-CHAMPION STEAKTUBE!
THIS ALLEY IS MUTANT GROUND AN' YOU BE TRESPASSIN'!
PLEASE, WE'RE FROM WISCONSIN...
HELP US! SOMEBODY, PLEASE...!
KEN
CREAMY SCREAMY!
WISCONSIN, YEH?
STEAKTUBE SINCERELY HOPES YEH TASTE LIKE *CHEEEEEESSE!*
LEAVE OFF HIM AN' THAT FAMILY!
OR DIE.
CA-CLICK
CA-CLICK
HAR! HAR!
COWBOYS AN' INJUNS, IS IT?
H'BOUT IT PLAYS OUT THIS WAY, COWBOYMAN...?
LIEGH CO.

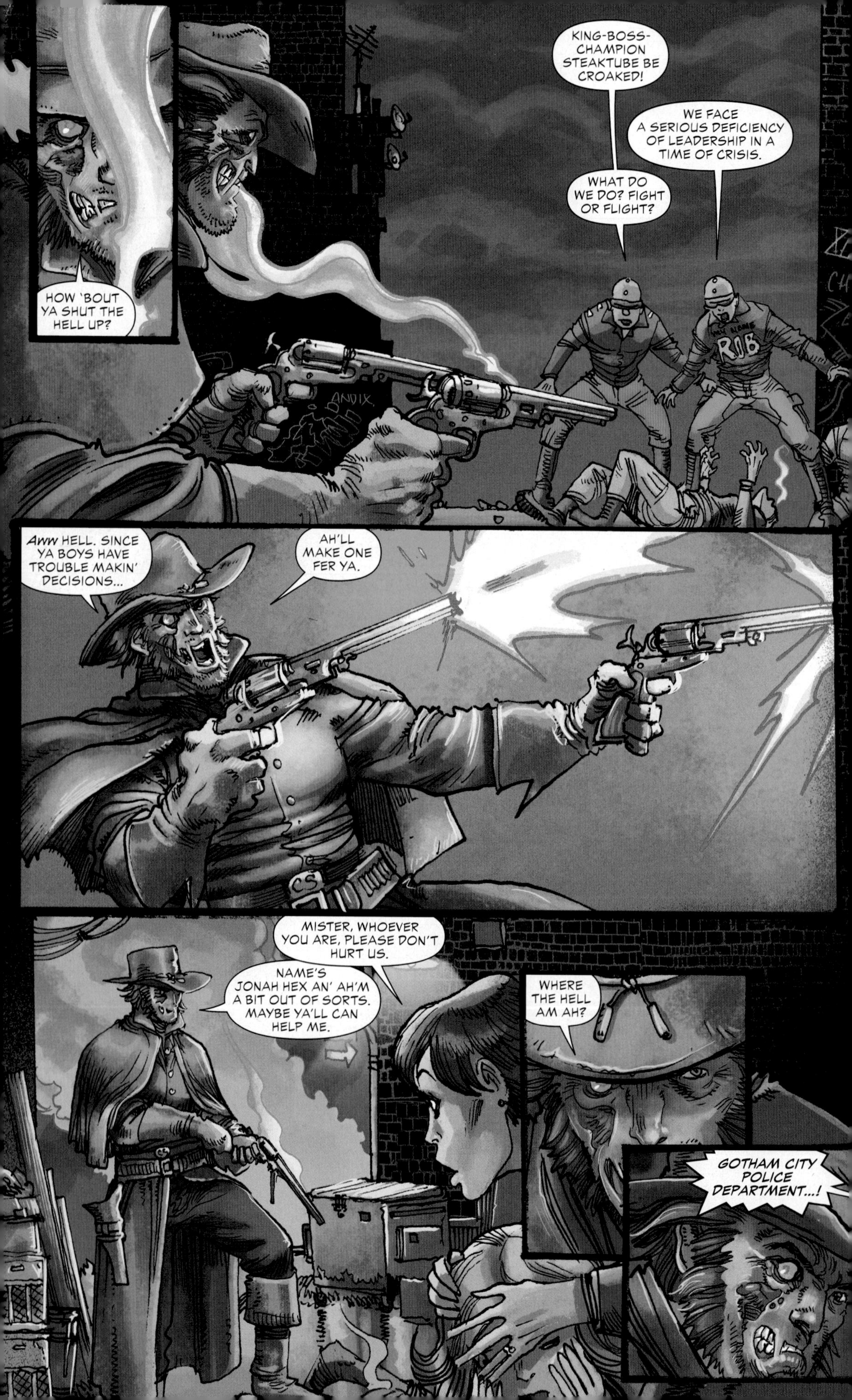
KING-BOSS-CHAMPION STEAKTUBE BE CROAKED!
WE FACE A SERIOUS DEFICIENCY OF LEADERSHIP IN A TIME OF CRISIS.
WHAT DO WE DO? FIGHT OR FLIGHT?
HOW 'BOUT YA SHUT THE HELL UP?
AWW HELL. SINCE YA BOYS HAVE TROUBLE MAKIN' DECISIONS...
AH'LL MAKE ONE FER YA.
MISTER, WHOEVER YOU ARE, PLEASE DON'T HURT US.
NAME'S JONAH HEX AN' AH'M A BIT OUT OF SORTS. MAYBE YA'LL CAN HELP ME.
WHERE THE HELL AM AH?
GOTHAM CITY POLICE DEPARTMENT...!

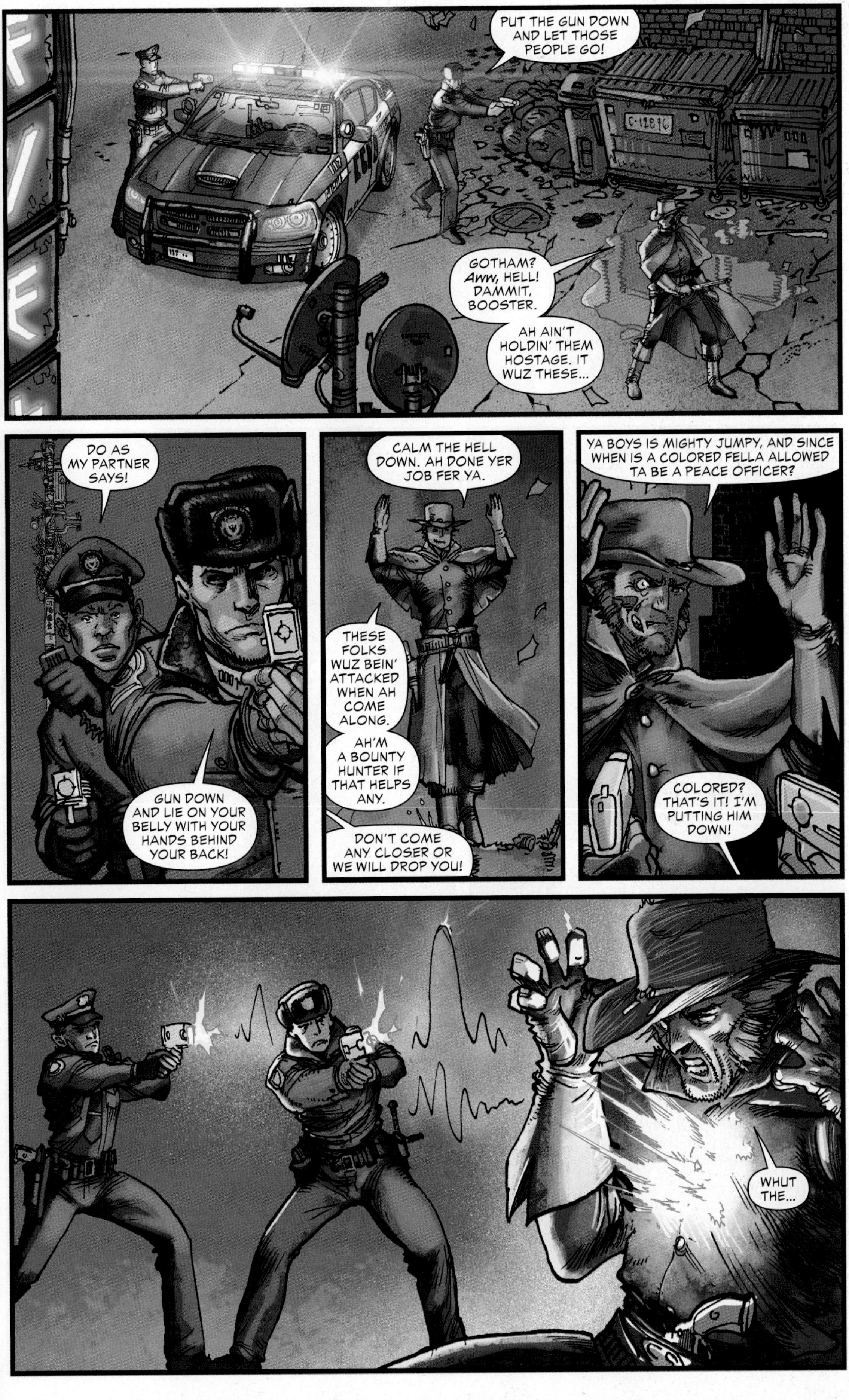
PUT THE GUN DOWN AND LET THOSE PEOPLE GO!
GOTHAM? *AWW*, HELL! DAMMIT, BOOSTER.
AH AIN'T HOLDIN' THEM HOSTAGE. IT WUZ THESE...
DO AS MY PARTNER SAYS!
GUN DOWN AND LIE ON YOUR BELLY WITH YOUR HANDS BEHIND YOUR BACK!
CALM THE HELL DOWN. AH DONE YER JOB FER YA.
THESE FOLKS WUZ BEIN' ATTACKED WHEN AH COME ALONG.
AH'M A BOUNTY HUNTER IF THAT HELPS ANY.
DON'T COME ANY CLOSER OR WE WILL DROP YOU!
YA BOYS IS MIGHTY JUMPY, AND SINCE WHEN IS A COLORED FELLA ALLOWED TA BE A PEACE OFFICER?
COLORED? THAT'S IT! I'M PUTTING HIM DOWN!
WHUT THE...

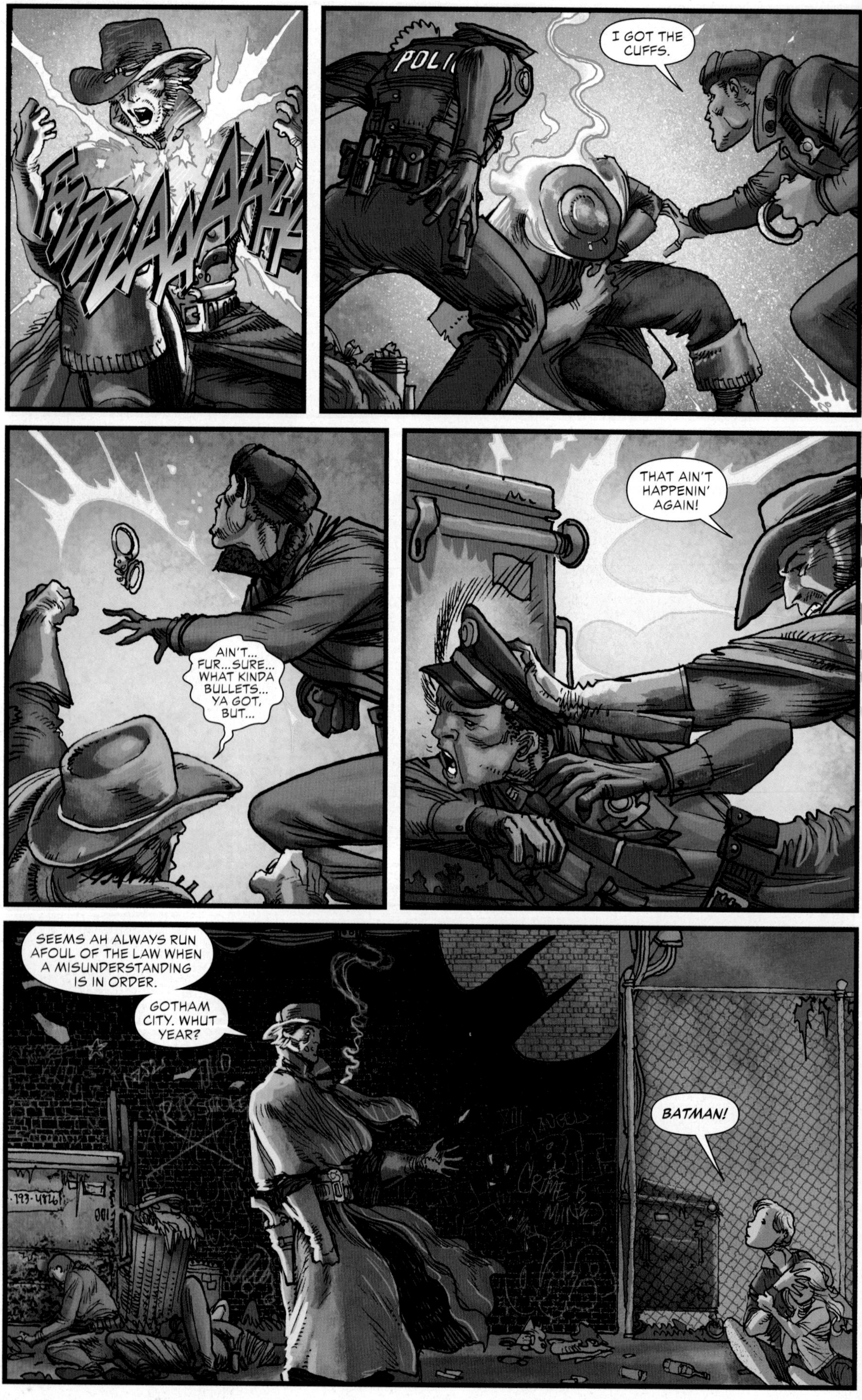
FZZAAAK!
I GOT THE CUFFS.
POLI
AIN'T... FUR...SURE... WHAT KINDA BULLETS... YA GOT, BUT...
THAT AIN'T HAPPENIN' AGAIN!
SEEMS AH ALWAYS RUN AFOUL OF THE LAW WHEN A MISUNDERSTANDING IS IN ORDER.
GOTHAM CITY. WHUT YEAR?
BATMAN!
CRIME IS MINE

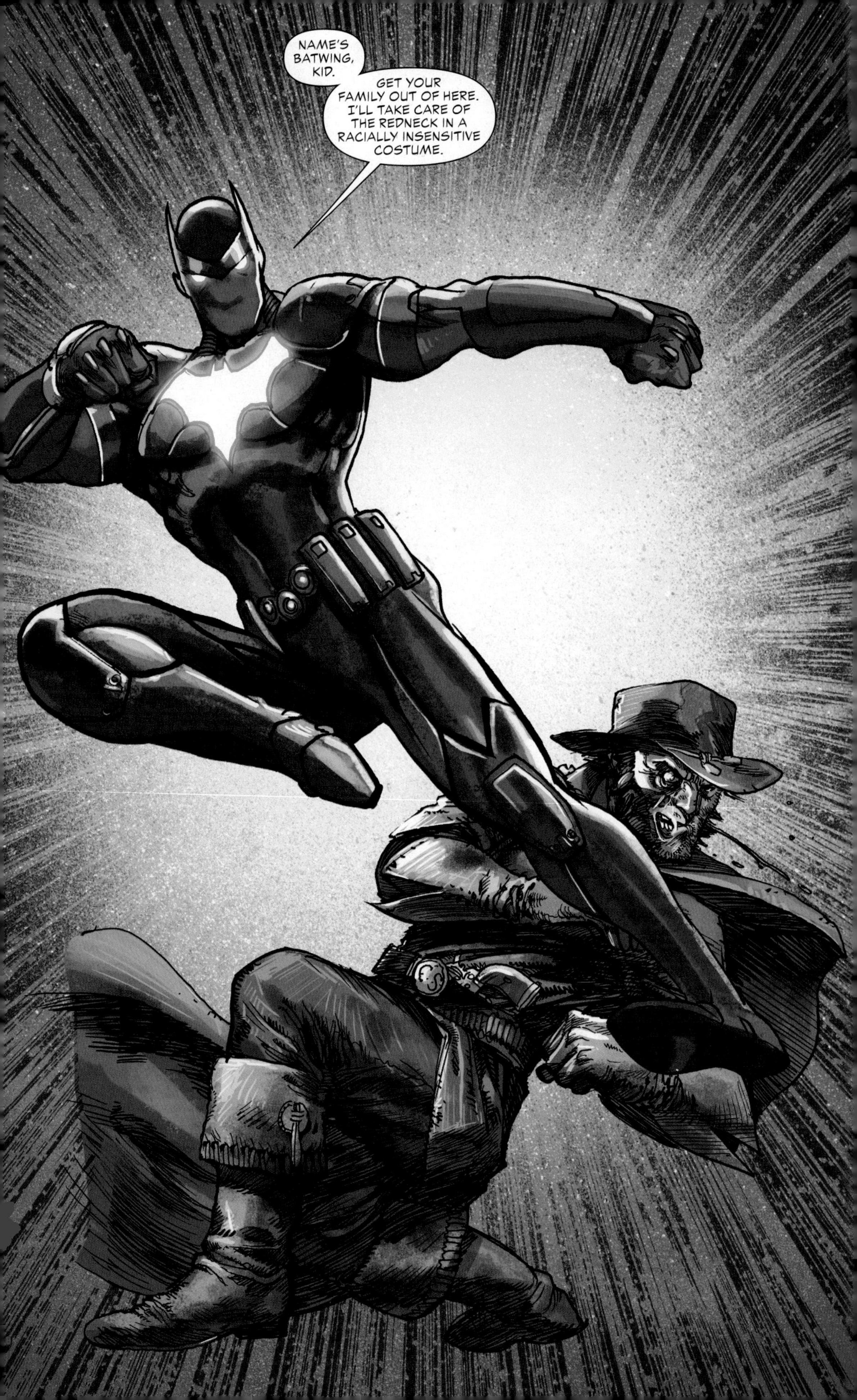
NAME'S BATWING, KID.
GET YOUR FAMILY OUT OF HERE. I'LL TAKE CARE OF THE REDNECK IN A RACIALLY INSENSITIVE COSTUME.

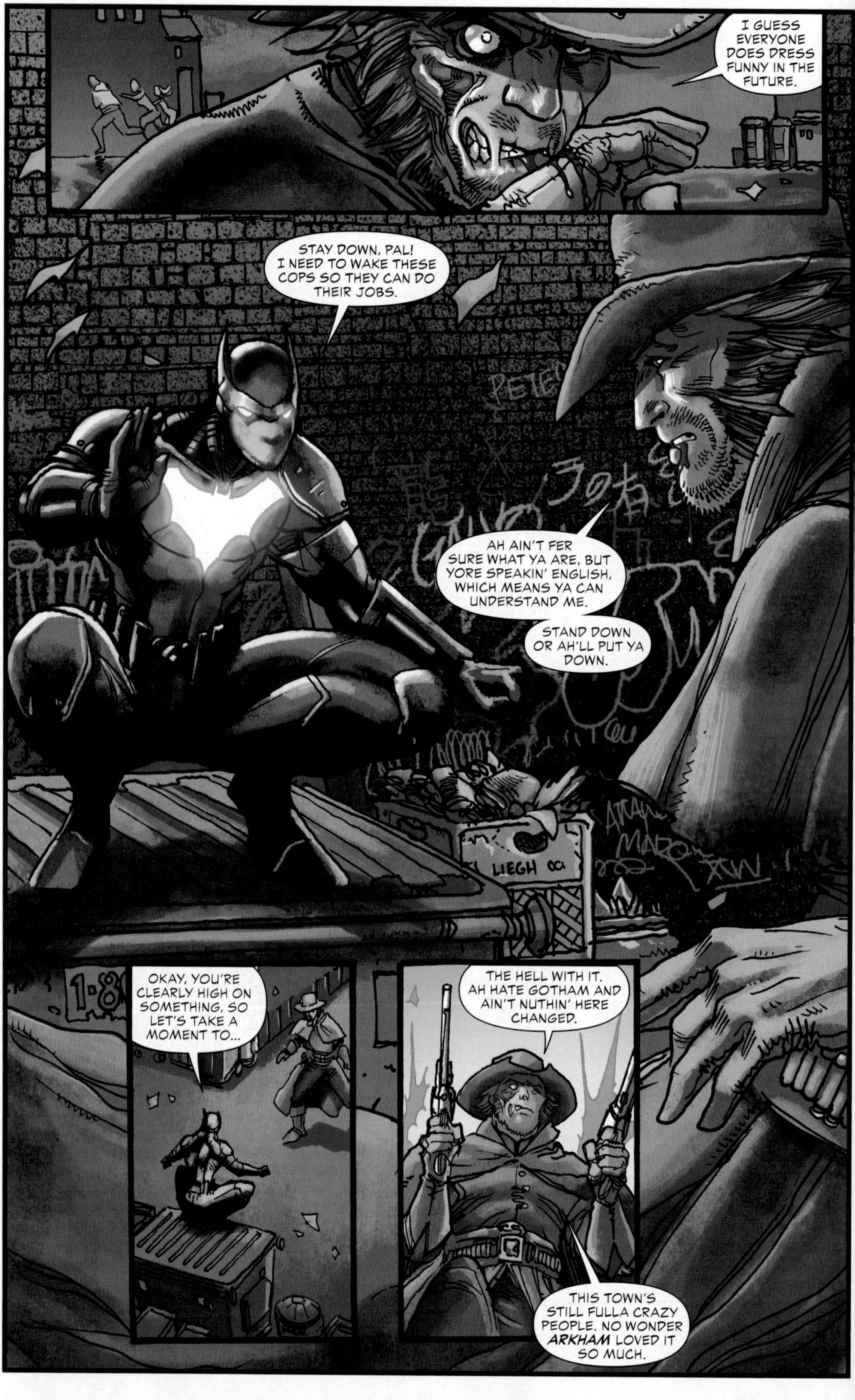
I GUESS EVERYONE DOES DRESS FUNNY IN THE FUTURE.
STAY DOWN, PAL! I NEED TO WAKE THESE COPS SO THEY CAN DO THEIR JOBS.
AH AIN'T FER SURE WHAT YA ARE, BUT YORE SPEAKIN' ENGLISH, WHICH MEANS YA CAN UNDERSTAND ME.
STAND DOWN OR AH'LL PUT YA DOWN.
LIEGH CO.
OKAY, YOU'RE CLEARLY HIGH ON SOMETHING, SO LET'S TAKE A MOMENT TO...
THE HELL WITH IT. AH HATE GOTHAM AND AIN'T NUTHIN' HERE CHANGED.
THIS TOWN'S STILL FULLA CRAZY PEOPLE. NO WONDER ARKHAM LOVED IT SO MUCH.

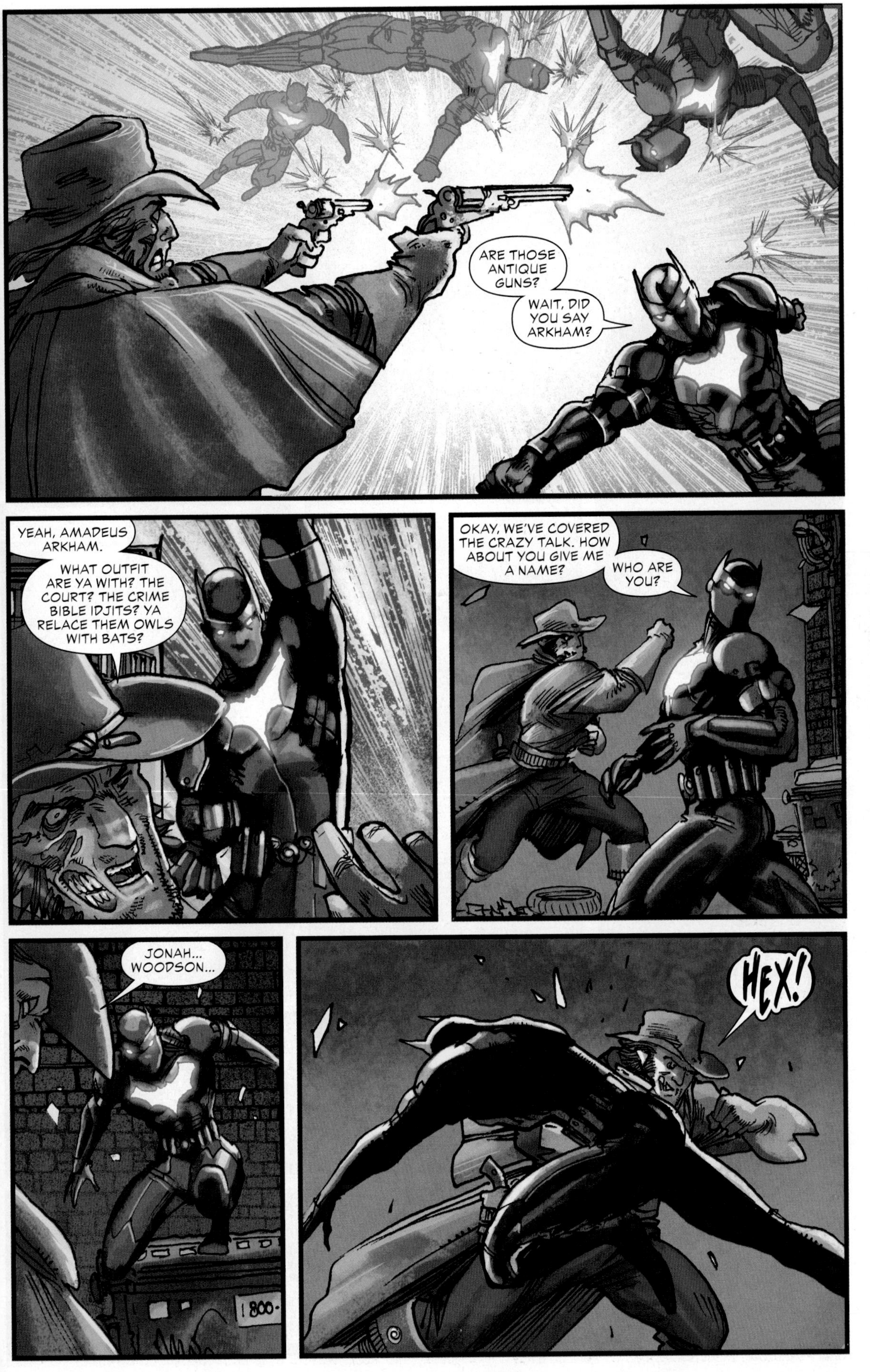
ARE THOSE ANTIQUE GUNS?
WAIT, DID YOU SAY ARKHAM?
YEAH, AMADEUS ARKHAM.
WHAT OUTFIT ARE YA WITH? THE COURT? THE CRIME BIBLE IDJITS? YA RELACE THEM OWLS WITH BATS?
OKAY, WE'VE COVERED THE CRAZY TALK. HOW ABOUT YOU GIVE ME A NAME?
WHO ARE YOU?
JONAH... WOODSON...
1800-
HEX!

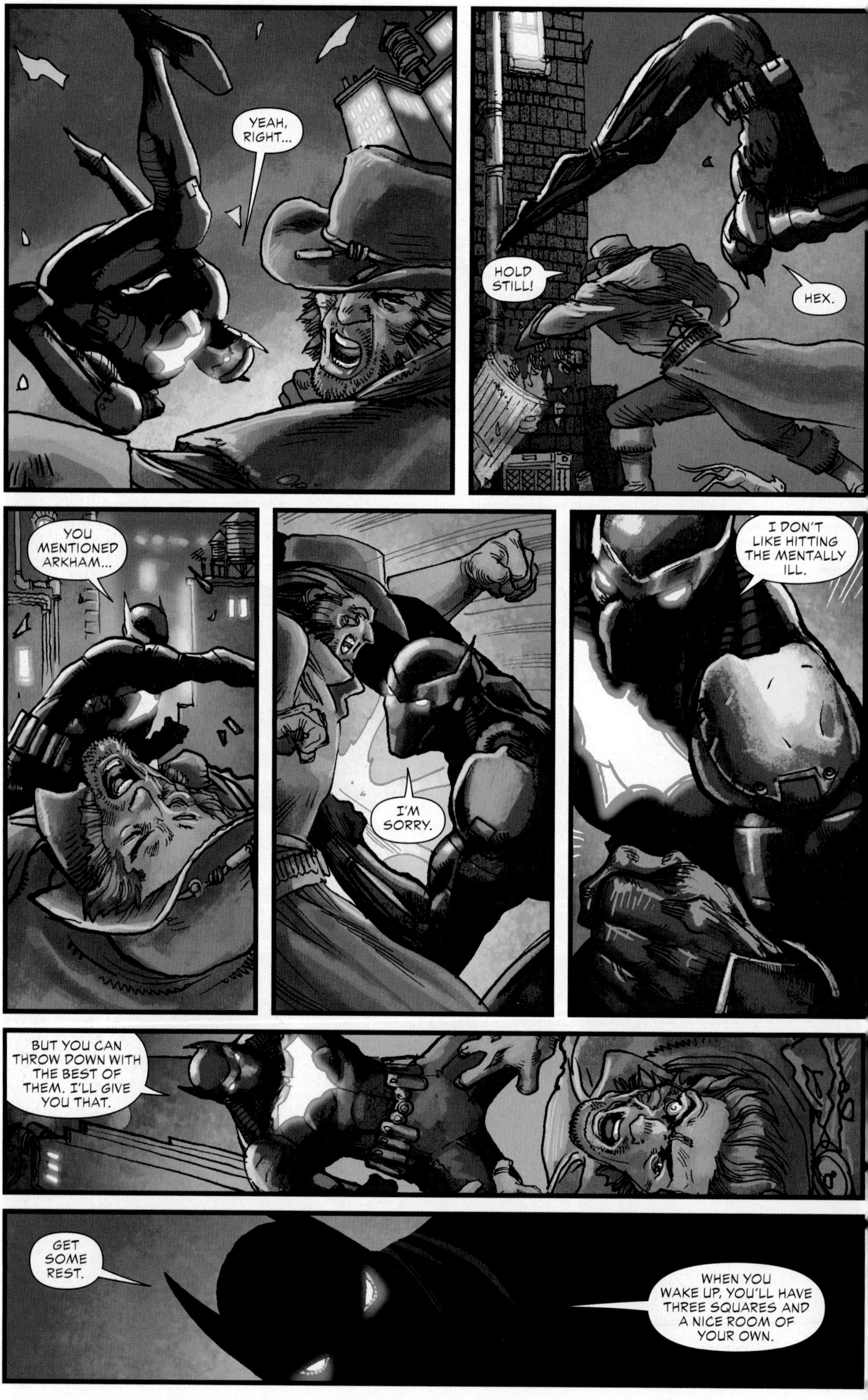
YEAH, RIGHT...
HOLD STILL!
HEX.
YOU MENTIONED ARKHAM...
I'M SORRY.
I DON'T LIKE HITTING THE MENTALLY ILL.
BUT YOU CAN THROW DOWN WITH THE BEST OF THEM. I'LL GIVE YOU THAT.
GET SOME REST.
WHEN YOU WAKE UP, YOU'LL HAVE THREE SQUARES AND A NICE ROOM OF YOUR OWN.

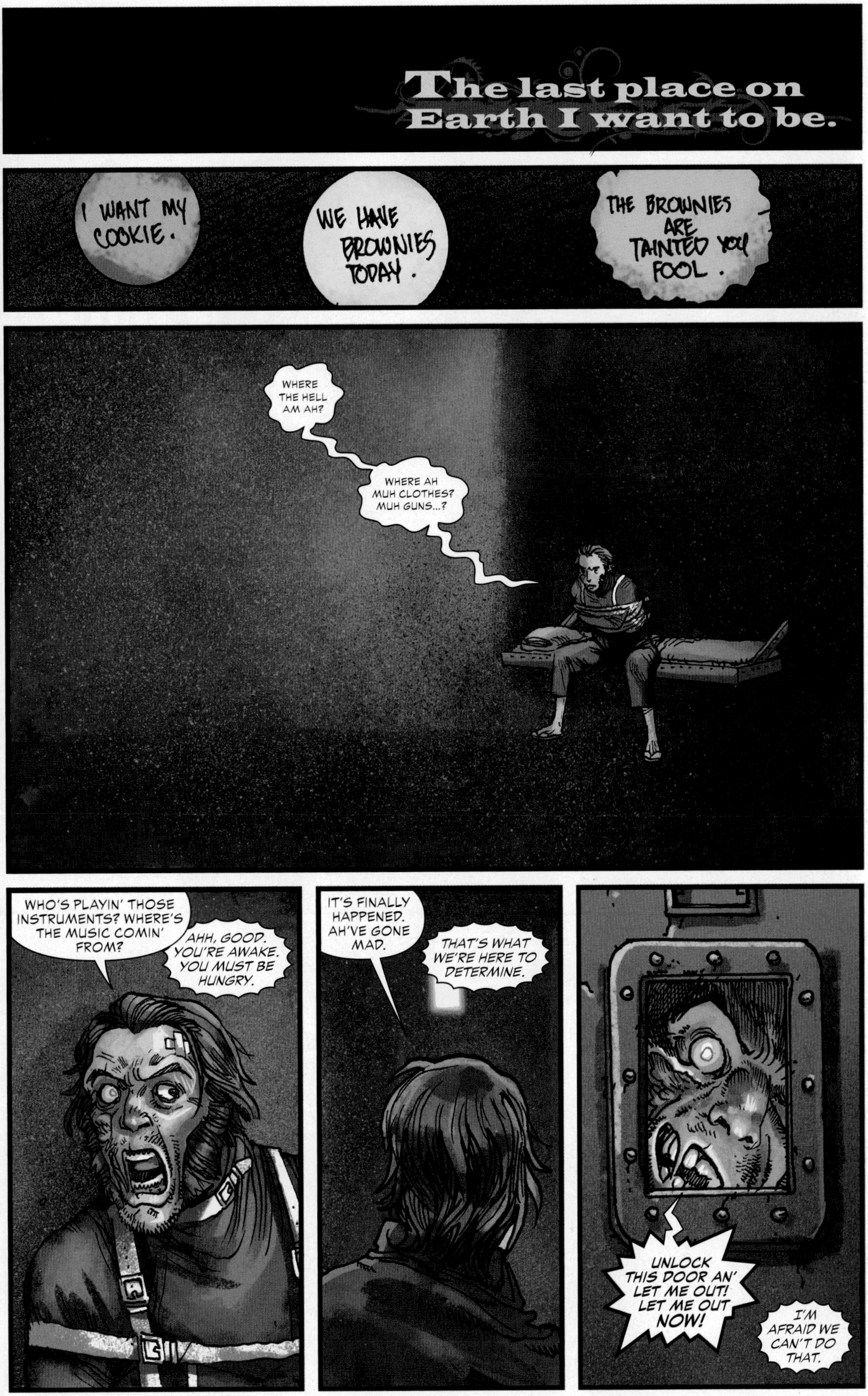
The last place on Earth I want to be.
I WANT MY COOKIE.
WE HAVE BROWNIES TODAY.
THE BROWNIES ARE TAINTED YOU FOOL.
WHERE THE HELL AM AH?
WHERE AH MUH CLOTHES? MUH GUNS...?
WHO'S PLAYIN' THOSE INSTRUMENTS? WHERE'S THE MUSIC COMIN' FROM?
AHH, GOOD. YOU'RE AWAKE. YOU MUST BE HUNGRY.
IT'S FINALLY HAPPENED. AH'VE GONE MAD.
THAT'S WHAT WE'RE HERE TO DETERMINE.
UNLOCK THIS DOOR AN' LET ME OUT! LET ME OUT NOW!
I'M AFRAID WE CAN'T DO THAT.

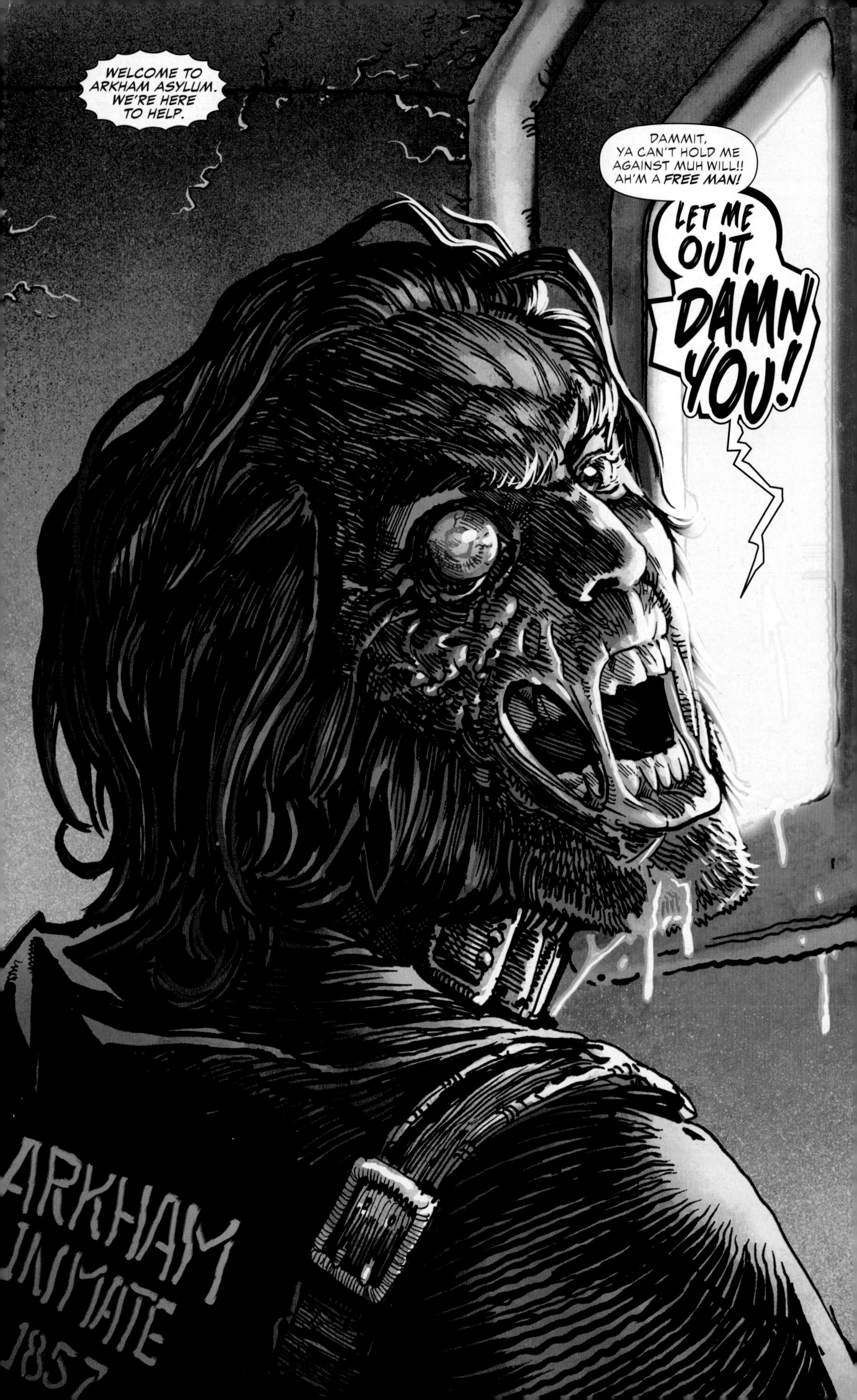
WELCOME TO ARKHAM ASYLUM. WE'RE HERE TO HELP.
DAMMIT, YA CAN'T HOLD ME AGAINST MUH WILL!! AH'M A *FREE MAN!*
LET ME OUT, DAMN YOU!
ARKHAM INMATE 1857

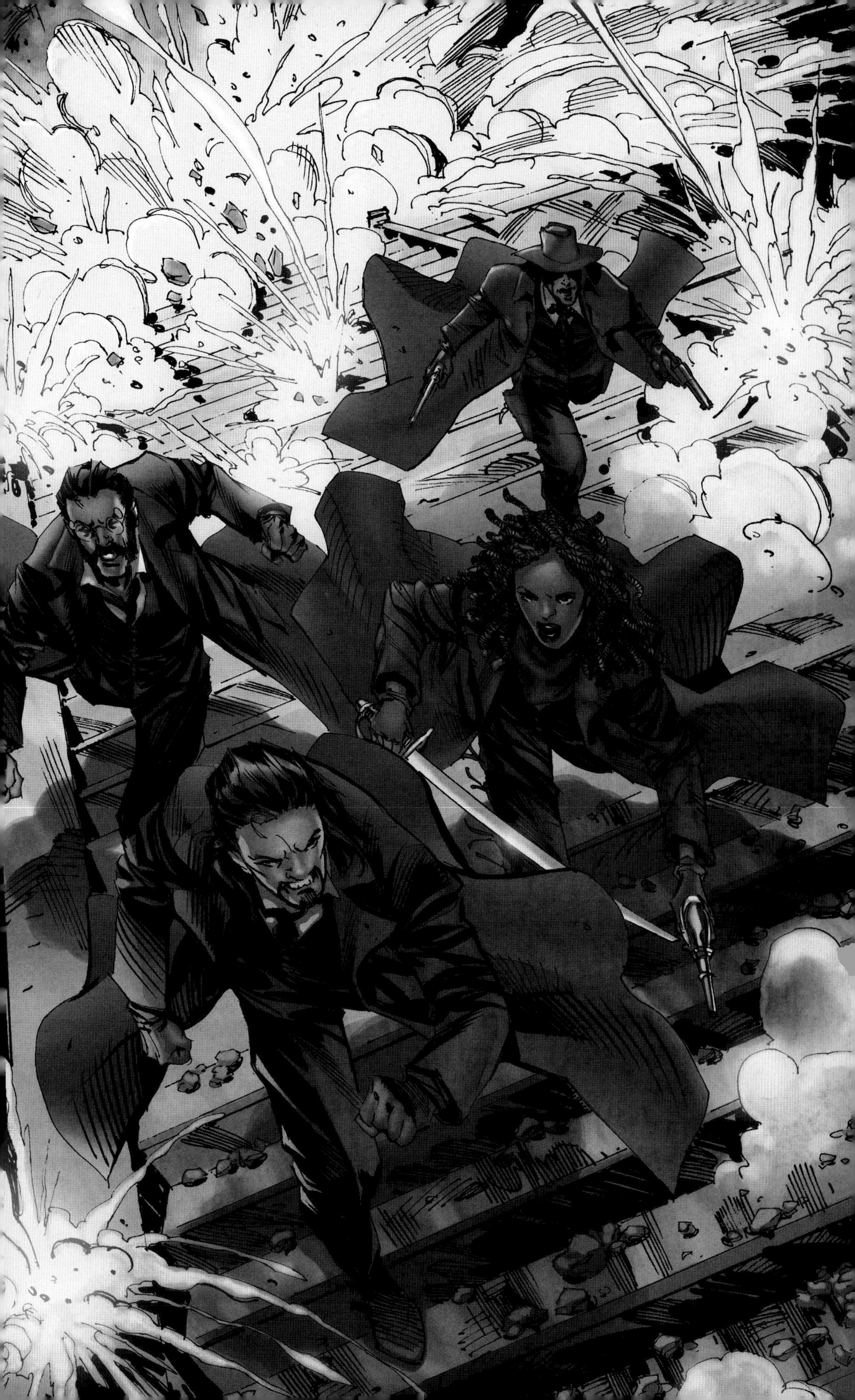

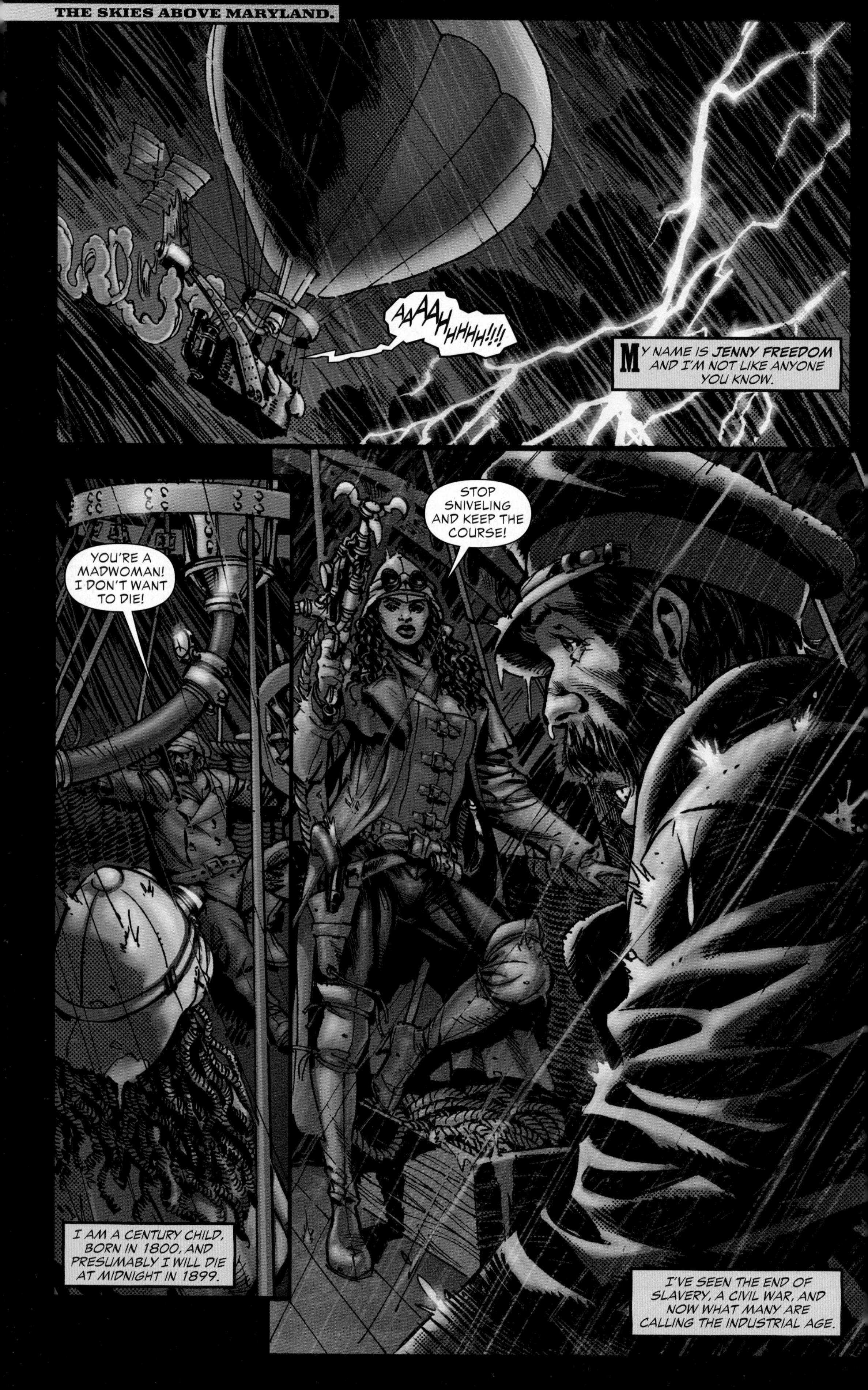
THE SKIES ABOVE MARYLAND.
AAAAHHHHH!!!!
MY NAME IS JENNY FREEDOM AND I'M NOT LIKE ANYONE YOU KNOW.
YOU'RE A MADWOMAN! I DON'T WANT TO DIE!
STOP SNIVELING AND KEEP THE COURSE!
I AM A CENTURY CHILD, BORN IN 1800, AND PRESUMABLY I WILL DIE AT MIDNIGHT IN 1899.
I'VE SEEN THE END OF SLAVERY, A CIVIL WAR, AND NOW WHAT MANY ARE CALLING THE INDUSTRIAL AGE.

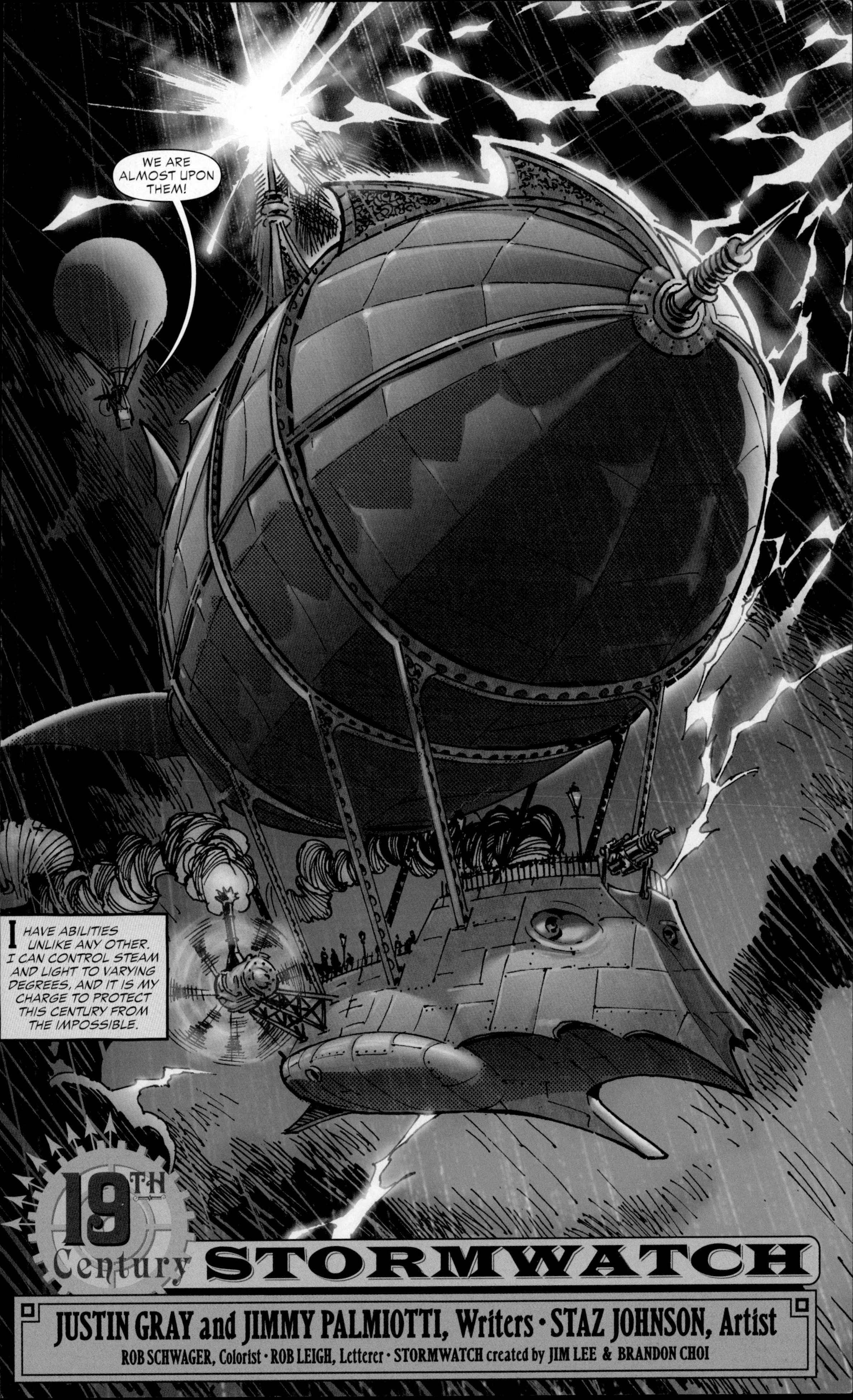
WE ARE ALMOST UPON THEM!
I HAVE ABILITIES UNLIKE ANY OTHER. I CAN CONTROL STEAM AND LIGHT TO VARYING DEGREES, AND IT IS MY CHARGE TO PROTECT THIS CENTURY FROM THE IMPOSSIBLE.
19TH Century STORMWATCH
JUSTIN GRAY and JIMMY PALMIOTTI, Writers • STAZ JOHNSON, Artist
ROB SCHWAGER, Colorist • ROB LEIGH, Letterer • STORMWATCH created by JIM LEE & BRANDON CHOI

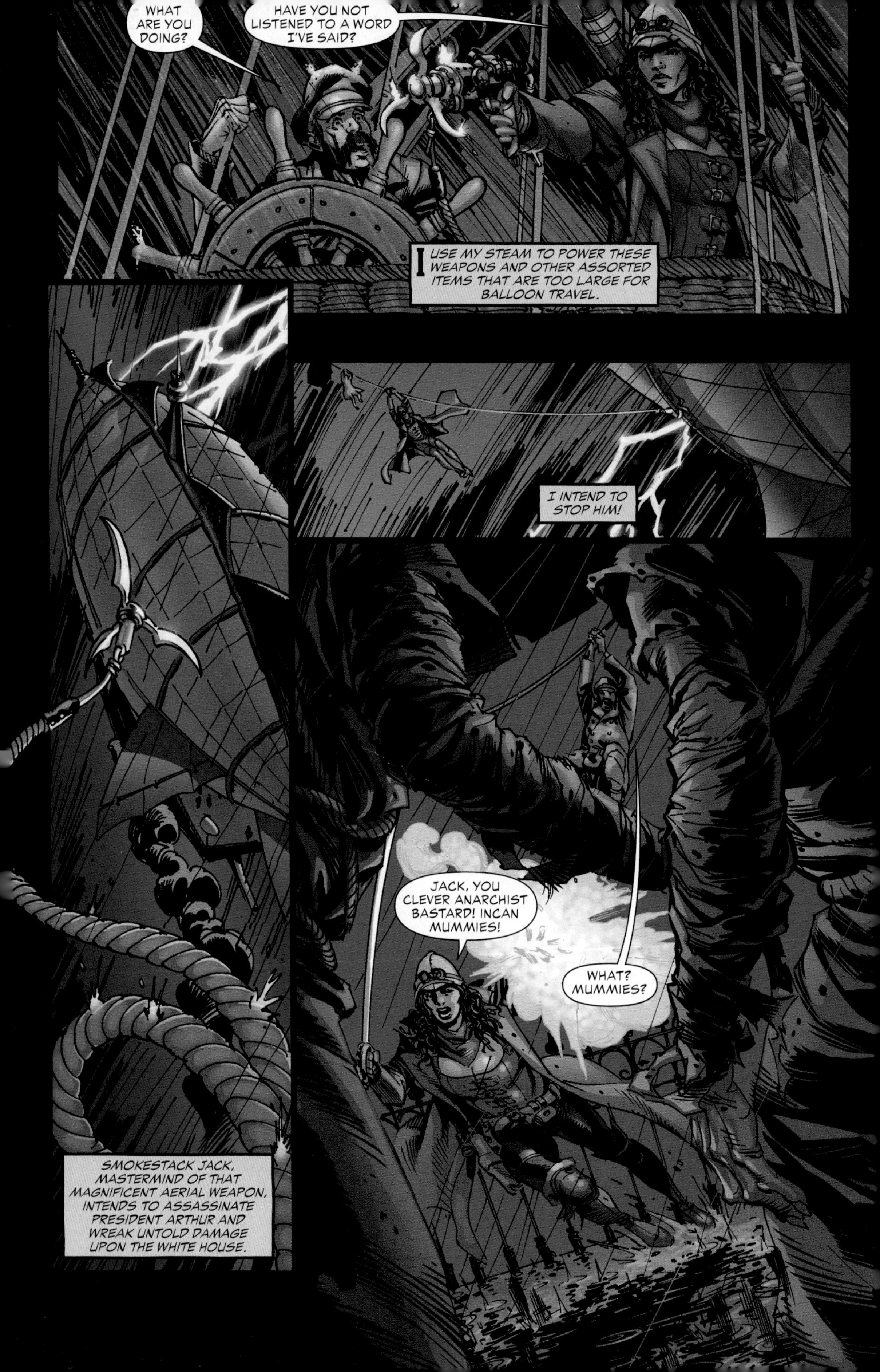

WHAT ARE YOU DOING?
HAVE YOU NOT LISTENED TO A WORD I'VE SAID?
I USE MY STEAM TO POWER THESE WEAPONS AND OTHER ASSORTED ITEMS THAT ARE TOO LARGE FOR BALLOON TRAVEL.
SMOKESTACK JACK, MASTERMIND OF THAT MAGNIFICENT AERIAL WEAPON, INTENDS TO ASSASSINATE PRESIDENT ARTHUR AND WREAK UNTOLD DAMAGE UPON THE WHITE HOUSE.
I INTEND TO STOP HIM!
JACK, YOU CLEVER ANARCHIST BASTARD! INCAN MUMMIES!
WHAT? MUMMIES?

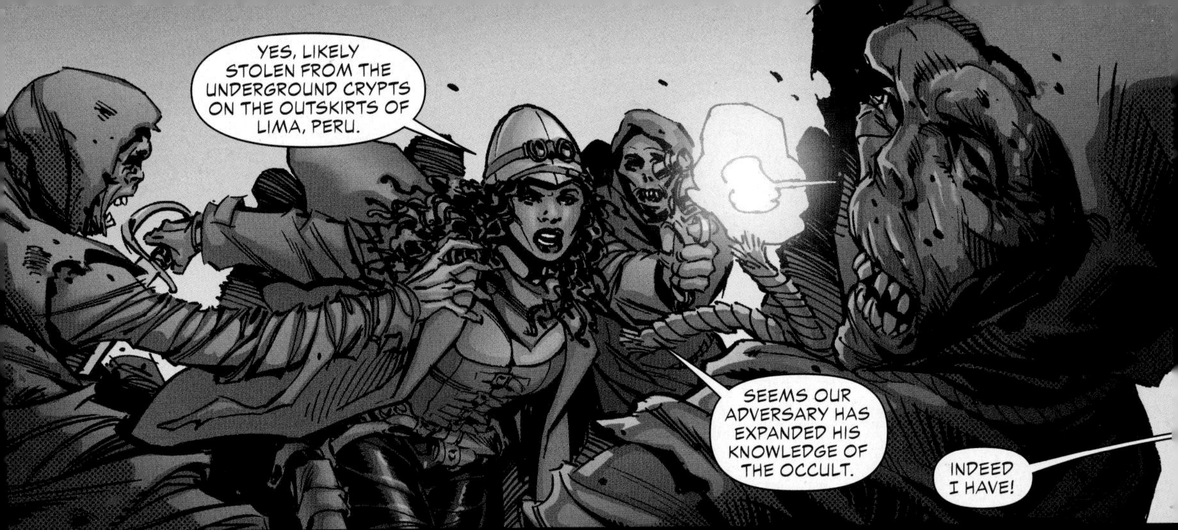
YES, LIKELY STOLEN FROM THE UNDERGROUND CRYPTS ON THE OUTSKIRTS OF LIMA, PERU.
SEEMS OUR ADVERSARY HAS EXPANDED HIS KNOWLEDGE OF THE OCCULT.
INDEED I HAVE!
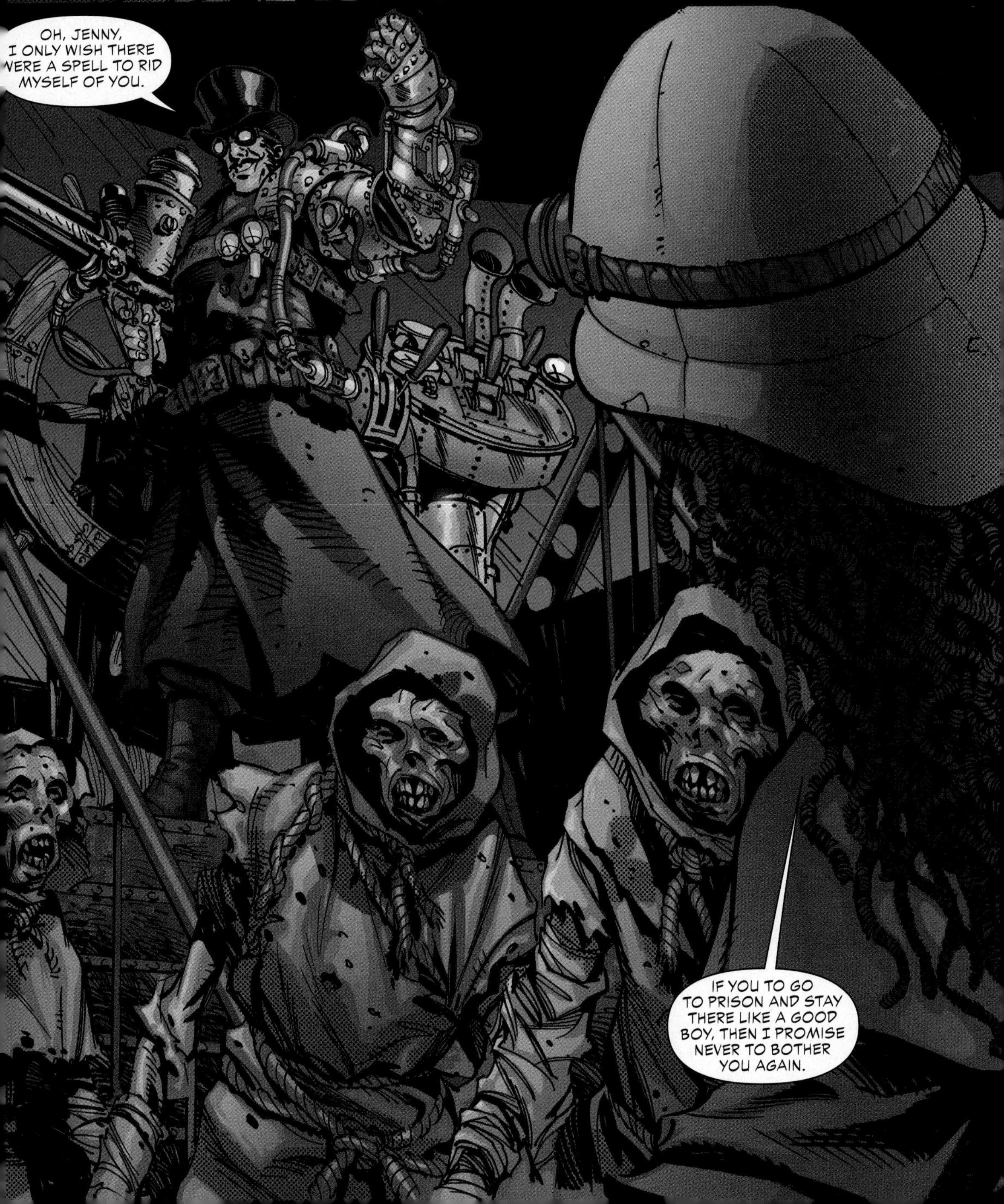
OH, JENNY, I ONLY WISH THERE WERE A SPELL TO RID MYSELF OF YOU.
IF YOU TO GO TO PRISON AND STAY THERE LIKE A GOOD BOY, THEN I PROMISE NEVER TO BOTHER YOU AGAIN.

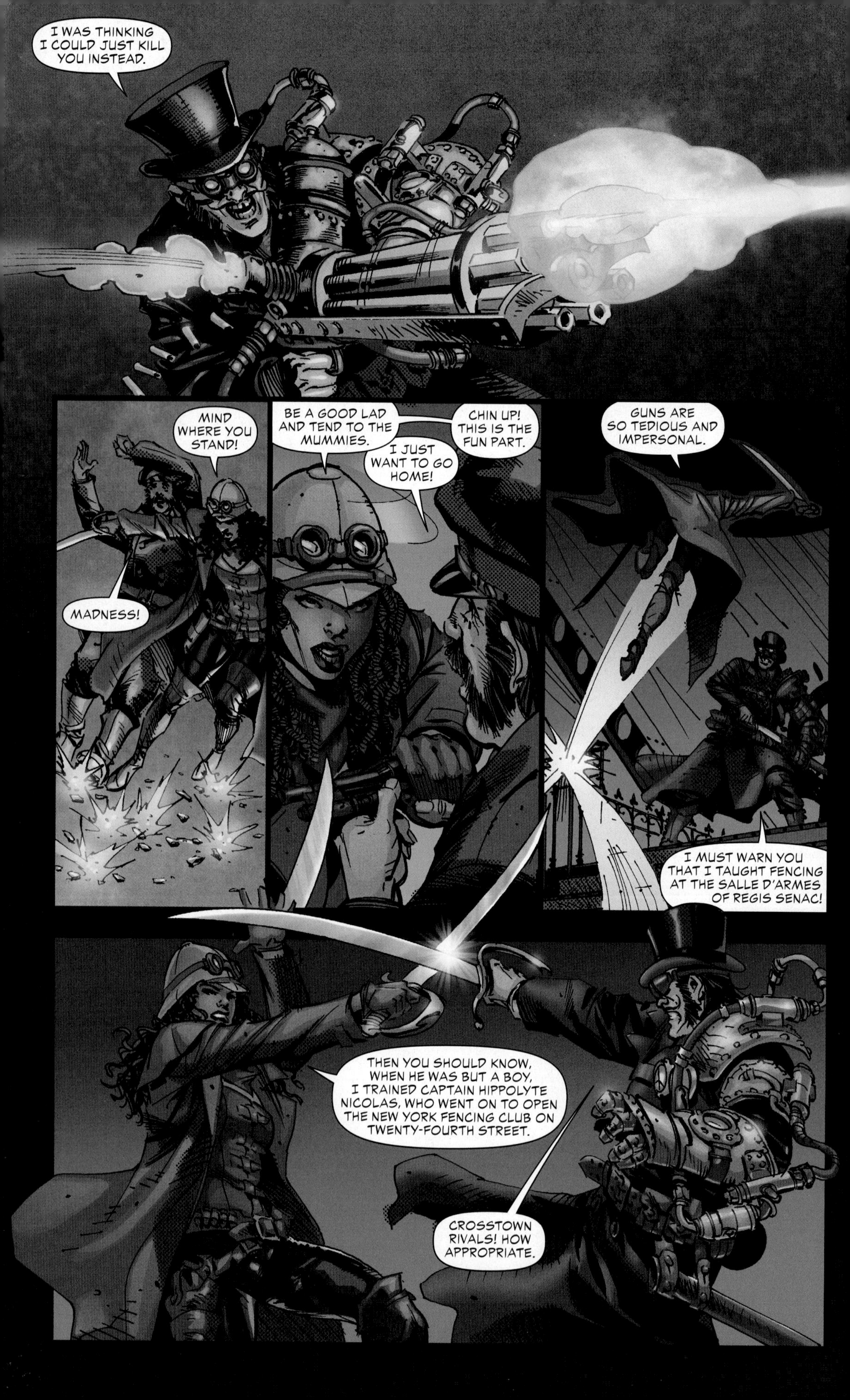
I WAS THINKING I COULD JUST KILL YOU INSTEAD.
MIND WHERE YOU STAND!
MADNESS!
BE A GOOD LAD AND TEND TO THE MUMMIES.
CHIN UP! THIS IS THE FUN PART.
I JUST WANT TO GO HOME!
GUNS ARE SO TEDIOUS AND IMPERSONAL.
I MUST WARN YOU THAT I TAUGHT FENCING AT THE SALLE D'ARMES OF REGIS SENAC!
THEN YOU SHOULD KNOW, WHEN HE WAS BUT A BOY, I TRAINED CAPTAIN HIPPOLYTE NICOLAS, WHO WENT ON TO OPEN THE NEW YORK FENCING CLUB ON TWENTY-FOURTH STREET.
CROSSTOWN RIVALS! HOW APPROPRIATE.

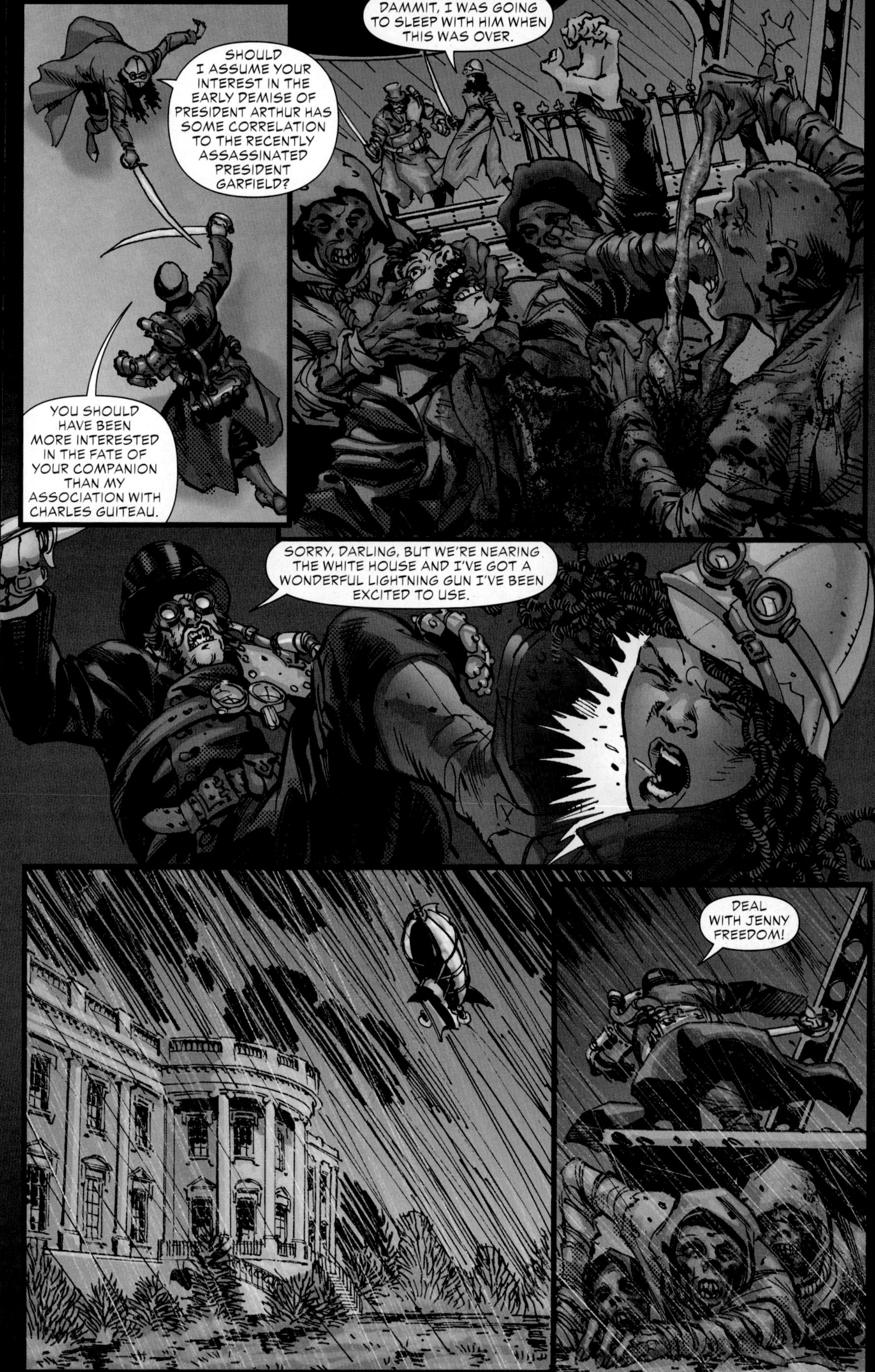
SHOULD I ASSUME YOUR INTEREST IN THE EARLY DEMISE OF PRESIDENT ARTHUR HAS SOME CORRELATION TO THE RECENTLY ASSASSINATED PRESIDENT GARFIELD?
YOU SHOULD HAVE BEEN MORE INTERESTED IN THE FATE OF YOUR COMPANION THAN MY ASSOCIATION WITH CHARLES GUITEAU.
DAMMIT, I WAS GOING TO SLEEP WITH HIM WHEN THIS WAS OVER.
SORRY, DARLING, BUT WE'RE NEARING THE WHITE HOUSE AND I'VE GOT A WONDERFUL LIGHTNING GUN I'VE BEEN EXCITED TO USE.
DEAL WITH JENNY FREEDOM!

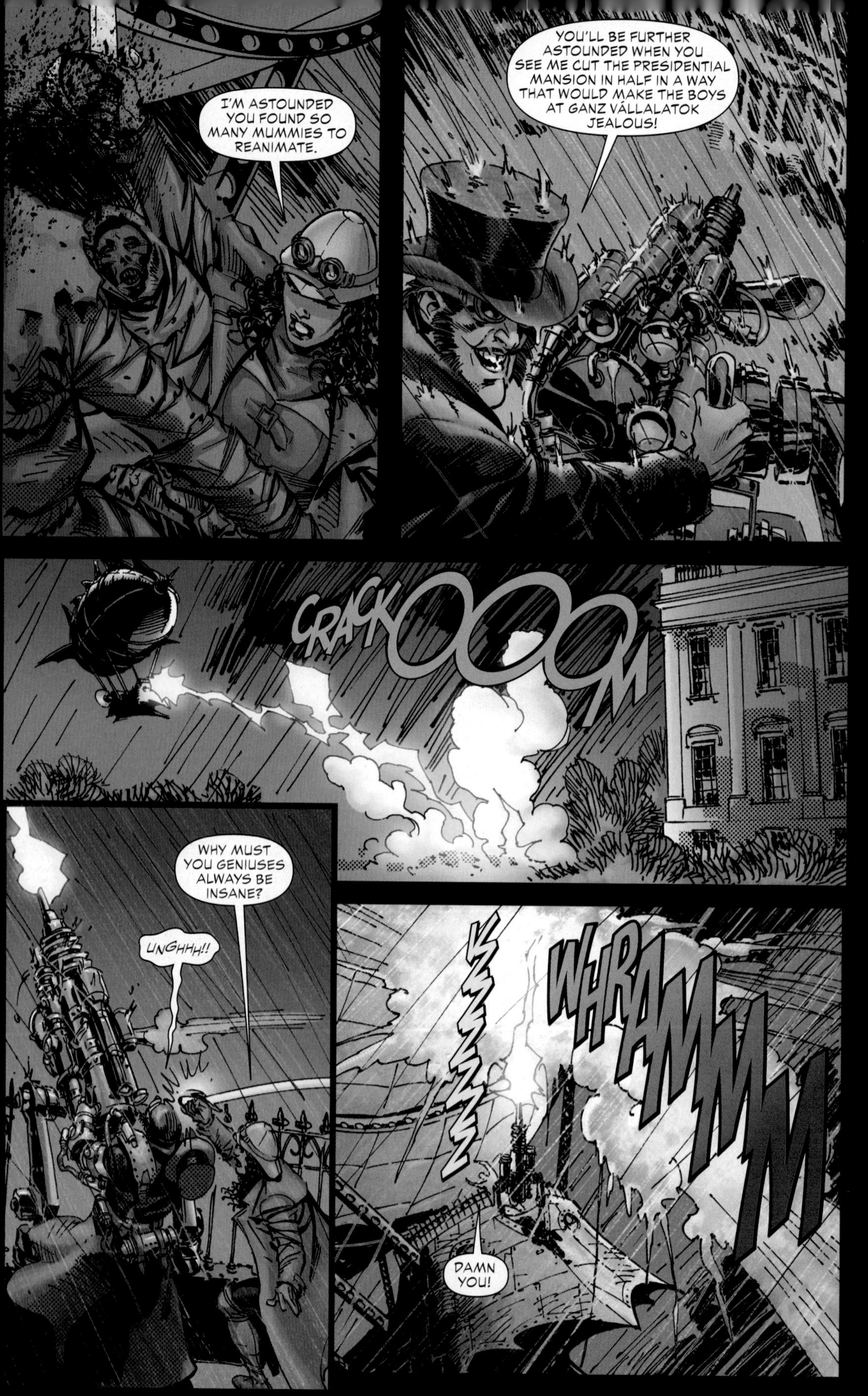
I'M ASTOUNDED YOU FOUND SO MANY MUMMIES TO REANIMATE.
YOU'LL BE FURTHER ASTOUNDED WHEN YOU SEE ME CUT THE PRESIDENTIAL MANSION IN HALF IN A WAY THAT WOULD MAKE THE BOYS AT GANZ VÁLLALATOK JEALOUS!
CRACKOOOM
WHY MUST YOU GENIUSES ALWAYS BE INSANE?
UNGHHH!!
WHRAMMMM
DAMN YOU!

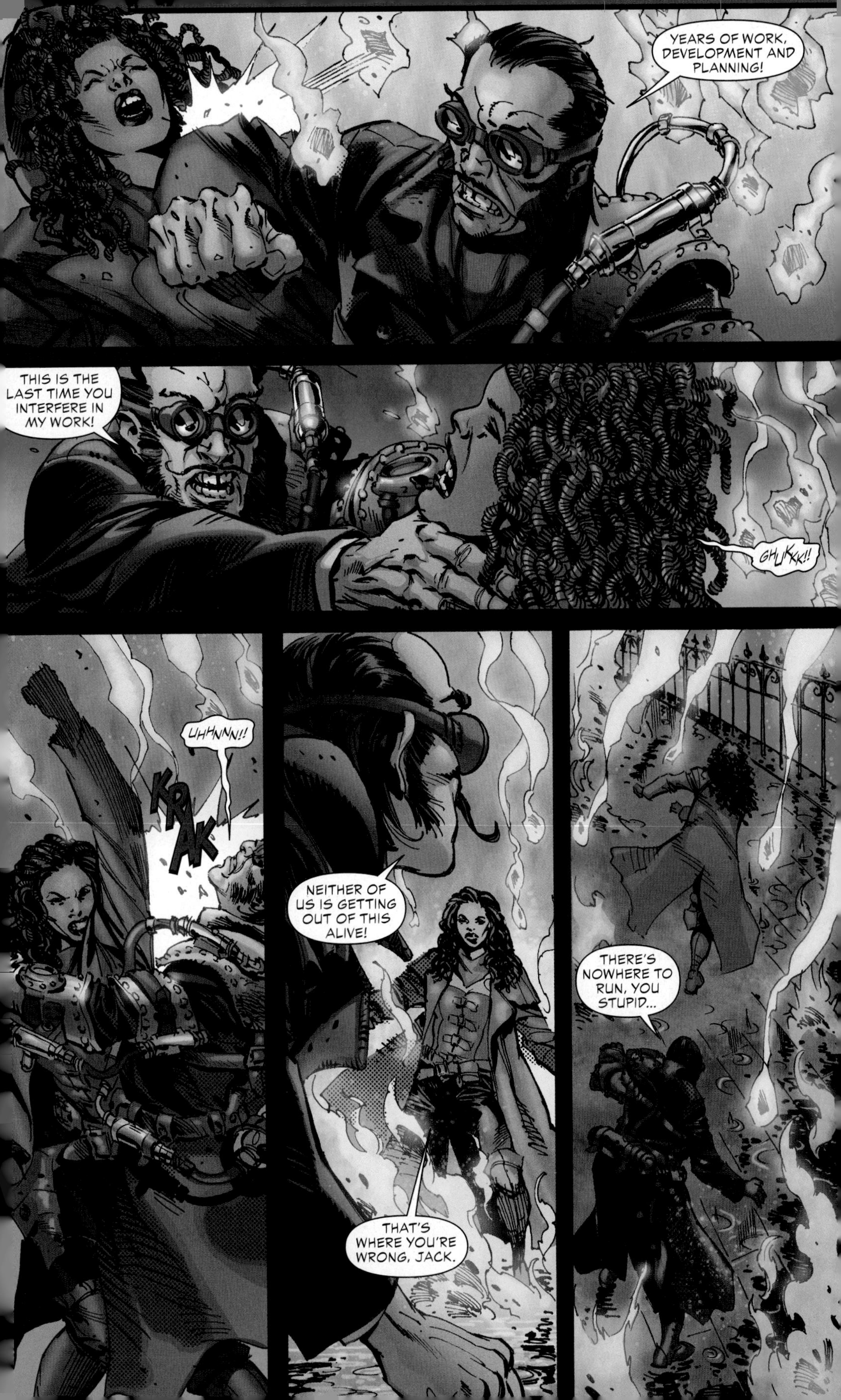
YEARS OF WORK, DEVELOPMENT AND PLANNING!
THIS IS THE LAST TIME YOU INTERFERE IN MY WORK!
GHUKKK!!
UHHNNN!!
KRAK
NEITHER OF US IS GETTING OUT OF THIS ALIVE!
THAT'S WHERE YOU'RE WRONG, JACK.
THERE'S NOWHERE TO RUN, YOU STUPID...

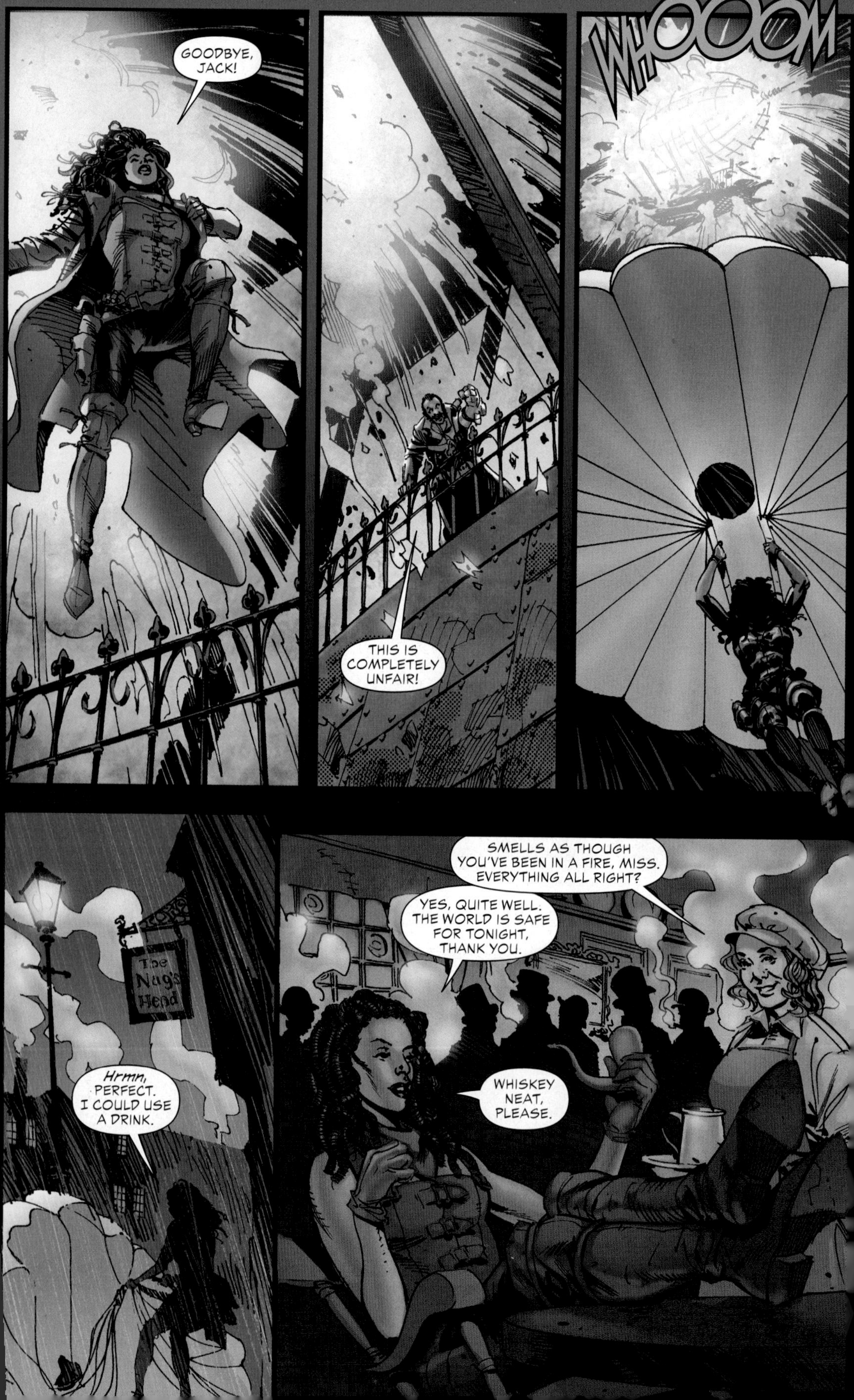
GOODBYE, JACK!
THIS IS COMPLETELY UNFAIR!
WHOOOOM
The Nag's Head
Hrmn, PERFECT. I COULD USE A DRINK.
SMELLS AS THOUGH YOU'VE BEEN IN A FIRE, MISS. EVERYTHING ALL RIGHT?
YES, QUITE WELL. THE WORLD IS SAFE FOR TONIGHT, THANK YOU.
WHISKEY NEAT, PLEASE.

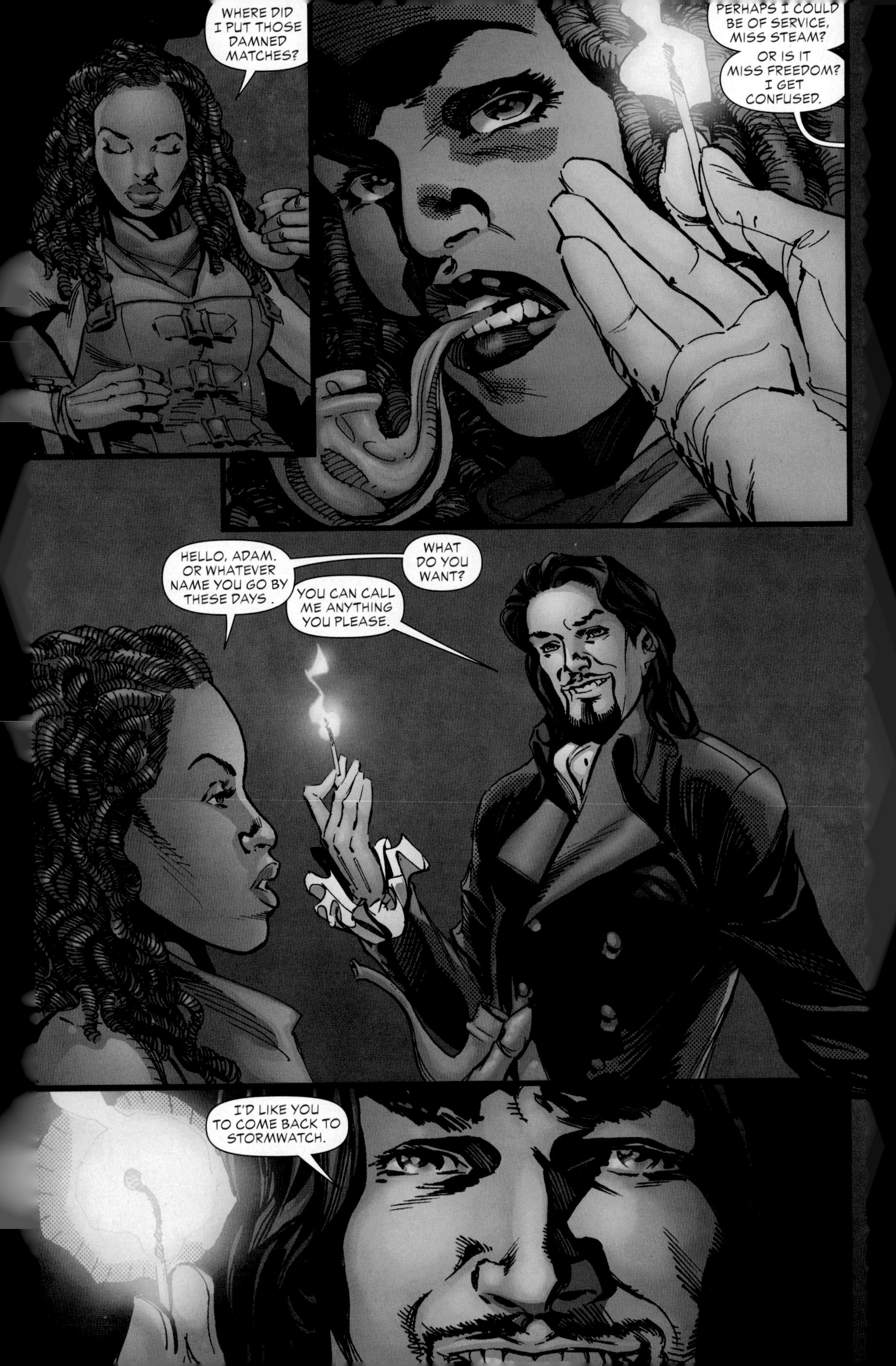
WHERE DID I PUT THOSE DAMNED MATCHES?
PERHAPS I COULD BE OF SERVICE, MISS STEAM?
OR IS IT MISS FREEDOM? I GET CONFUSED.
HELLO, ADAM. OR WHATEVER NAME YOU GO BY THESE DAYS .
WHAT DO YOU WANT?
YOU CAN CALL ME ANYTHING YOU PLEASE.
I'D LIKE YOU TO COME BACK TO STORMWATCH.

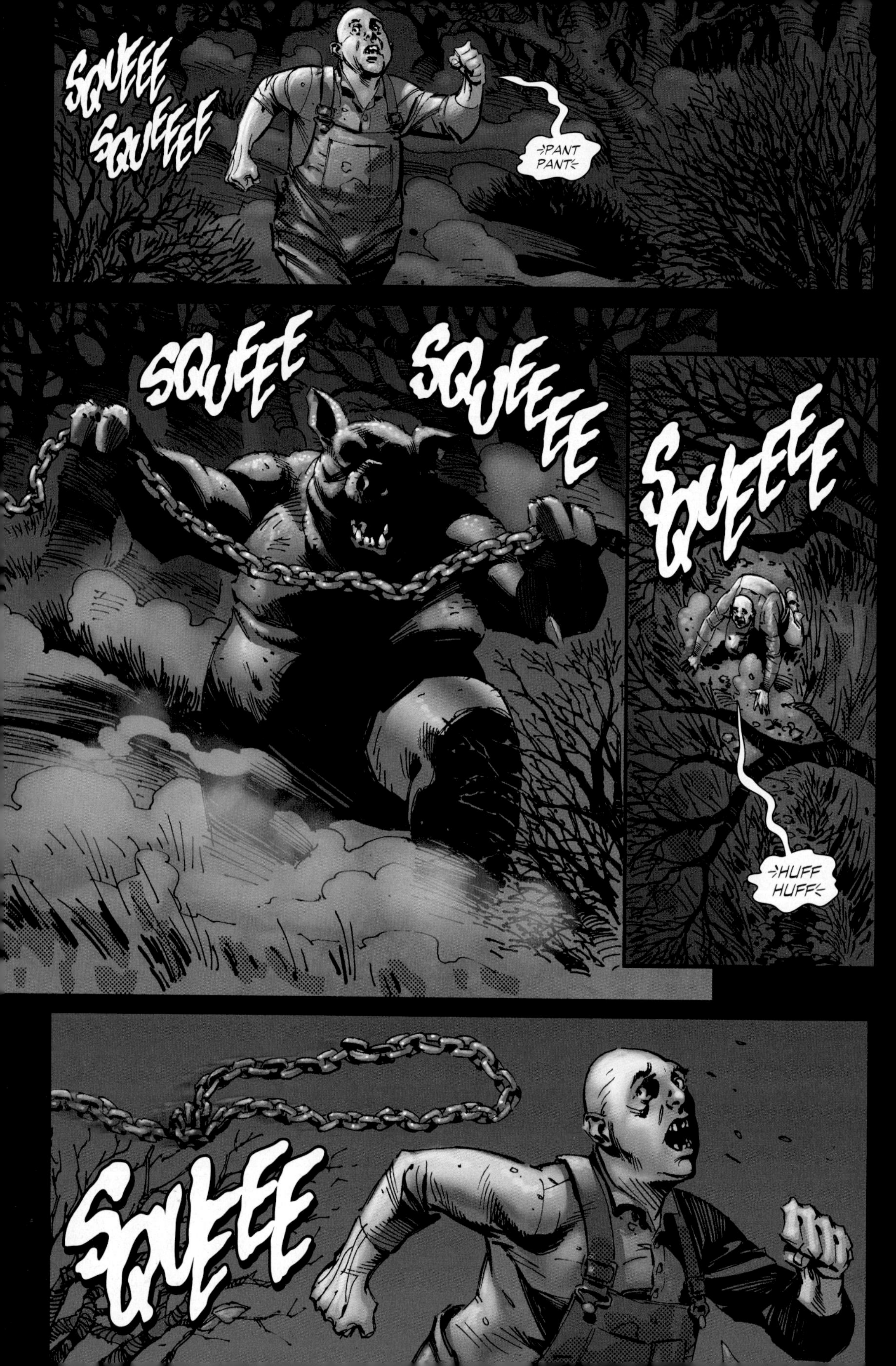
SQUEEE
SQUEEEE
PANT PANT
SQUEEE
SQUEEEEE
SQUEEEE
HUFF HUFF
SQUEEE

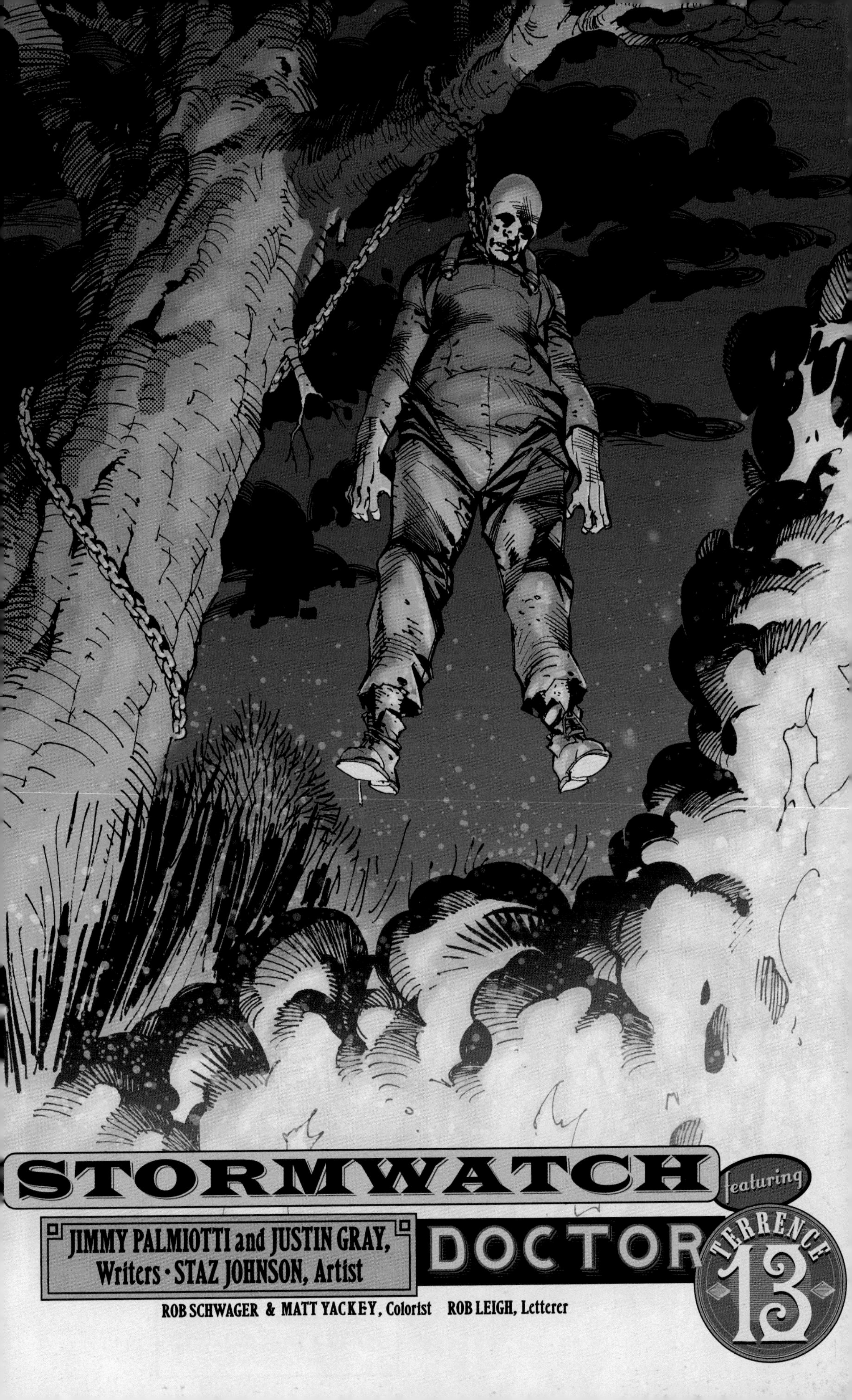
STORMWATCH
featuring
DOCTOR
TERRENCE 13
JIMMY PALMIOTTI and JUSTIN GRAY, Writers • STAZ JOHNSON, Artist
ROB SCHWAGER & MATT YACKEY, Colorist ROB LEIGH, Letterer

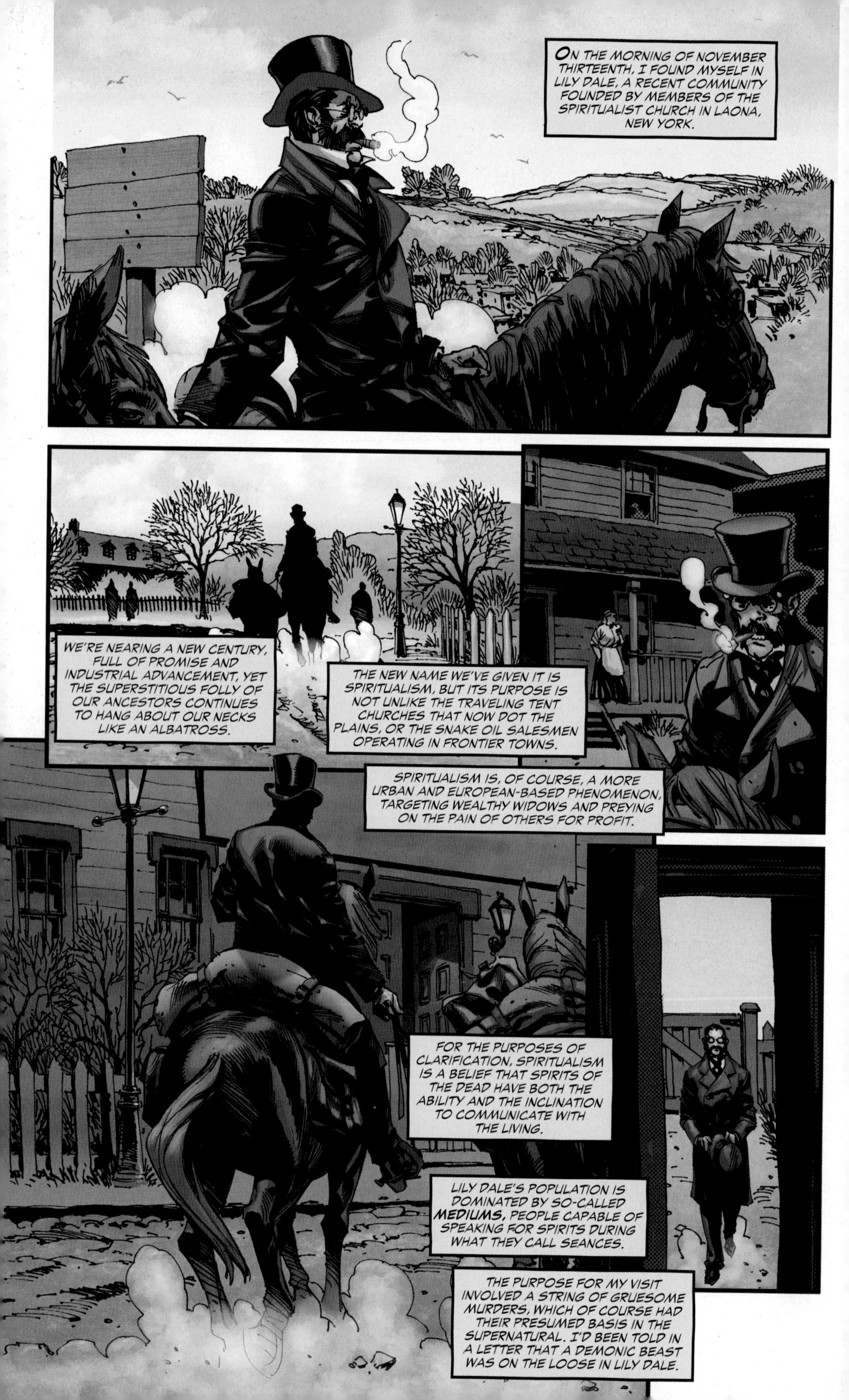
ON THE MORNING OF NOVEMBER THIRTEENTH, I FOUND MYSELF IN LILY DALE, A RECENT COMMUNITY FOUNDED BY MEMBERS OF THE SPIRITUALIST CHURCH IN LAONA, NEW YORK.
WE'RE NEARING A NEW CENTURY, FULL OF PROMISE AND INDUSTRIAL ADVANCEMENT, YET THE SUPERSTITIOUS FOLLY OF OUR ANCESTORS CONTINUES TO HANG ABOUT OUR NECKS LIKE AN ALBATROSS.
THE NEW NAME WE'VE GIVEN IT IS SPIRITUALISM, BUT ITS PURPOSE IS NOT UNLIKE THE TRAVELING TENT CHURCHES THAT NOW DOT THE PLAINS, OR THE SNAKE OIL SALESMEN OPERATING IN FRONTIER TOWNS.
SPIRITUALISM IS, OF COURSE, A MORE URBAN AND EUROPEAN-BASED PHENOMENON, TARGETING WEALTHY WIDOWS AND PREYING ON THE PAIN OF OTHERS FOR PROFIT.
FOR THE PURPOSES OF CLARIFICATION, SPIRITUALISM IS A BELIEF THAT SPIRITS OF THE DEAD HAVE BOTH THE ABILITY AND THE INCLINATION TO COMMUNICATE WITH THE LIVING.
LILY DALE'S POPULATION IS DOMINATED BY SO-CALLED **MEDIUMS**, PEOPLE CAPABLE OF SPEAKING FOR SPIRITS DURING WHAT THEY CALL SEANCES.
THE PURPOSE FOR MY VISIT INVOLVED A STRING OF GRUESOME MURDERS, WHICH OF COURSE HAD THEIR PRESUMED BASIS IN THE SUPERNATURAL. I'D BEEN TOLD IN A LETTER THAT A DEMONIC BEAST WAS ON THE LOOSE IN LILY DALE.

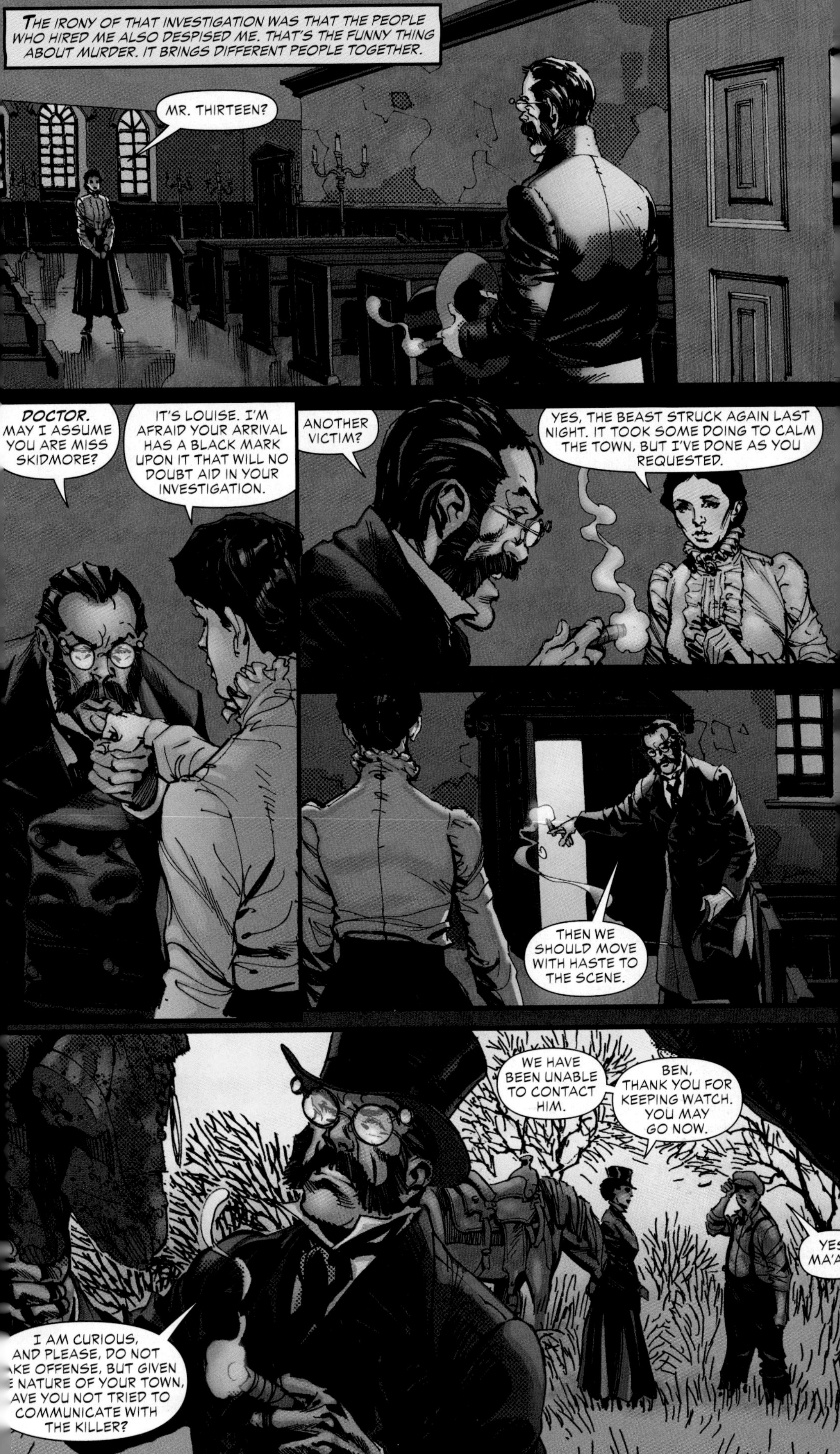
THE IRONY OF THAT INVESTIGATION WAS THAT THE PEOPLE WHO HIRED ME ALSO DESPISED ME. THAT'S THE FUNNY THING ABOUT MURDER. IT BRINGS DIFFERENT PEOPLE TOGETHER.
MR. THIRTEEN?
DOCTOR. MAY I ASSUME YOU ARE MISS SKIDMORE?
IT'S LOUISE. I'M AFRAID YOUR ARRIVAL HAS A BLACK MARK UPON IT THAT WILL NO DOUBT AID IN YOUR INVESTIGATION.
ANOTHER VICTIM?
YES, THE BEAST STRUCK AGAIN LAST NIGHT. IT TOOK SOME DOING TO CALM THE TOWN, BUT I'VE DONE AS YOU REQUESTED.
THEN WE SHOULD MOVE WITH HASTE TO THE SCENE.
I AM CURIOUS, AND PLEASE, DO NOT AKE OFFENSE, BUT GIVEN E NATURE OF YOUR TOWN, AVE YOU NOT TRIED TO COMMUNICATE WITH THE KILLER?
WE HAVE BEEN UNABLE TO CONTACT HIM.
BEN, THANK YOU FOR KEEPING WATCH. YOU MAY GO NOW.
YES MA'A

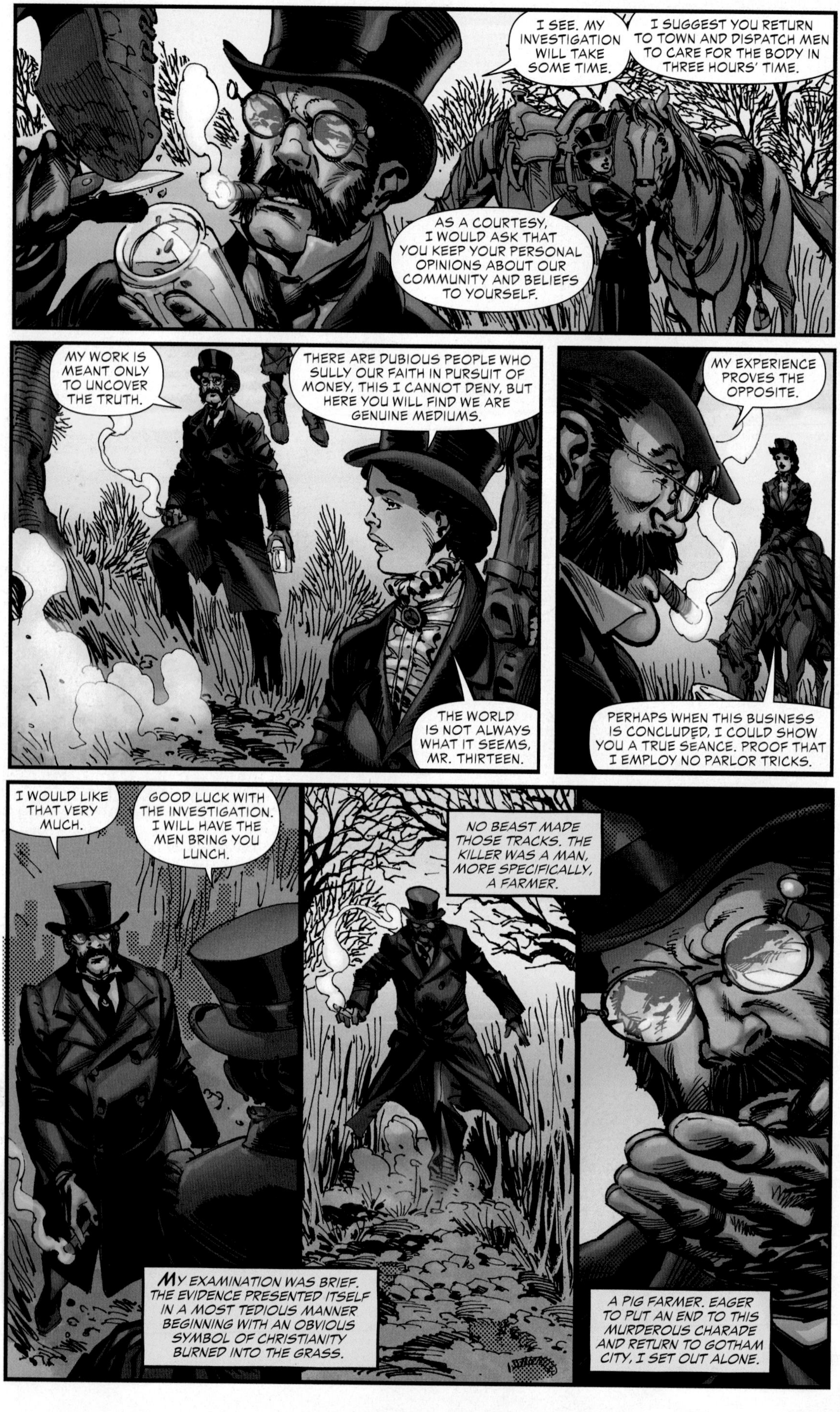
I SEE. MY INVESTIGATION WILL TAKE SOME TIME.
I SUGGEST YOU RETURN TO TOWN AND DISPATCH MEN TO CARE FOR THE BODY IN THREE HOURS' TIME.
AS A COURTESY, I WOULD ASK THAT YOU KEEP YOUR PERSONAL OPINIONS ABOUT OUR COMMUNITY AND BELIEFS TO YOURSELF.
MY WORK IS MEANT ONLY TO UNCOVER THE TRUTH.
THERE ARE DUBIOUS PEOPLE WHO SULLY OUR FAITH IN PURSUIT OF MONEY, THIS I CANNOT DENY, BUT HERE YOU WILL FIND WE ARE GENUINE MEDIUMS.
THE WORLD IS NOT ALWAYS WHAT IT SEEMS, MR. THIRTEEN.
MY EXPERIENCE PROVES THE OPPOSITE.
PERHAPS WHEN THIS BUSINESS IS CONCLUDED, I COULD SHOW YOU A TRUE SEANCE. PROOF THAT I EMPLOY NO PARLOR TRICKS.
I WOULD LIKE THAT VERY MUCH.
GOOD LUCK WITH THE INVESTIGATION. I WILL HAVE THE MEN BRING YOU LUNCH.
MY EXAMINATION WAS BRIEF. THE EVIDENCE PRESENTED ITSELF IN A MOST TEDIOUS MANNER BEGINNING WITH AN OBVIOUS SYMBOL OF CHRISTIANITY BURNED INTO THE GRASS.
NO BEAST MADE THOSE TRACKS. THE KILLER WAS A MAN, MORE SPECIFICALLY, A FARMER.
A PIG FARMER. EAGER TO PUT AN END TO THIS MURDEROUS CHARADE AND RETURN TO GOTHAM CITY, I SET OUT ALONE.

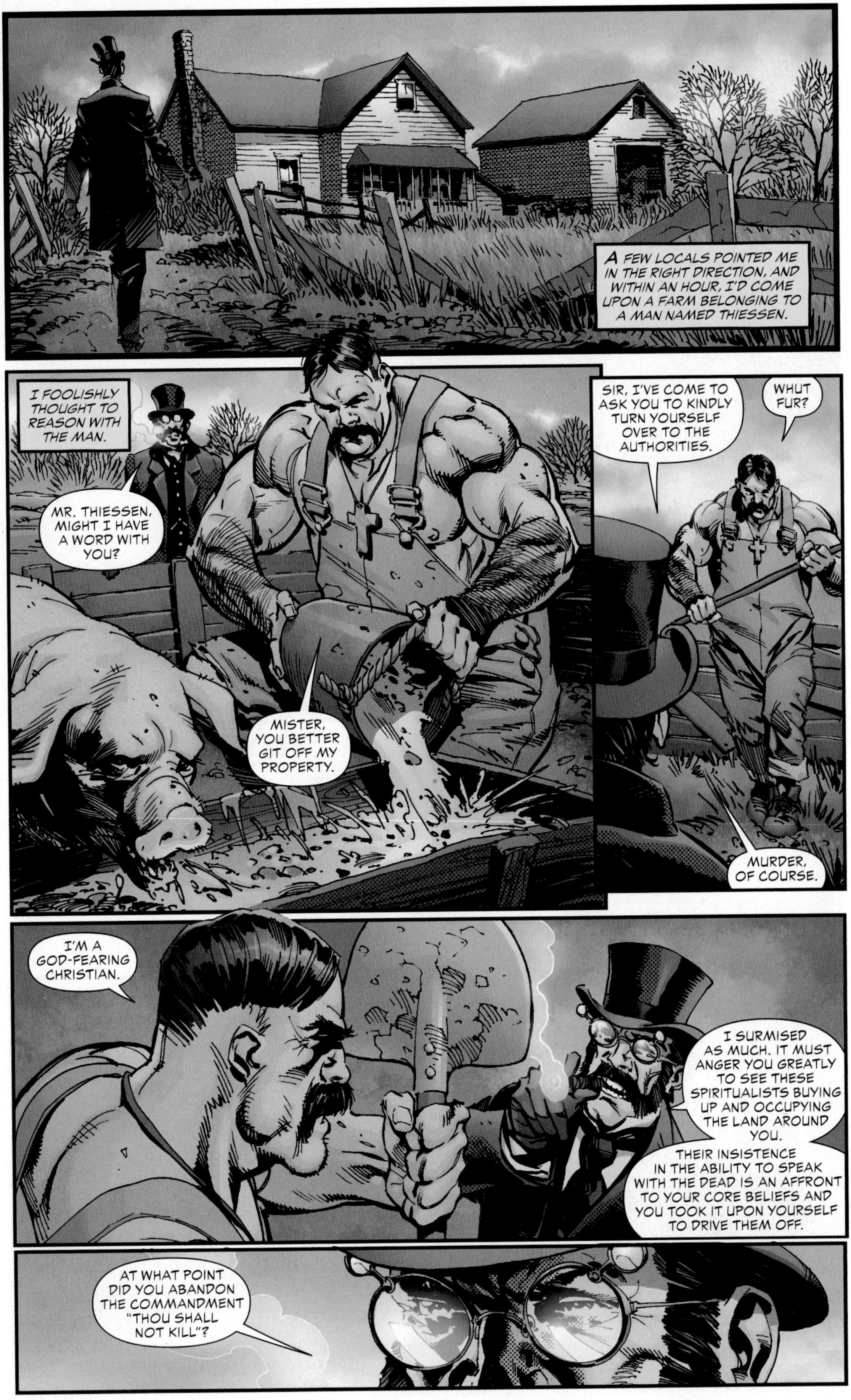
A FEW LOCALS POINTED ME IN THE RIGHT DIRECTION, AND WITHIN AN HOUR, I'D COME UPON A FARM BELONGING TO A MAN NAMED THIESSEN.
I FOOLISHLY THOUGHT TO REASON WITH THE MAN.
MR. THIESSEN, MIGHT I HAVE A WORD WITH YOU?
MISTER, YOU BETTER GIT OFF MY PROPERTY.
SIR, I'VE COME TO ASK YOU TO KINDLY TURN YOURSELF OVER TO THE AUTHORITIES.
WHUT FUR?
MURDER, OF COURSE.
I'M A GOD-FEARING CHRISTIAN.
I SURMISED AS MUCH. IT MUST ANGER YOU GREATLY TO SEE THESE SPIRITUALISTS BUYING UP AND OCCUPYING THE LAND AROUND YOU.
THEIR INSISTENCE IN THE ABILITY TO SPEAK WITH THE DEAD IS AN AFFRONT TO YOUR CORE BELIEFS AND YOU TOOK IT UPON YOURSELF TO DRIVE THEM OFF.
AT WHAT POINT DID YOU ABANDON THE COMMANDMENT "THOU SHALL NOT KILL"?

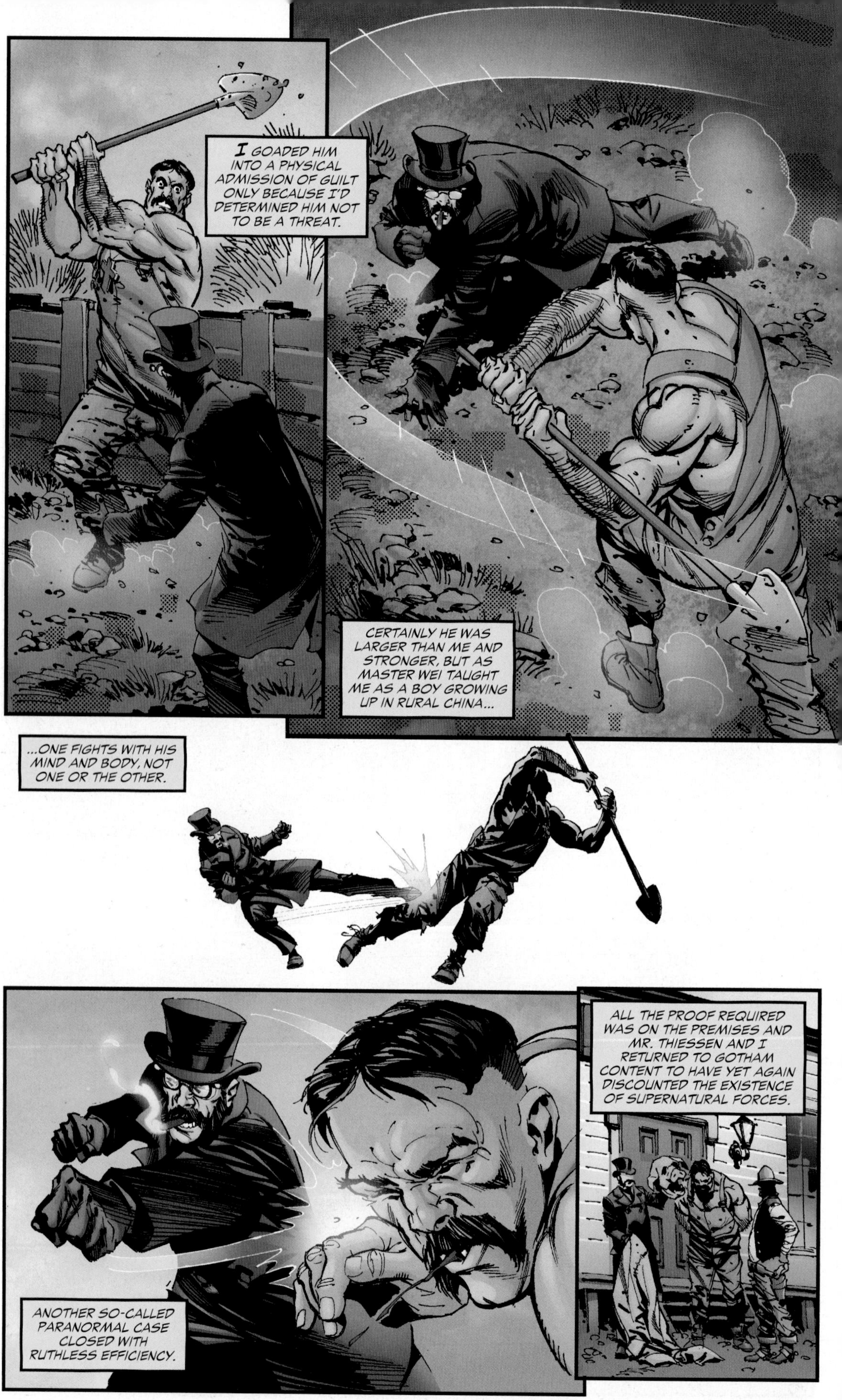
I GOADED HIM INTO A PHYSICAL ADMISSION OF GUILT ONLY BECAUSE I'D DETERMINED HIM NOT TO BE A THREAT.
CERTAINLY HE WAS LARGER THAN ME AND STRONGER, BUT AS MASTER WEI TAUGHT ME AS A BOY GROWING UP IN RURAL CHINA...
...ONE FIGHTS WITH HIS MIND AND BODY, NOT ONE OR THE OTHER.
ANOTHER SO-CALLED PARANORMAL CASE CLOSED WITH RUTHLESS EFFICIENCY.
ALL THE PROOF REQUIRED WAS ON THE PREMISES AND MR. THIESSEN AND I RETURNED TO GOTHAM CONTENT TO HAVE YET AGAIN DISCOUNTED THE EXISTENCE OF SUPERNATURAL FORCES.

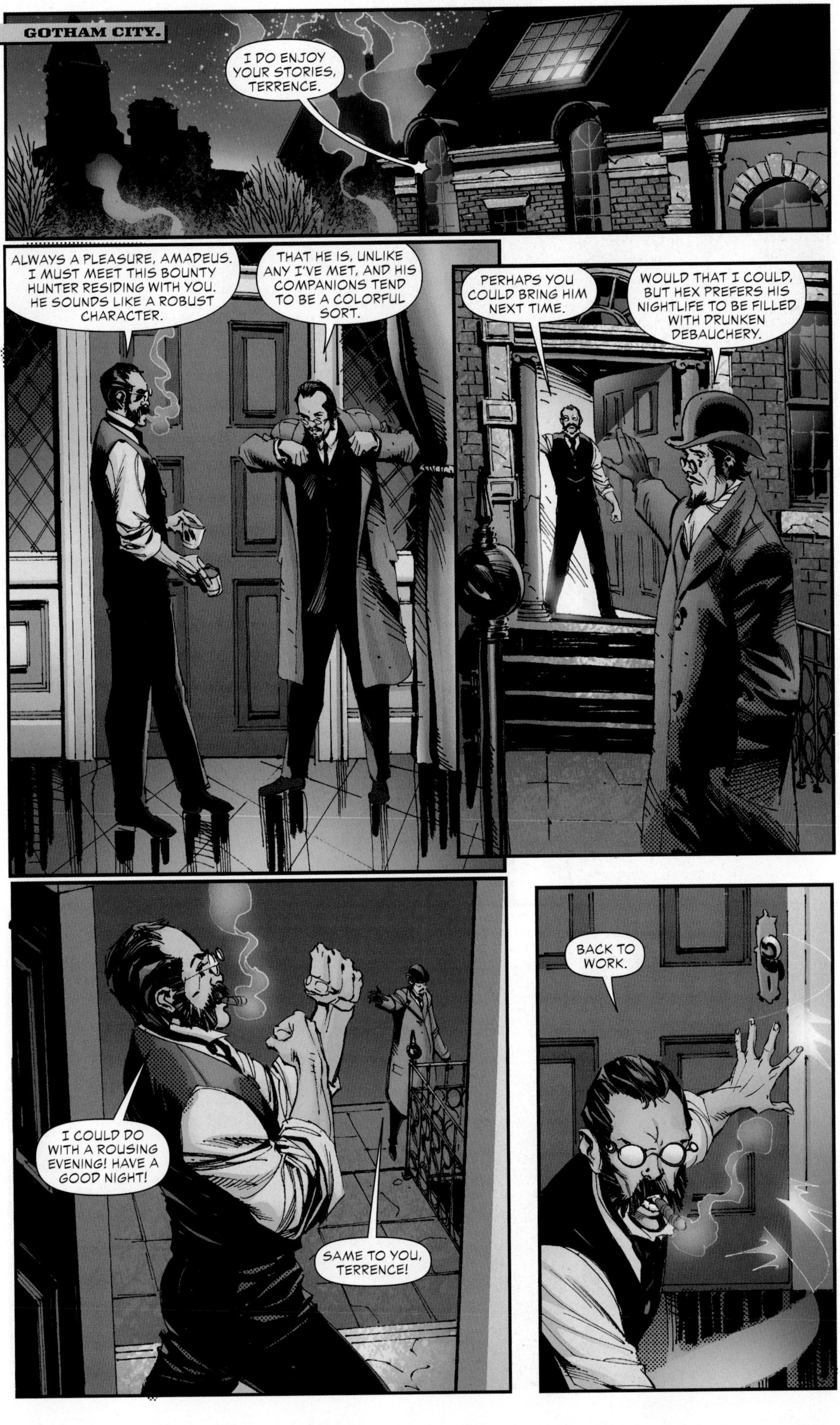
GOTHAM CITY.
I DO ENJOY YOUR STORIES, TERRENCE.
ALWAYS A PLEASURE, AMADEUS. I MUST MEET THIS BOUNTY HUNTER RESIDING WITH YOU. HE SOUNDS LIKE A ROBUST CHARACTER.
THAT HE IS, UNLIKE ANY I'VE MET, AND HIS COMPANIONS TEND TO BE A COLORFUL SORT.
PERHAPS YOU COULD BRING HIM NEXT TIME.
WOULD THAT I COULD, BUT HEX PREFERS HIS NIGHTLIFE TO BE FILLED WITH DRUNKEN DEBAUCHERY.
I COULD DO WITH A ROUSING EVENING! HAVE A GOOD NIGHT!
SAME TO YOU, TERRENCE!
BACK TO WORK.

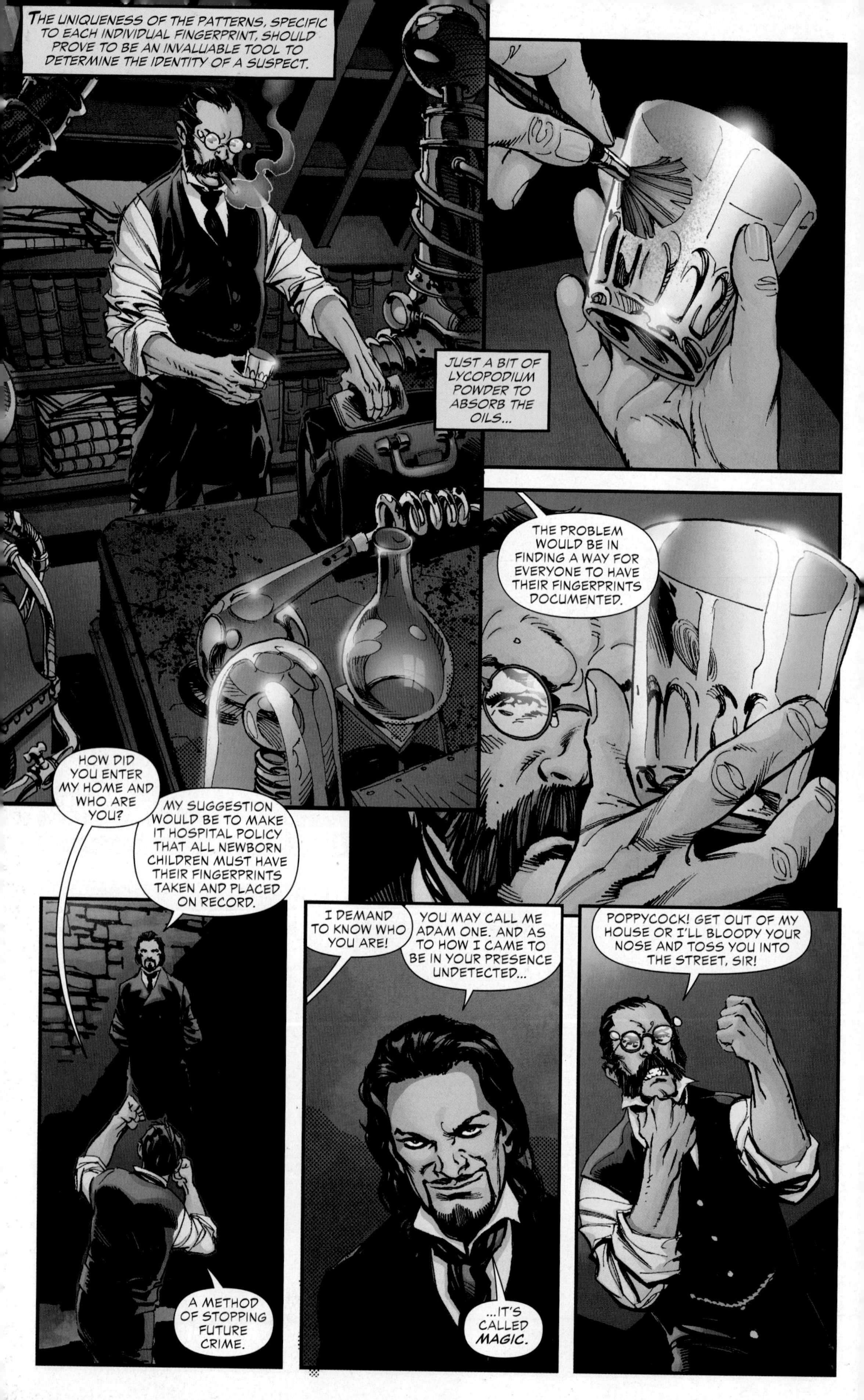

THE UNIQUENESS OF THE PATTERNS, SPECIFIC TO EACH INDIVIDUAL FINGERPRINT, SHOULD PROVE TO BE AN INVALUABLE TOOL TO DETERMINE THE IDENTITY OF A SUSPECT.
JUST A BIT OF LYCOPODIUM POWDER TO ABSORB THE OILS...
THE PROBLEM WOULD BE IN FINDING A WAY FOR EVERYONE TO HAVE THEIR FINGERPRINTS DOCUMENTED.
HOW DID YOU ENTER MY HOME AND WHO ARE YOU?
MY SUGGESTION WOULD BE TO MAKE IT HOSPITAL POLICY THAT ALL NEWBORN CHILDREN MUST HAVE THEIR FINGERPRINTS TAKEN AND PLACED ON RECORD.
A METHOD OF STOPPING FUTURE CRIME.
I DEMAND TO KNOW WHO YOU ARE!
YOU MAY CALL ME ADAM ONE. AND AS TO HOW I CAME TO BE IN YOUR PRESENCE UNDETECTED...
...IT'S CALLED *MAGIC*.
POPPYCOCK! GET OUT OF MY HOUSE OR I'LL BLOODY YOUR NOSE AND TOSS YOU INTO THE STREET, SIR!

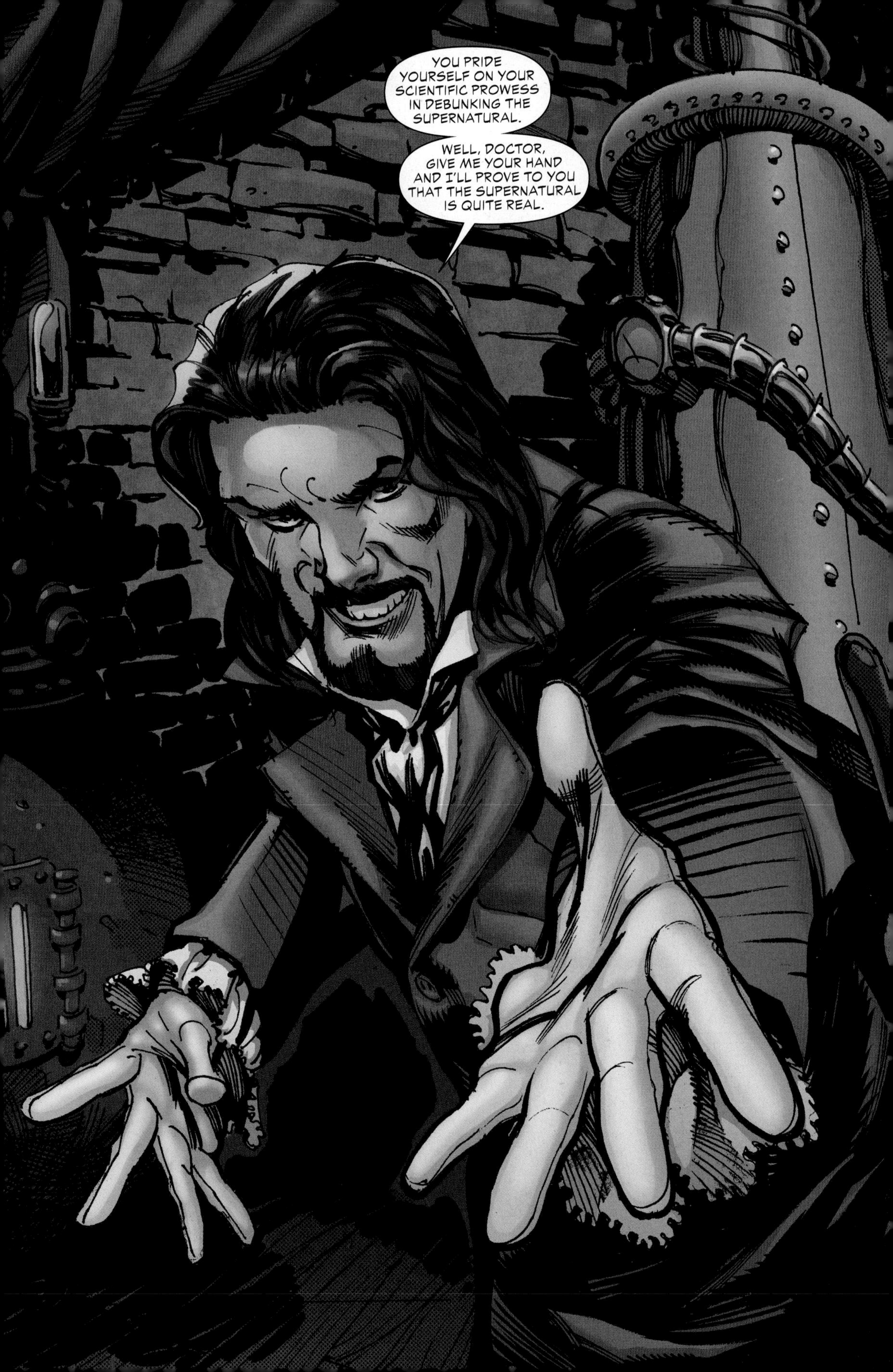
YOU PRIDE YOURSELF ON YOUR SCIENTIFIC PROWESS IN DEBUNKING THE SUPERNATURAL.
WELL, DOCTOR, GIVE ME YOUR HAND AND I'LL PROVE TO YOU THAT THE SUPERNATURAL IS QUITE REAL.

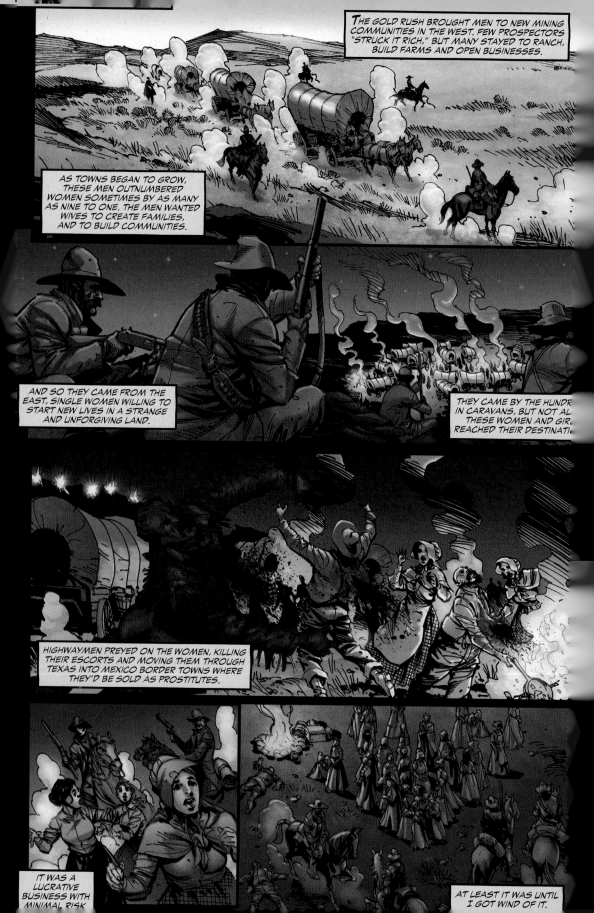

THE GOLD RUSH BROUGHT MEN TO NEW MINING COMMUNITIES IN THE WEST. FEW PROSPECTORS "STRUCK IT RICH," BUT MANY STAYED TO RANCH, BUILD FARMS AND OPEN BUSINESSES.

AS TOWNS BEGAN TO GROW, THESE MEN OUTNUMBERED WOMEN SOMETIMES BY AS MANY AS NINE TO ONE. THE MEN WANTED WIVES TO CREATE FAMILIES, AND TO BUILD COMMUNITIES.

AND SO THEY CAME FROM THE EAST, SINGLE WOMEN WILLING TO START NEW LIVES IN A STRANGE AND UNFORGIVING LAND.

THEY CAME BY THE HUNDR[E] IN CARAVANS, BUT NOT AL[L] THESE WOMEN AND GIR[LS] REACHED THEIR DESTINATI[ON]

HIGHWAYMEN PREYED ON THE WOMEN, KILLING THEIR ESCORTS AND MOVING THEM THROUGH TEXAS INTO MEXICO BORDER TOWNS WHERE THEY'D BE SOLD AS PROSTITUTES.

IT WAS A LUCRATIVE BUSINESS WITH MINIMAL RISK

AT LEAST IT WAS UNTIL I GOT WIND OF IT.

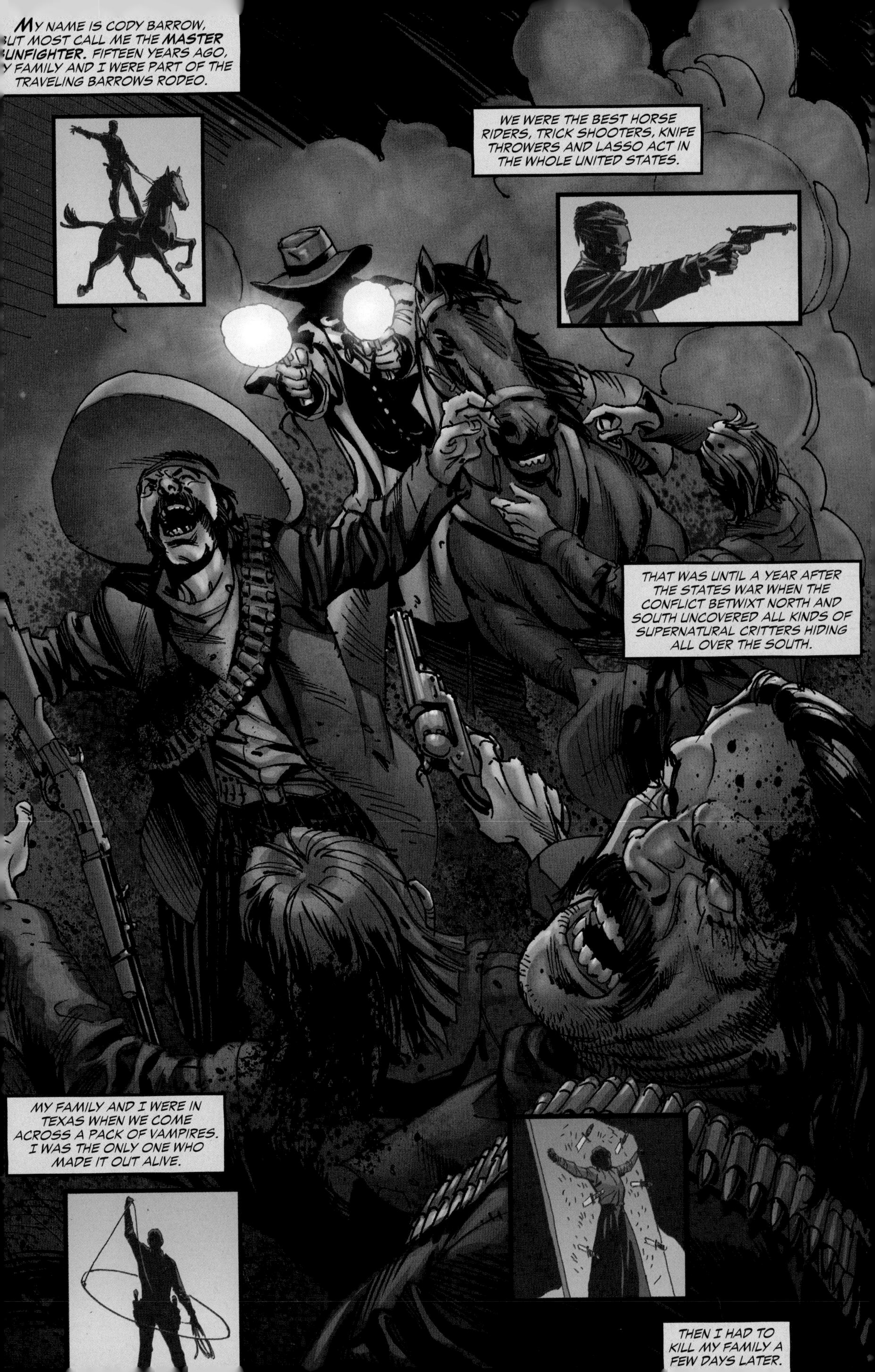
MY NAME IS CODY BARROW,
UT MOST CALL ME THE MASTER
UNFIGHTER. FIFTEEN YEARS AGO,
Y FAMILY AND I WERE PART OF THE
TRAVELING BARROWS RODEO.
WE WERE THE BEST HORSE RIDERS, TRICK SHOOTERS, KNIFE THROWERS AND LASSO ACT IN THE WHOLE UNITED STATES.
THAT WAS UNTIL A YEAR AFTER THE STATES WAR WHEN THE CONFLICT BETWIXT NORTH AND SOUTH UNCOVERED ALL KINDS OF SUPERNATURAL CRITTERS HIDING ALL OVER THE SOUTH.
MY FAMILY AND I WERE IN TEXAS WHEN WE COME ACROSS A PACK OF VAMPIRES. I WAS THE ONLY ONE WHO MADE IT OUT ALIVE.
THEN I HAD TO KILL MY FAMILY A FEW DAYS LATER.

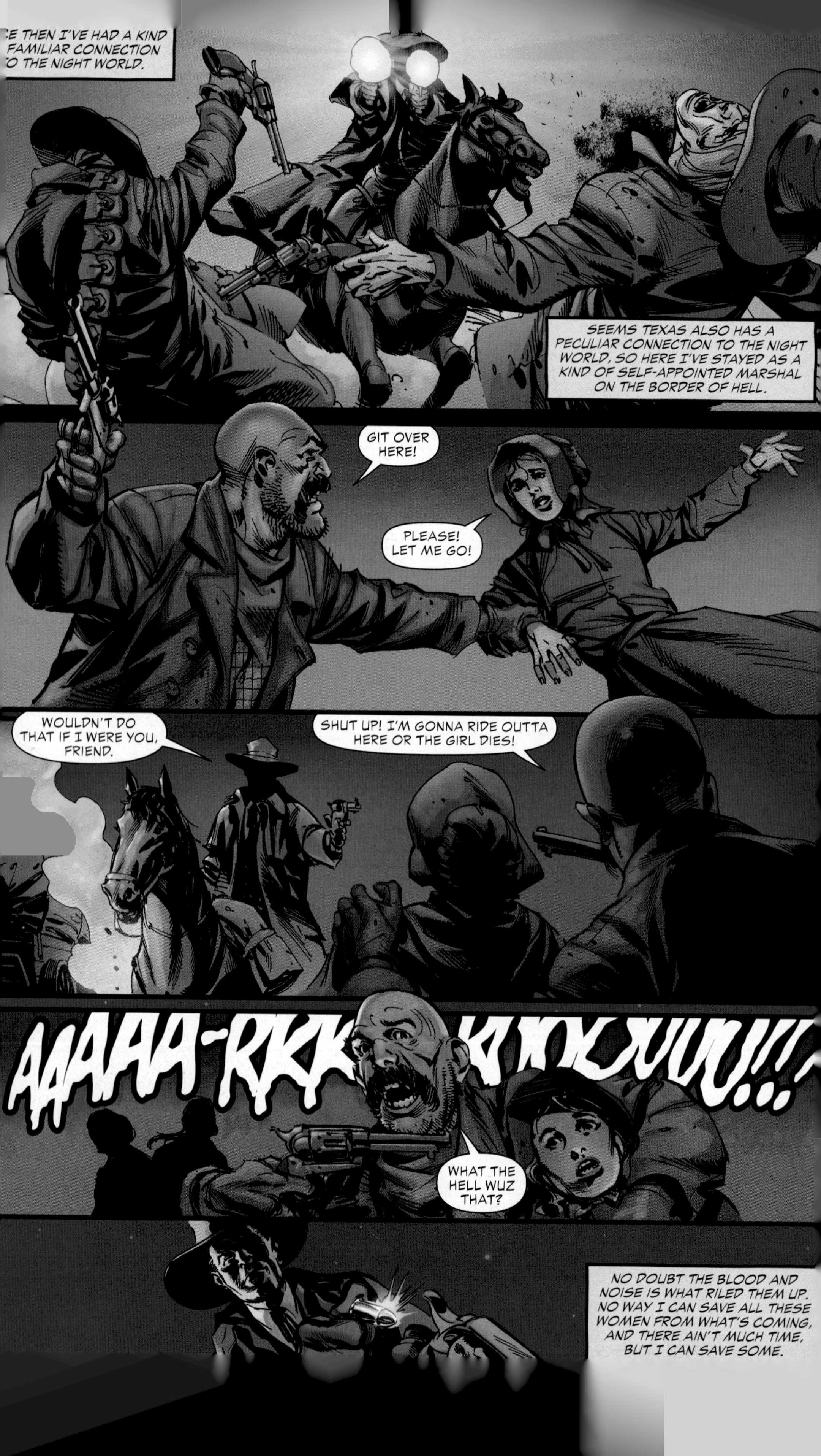

E THEN I'VE HAD A KIND FAMILIAR CONNECTION TO THE NIGHT WORLD.
SEEMS TEXAS ALSO HAS A PECULIAR CONNECTION TO THE NIGHT WORLD, SO HERE I'VE STAYED AS A KIND OF SELF-APPOINTED MARSHAL ON THE BORDER OF HELL.
GIT OVER HERE!
PLEASE! LET ME GO!
WOULDN'T DO THAT IF I WERE YOU, FRIEND.
SHUT UP! I'M GONNA RIDE OUTTA HERE OR THE GIRL DIES!
AAAAA-RKK
WHAT THE HELL WUZ THAT?
NO DOUBT THE BLOOD AND NOISE IS WHAT RILED THEM UP. NO WAY I CAN SAVE ALL THESE WOMEN FROM WHAT'S COMING, AND THERE AIN'T MUCH TIME, BUT I CAN SAVE SOME.

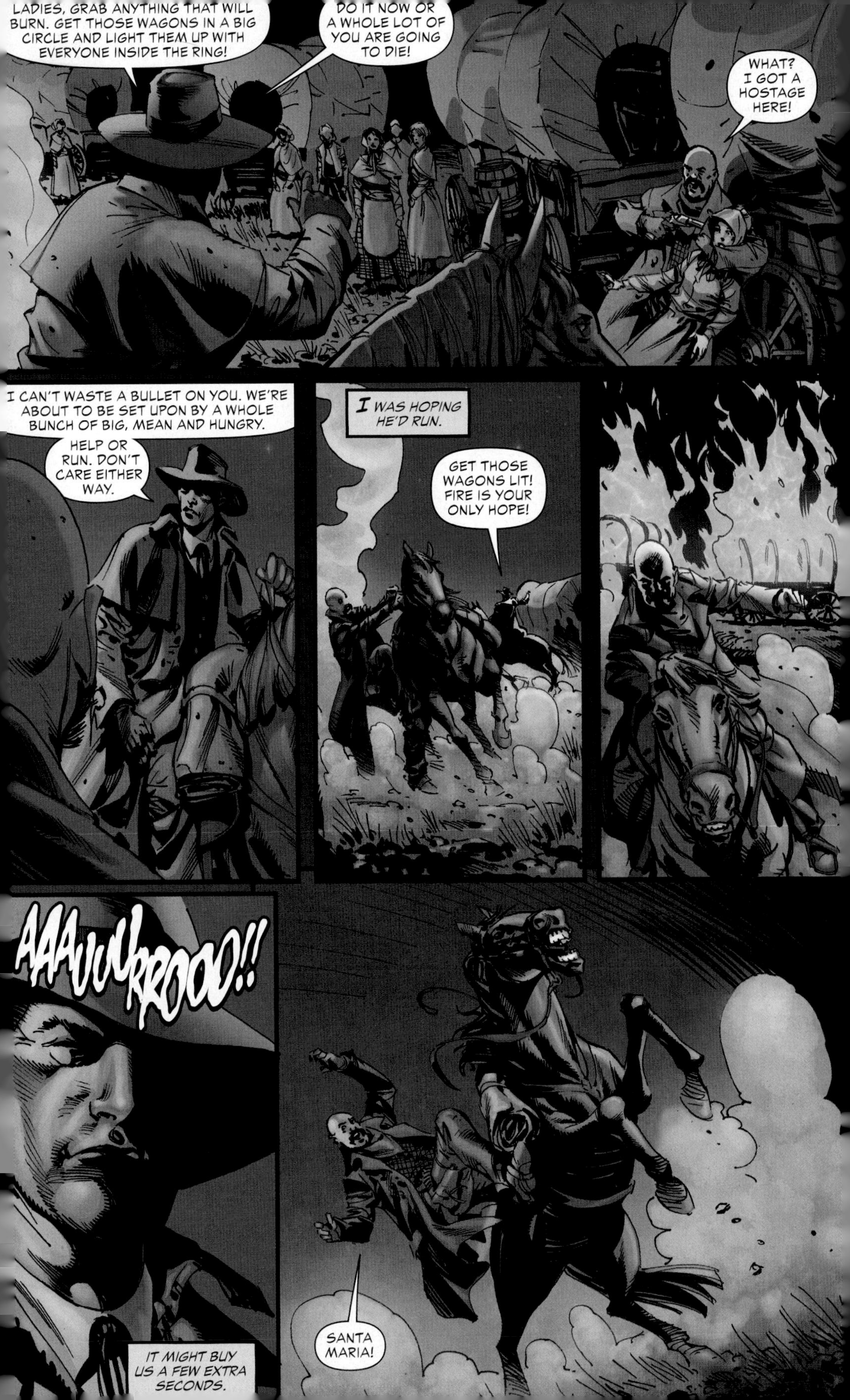

LADIES, GRAB ANYTHING THAT WILL BURN. GET THOSE WAGONS IN A BIG CIRCLE AND LIGHT THEM UP WITH EVERYONE INSIDE THE RING!
DO IT NOW OR A WHOLE LOT OF YOU ARE GOING TO DIE!
WHAT? I GOT A HOSTAGE HERE!
I CAN'T WASTE A BULLET ON YOU. WE'RE ABOUT TO BE SET UPON BY A WHOLE BUNCH OF BIG, MEAN AND HUNGRY.
HELP OR RUN. DON'T CARE EITHER WAY.
I WAS HOPING HE'D RUN.
GET THOSE WAGONS LIT! FIRE IS YOUR ONLY HOPE!
AAAVUURROOO!!
SANTA MARIA!
IT MIGHT BUY US A FEW EXTRA SECONDS.

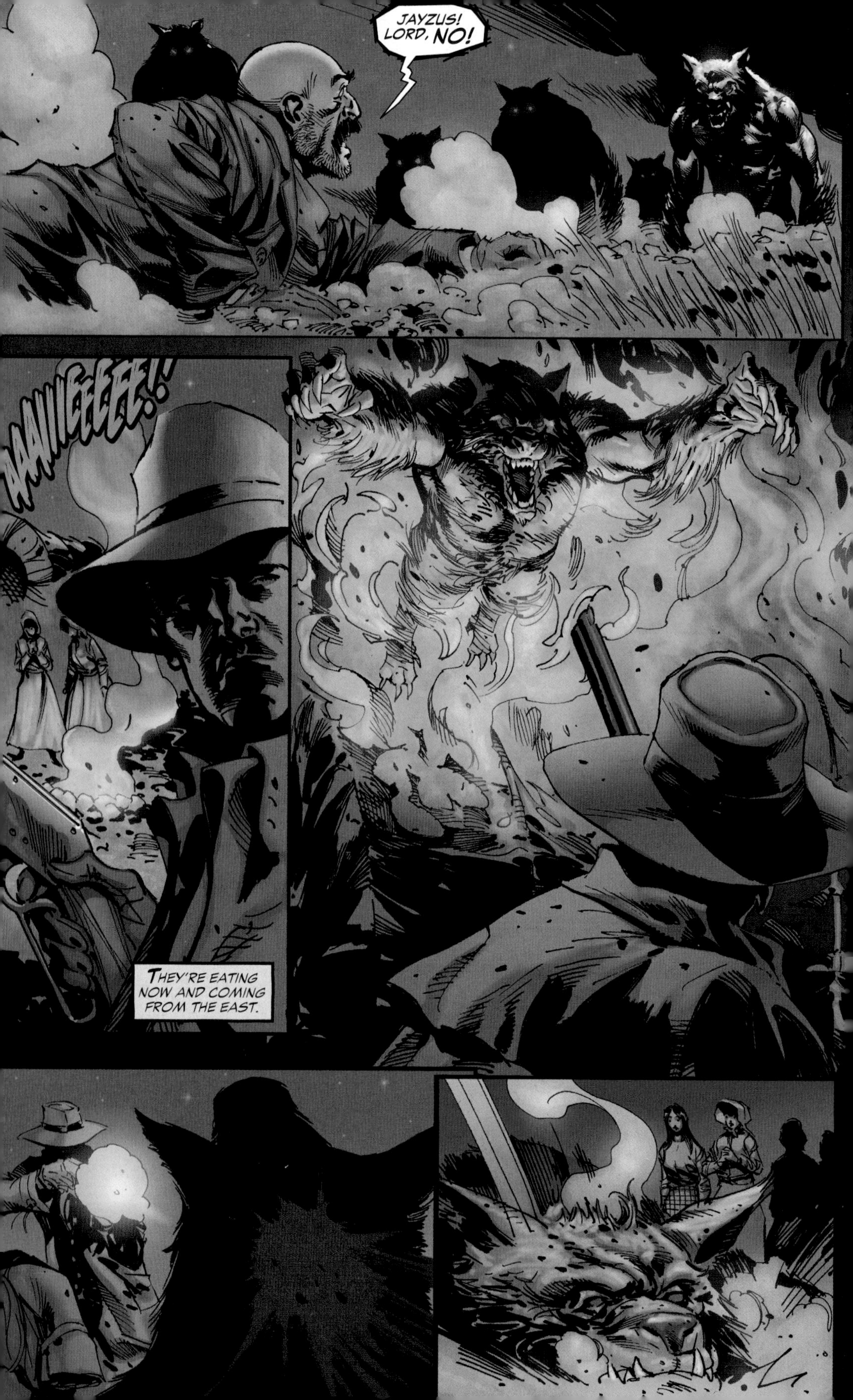

JAYZUS! LORD, NO!
AAIIIEEEEE!!
THEY'RE EATING NOW AND COMING FROM THE EAST.

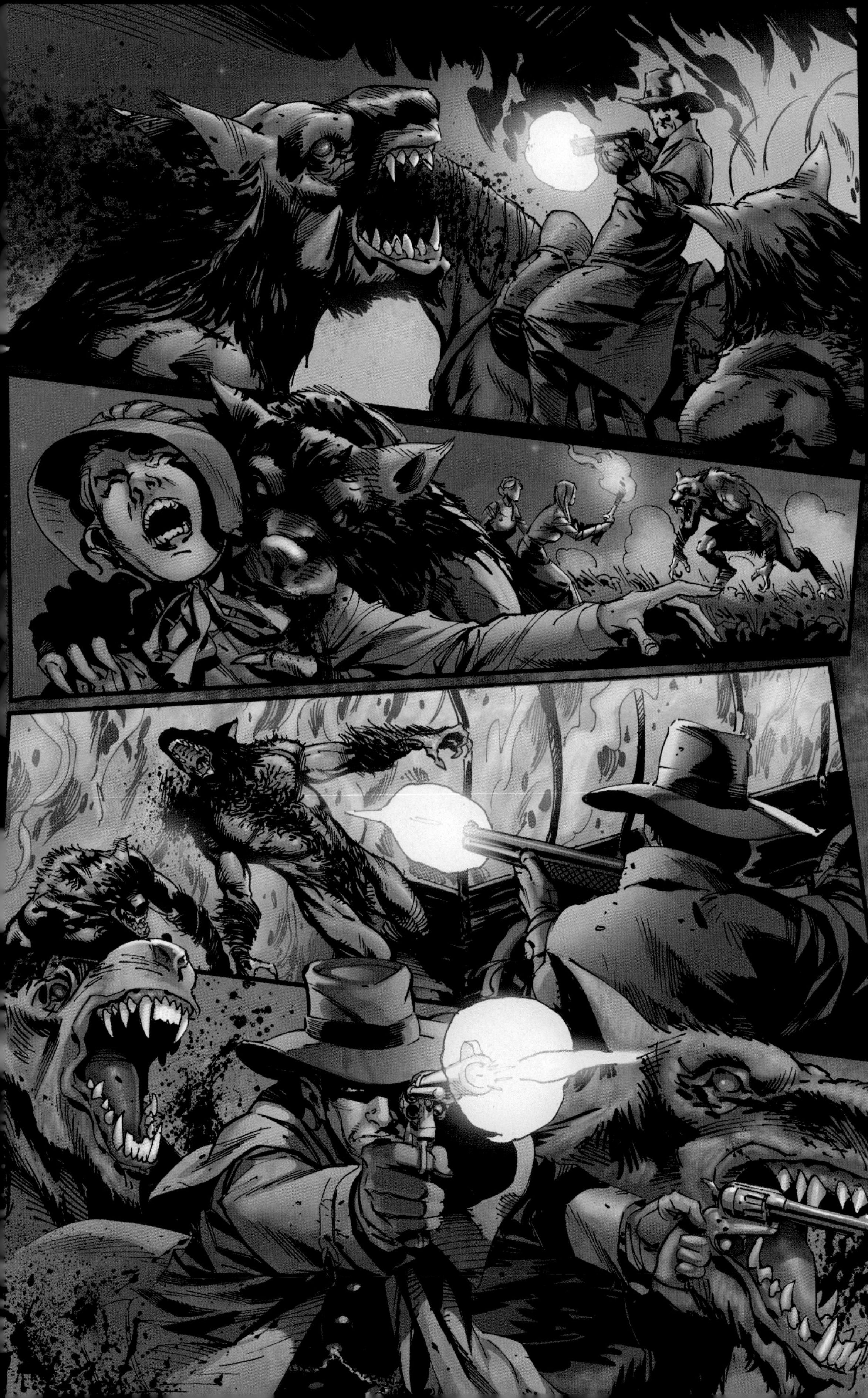

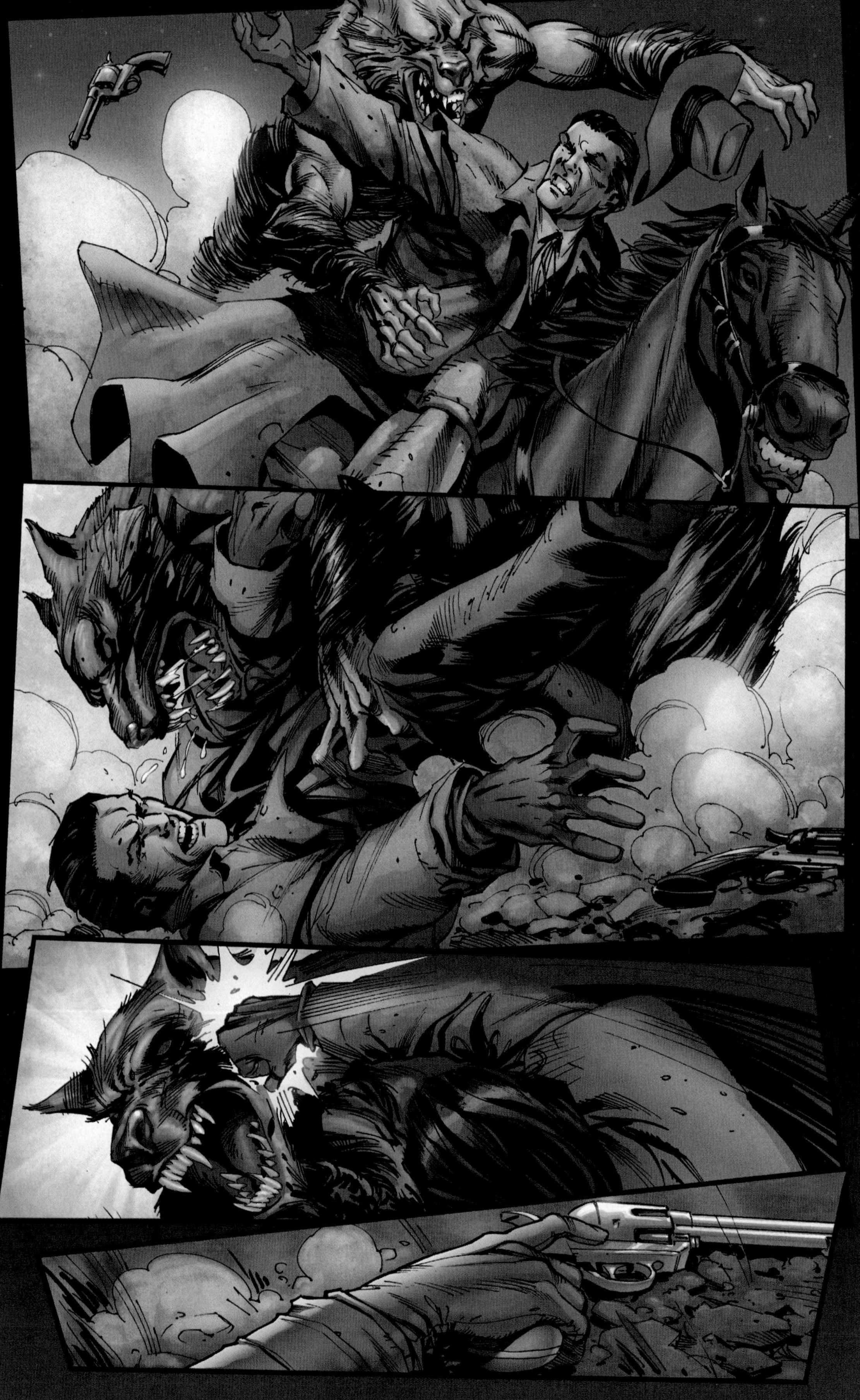

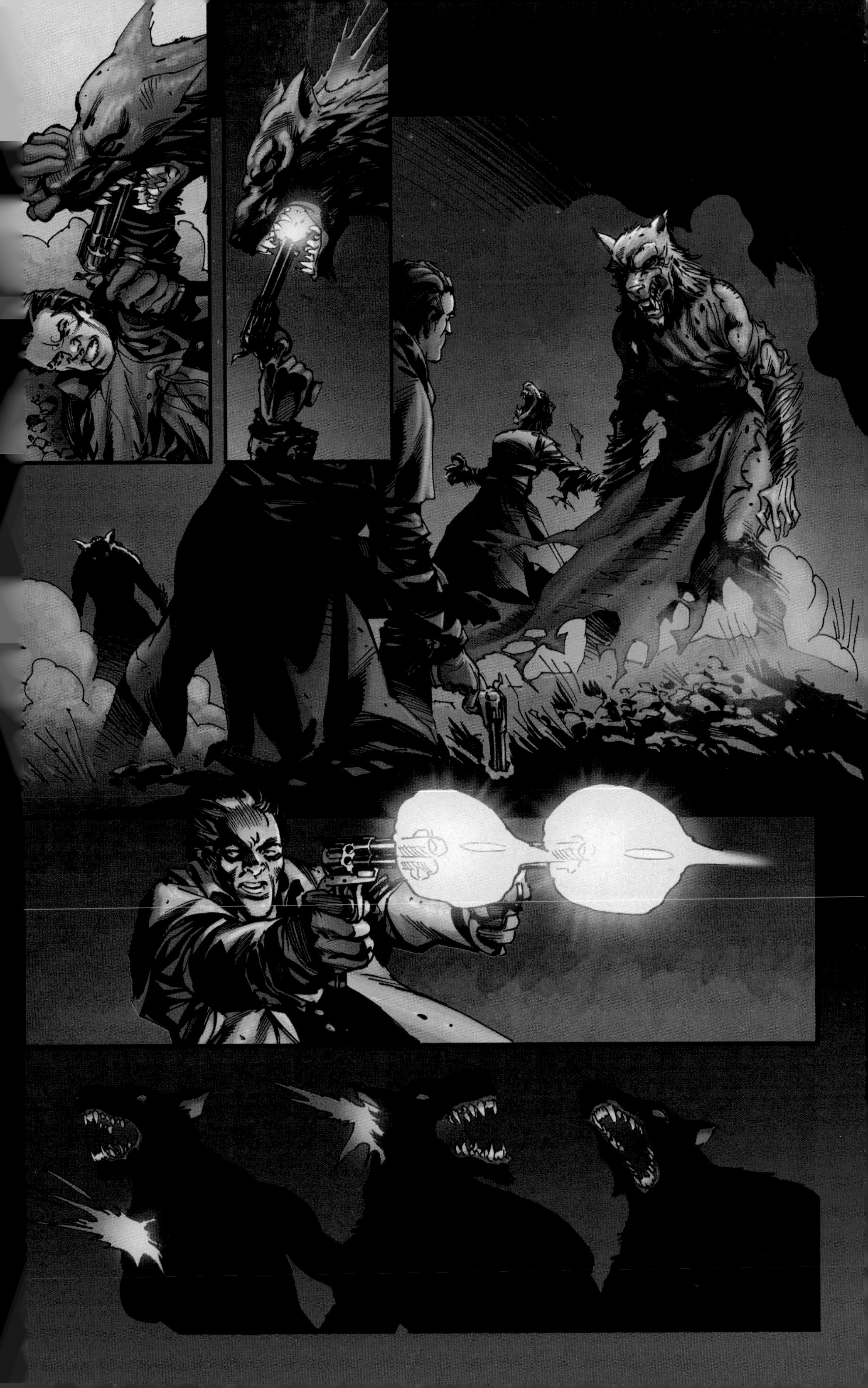

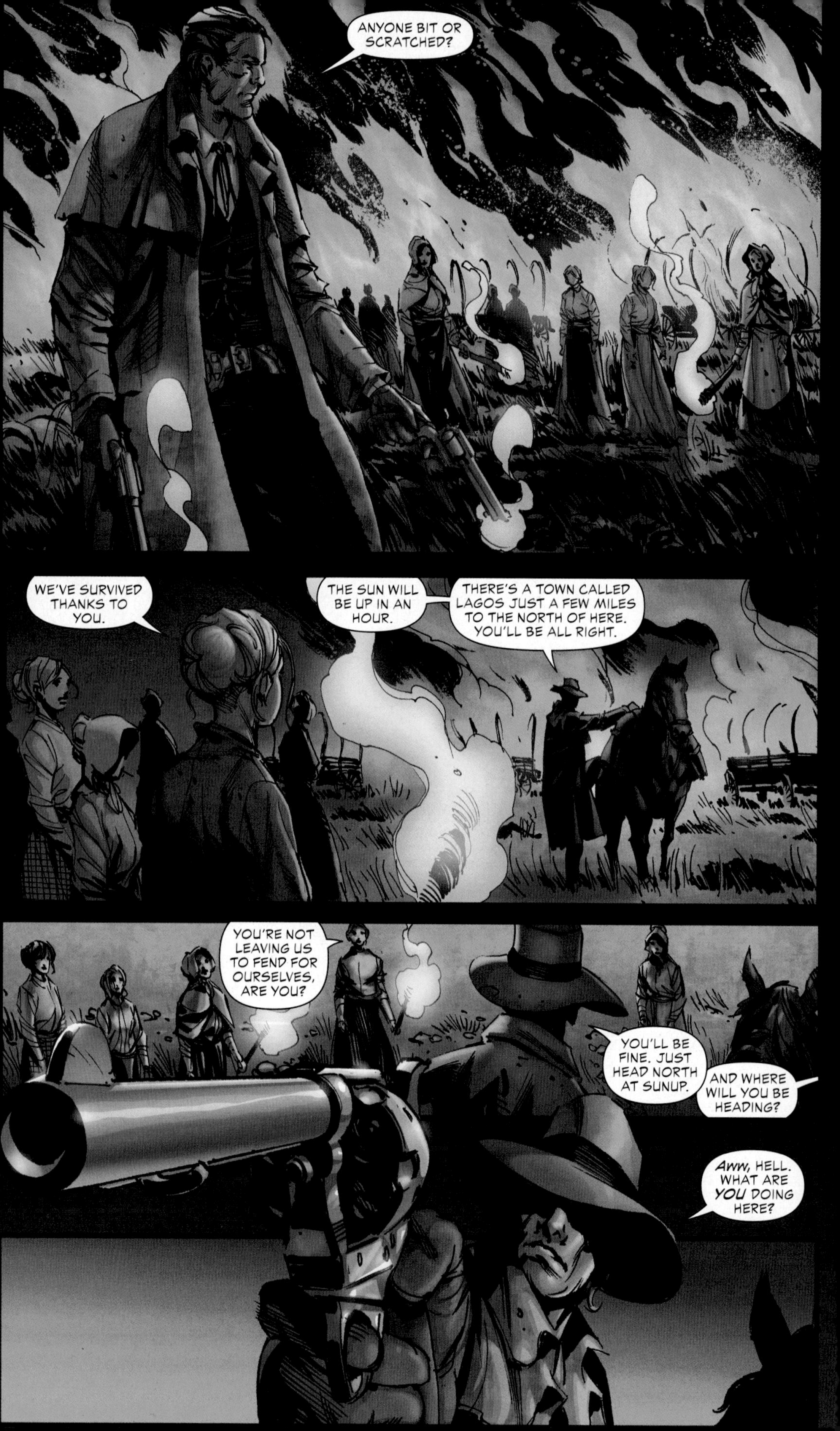
ANYONE BIT OR SCRATCHED?
WE'VE SURVIVED THANKS TO YOU.
THE SUN WILL BE UP IN AN HOUR.
THERE'S A TOWN CALLED LAGOS JUST A FEW MILES TO THE NORTH OF HERE. YOU'LL BE ALL RIGHT.
YOU'RE NOT LEAVING US TO FEND FOR OURSELVES, ARE YOU?
YOU'LL BE FINE. JUST HEAD NORTH AT SUNUP.
AND WHERE WILL YOU BE HEADING?
Aww, HELL. WHAT ARE *YOU* DOING HERE?

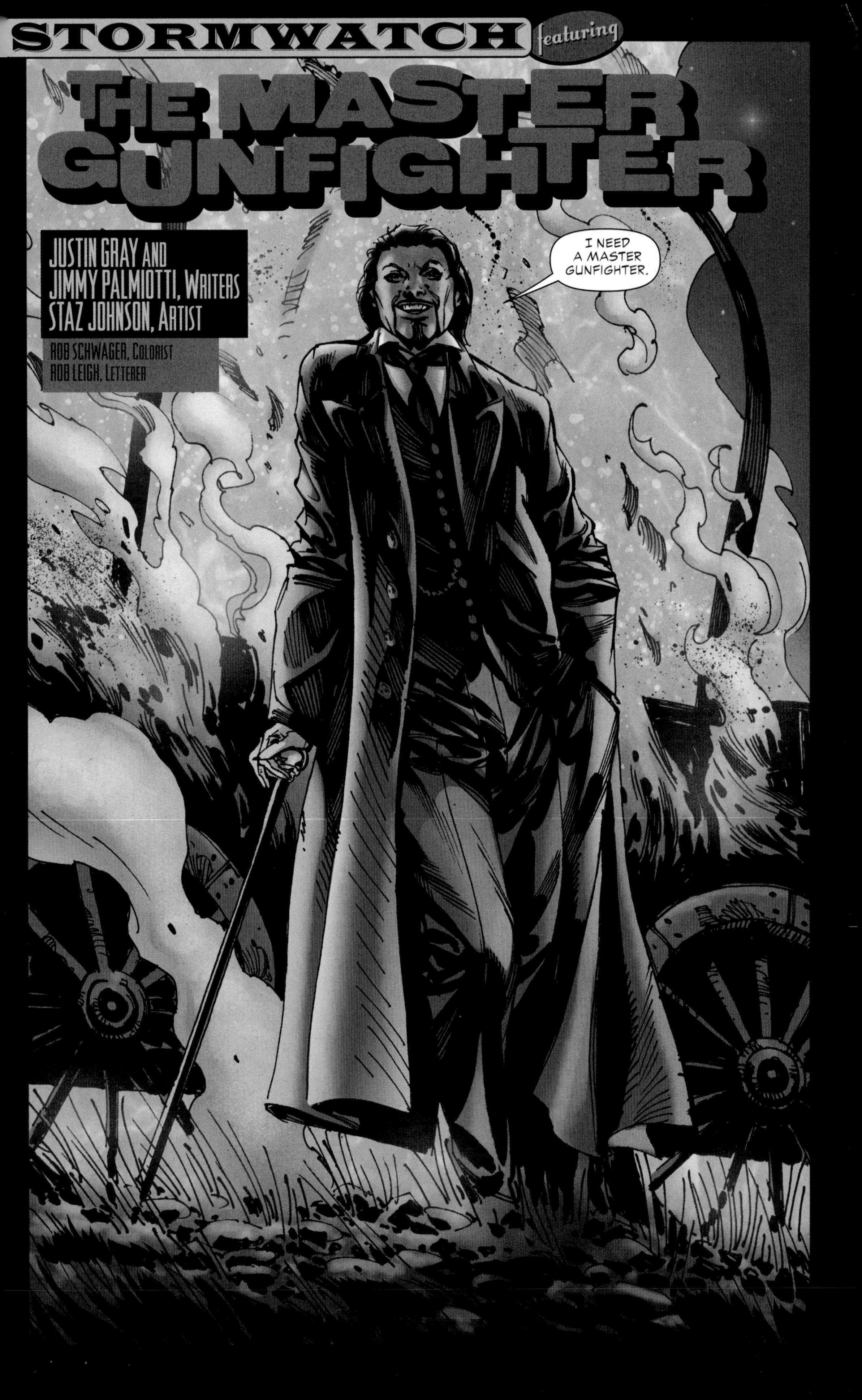
STORMWATCH featuring
THE MASTER GUNFIGHTER
JUSTIN GRAY AND JIMMY PALMIOTTI, WRITERS
STAZ JOHNSON, ARTIST
ROB SCHWAGER, COLORIST
ROB LEIGH, LETTERER
I NEED A MASTER GUNFIGHTER.

STORMWATCH

The LOST CITY of GOLD

JIMMY PALMIOTTI and JUSTIN GRAY, Writers · STAZ JOHNSON, Artist · ROB SCHWAGER, Colorist · ROB LEIGH, Letterer

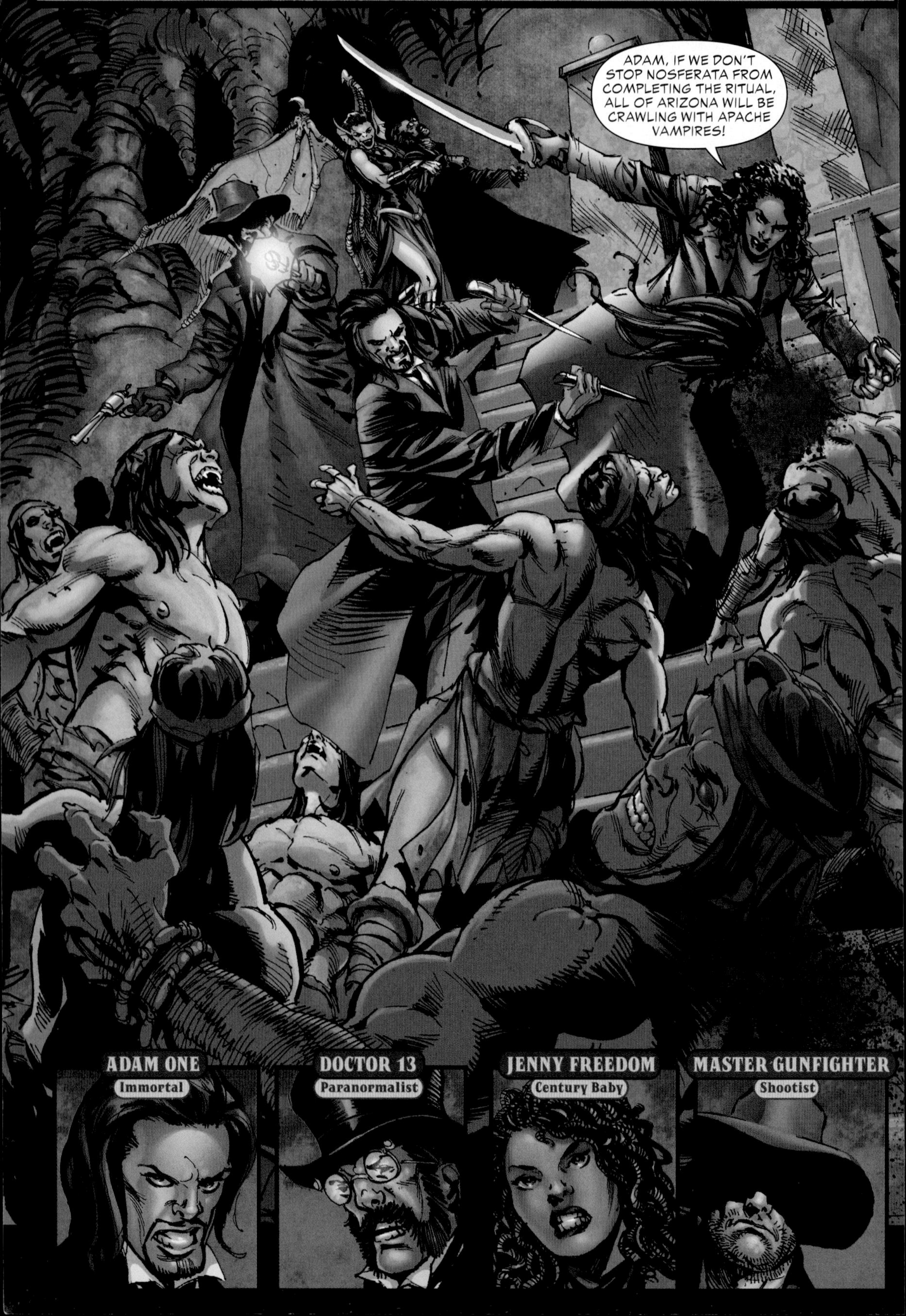

ADAM, IF WE DON'T STOP NOSFERATA FROM COMPLETING THE RITUAL, ALL OF ARIZONA WILL BE CRAWLING WITH APACHE VAMPIRES!
ADAM ONE
Immortal
DOCTOR 13
Paranormalist
JENNY FREEDOM
Century Baby
MASTER GUNFIGHTER
Shootist

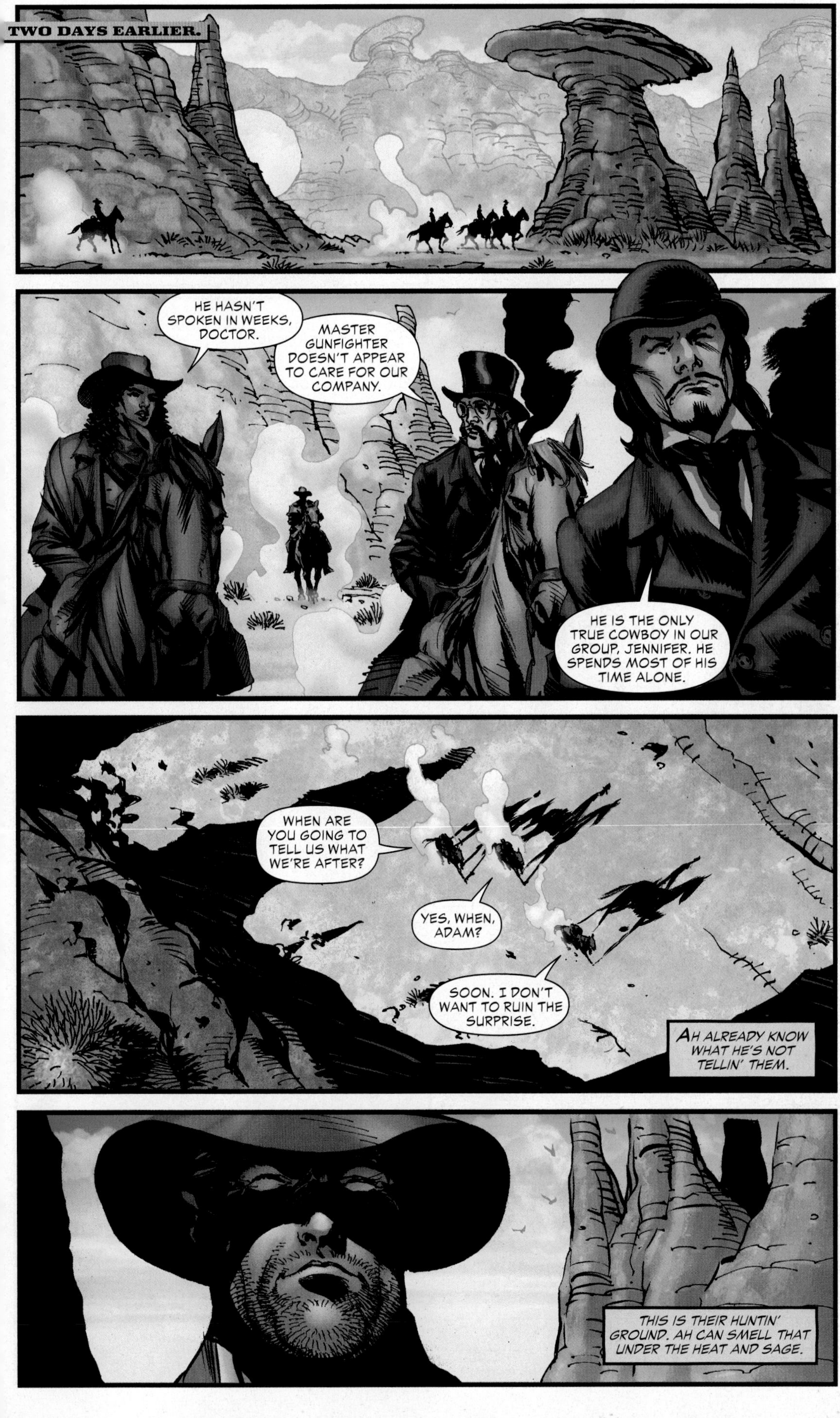
TWO DAYS EARLIER.
HE HASN'T SPOKEN IN WEEKS, DOCTOR.
MASTER GUNFIGHTER DOESN'T APPEAR TO CARE FOR OUR COMPANY.
HE IS THE ONLY TRUE COWBOY IN OUR GROUP, JENNIFER. HE SPENDS MOST OF HIS TIME ALONE.
WHEN ARE YOU GOING TO TELL US WHAT WE'RE AFTER?
YES, WHEN, ADAM?
SOON. I DON'T WANT TO RUIN THE SURPRISE.
AH ALREADY KNOW WHAT HE'S NOT TELLIN' THEM.
THIS IS THEIR HUNTIN' GROUND. AH CAN SMELL THAT UNDER THE HEAT AND SAGE.

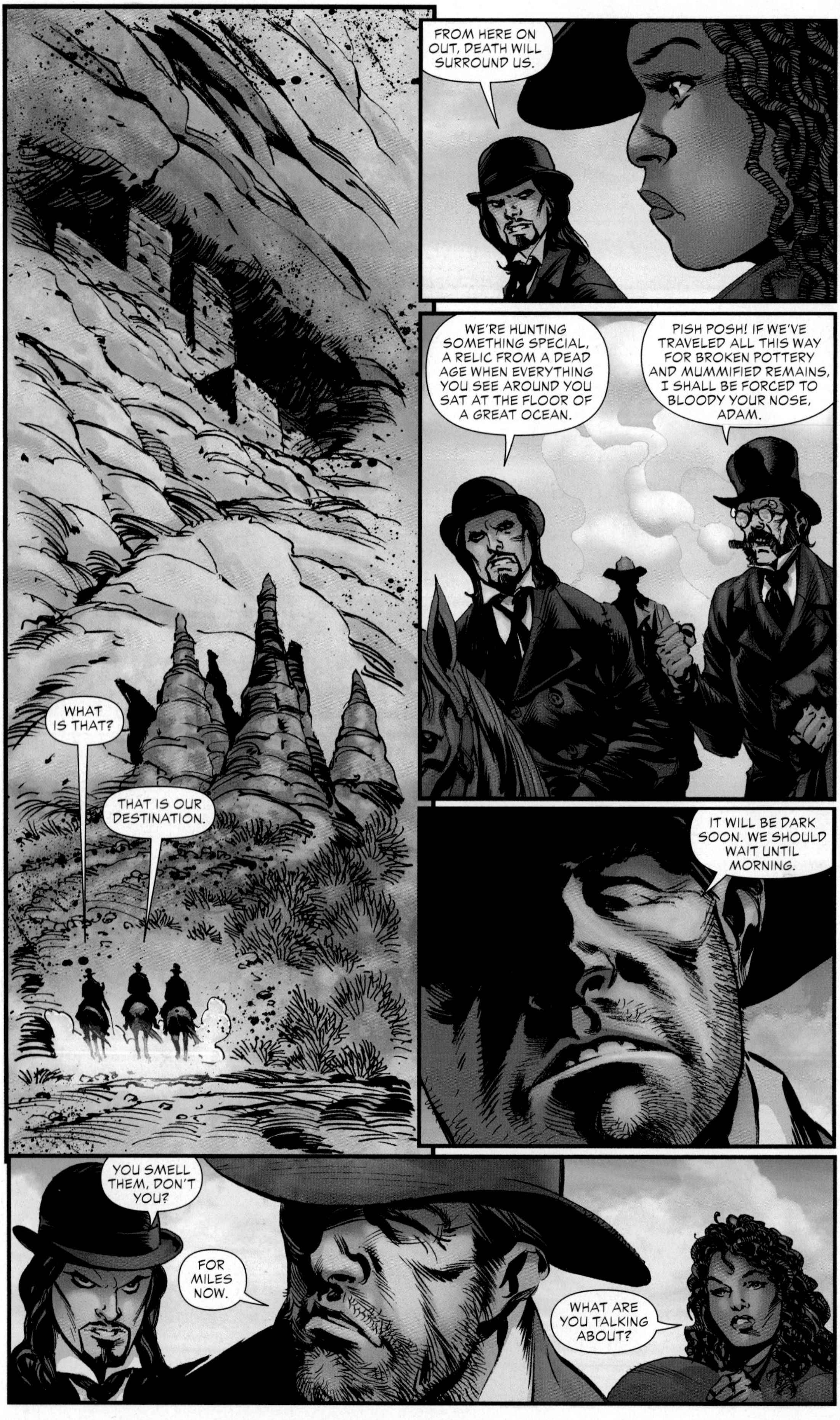
WHAT IS THAT?
THAT IS OUR DESTINATION.
FROM HERE ON OUT, DEATH WILL SURROUND US.
WE'RE HUNTING SOMETHING SPECIAL, A RELIC FROM A DEAD AGE WHEN EVERYTHING YOU SEE AROUND YOU SAT AT THE FLOOR OF A GREAT OCEAN.
PISH POSH! IF WE'VE TRAVELED ALL THIS WAY FOR BROKEN POTTERY AND MUMMIFIED REMAINS, I SHALL BE FORCED TO BLOODY YOUR NOSE, ADAM.
IT WILL BE DARK SOON. WE SHOULD WAIT UNTIL MORNING.
YOU SMELL THEM, DON'T YOU?
FOR MILES NOW.
WHAT ARE YOU TALKING ABOUT?

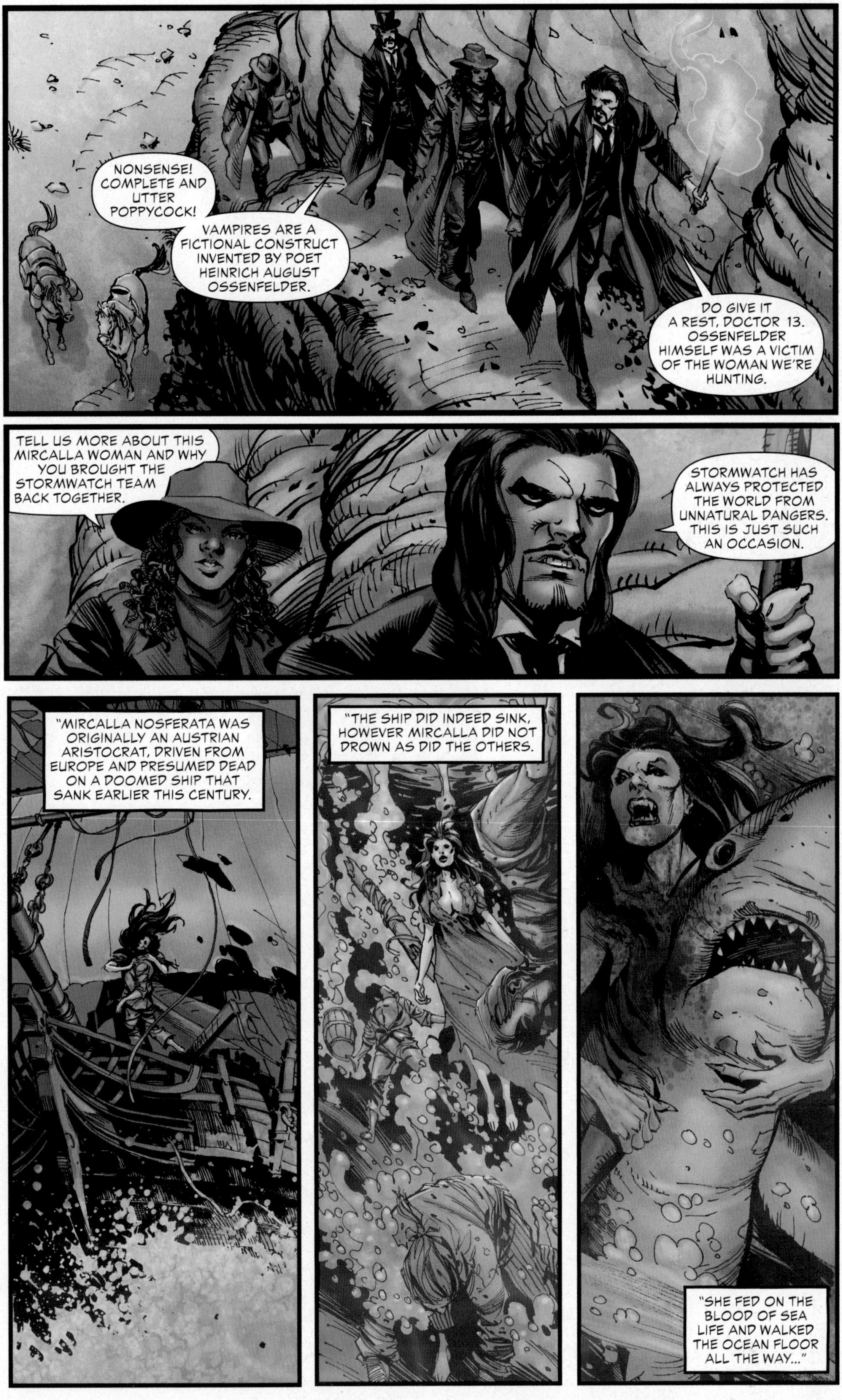
NONSENSE! COMPLETE AND UTTER POPPYCOCK!
VAMPIRES ARE A FICTIONAL CONSTRUCT INVENTED BY POET HEINRICH AUGUST OSSENFELDER.
DO GIVE IT A REST, DOCTOR 13. OSSENFELDER HIMSELF WAS A VICTIM OF THE WOMAN WE'RE HUNTING.
TELL US MORE ABOUT THIS MIRCALLA WOMAN AND WHY YOU BROUGHT THE STORMWATCH TEAM BACK TOGETHER.
STORMWATCH HAS ALWAYS PROTECTED THE WORLD FROM UNNATURAL DANGERS. THIS IS JUST SUCH AN OCCASION.
"MIRCALLA NOSFERATA WAS ORIGINALLY AN AUSTRIAN ARISTOCRAT, DRIVEN FROM EUROPE AND PRESUMED DEAD ON A DOOMED SHIP THAT SANK EARLIER THIS CENTURY.
"THE SHIP DID INDEED SINK, HOWEVER MIRCALLA DID NOT DROWN AS DID THE OTHERS.
"SHE FED ON THE BLOOD OF SEA LIFE AND WALKED THE OCEAN FLOOR ALL THE WAY..."

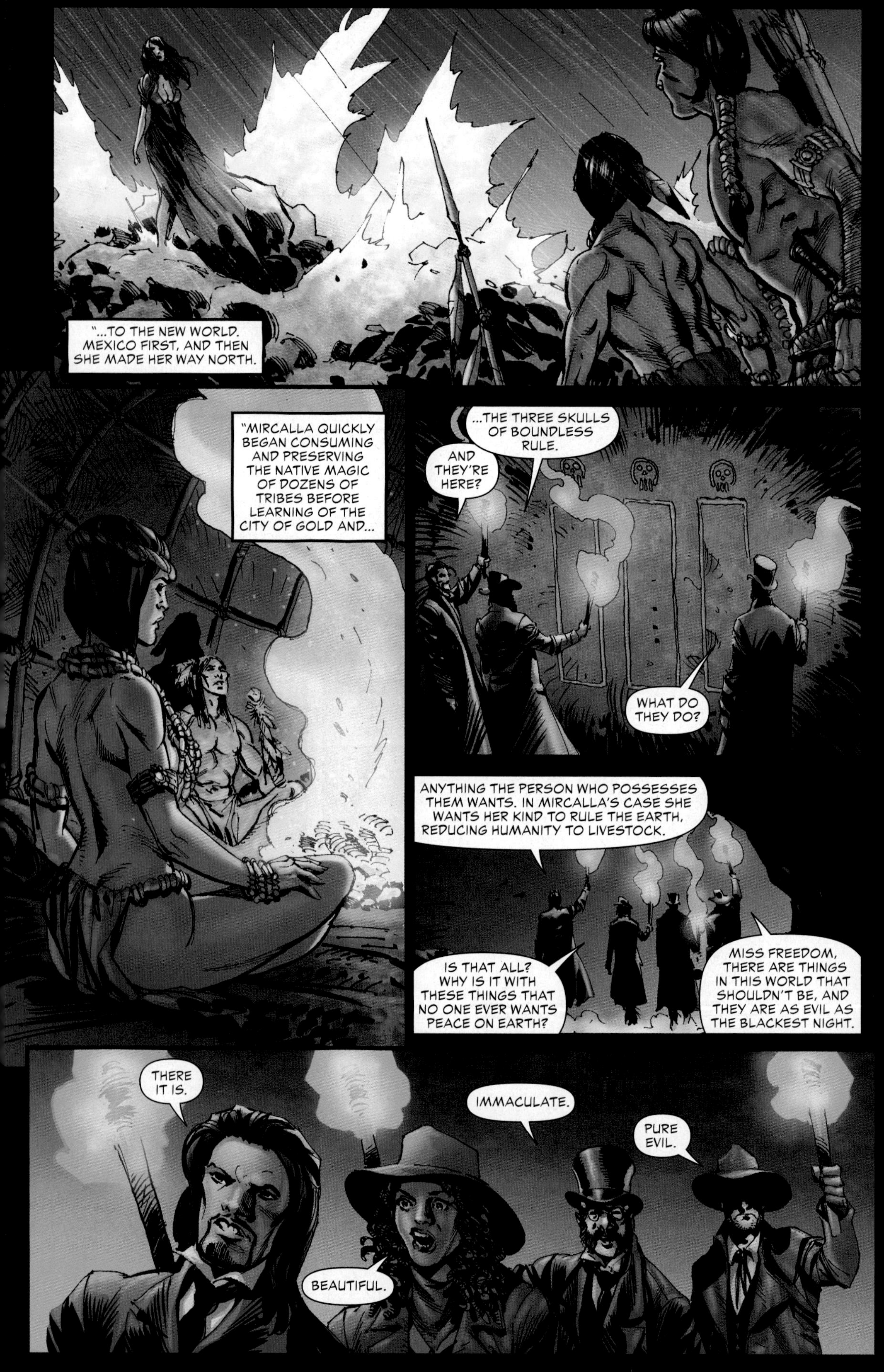
"...TO THE NEW WORLD. MEXICO FIRST, AND THEN SHE MADE HER WAY NORTH.
"MIRCALLA QUICKLY BEGAN CONSUMING AND PRESERVING THE NATIVE MAGIC OF DOZENS OF TRIBES BEFORE LEARNING OF THE CITY OF GOLD AND...
...THE THREE SKULLS OF BOUNDLESS RULE.
AND THEY'RE HERE?
WHAT DO THEY DO?
ANYTHING THE PERSON WHO POSSESSES THEM WANTS. IN MIRCALLA'S CASE SHE WANTS HER KIND TO RULE THE EARTH, REDUCING HUMANITY TO LIVESTOCK.
IS THAT ALL? WHY IS IT WITH THESE THINGS THAT NO ONE EVER WANTS PEACE ON EARTH?
MISS FREEDOM, THERE ARE THINGS IN THIS WORLD THAT SHOULDN'T BE, AND THEY ARE AS EVIL AS THE BLACKEST NIGHT.
THERE IT IS.
IMMACULATE.
PURE EVIL.
BEAUTIFUL.

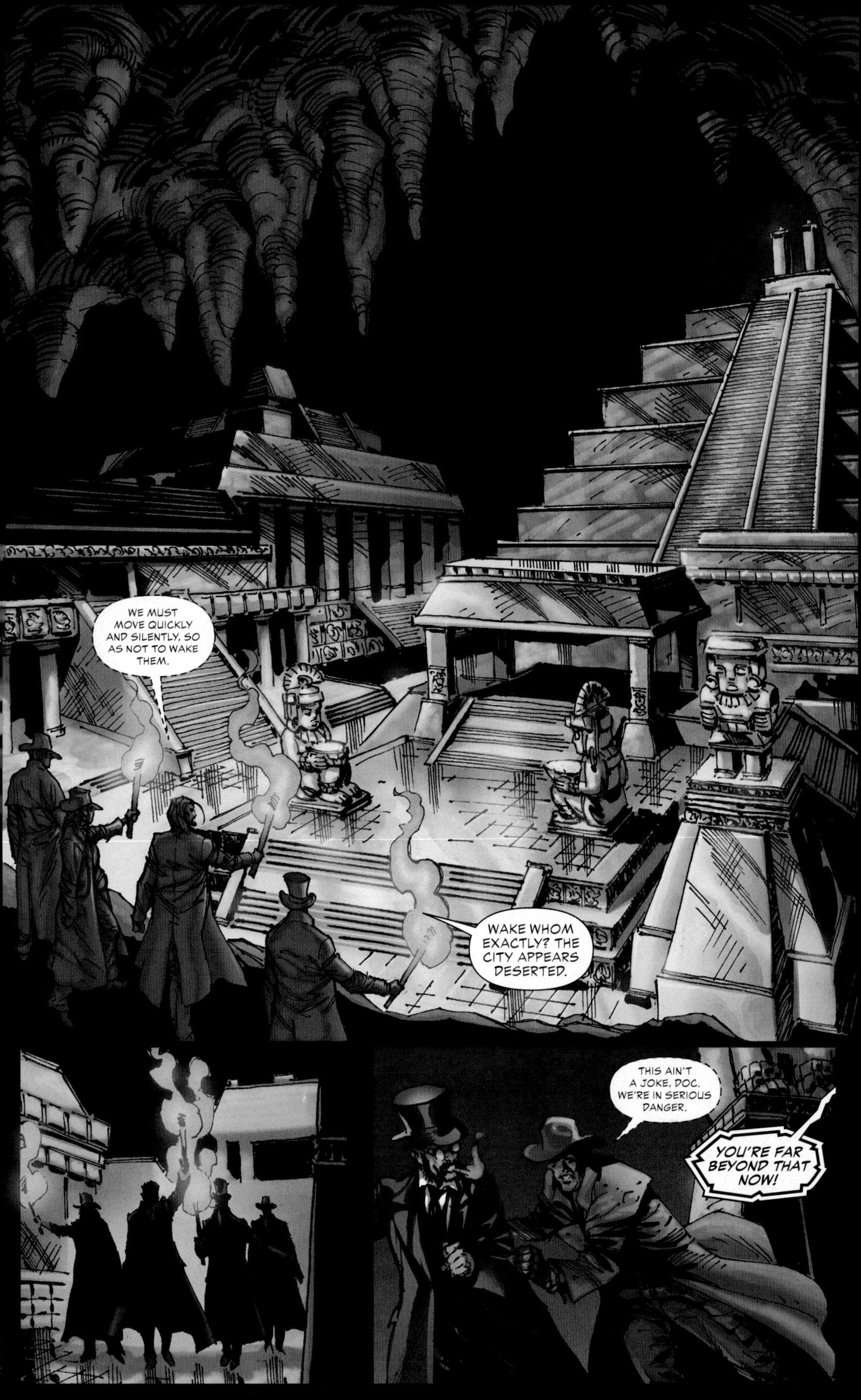
WE MUST MOVE QUICKLY AND SILENTLY, SO AS NOT TO WAKE THEM.
WAKE WHOM EXACTLY? THE CITY APPEARS DESERTED.
THIS AIN'T A JOKE, DOC. WE'RE IN SERIOUS DANGER.
YOU'RE FAR BEYOND THAT NOW!

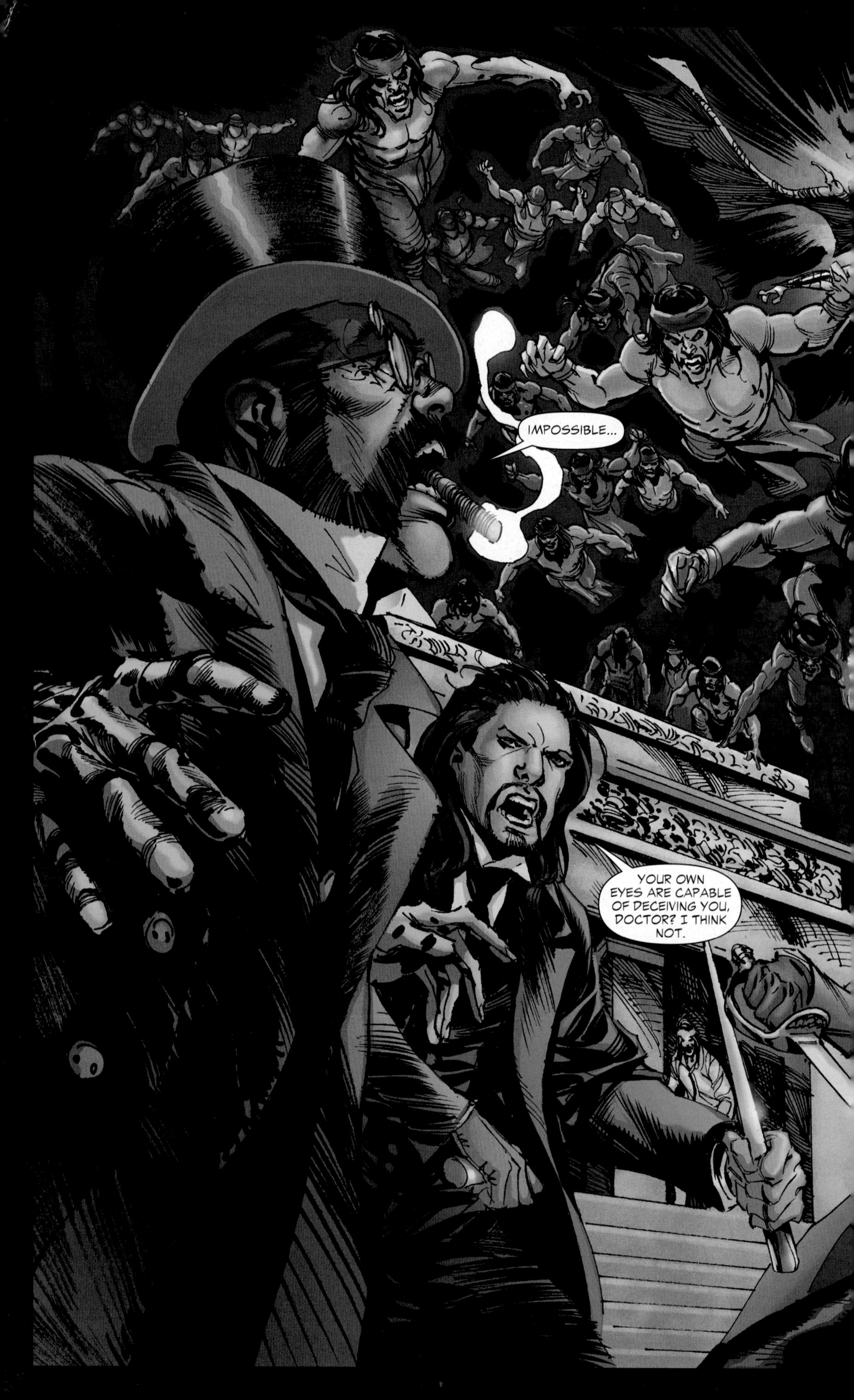
IMPOSSIBLE...
YOUR OWN EYES ARE CAPABLE OF DECEIVING YOU, DOCTOR? I THINK NOT.

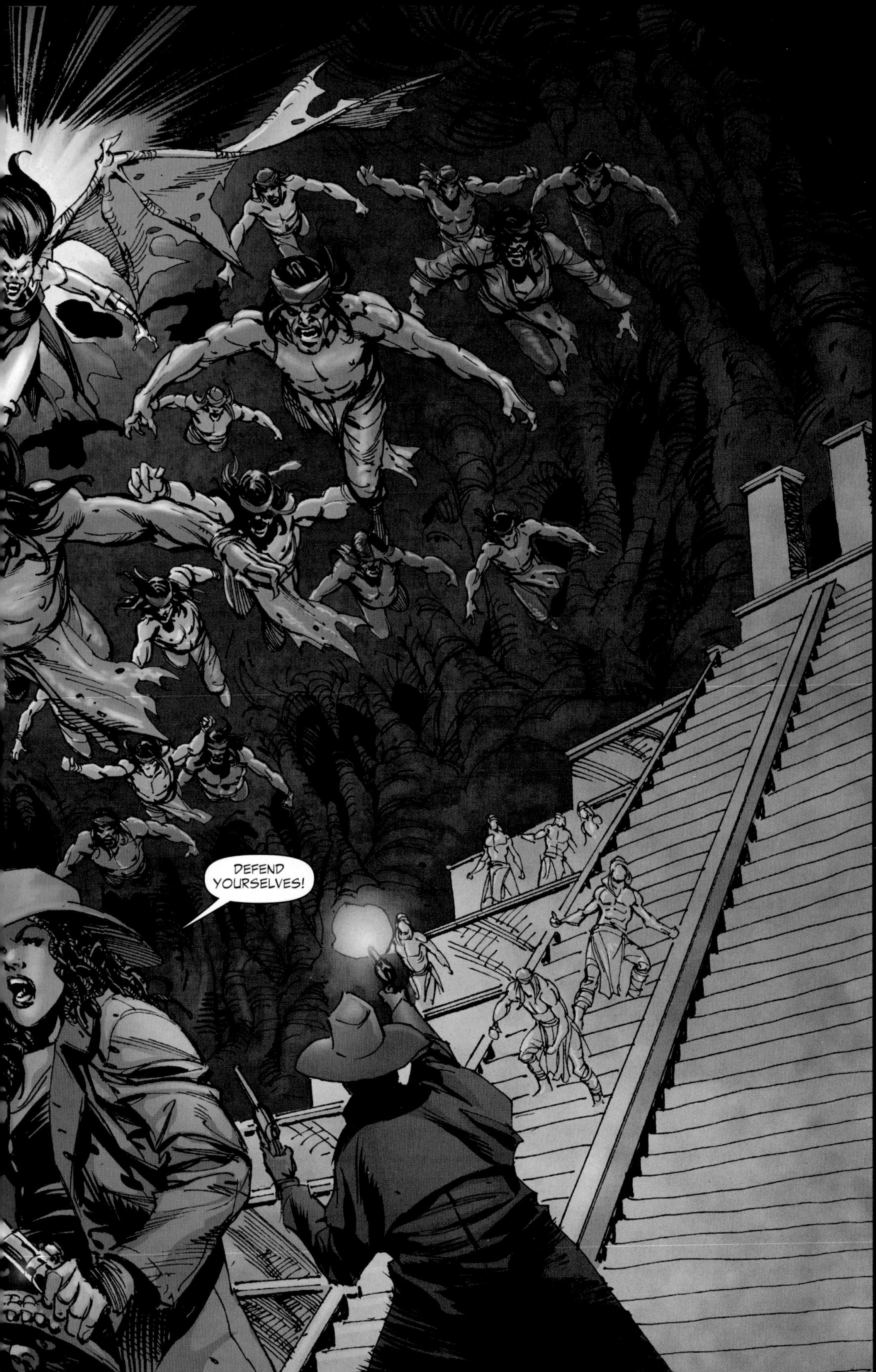
DEFEND YOURSELVES!

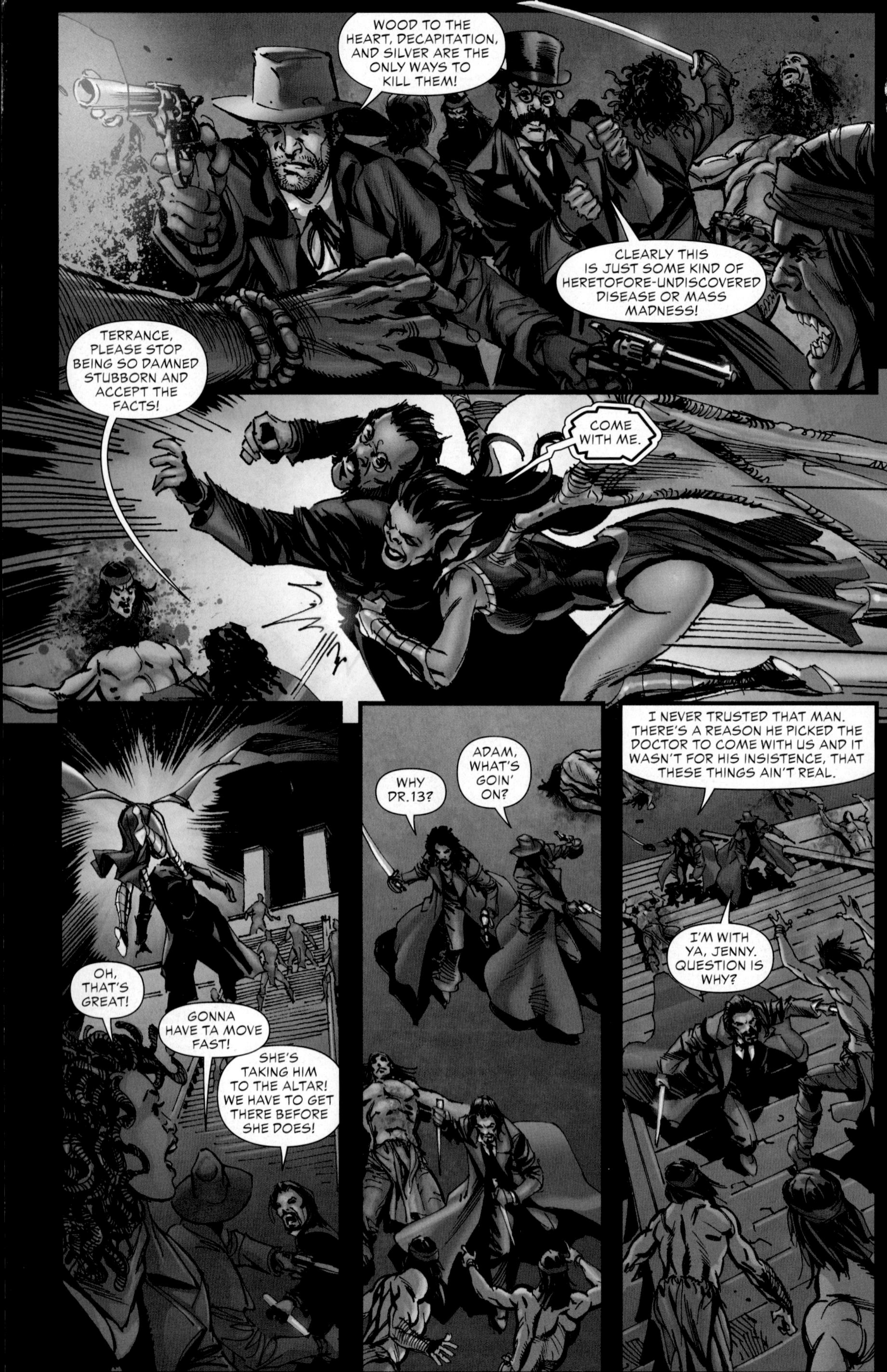

WOOD TO THE HEART, DECAPITATION, AND SILVER ARE THE ONLY WAYS TO KILL THEM!
CLEARLY THIS IS JUST SOME KIND OF HERETOFORE-UNDISCOVERED DISEASE OR MASS MADNESS!
TERRANCE, PLEASE STOP BEING SO DAMNED STUBBORN AND ACCEPT THE FACTS!
COME WITH ME.
OH, THAT'S GREAT!
GONNA HAVE TA MOVE FAST!
SHE'S TAKING HIM TO THE ALTAR! WE HAVE TO GET THERE BEFORE SHE DOES!
ADAM, WHAT'S GOIN' ON?
WHY DR.13?
I NEVER TRUSTED THAT MAN. THERE'S A REASON HE PICKED THE DOCTOR TO COME WITH US AND IT WASN'T FOR HIS INSISTENCE, THAT THESE THINGS AIN'T REAL.
I'M WITH YA, JENNY. QUESTION IS WHY?

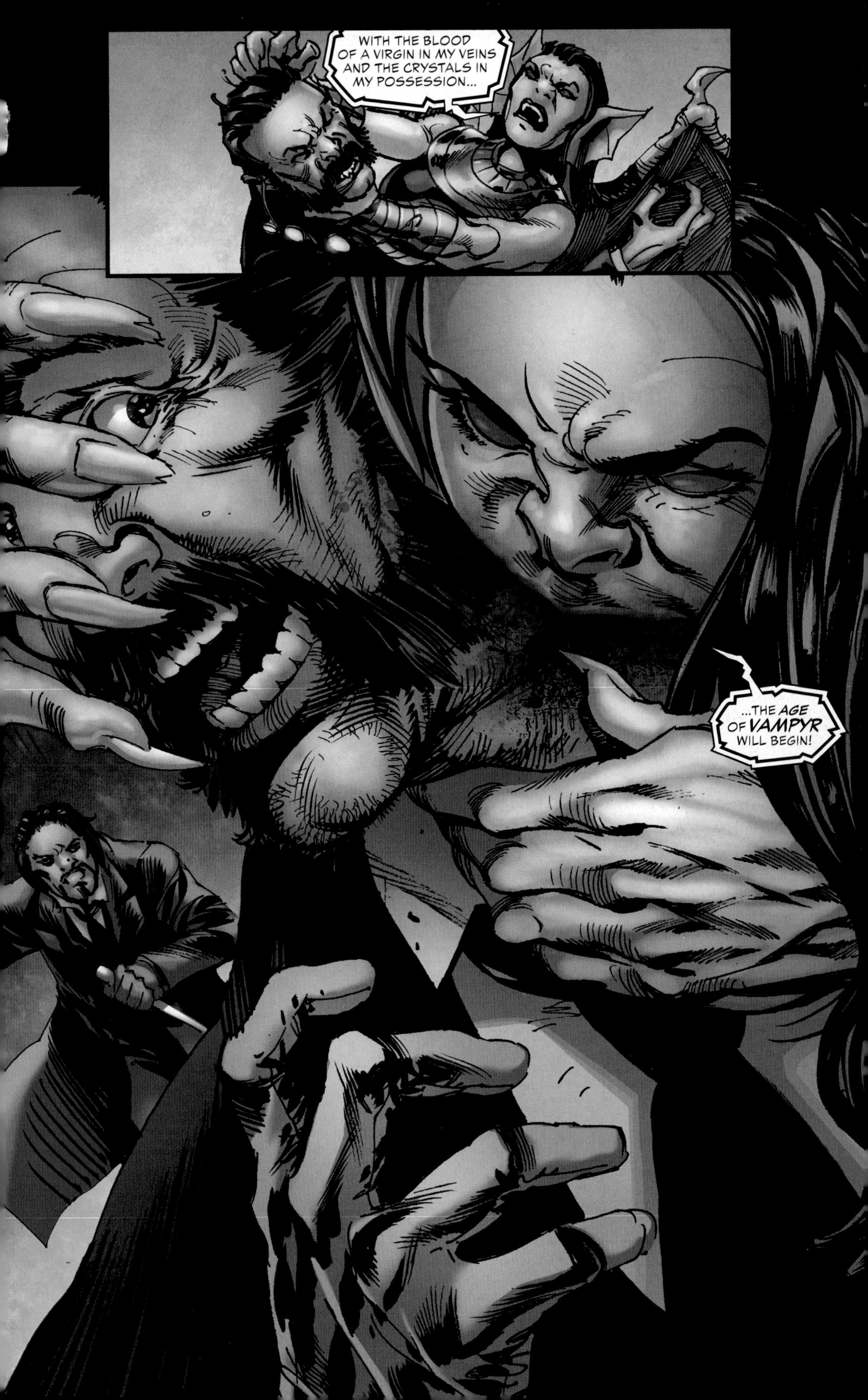
WITH THE BLOOD OF A VIRGIN IN MY VEINS AND THE CRYSTALS IN MY POSSESSION...
...THE AGE OF VAMPYR WILL BEGIN!

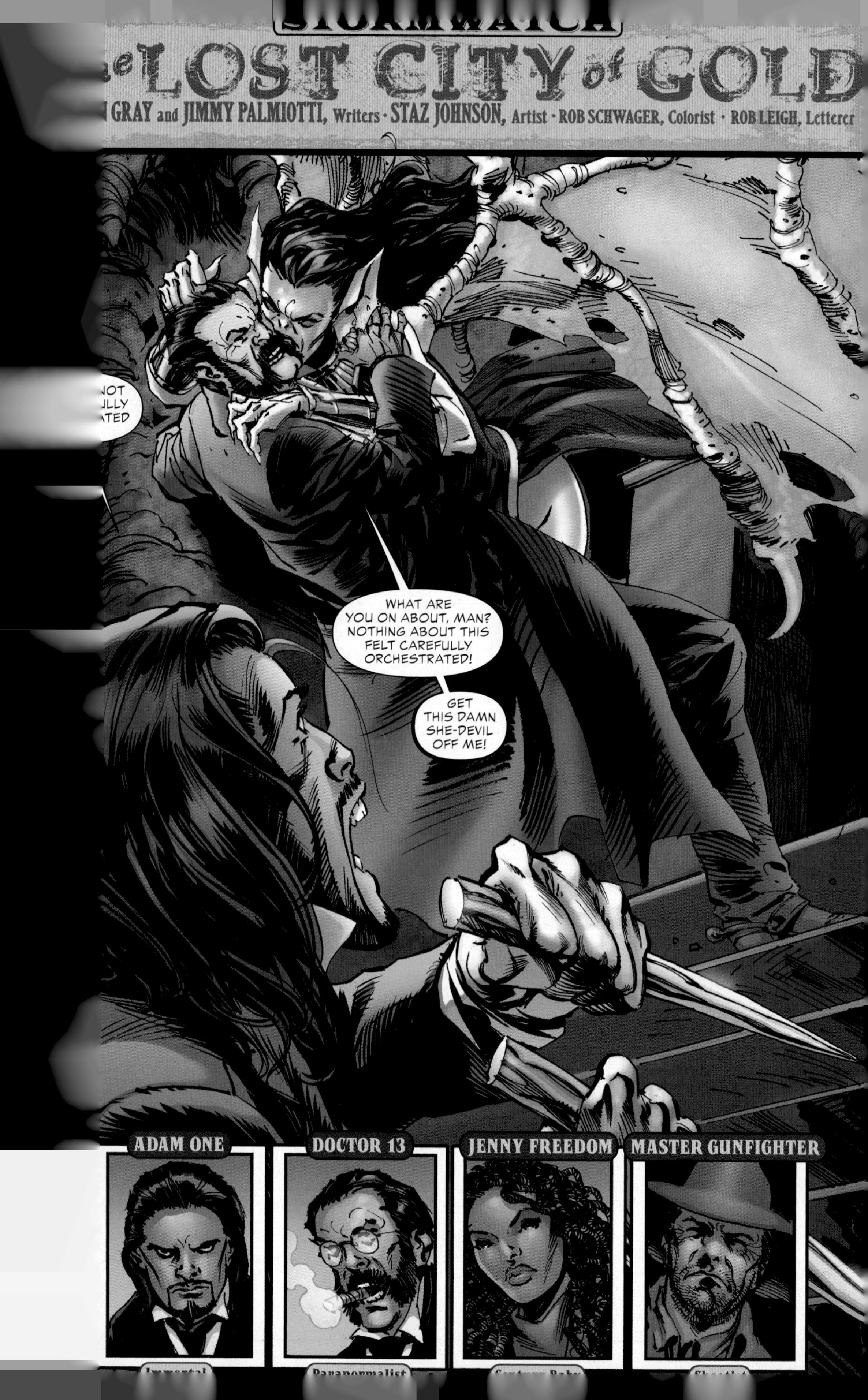
LOST CITY of GOLD
GRAY and JIMMY PALMIOTTI, Writers · STAZ JOHNSON, Artist · ROB SCHWAGER, Colorist · ROB LEIGH, Letterer
WHAT ARE YOU ON ABOUT, MAN? NOTHING ABOUT THIS FELT CAREFULLY ORCHESTRATED!
GET THIS DAMN SHE-DEVIL OFF ME!
ADAM ONE
DOCTOR 13
JENNY FREEDOM
MASTER GUNFIGHTER

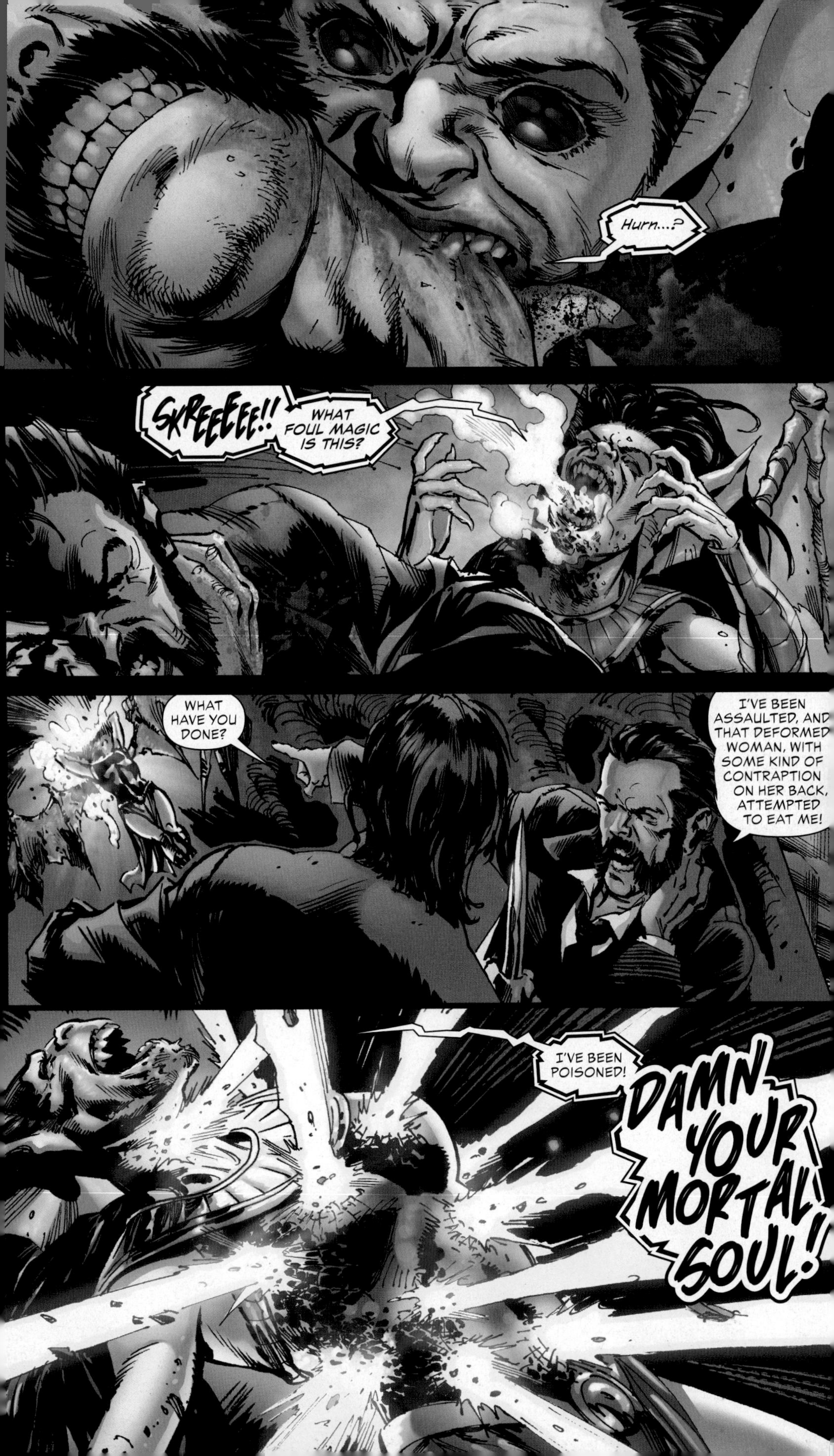
Hurn...?
SKREEEEEE!!
WHAT FOUL MAGIC IS THIS?
WHAT HAVE YOU DONE?
I'VE BEEN ASSAULTED, AND THAT DEFORMED WOMAN, WITH SOME KIND OF CONTRAPTION ON HER BACK, ATTEMPTED TO EAT ME!
I'VE BEEN POISONED!
DAMN YOUR MORTAL SOUL!

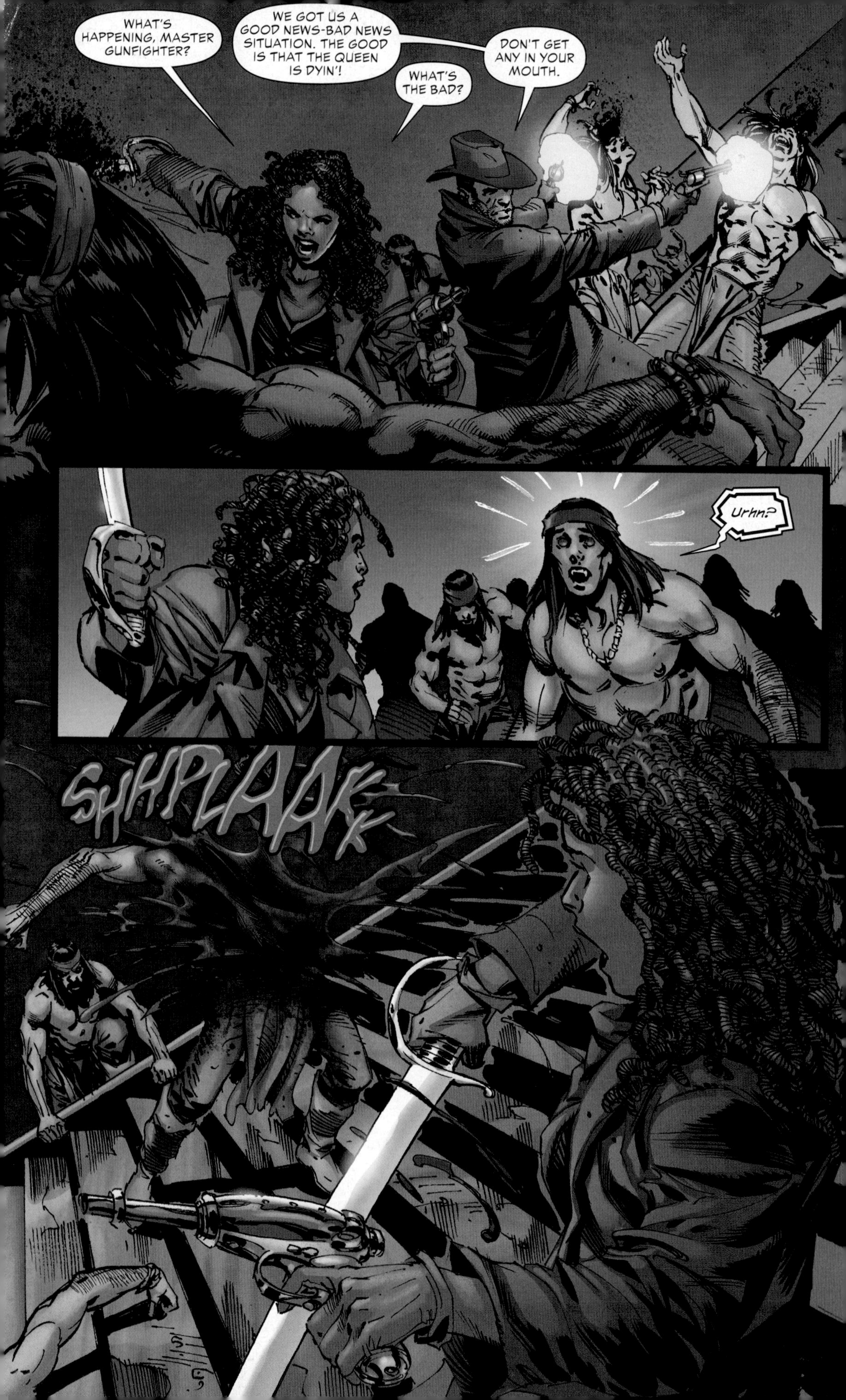
WHAT'S HAPPENING, MASTER GUNFIGHTER?
WE GOT US A GOOD NEWS-BAD NEWS SITUATION. THE GOOD IS THAT THE QUEEN IS DYIN'!
WHAT'S THE BAD?
DON'T GET ANY IN YOUR MOUTH.
Urhn?
SHHPLAAKK

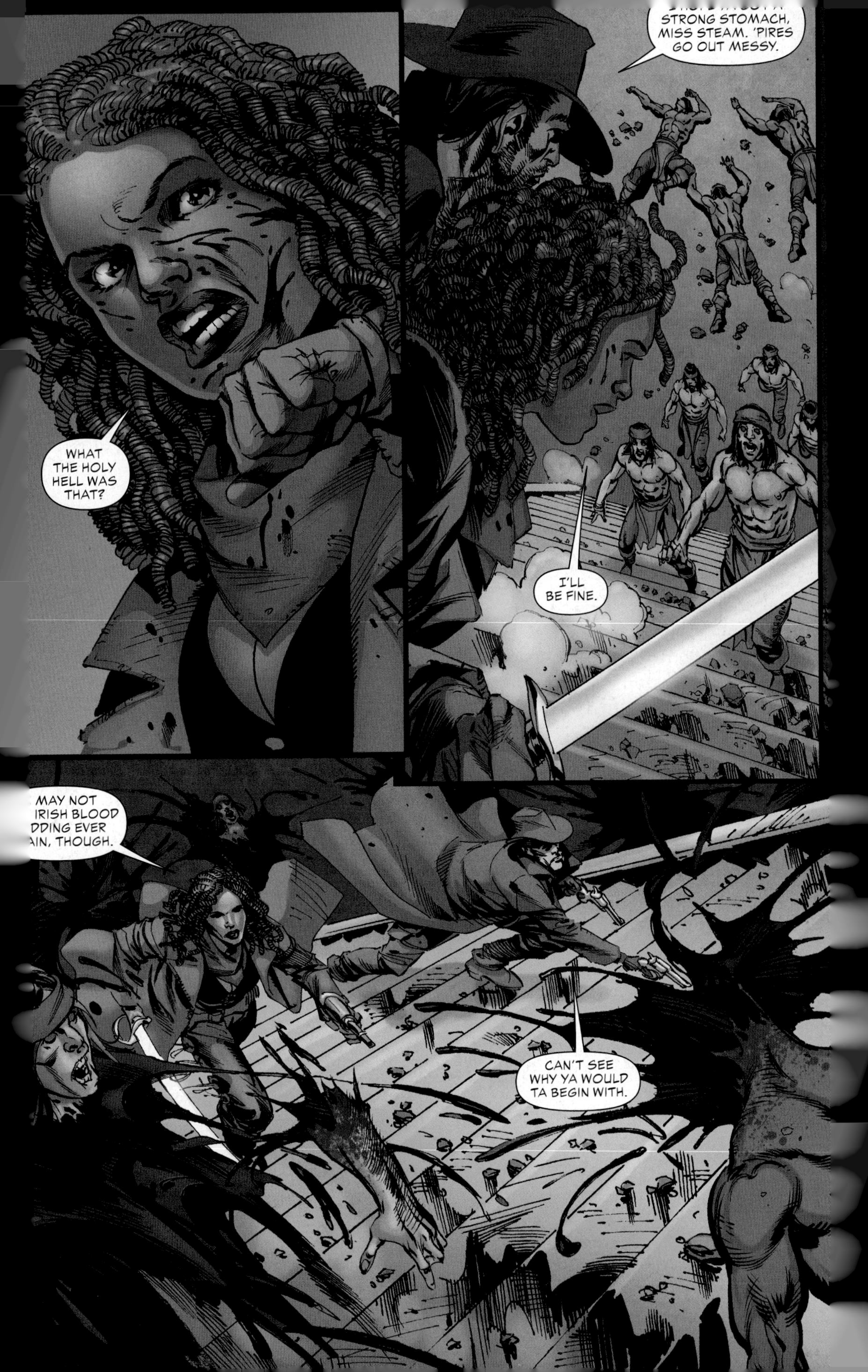
WHAT THE HOLY HELL WAS THAT?
STRONG STOMACH, MISS STEAM. 'PIRES GO OUT MESSY.
I'LL BE FINE.
MAY NOT IRISH BLOOD DDING EVER AIN, THOUGH.
CAN'T SEE WHY YA WOULD TA BEGIN WITH.

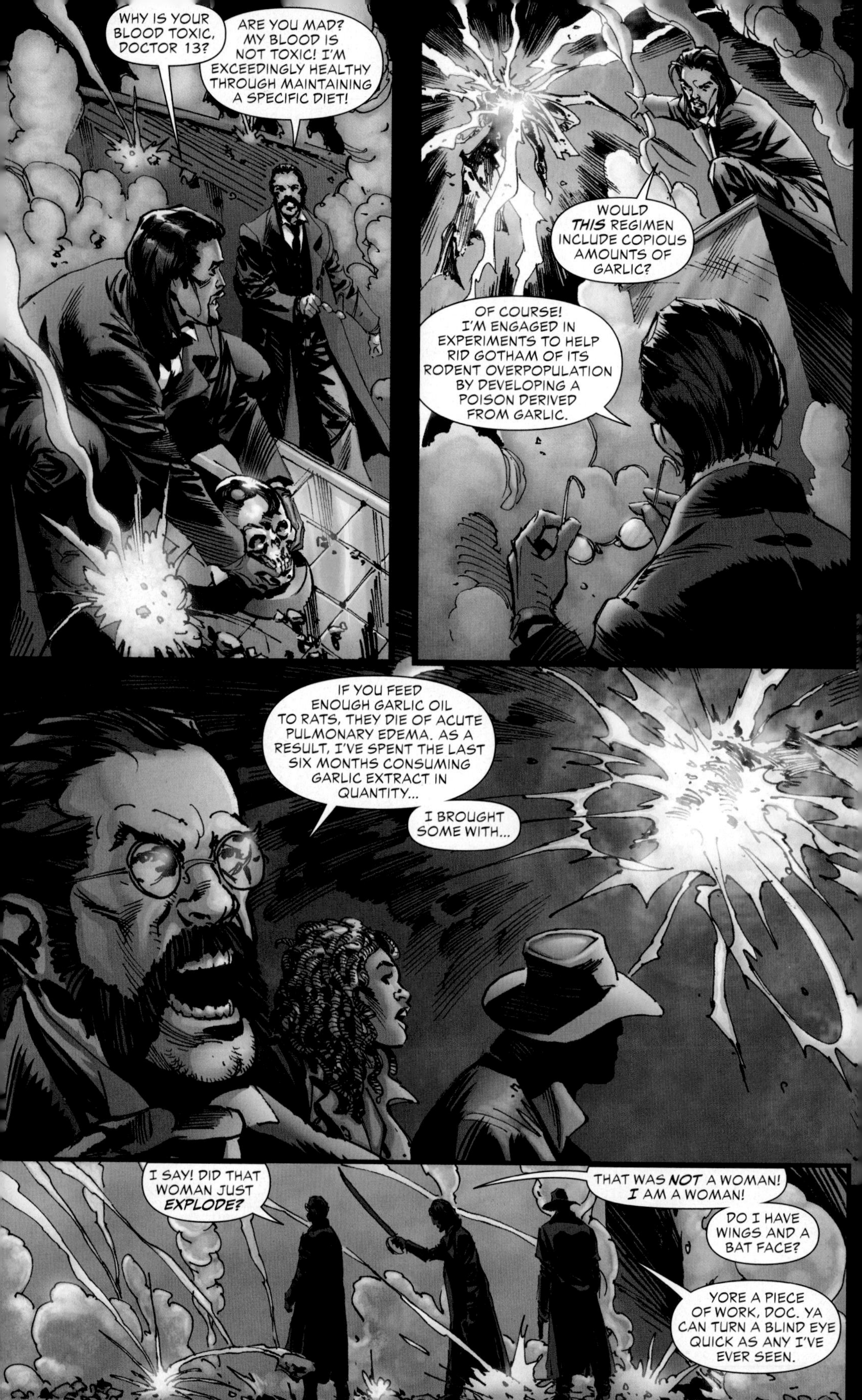
WHY IS YOUR BLOOD TOXIC, DOCTOR 13?
ARE YOU MAD? MY BLOOD IS NOT TOXIC! I'M EXCEEDINGLY HEALTHY THROUGH MAINTAINING A SPECIFIC DIET!
WOULD THIS REGIMEN INCLUDE COPIOUS AMOUNTS OF GARLIC?
OF COURSE! I'M ENGAGED IN EXPERIMENTS TO HELP RID GOTHAM OF ITS RODENT OVERPOPULATION BY DEVELOPING A POISON DERIVED FROM GARLIC.
IF YOU FEED ENOUGH GARLIC OIL TO RATS, THEY DIE OF ACUTE PULMONARY EDEMA. AS A RESULT, I'VE SPENT THE LAST SIX MONTHS CONSUMING GARLIC EXTRACT IN QUANTITY...
I BROUGHT SOME WITH...
I SAY! DID THAT WOMAN JUST EXPLODE?
THAT WAS NOT A WOMAN! I AM A WOMAN!
DO I HAVE WINGS AND A BAT FACE?
YORE A PIECE OF WORK, DOC. YA CAN TURN A BLIND EYE QUICK AS ANY I'VE EVER SEEN.

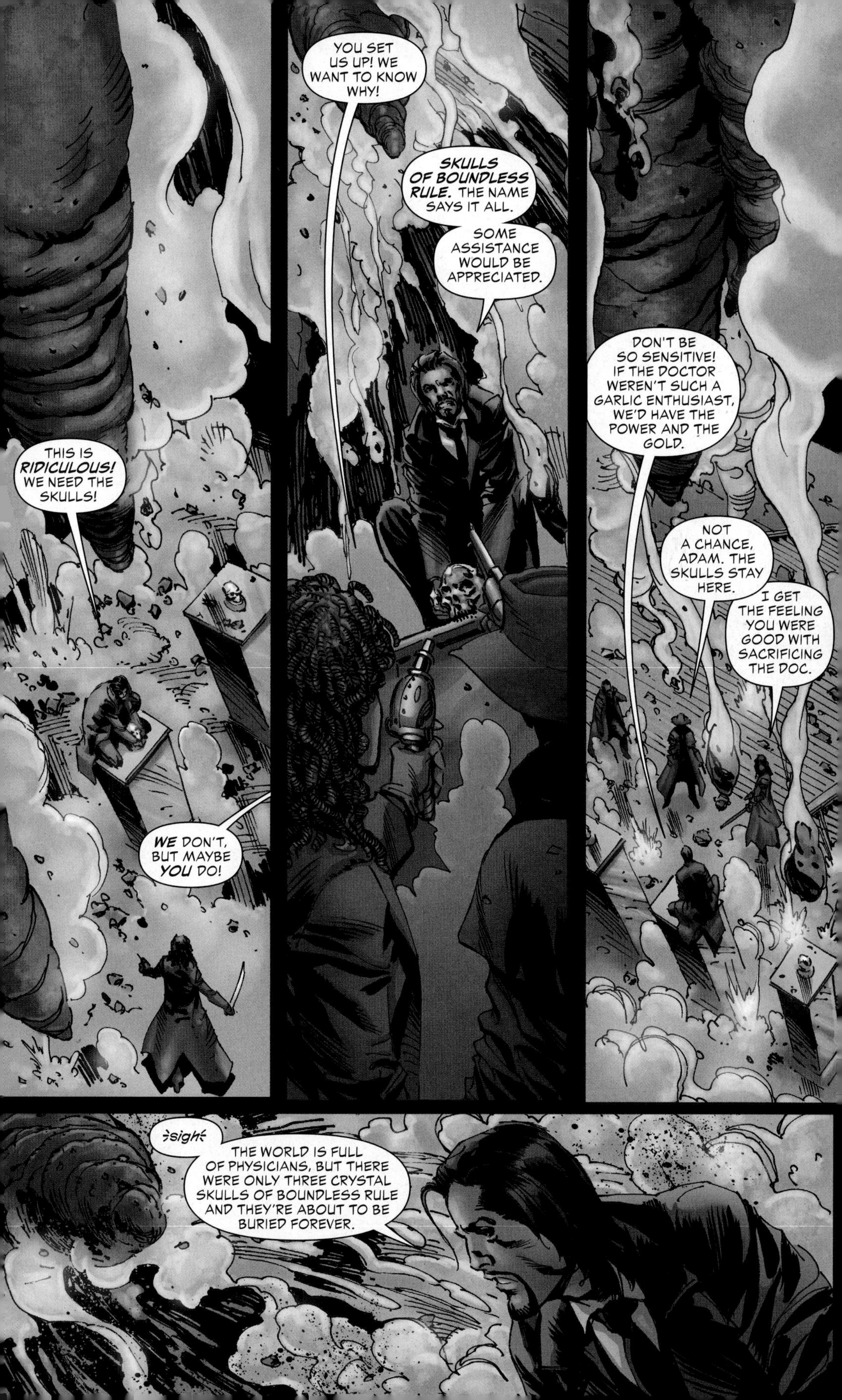
THIS IS RIDICULOUS! WE NEED THE SKULLS!
WE DON'T, BUT MAYBE YOU DO!
YOU SET US UP! WE WANT TO KNOW WHY!
SKULLS OF BOUNDLESS RULE. THE NAME SAYS IT ALL.
SOME ASSISTANCE WOULD BE APPRECIATED.
DON'T BE SO SENSITIVE! IF THE DOCTOR WEREN'T SUCH A GARLIC ENTHUSIAST, WE'D HAVE THE POWER AND THE GOLD.
NOT A CHANCE, ADAM. THE SKULLS STAY HERE.
I GET THE FEELING YOU WERE GOOD WITH SACRIFICING THE DOC.
sigh
THE WORLD IS FULL OF PHYSICIANS, BUT THERE WERE ONLY THREE CRYSTAL SKULLS OF BOUNDLESS RULE AND THEY'RE ABOUT TO BE BURIED FOREVER.

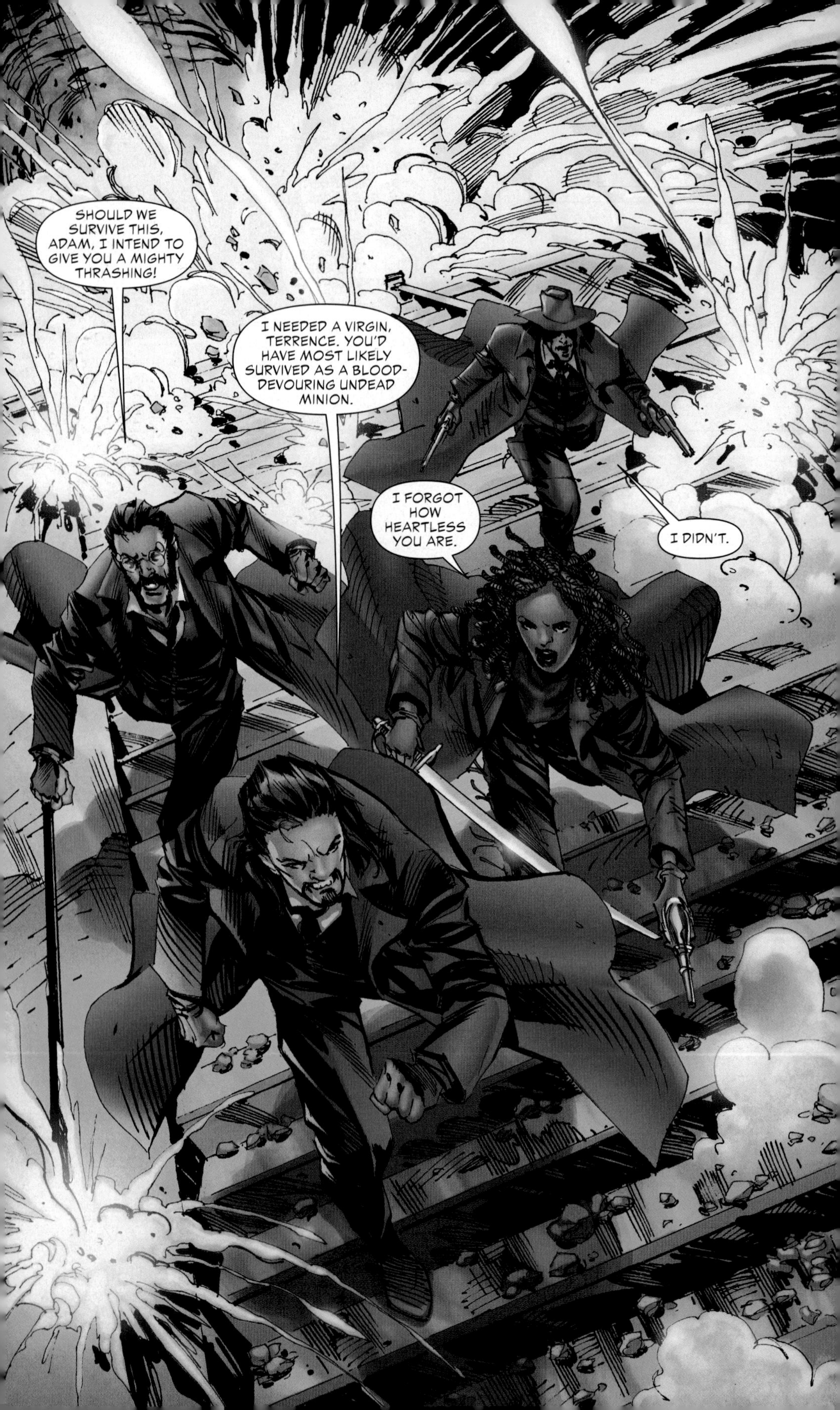
SHOULD WE SURVIVE THIS, ADAM, I INTEND TO GIVE YOU A MIGHTY THRASHING!
I NEEDED A VIRGIN, TERRENCE. YOU'D HAVE MOST LIKELY SURVIVED AS A BLOOD-DEVOURING UNDEAD MINION.
I FORGOT HOW HEARTLESS YOU ARE.
I DIDN'T.

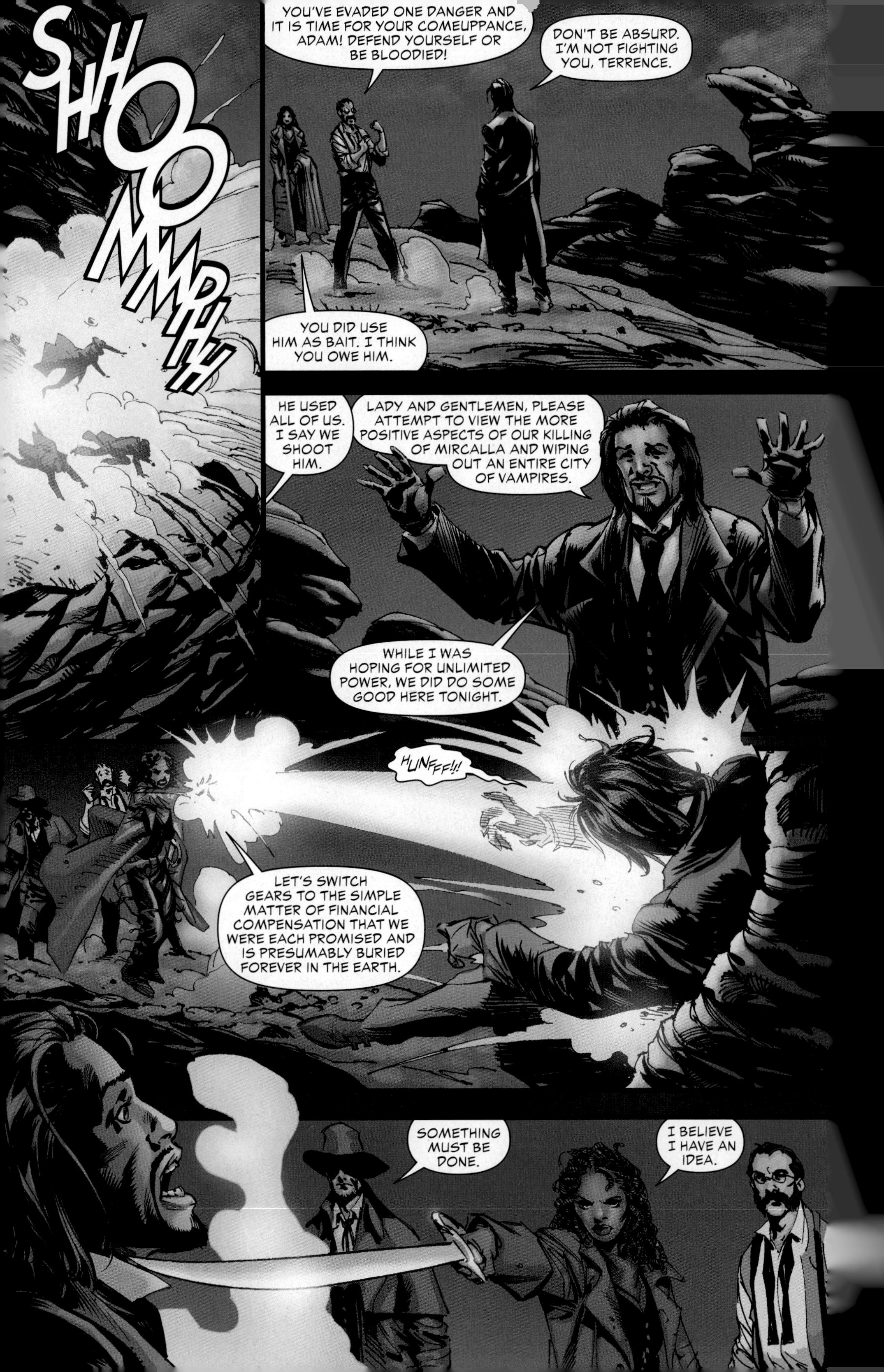
SHOOOMMMPHH
YOU'VE EVADED ONE DANGER AND IT IS TIME FOR YOUR COMEUPPANCE, ADAM! DEFEND YOURSELF OR BE BLOODIED!
DON'T BE ABSURD. I'M NOT FIGHTING YOU, TERRENCE.
YOU DID USE HIM AS BAIT. I THINK YOU OWE HIM.
HE USED ALL OF US. I SAY WE SHOOT HIM.
LADY AND GENTLEMEN, PLEASE ATTEMPT TO VIEW THE MORE POSITIVE ASPECTS OF OUR KILLING OF MIRCALLA AND WIPING OUT AN ENTIRE CITY OF VAMPIRES.
WHILE I WAS HOPING FOR UNLIMITED POWER, WE DID DO SOME GOOD HERE TONIGHT.
HUNFFF!!!
LET'S SWITCH GEARS TO THE SIMPLE MATTER OF FINANCIAL COMPENSATION THAT WE WERE EACH PROMISED AND IS PRESUMABLY BURIED FOREVER IN THE EARTH.
SOMETHING MUST BE DONE.
I BELIEVE I HAVE AN IDEA.

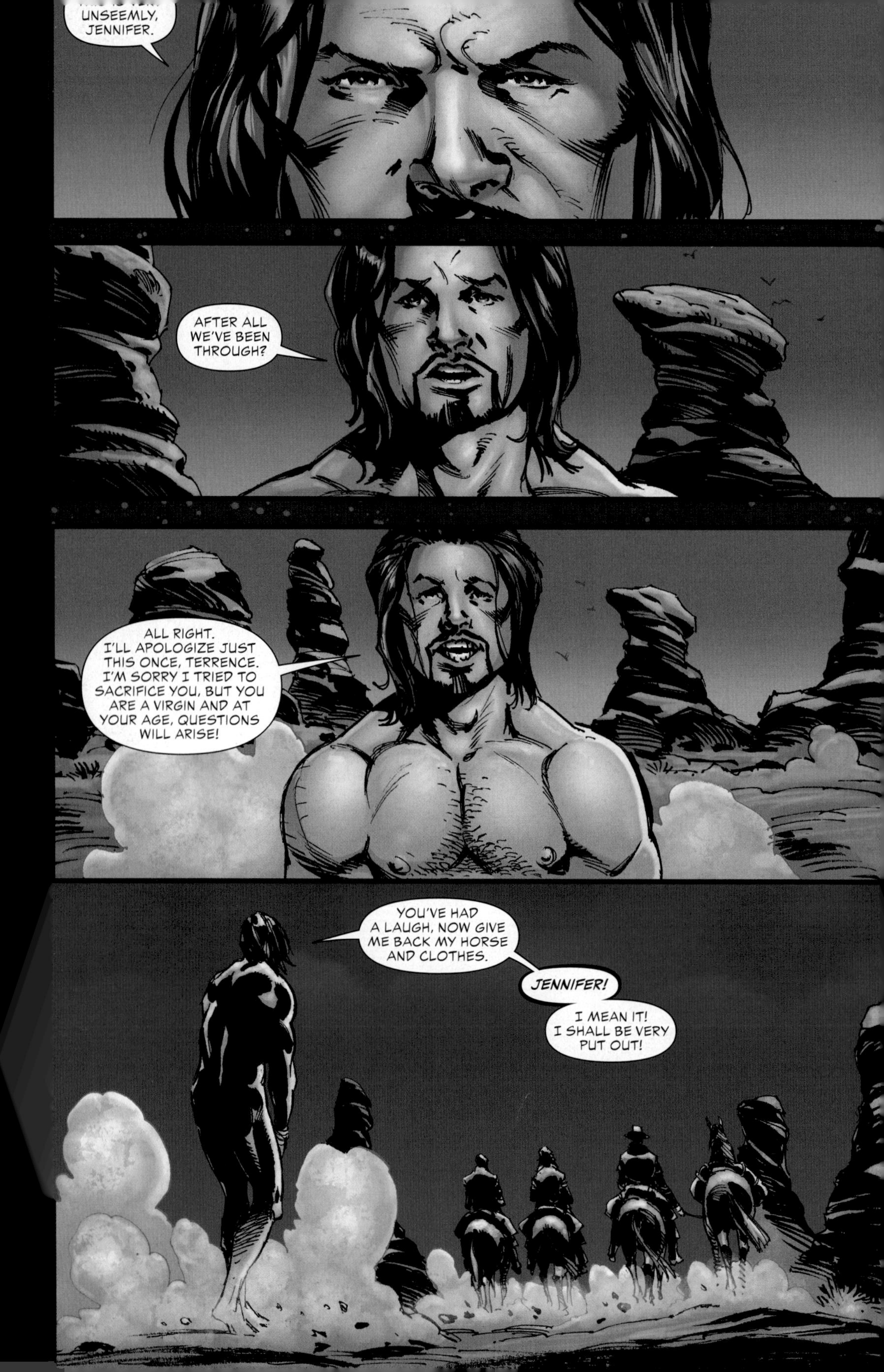
UNSEEMLY, JENNIFER.
AFTER ALL WE'VE BEEN THROUGH?
ALL RIGHT. I'LL APOLOGIZE JUST THIS ONCE, TERRENCE. I'M SORRY I TRIED TO SACRIFICE YOU, BUT YOU ARE A VIRGIN AND AT YOUR AGE, QUESTIONS WILL ARISE!
YOU'VE HAD A LAUGH, NOW GIVE ME BACK MY HORSE AND CLOTHES.
JENNIFER!
I MEAN IT! I SHALL BE VERY PUT OUT!

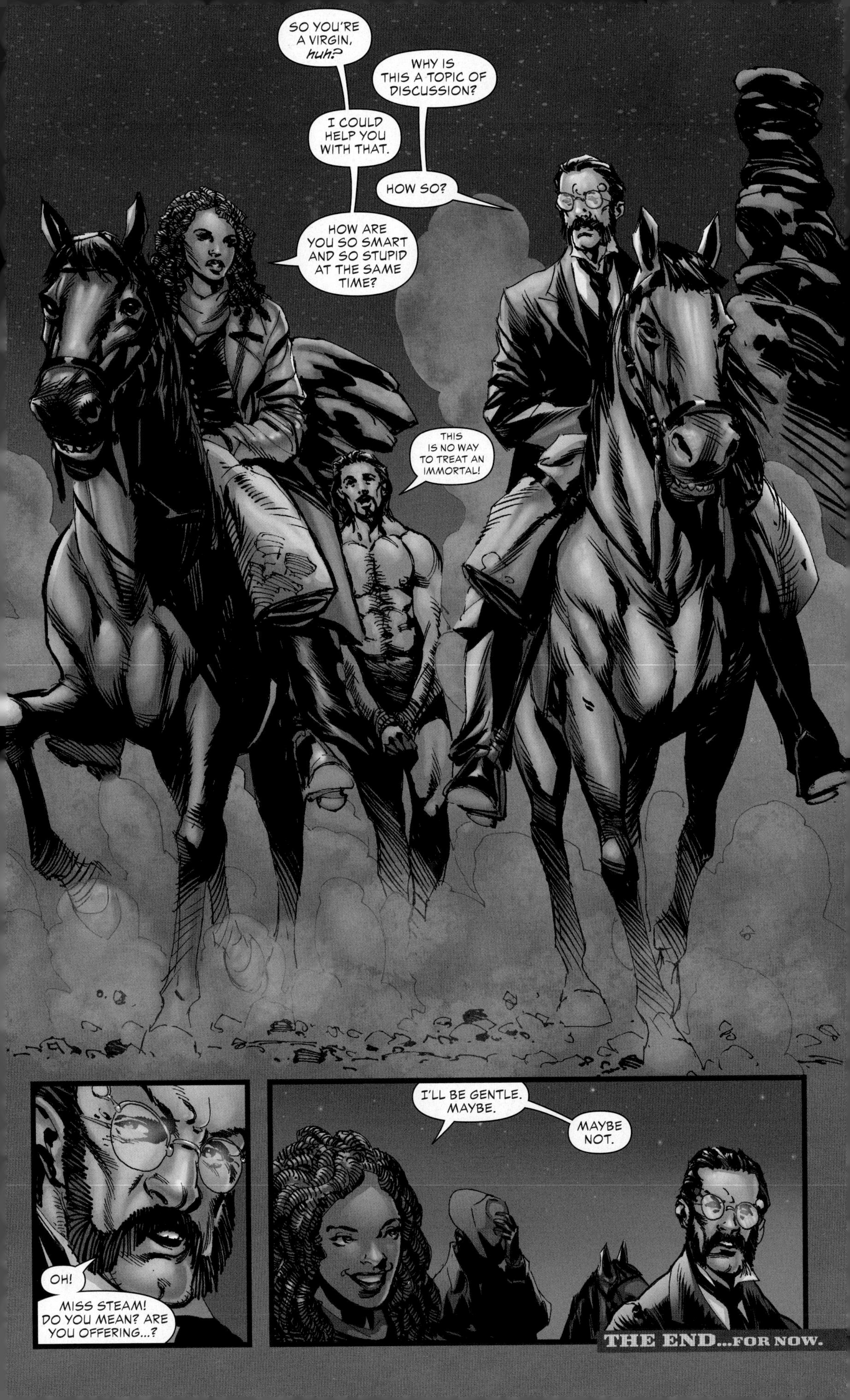
SO YOU'RE A VIRGIN, *huh?*
WHY IS THIS A TOPIC OF DISCUSSION?
I COULD HELP YOU WITH THAT.
HOW SO?
HOW ARE YOU SO SMART AND SO STUPID AT THE SAME TIME?
THIS IS NO WAY TO TREAT AN IMMORTAL!
OH!
MISS STEAM! DO YOU MEAN? ARE YOU OFFERING...?
I'LL BE GENTLE. MAYBE.
MAYBE NOT.
THE END...FOR NOW.

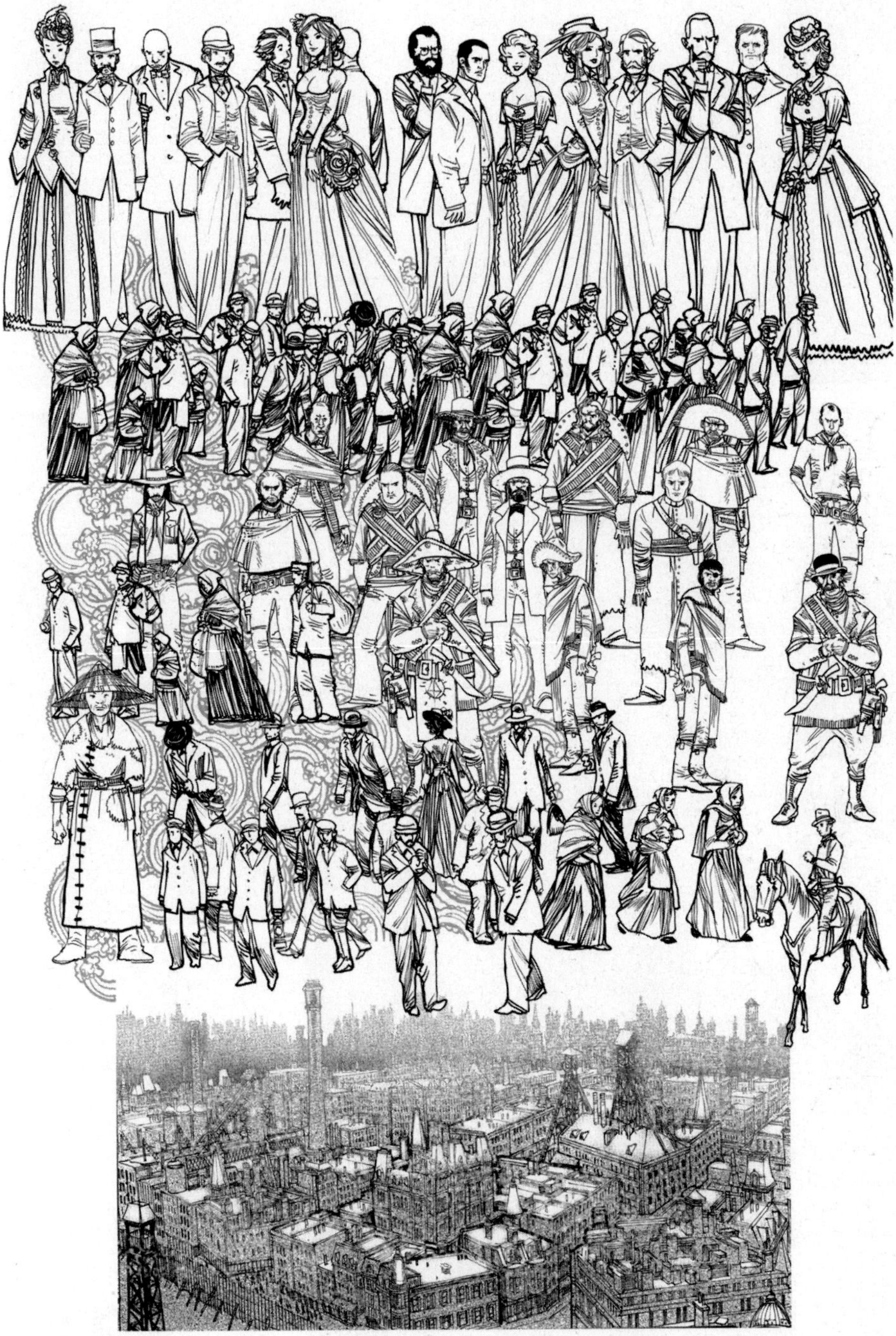

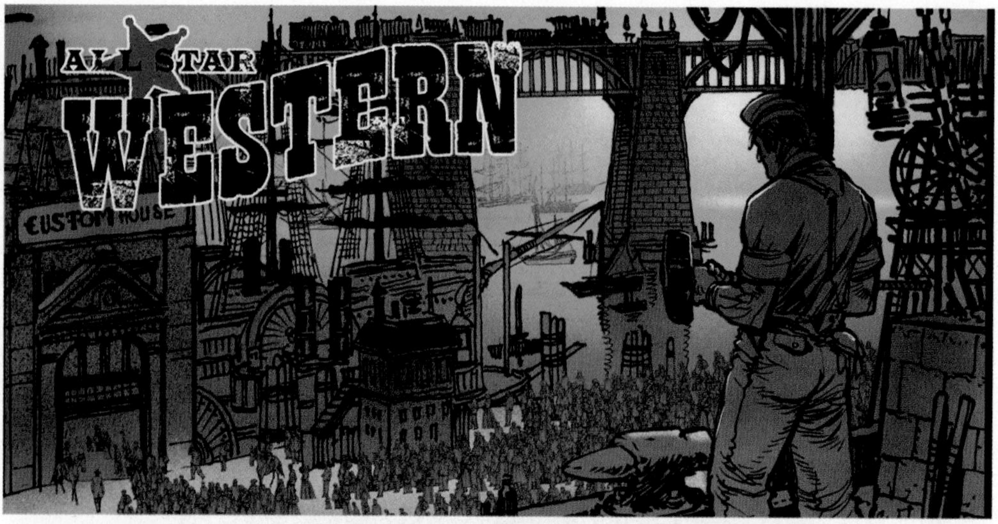
ALL STAR
WESTERN
CUSTOM HOUSE

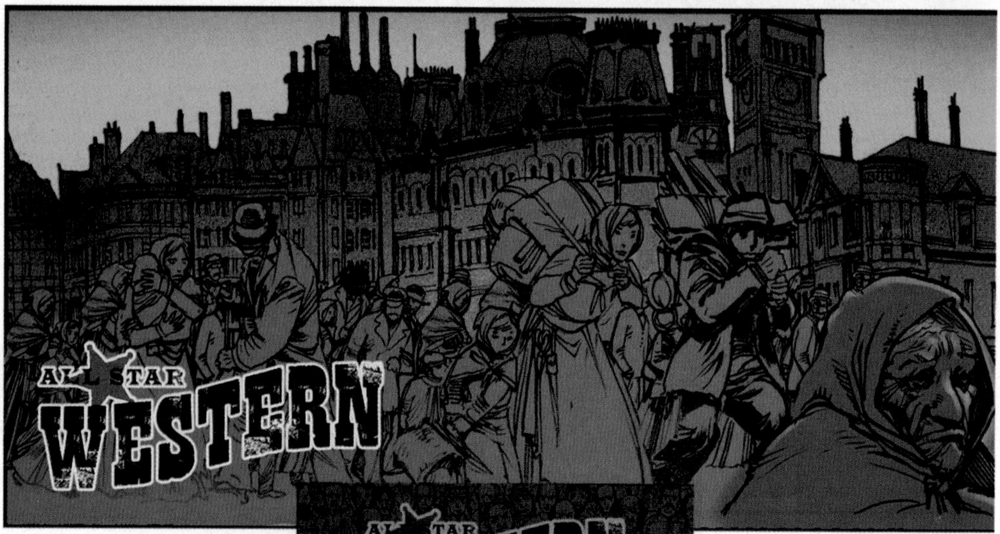
ALL STAR
WESTERN

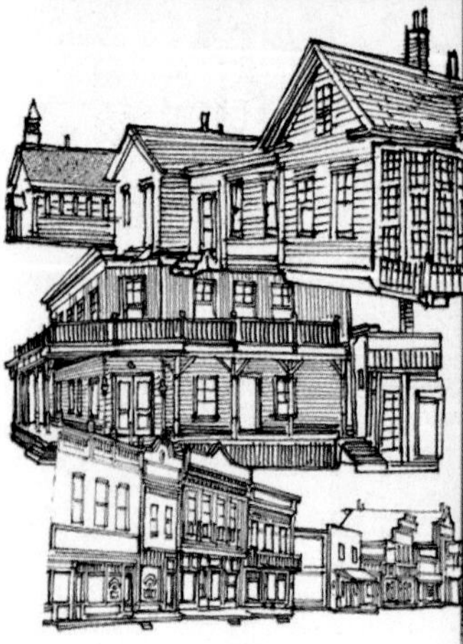

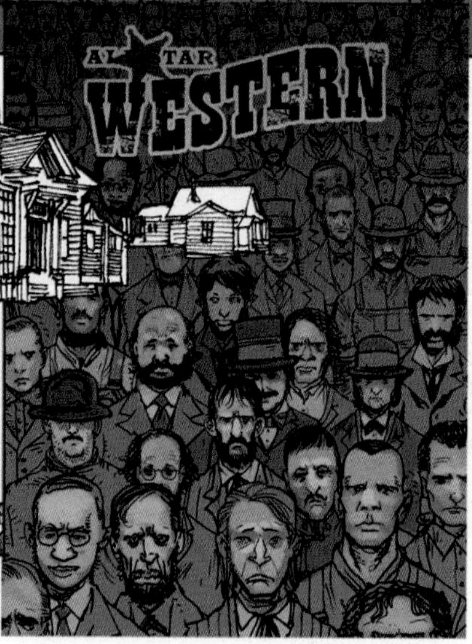
ALL STAR
WESTERN

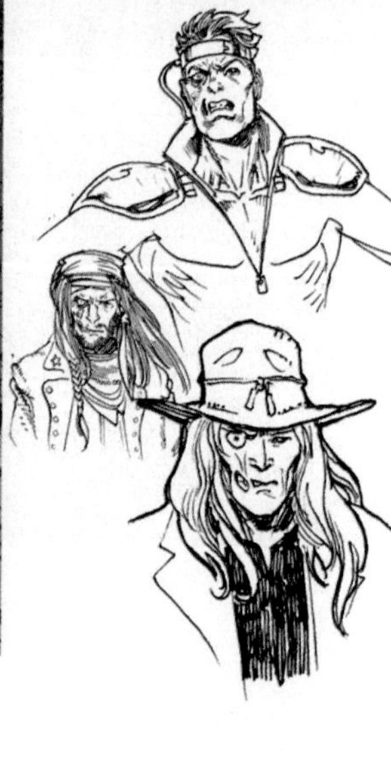

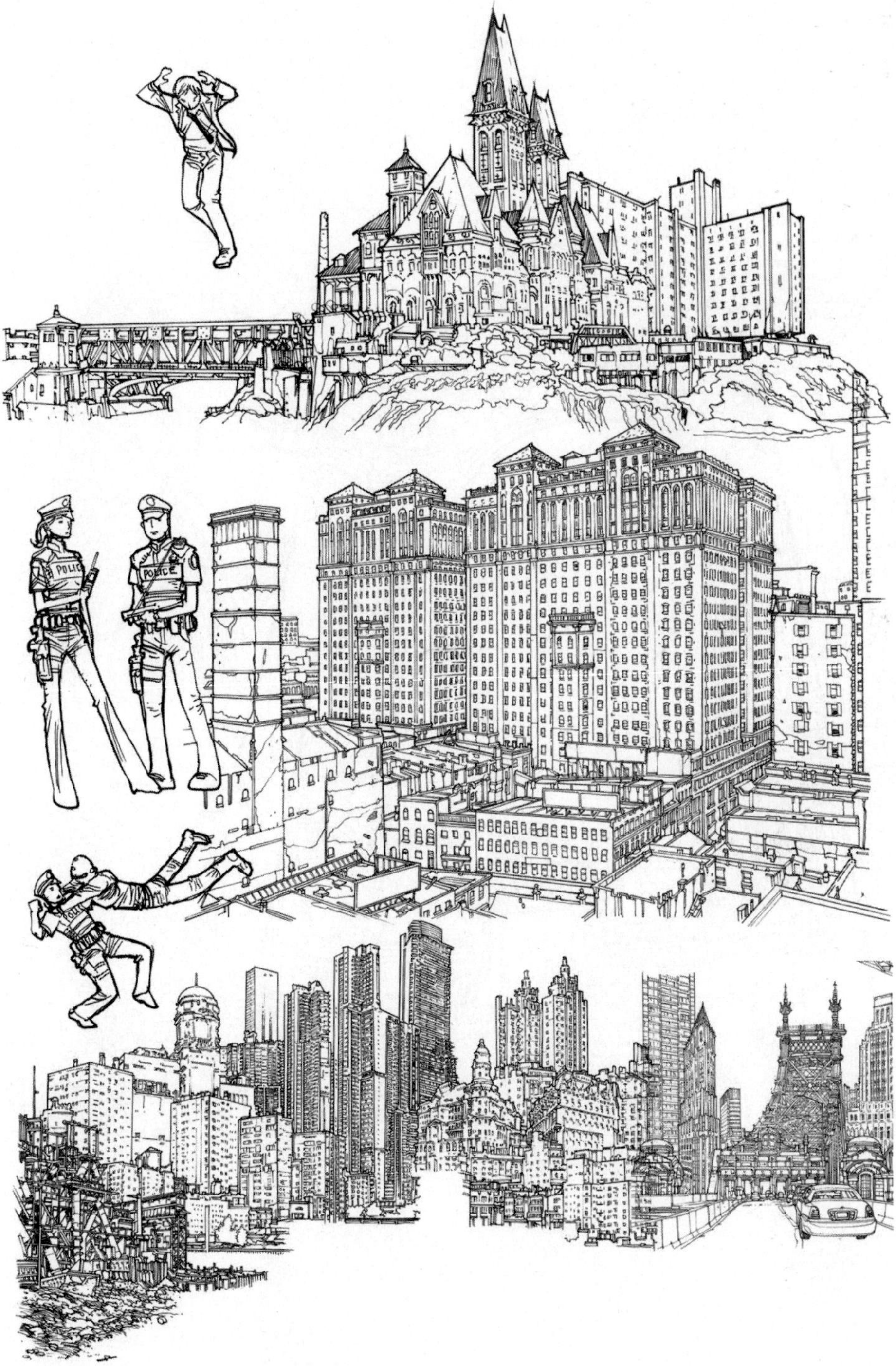
POLICE

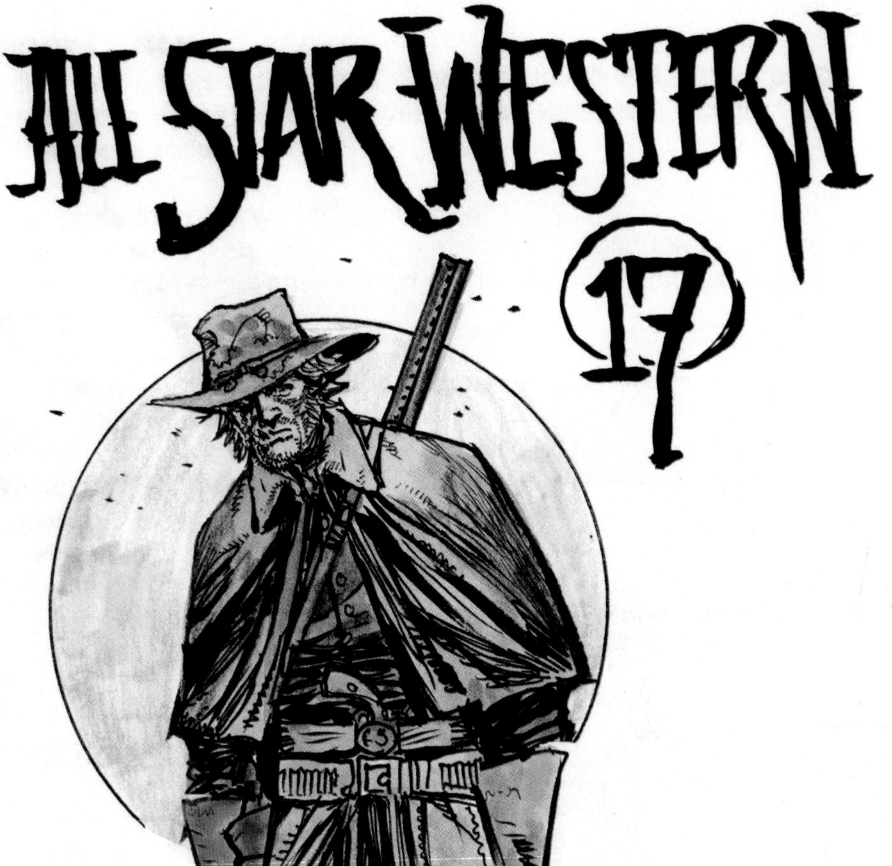
ALL STAR WESTERN
17

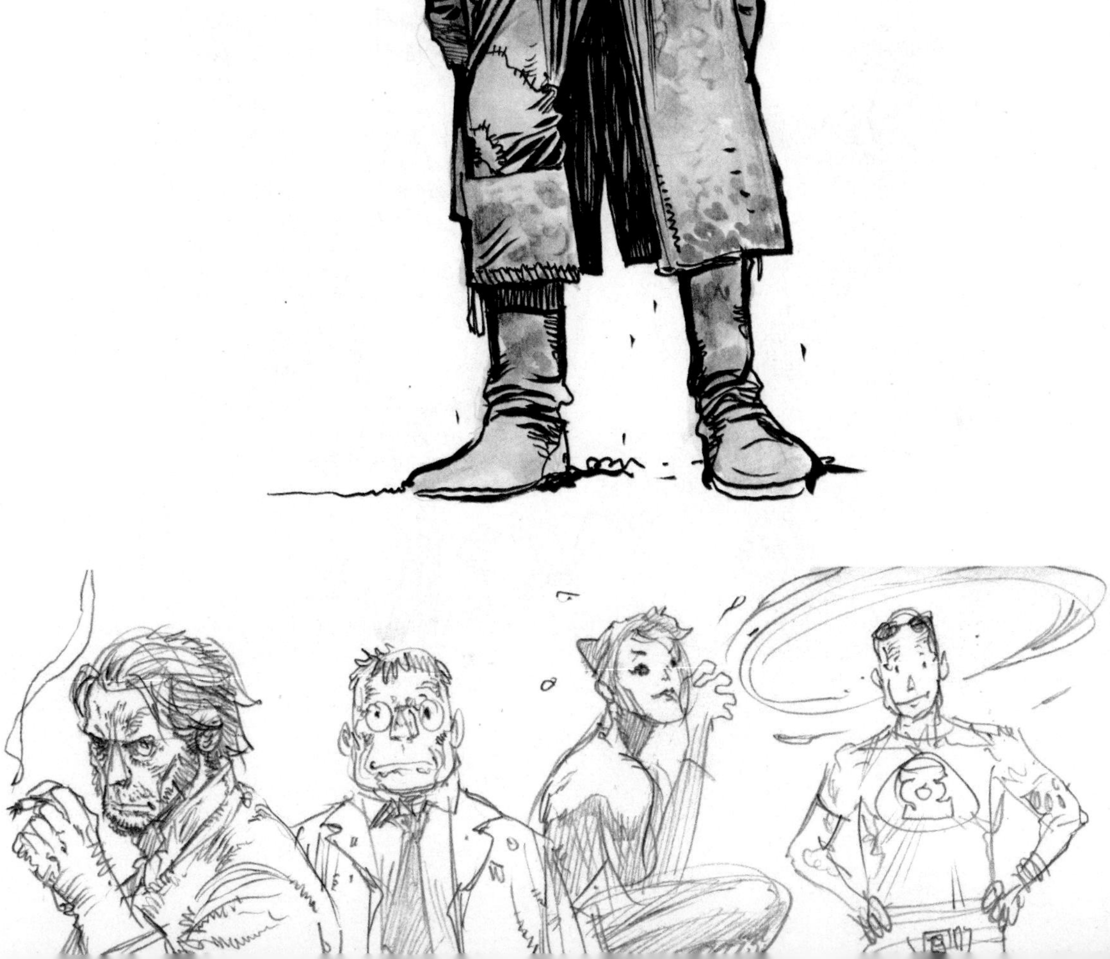

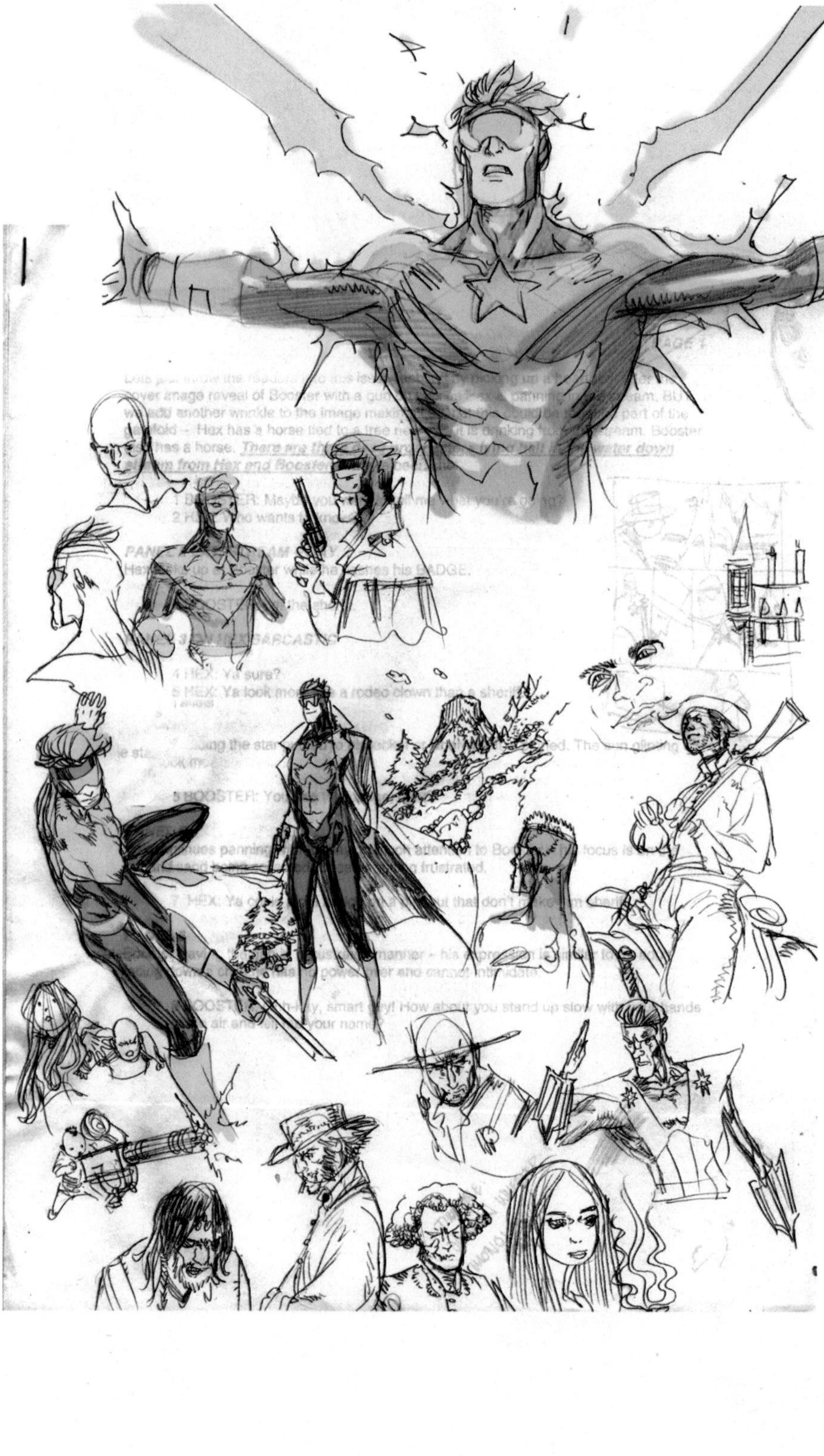

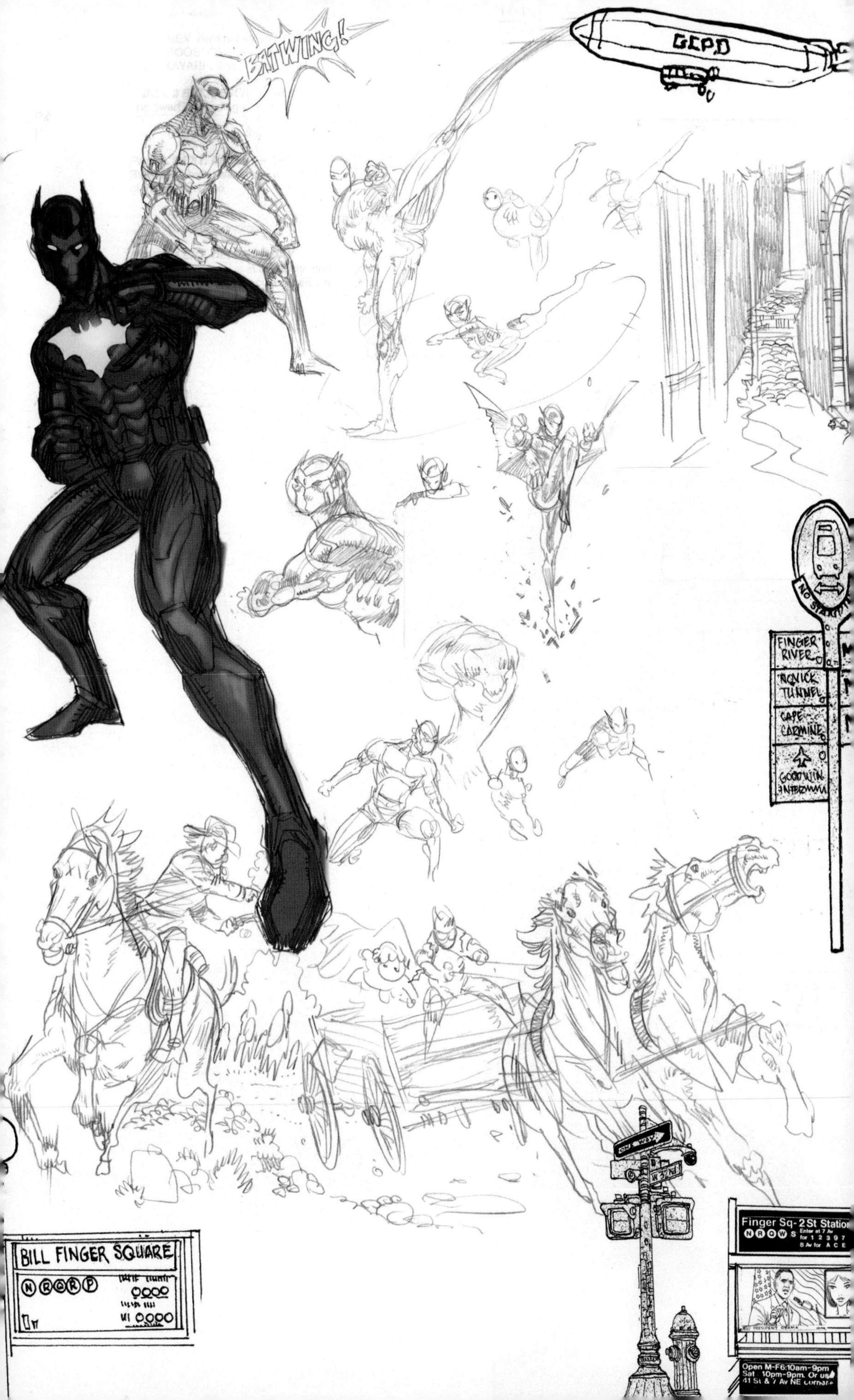

BATWING!
GCPD
FINGER RIVER
CAPE CARMINE
BILL FINGER SQUARE
Finger Sq-2St Station
N R Q W S
Enter at 7 Av for 1 2 3 9 7
8 Av for A C E
Open M-F6:10am-9pm
Sat 10pm-9pm. Or use
41 St & 7 Av NE corner

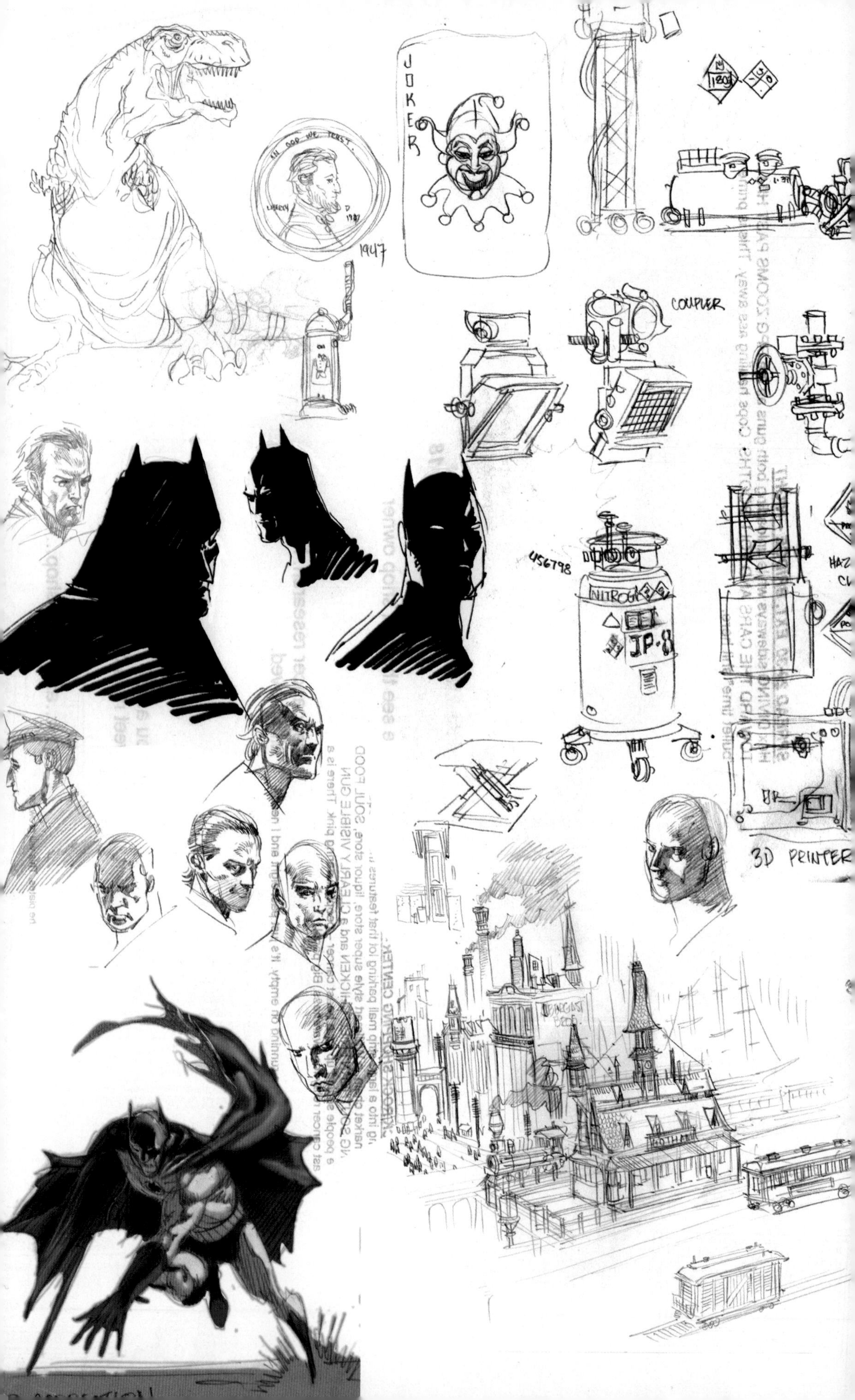
JOKER
1947
COUPLER
456798
JP-8
3D PRINTER

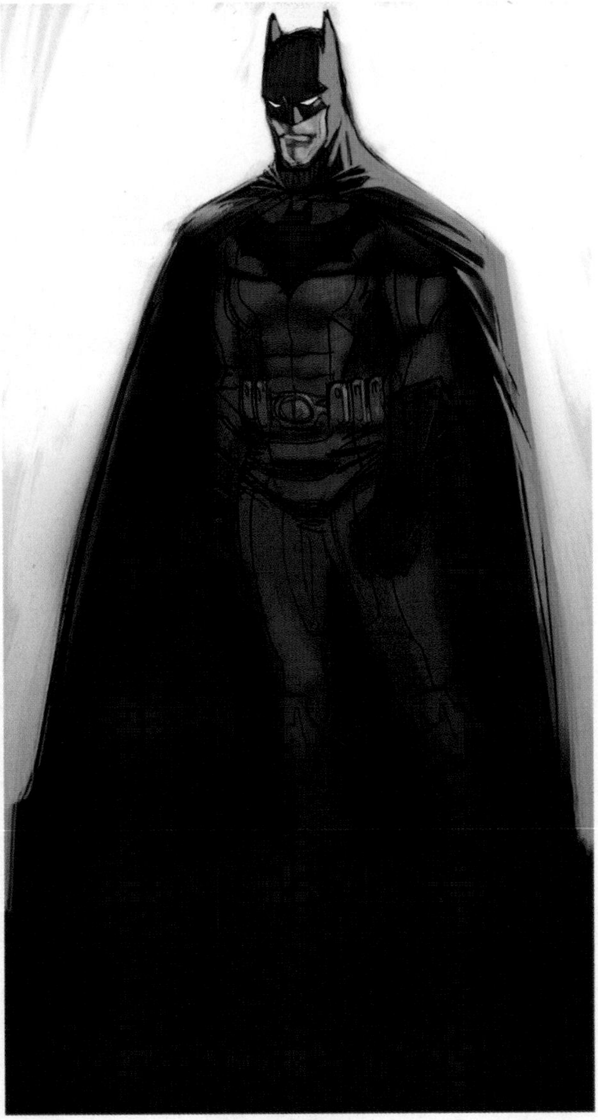
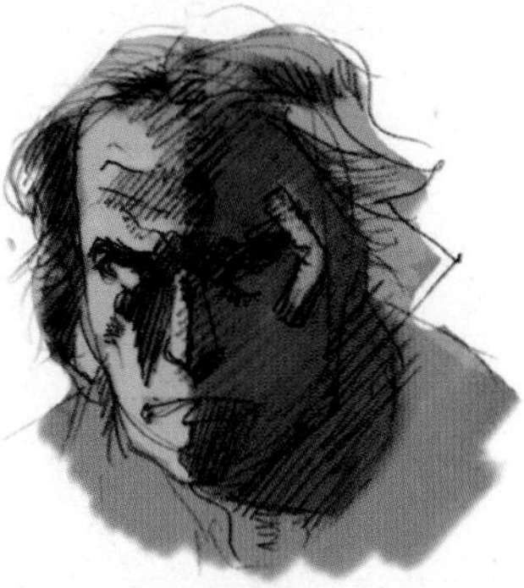
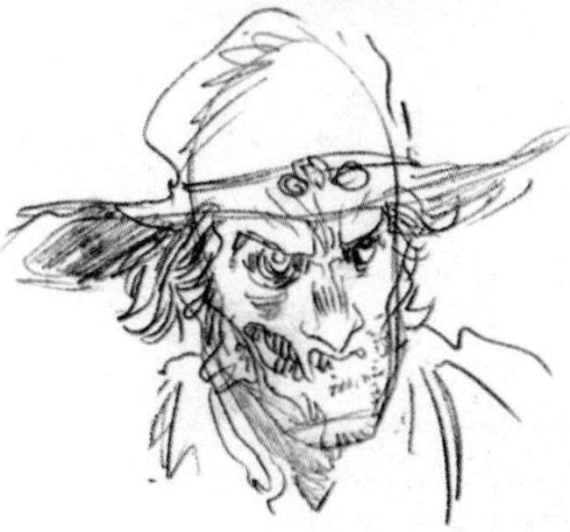
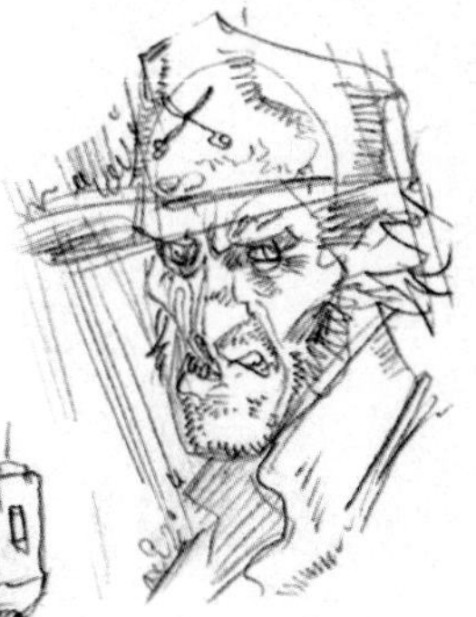
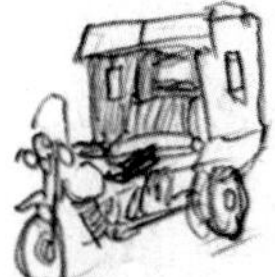
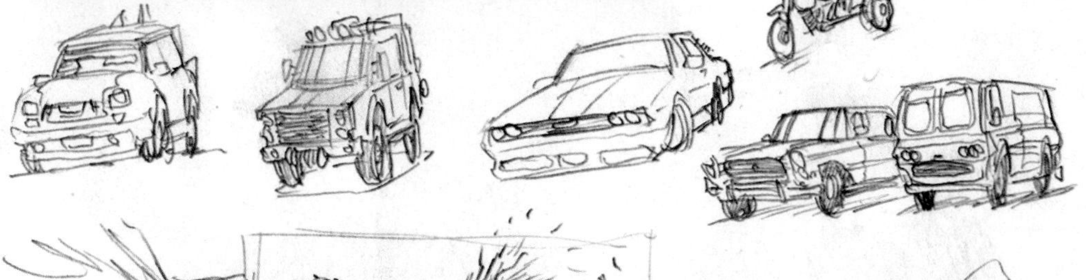
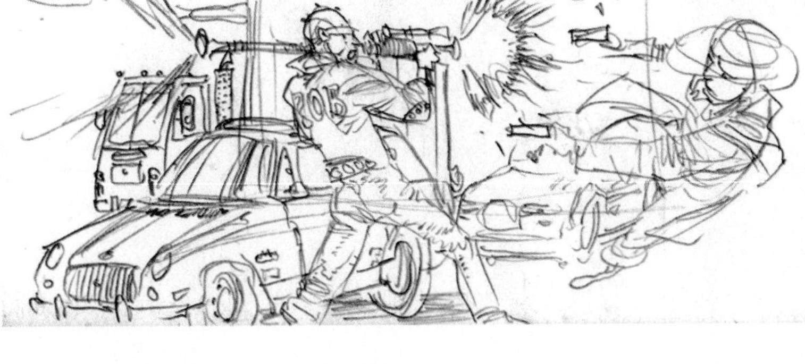
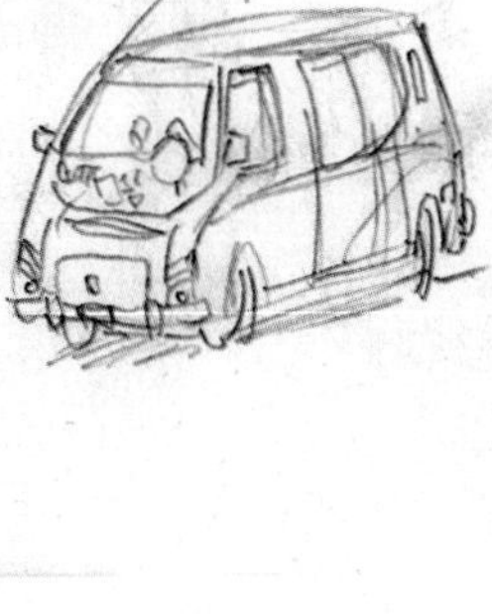

ROMIO SANTARIA
ASW #20

HIGH WALL
.45/70 CAL

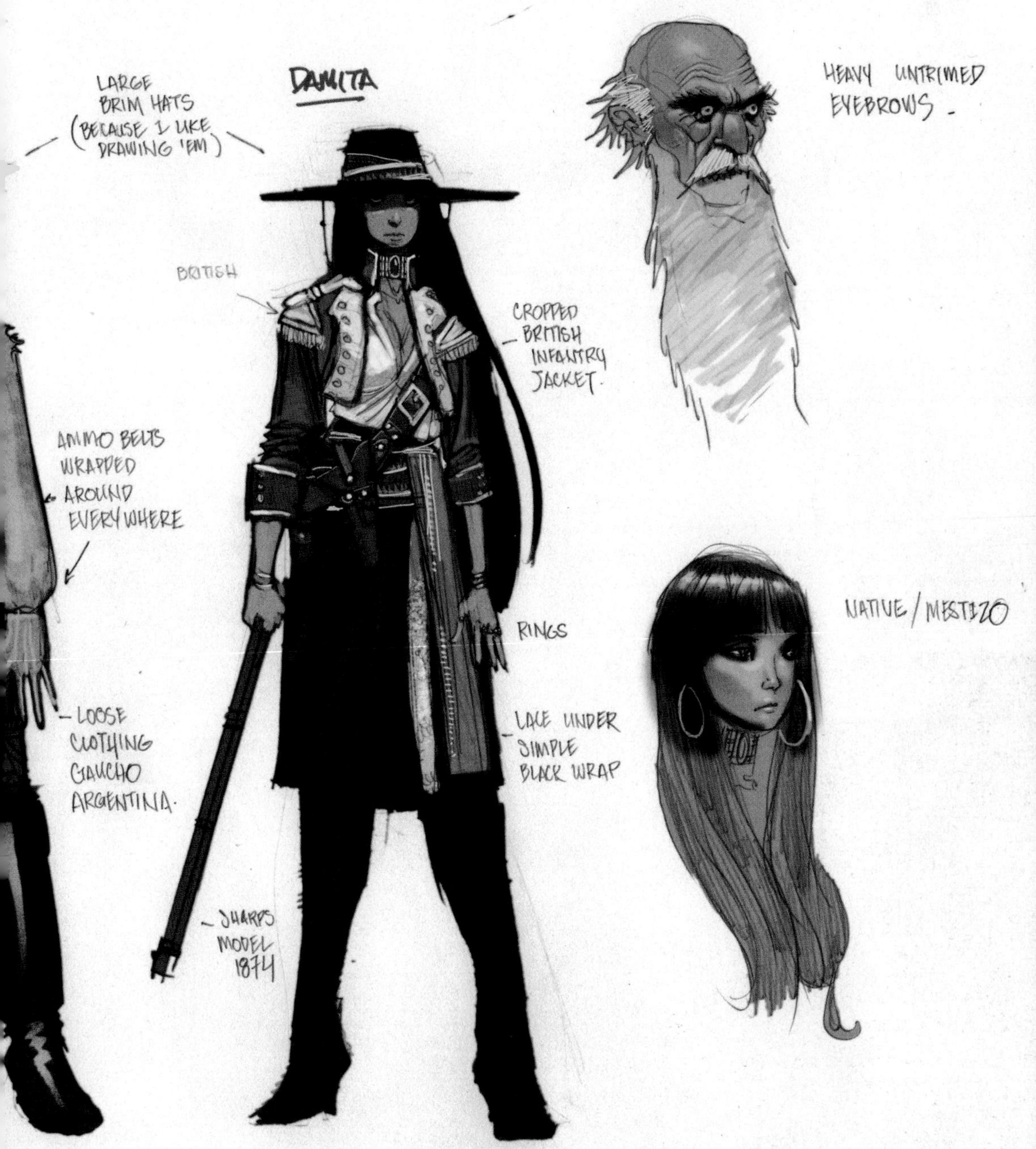
DAMITA
LARGE BRIM HATS (BECAUSE I LIKE DRAWING 'EM)
BRITISH
CROPPED BRITISH INFANTRY JACKET.
AMMO BELTS WRAPPED AROUND EVERYWHERE
RINGS
LOOSE CLOTHING GAUCHO ARGENTINA.
LACE UNDER SIMPLE BLACK WRAP
SHARPS MODEL 1874
HEAVY UNTRIMED EYEBROWS -
NATIVE / MESTIZO

Full spread cover for ALL STAR WESTERN #19 by Howard Porter

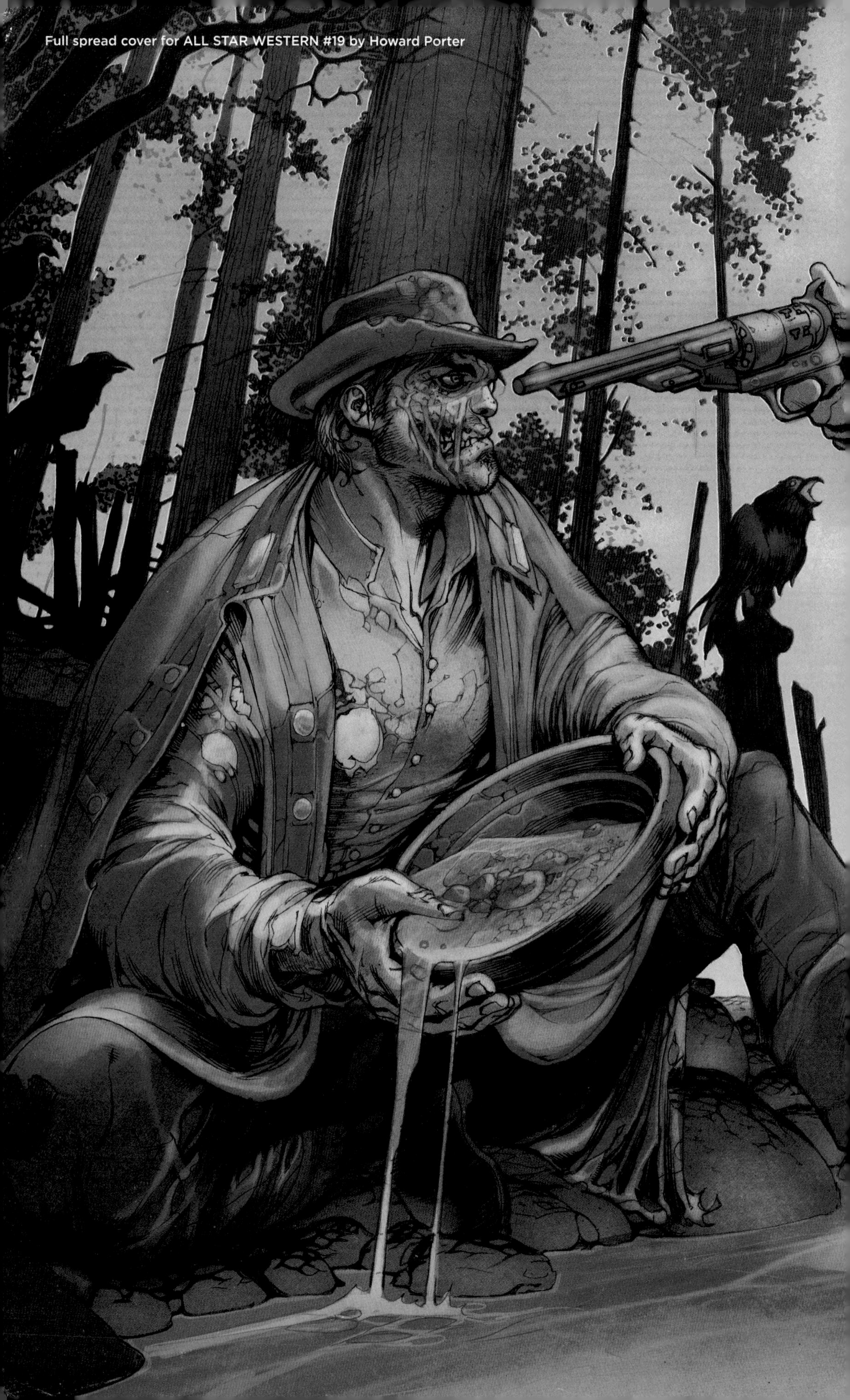

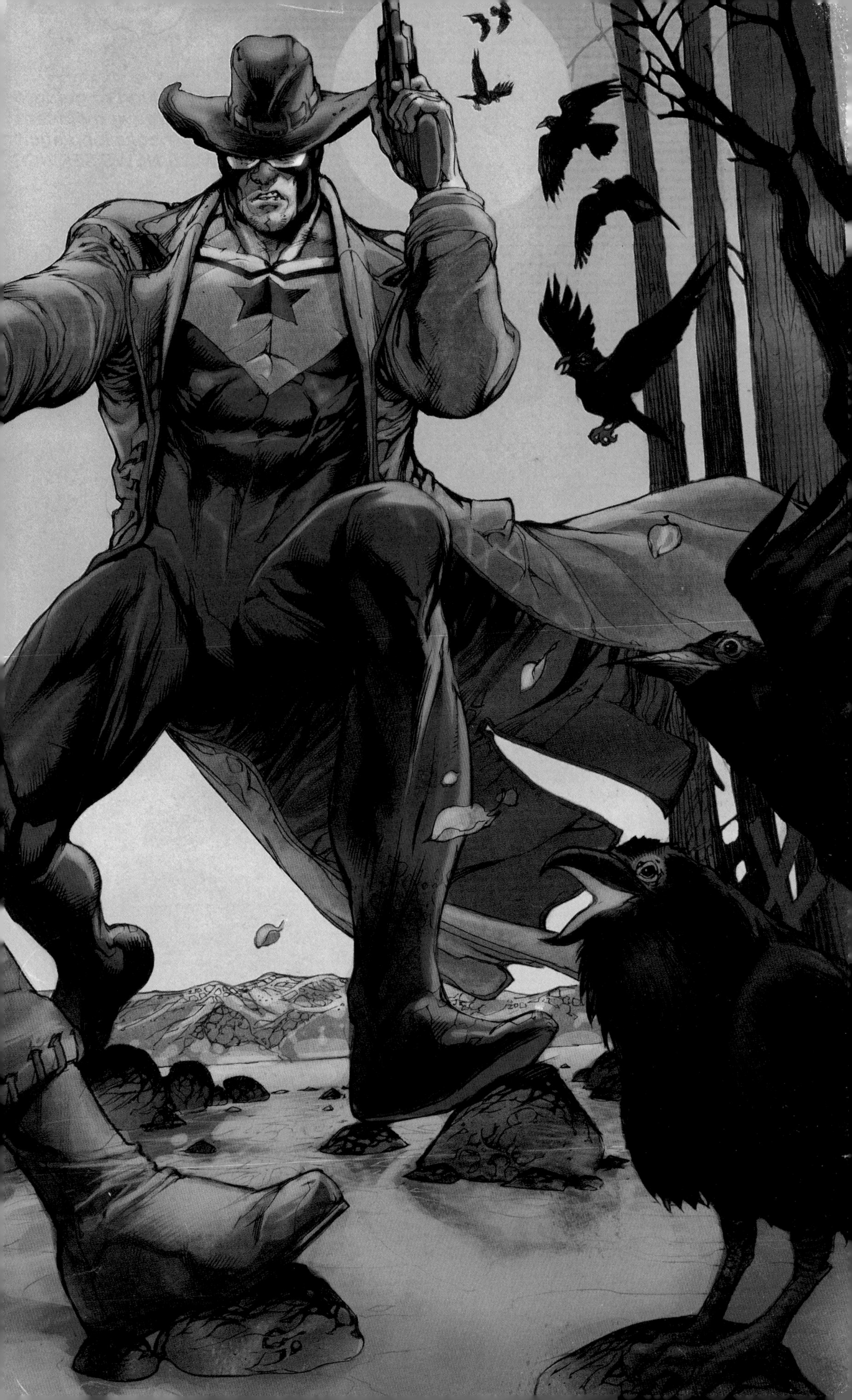

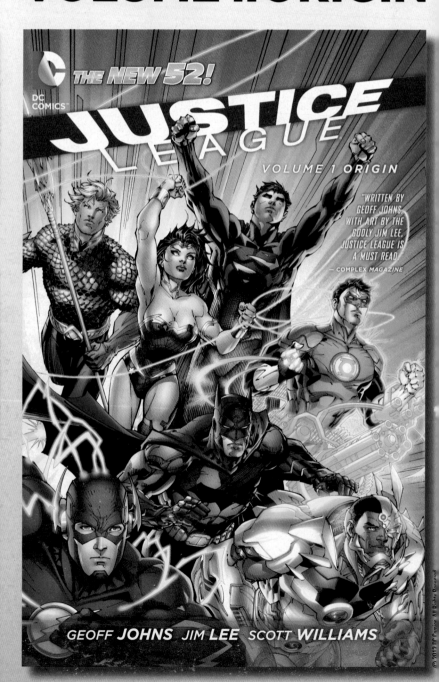